The Song at the Sea

The Song at the Sea

being a Commentary on a Commentary in Two Parts

by Judah Goldin

New Haven and London, Yale University Press, 1971

Library of Congress catalog card number: 73-140530
International standard book number: 0-300-01409-0
Designed by Marvin Howard Simmons
and set in Baskerville type.
Printed in the United States of America by
The Vail-Ballou Press, Binghamton, N.Y.
Distributed in Great Britain, Europe, and Africa by
Yale University Press, Ltd., London; in Canada by
McGill-Queen's University Press, Montreal; in Mexico
by Centro Interamericano de Libros Academicos,
Mexico City; in Central and South America by
Kaiman & Polon, Inc., New York City; in Australasia
by Australia and New Zealand Book Co., Pty., Ltd.,
Artarmon, New South Wales; in India by UBS
Publishers' Distributors Pvt., Ltd., Delhi; in Japan
by John Weatherhill, Inc., Tokyo.

FOR PAUL FRIEDMAN

Contents

Preface

There is something unique about every book, certainly about every biblical book. What is unique about the Book of Exodus is that it tells the stories of the Redemption of Israel from Egyptian bondage and the Revelation of the Law at Mount Sinai. These two stories are decisive themes for both Judaism and Christianity, and their influence has spilled over onto Islam as well. For Judaism these two themes have been primary historical events and a permanent preoccupation.

To the Revelation at Sinai there are a few references and attestations in several books beyond the Pentateuch also. One thing, however, is unmistakable, even for the casual reader of Scripture: the exodus from Egypt is not simply referred to occasionally, but recalled countless times and in a variety of connections, by lawgiver and prophet and historian and psalmist. As a matter of fact, the divine proclamation at the very head of the Ten Commandments at Mount Sinai is made in these terms: "I the Lord am your God who brought you out of the land of Egypt, the house of bondage." In the seventh century B.C. there was current a popular exclamation, "As the Lord liveth who brought up the Israelites out of the land of Egypt." In the second century A.D. you might frequently run into sundry people who, to overcome demons or evil powers, would recite the formula, "The God who drowned the king of Egypt and the Egyptians in the Red Sea." Rabbis of the same century said that "In every single generation a person must look upon himself as though *he* had gone forth from Egypt," and to this day the Jews recite this statement as they celebrate Passover. "Let my people go" is the refrain of a long-favorite and familiar Negro spiritual.

According to Scripture, the climax of that deliverance occurred at the miracle of the splitting of the Reed Sea (commonly called the Red Sea), and on that occasion Moses and the children of Israel sang the stirring song recorded in the fifteenth chapter of the Book of Exodus. Like the exodus story as a whole (indeed, like the Scriptures as a whole), that song has been commented on by one generation after another of Bible commentators, Jewish and Christian. The earliest extant and complete commentary on the Song at the Sea is *Shirta,* which means "The Song." This is one of the treatises in a composite work, devoted to the Book of Exodus and known as *Mekilta* (treatise of interpretation), which contains the interpretations and views of the rabbis who are called Tannaim—that is, the Palestinian-Jewish teachers of the first two centuries A.D. All subsequent interpretation of the Song has been affected by their interpretation, either directly or indirectly.

Although "Shirta" is an Aramaic word, the treatise itself is in Hebrew, the language of all tannaite sources, the Mishnah, the Tosefta, and the other tannaite Midrashim. The Aramaic title was very likely given to the treatise in posttannaite times,* when the Mekilta as we have it was compiled.

The present volume is the outgrowth of the Midrash Seminar at Yale, where during the past decade I studied Shirta and the other tannaite Midrashim with my students. Through their lively give-and-take and refusal to take anything for granted, the meaning of the texts became clearer, and I came to feel that a commentary like the present one could be useful in written form no less than orally. I am grateful to the members of the Seminar (and among them Professor Rowan A. Greer, III) for the challenge they provided. The growing interest in Judaica Studies in American universities, along with the growing numbers desiring to read classical Hebrew texts, underscores that for studies in

---

* Horovitz-Rabin call the treatise by the Hebrew title, *Shirah* (*Massekta de-Shirah*), but even they record *Shirta* in the colophon at the end of the treatise.

depth, interpretation must accompany translation. For example, some fine translations of the Bible exist, but running commentaries have always been required, and produced, for study; in fact, it is through these that the translations themselves have been improved. The postbiblical Hebrew classics require no less. Of course, intensive exegetical works have been composed right along—in Hebrew. What we need is detailed, critical commentaries in English.* And painstaking analysis of a tannaite commentary will prove rewarding to all students of the history of biblical exegesis.

The present work is in two parts: first, a discussion of the character and significance of Shirta as a whole; second, a translation accompanied by detailed interpretation of the treatise. The totality and its parts are thus meant to illuminate each other. Obviously I did not find the translation by Lauterbach altogether satisfactory; otherwise I would not have undertaken translation anew. (Nor is the German translation published in 1909 [Leipzig] by Winter and Wünsche satisfactory, prepared as it was before the critical editions of the Mekilta and of Mekilta de-Rabbi Simeon were published.) It seems to me that we fail to suggest what Shirta is like unless, somehow, we make visible its poetic elements.

The text adopted for translation is that edited by J. Z. Lauterbach (Philadelphia, 1933–35), which, in my opinion, qua text, is the best available, although its readings too can be improved in a number of instances (see, for particulars, S. Lieberman's review in *Kirjath Sepher*, xii [1935–36], pp. 54–65). Needless to say, I constantly kept referring to the H. S. Horovitz–I. A. Rabin edition as well (Frankfurt am Main, 1928), because of its fuller critical apparatus and its notes, but these are far from adding up to full commentary.

Because in Shirta especially, our Mekilta is so closely related to—practically identical with—Mekilta de-Rabbi Simeon, it seemed to me important to call attention to all the variants between the two Mekiltas (except for minor

---

* A recent commentary in English on the first two treatises of the Mekilta, Pisha and Be-Shallaḥ, is M. Kadushin, *A Conceptual Approach to the Mekilta* (New York, 1969).

differences of spelling). I hope I have not overlooked any. Doubtless this will appear pedantic. But these minutiae, even in translation, may often teach us important lessons about the nature of the Hebrew language, and about the oral transmission of a text. The Mekilta de-Rabbi Simeon edition to which reference is always made is that prepared by J. N. Epstein–E. Z. Melamed (Jerusalem, 1955).

It seemed unnecessary to reproduce the references to parallel passages which the student can easily get by consulting either Lauterbach or Horovitz–Rabin. When I did supply such references, it was because they contributed immediately to the solution of a problem in the text under discussion. On the other hand, I tried to refer to every single passage in every treatise of the Mekilta related to or clarifying the text of Shirta. These references are given in the following way: for example, "Pisḥa, 1 (1, 15)," which means: the first chapter of the treatise Pisḥa, and in Lauterbach's edition, Volume 1, page 15. I have also tried to provide relevant references to sources published since the publication of the Horovitz-Rabin and Lauterbach editions.

In order to economize on printing costs, I have transliterated when Hebrew (or Greek) had to be quoted (the accent on the Greek word is only meant to indicate where the accent is placed, not the kind of accent it is). Titles of works have been abbreviated, but they are spelled out in full in the List of Abbreviations and Short Titles, page xv.

A word about biblical citations: Verses are always rendered in accordance with the specific midrashic requirements. Otherwise the translation adopted was the one that seemed to me most appropriate in the particular context —either *RSV* or 1917 Jewish Publication Society Version or New *JPS* Version. In the end, I suppose, for the most part I used the 1917 *JPS*.

A suggestion to students. Whenever a biblical verse is quoted, and all the more when only part of the verse is quoted, the biblical text should be consulted, for the *context* (verses before and after) will prove more revealing than any commentator's paraphrase.

It is not mere protocol which makes me say that much in the following pages could not have been written if I did not enjoy the instruction and stimulation of four erudite and acute friends, Professors Elias Bickerman, Louis Finkelstein, Saul Lieberman, and Shalom Spiegel. They teach one not only how to read primary sources but why one must come back to these again and again. For the views expressed in this volume, however, I alone am responsible. For their many acts of assistance I would like to thank the staffs of the Royal Library in Copenhagen, the Library of the Jewish Theological Seminary of America, and especially the Yale University Library. Nor must I neglect to say thanks to the chairman of the Department of Religious Studies at Yale, Professor Julian N. Hartt, for help and encouragement, particularly when the mood was winter and the work would not go. My friend Philip Kuttner was good enough to transcribe for me the musical passage which appears on the title page with the permission of G. Schirmer, Inc. I am indebted to Chester Kerr, director of the Yale University Press, to Wayland Schmitt, editor, and not least to Jennifer Alkire, editor, for all they did to put this book into shape for publication. I am also indebted to the Fulbright Commission for the research fellowship which made possible a good deal of the work in connection with this volume. And as always I remain indebted to Grace Goldin.

New Haven, Conn.
October, 1969

J. G.
Davenport College
Yale University

Abbreviations and Short Titles

AA	*Alei Ayin: The Salman Schocken Jubilee Volume.* Jerusalem, 5708–12.
AAJR	American Academy for Jewish Research.
AhB	*Sefer Arugat Habosem by Abraham ben Azriel* (thirteenth century), ed. E. E. Urbach. Jerusalem, 1939–63.
AhT	B. Z. Bacher. *Aggadot ha-Tannaim.* Berlin, 5682–88.
Aknin	*Joseph ben Judah ben Jacob ibn ʿAknin, Divulgatio Mysteriorum Luminumque Apparentia,* ed. A. S. Halkin. Jerusalem, 1964.
Alon, *Toledot*	G. Alon. *Toledot ha-Yehudim be-ʾEreṣ Yiśraʾel bi-Tekufath ha-Mishnah we-ha-Talmud.* 2 vols. Tel Aviv, 1952–55.
ANEP	J. B. Pritchard, ed. *The Ancient Near East in Pictures.* Princeton, 1954.
ANET	J. B. Pritchard, ed., *Ancient Near Eastern Texts.* Princeton, 1950.
Antiquities	Josephus. *Jewish Antiquities,* trans. H. St. J. Thackeray, R. Marcus, and L. Feldman. London and New York, 1930–65.
ARN	*Abot de-Rabbi Natan,* ed. S. Schechter. Vienna, 1887.
ARNA	Version A of *ARN.*
ARNB	Version B of *ARN.*
B	Babylonian Talmud (cited by treatise and folio).
Baer	S. Baer. *Seder ʿAbodat Yisrael.* Schocken, Germany, 5697.
Bamberger	B. J. Bamberger. *Fallen Angels.* Philadelphia, 1952.

Barhebraeus	*Barhebraeus' Scholia on the Old Testament,* ed. M. Sprengling and W. C. Graham. Chicago, 1931.
BASOR	*Bulletin of the American Schools of Oriental Research.*
BDB	F. Brown, S. R. Driver, and C. A. Briggs. *Hebrew and English Lexicon.* Boston and New York, 1907.
Beginnings of Christianity	F. J. Foakes Jackson and K. Lake. *The Beginnings of Christianity.* 5 vols. London, 1920–33.
Blau, *Altjüdische Zauberwesen*	L. Blau. *Das altjüdische Zauberwesen.* Strasbourg, 1898.
Bonsirven	J. Bonsirven. *Le Judaisme palestinien.* Paris, 1934.
Büchler, *Types*	A. Büchler. *Types of Jewish-Palestinian Piety from 70 B.C.E. to 70 C.E.* New York, 1968.
Cant. R.	*Canticles Rabba.*
Cross, "SSCM"	F. M. Cross, Jr. "The Song of the Sea and Canaanite Myth." *Journal for Theology and the Church* (1968), pp. 1 ff.
Cross, *Studies*	F. M. Cross, Jr. *Studies in Ancient Yahwistic Poetry.* Baltimore, 1950.
Daremberg and Saglio	C. V. Daremberg and E. Saglio. *Dictionnaire des antiquités grecques et romaines.* Paris, 1877–1917.
de Lubac	H. de Lubac, *Exégèse médiévale,* Paris, 1964.
Deut. R., ed. Liebermann	*Midrash Debarim Rabbah,* ed. S. Liebermann. Jerusalem, 1940.
DS	*Diqduqe Soferim* (Variae Lectiones in Mischnam et in Talmud Babylonicum), recorded by R. Rabinowitz (in reprint edition). Brooklyn, N.Y., 5720 et seq.
EJ	*Encyclopaedia Judaica.* 10 vols. Berlin, 1928 ff.
Eccl. R.	*Ecclesiastes Rabba.*
Elbogen	I. Elbogen. *Der jüdische Gottesdienst in seiner geschichtlichen Entwicklung.* 3d ed. Frankfurt am Main, 1931.
EM	B. Z. Bacher. *ʿErke Midrash.* Tel Aviv, 5683.
Epstein, *Mabo*	J. N. Epstein. *Mabo le-Nusaḥ ha-Mishnah.* Jerusalem, 5708.
Epstein, *Mebo'ot*	J. N. Epstein. *Meboʾot le-Sifrut ha-Tannaim.* Jerusalem and Tel Aviv, 1957.

Exod. R.	Exodus Rabba.
Field	F. Field. *Origenis Hexaplorum.* Oxford, 1875.
Finkelstein, *The Jews*	L. Finkelstein. *The Jews: Their History, Culture, and Religion.* 2 vols. 3d ed. New York, 1960.
Geiger, *Ha-Miqra' we-Targumaw*	A. Geiger. *Ha-Miqra' we-Targumaw.* Jerusalem, 1949.
Gen. R.	*Genesis Rabba,* ed. J. Theodor and C. Albeck. Berlin, 1912–27.
Gevirtz	S. Gevirtz. *Patterns in the Early Poetry of Israel.* Chicago, 1963.
Ginzberg, *Legends*	Louis Ginzberg. *Legends of the Jews.* 7 vols. Philadelphia, 1913–38.
GJP	Saul Lieberman. *Greek in Jewish Palestine.* New York, 1942.
Goodenough, *Jewish Symbols*	E. R. Goodenough. *Jewish Symbols in the Greco-Roman Period.* New York, 1953–65.
GS	L. Ginzberg. *Ginze Schechter.* Vol. 1. New York, 1928.
Heinemann	I. Heinemann. *Darke ha-'Aggadah.* Jerusalem, 5710.
Hengel	M. Hengel. *Die Zeloten.* Leiden and Cologne, 1961.
Ḥizquni	R. Ḥizqiah ben Manoah: Bible Commentator, 13th century.
HJP	S. Lieberman. *Hellenism in Jewish Palestine.* New York, 1962.
Hodayot	J. Licht. *The Thanksgiving Scroll.* Jerusalem, 1957.
HR	*Mechilta d'Rabbi Ismael,* ed. H. S. Horovitz-I. A. Rabin. Frankfurt am Main, 1931.
HUCA	*Hebrew Union College Annual.*
ICC	International Critical Commentary (on the Bible).
I Mac	I Maccabees.
Jastrow	M. Jastrow. *Dictionary of the Targumim, the Talmud Babli and Yerushalmi, and the Midrashic Literature.* New York and London, 1926.
JBL	*Journal of Biblical Literature.*
JE	*Jewish Encyclopaedia.*
JNES	*Journal of Near Eastern Studies.*
Josephus, *War*	Josephus. *The Jewish War,* trans. H. St. J. Thackeray. New York and London, 1927–28.

JPS	Jewish Publication Society of America.
JQR	*Jewish Quarterly Review.*
Kasher	Menahem M. Kasher. *Torah Shelemah.* 23 vols. New York, 5709 et seq.
Klausner	*Sefer Klausner* (essays in honor of Joseph Klausner). Tel Aviv, 5697.
Koehler-Baumgartner	L. Koehler and W. Baumgartner. *Lexicon in Veteris Testamenti Libros.* Leiden, 1948 et seq.
Krauss, *Persia and Rome*	S. Krauss, *Persia and Rome in the Talmud and Midrashim* (in Hebrew). Jerusalem, 5708.
Kutscher	Yehezkel Kutscher. *Milim we-Toledotehem.* Jerusalem, 1961.
Lam. R.	Lamentations Rabba.
Landau	Isaac Elijah Landau. *Berure ha-Middot* (a commentary on the Mekilta). Wilna, 1844.
Lekaḥ Tob	*Lekaḥ Tob* (a commentary on the Pentateuch) by R. Tobia ben Elieser (11th century), ed. S. Buber and R. Aaron Moses Padua. Wilna, 1884.
Lev. R.	*Leviticus Rabba,* ed. M. Margulies. Jerusalem, 5713–20.
Levi	E. Levi. *Yesodot ha-Tefillah.* 2d ed. Tel Aviv, 5712.
LGJV	*Louis Ginzberg Jubilee Volume.* New York, 1945.
Liddel and Scott	H. G. Liddell and R. Scott. *A Greek-English Lexicon.* Oxford, 1958.
Lieberman, "After Life"	S. Lieberman. "Some Aspects of After Life in Early Rabbinic Literature." *H. A. Wolfson Jubilee Volume* (Jerusalem, 1965), pp. 495 ff.
Lieberman, *Yemenite Midrashim*	S. Lieberman. *Yemenite Midrashim* (in Hebrew). Jerusalem, 1940.
Loeb	Loeb Classics.
Loewe	R. Loewe. "The Targum to the Song of Songs." A. Altmann, ed., *Biblical Motifs.* Cambridge, Mass., 1966, pp. 159–96.
Loewenstamm	S. E. Loewenstamm. *The Tradition of the Exodus in Its Development* (in Hebrew). Jerusalem, 1965.
Luzzatto	S. D. Luzzatto. *Commentary to the Pentateuch* (Heb.). Tel Aviv, 1965.
LXX	*The Septuagint,* ed. A. Rahlfs. 6th ed. Stuttgart, 1959.

M	Mishnah.
Mabo	L. Finkelstein. *Mabo le-Massektot Abot ve-Abot d'Rabbi Natan.* New York, 1950.
Maḥzor Vitry	R. Simḥah (a pupil of Rashi's). *Maḥzor Vitry,* ed. S. Hurwitz. Nuremberg, 1923.
Mann, *Bible as Read*	J. Mann. *The Bible as Read and Preached in the Old Synagogue.* Vol. I. Cincinnati, 1940.
Marmorstein, *Studies in Jewish Theology*	A. Marmorstein. *Studies in Jewish Theology.* Oxford, 1950.
Melamed, *Ha-Yaḥas*	E. Z. Melamed, *Ha-Yaḥas sheben Midrashe Halakah la-Mishnah we-la-Tosefta,* Jerusalem, 5727.
Memar Marqah	J. Macdonald, ed., *Memar Marqah.* 2 vols. Berlin, 1963.
Meṣudat Dawid	A commentary on the Bible by R. David ben Aryeh Loeb Altschul, completed by his son; R. David lived toward the end of the seventeenth century, in Prague.
MhG	Midrash ha-Gadol.
MhG, Exod.	*Midrash ha-Gadol, Exodus,* ed. M. Margulies. Jerusalem, 1956.
MhG, Num.	*Midrash ha-Gadol, Numbers,* ed. S. Fisch. London, 1957–63.
MhM	R. Israel ibn Al-Nakawa. *Menorat ha-Maor,* ed. H. G. Enelow. New York, 1929–32.
MHRZW	R. Zeeb Wolf ben Israel Issar Einhorn, d. 1862. A commentary on Midrash Rabba (in the Wilna editions).
Midrash Ps.	*Midrash Tehillim* (Psalms), ed. S. Buber. Wilna, 1891.
Mid. Tan.	*Midrash Tannaim,* ed. D. Hoffmann. Berlin, 1909.
Migne, *PG*	J. P. Migne. *Patrologia Graeca.* Paris, 1844 et seq.
Mirsky	A. Mirsky. "The Origins of the Forms of Liturgical Poetry." *Studies of the Research Institute for Hebrew Poetry in Jerusalem.* Vol. VII. Jerusalem and Tel Aviv, 1958.
Mishnah ed. Lowe	*The Mishnah on Which the Palestinian Talmud Rests,* ed. W. H. Lowe. Cambridge, 1883.
MMKJV	*Mordecai M. Kaplan Jubilee Volume.* New York, 1953.

Montgomery	J. A. Montgomery. *Critical and Exegetical Commentary on the Books of Kings,* ed. H. G. Gehman. Edinburgh, 1960.
Moore	G. F. Moore. *Judaism.* 3 vols. Cambridge, Mass., 1927–40.
MRS	*Mekilta de-Rabbi Simeon,* ed. J. N. Epstein and E. Z. Melamed. Jerusalem, 1955.
MT	Masoretic Text of the Hebrew Bible.
Num. R.	Numbers Rabba.
OED	*The Oxford English Dictionary.* Oxford, 1961.
P	Palestinian Talmud.
PA	Pirqe ʾAbot (the treatise ʾAbot of the Mishnah, referred to by chapter and paragraph).
PAAJR	*Proceedings, American Academy for Jewish Research.*
Pauly-Wissowa	*Paulys Realencyclopädie der classischen altertumswissenschaft . . . hrsg. von G. Wissowa.* Stuttgart, 1894–1963.
Pesikta Kahana	*Pesikta de Rav Kahana,* ed. B. Mandelbaum. New York, 1962.
Pesikta R.	*Pesikta Rabbati,* ed. M. Friedmann. Vienna, 1880.
Pfeiffer	Robert H. Pfeiffer. *Introduction to the Old Testament.* New York and London, 1941.
PRE	*Pirke de-Rabbi Eliezer,* with commentary by R. David Luria. Warsaw ed. repro. in New York, 1946.
R	Rabbi (when preceding person's name). Rabba (when following the title of a biblical book—e.g. Gen R. = Genesis Rabba).
Rabinowitz, Halakah we-Aggadah	Z. M. Rabinowitz. *Halakah we-Aggadah be-Piyyute Yannai.* Tel Aviv, 1965.
Rashbam	R. Samuel ben Meir (Bible Commentator), 1080–1158.
RB	*Revue Biblique.*
Rostovtzeff, SEHHW	M. Rostovtzeff. *The Social and Economic History of the Hellenistic World.* Oxford, 1964.
RSV	*Revised Standard Version of the Bible.* New York, 1952.
Schechter, Aspects	S. Schechter. *Some Aspects of Rabbinic Theology,* New York, 1936.

Scholem, Gnosticism	G. G. Scholem. *Jewish Gnosticism, Merkabah Mysticism and Talmudic Tradition.* New York, 1960.
Scholem, *RhK*	G. Scholem. *Reshit ha-Kabbala (1150–1250).* Jerusalem and Tel Aviv, 1948.
Schürer	E. Schürer. *Geschichte des jüdischen Volkes.* Leipzig, 1901–09.
Sekel Tob	*Midrasch Sekel Tob,* ed. S. Buber. New York, 5719.
Sforno	R. Obadiah ben Jacob, biblical exegete, 1475–1550.
Sifra	*Sifra,* ed. I. H. Weiss. Vienna, 1862.
Sifre Deut.	*Siphre ad Deuteronomium,* ed. L. Finkelstein. Berlin, 1939.
Sifre Num.	*Siphre d'be Rab, Siphre ad Numeros,* ed. H. S. Horovitz. Jerusalem, 1966.
Sifre Z.	*Sifre Zutta zum IV. Buch Moses,* ed. H. S. Horovitz. Jerusalem, 1966.
Strack-Billerbeck	H. L. Strack and P. Billerbeck. *Kommentar zum Neuen Testament.* Munich, 1922.
SY	R. Judah Najar. *Shebut Yehudah* (a commentary on the Mekilta). Leghorn, 1801.
T	*Tosefta,* ed. M. S. Zuckermandel and S. Lieberman. Jerusalem, 5698.
Talmudic Encyclopedia	(in Hebrew). 12 vols. Jerusalem, 1947 et seq.
Tanḥuma B.	*Tanḥuma,* ed. S. Buber. Wilna, 1885.
Tg	Targum (Aramaic translations of Scripture).
Tg Jon.	*Targum Jonathan on Pentateuch,* ed. M. Ginsburger. Berlin, 1903.
TK	S. Lieberman. *Tosefta Ki-Fshuṭah.* New York, 1955–67.
TR	S. Lieberman. *Tosefeth Rishonim.* 4 vols. Jerusalem, 1937–39.
VT	*Vetus Testamentum.* Leiden, 1951 et seq.
Yalkut Shimeoni	Simeon Kara. *Yalkut Shimeoni.* Salonica, 1521 (on Prophets and Hagiographa) and 1526–27 (on Pentateuch).
Yalon, *Bulletin*	H. Yalon. *Bulletin of Hebrew Language Studies,* Jerusalem. 1963.
Yannai	*Piyyute Yannai,* ed. M. Zulay. Berlin, 1938.
ZAW	*Zeitschrift für die alttestamentliche Wissenschaft.*

Ziegler   Ignaz Ziegler. *Die königsgleichnisse des Mid-*
               rasch. Breslau, 1903.

ZY   *Zeh Yenaḥamenu* (a commentary on the
               Mekilta by R. Moses of Frankfort). Amster-
               dam, 1712.

Part I. An Introduction to Shirta

"The exodus from Egypt outweighs
all the miracles and mighty acts which
the Holy One, blessed be He, wrought
in behalf of Israel."

1. Shirta

The treatise Shirta [1] is the third of nine treatises which together make up the tannaite Midrash called Mekilta [2] de-Rabbi Ishmael. "Shirta" is an Aramaic word, meaning "The Song" (in Hebrew one would say *Ha-Shirah*); [3] and

1. I do not understand why J. Z. Lauterbach feels compelled to vocalize the consonants *š y r t ʾ* , Shirata, in the determined state of the feminine plural. He himself reports (in "The Arrangement and Division," *HUCA*, I [1924], 440) that "both the manuscripts and the editions have the closing phrase" *ḥslt šyrtʾ* (note also on p. 452 his quotation from the Oxford MS of the mnemotechnical statement at the end of the treatise), and the verb *ḥslt* is clearly in the singular, 3 feminine *peʿal*. To say as he does in the footnote (p. 440, n. 12) that the word "is no doubt to be read in the plural because the tractate covers the two songs, the song of Moses and the song of Miriam," seems to me entirely unnecessary. While Shirta (!) underscores that the women's choir did not form one choir with the men, the Song (according to the Midrash) was one and the same song. Hence when Lauterbach, in the same note, continues, "The closing phrase *ḥslt šyrtʾ* is shortened from" *ḥslt msktʾ šyrtʾ*, he is essentially arguing in circles. *Ḥslt šyrtʾ* may or may not represent *ḥslt msktʾ šyrtʾ* or *ḥslt msktʾ dšyrtʾ* (which is irrelevant here), but had the reading been Shirata, as he argues, it is more than likely that the verb would appear in the feminine plural (*ḥslh/ḥslw* if biblical, but much more likely as *ḥsln* or *ḥslyn* or *ḥslwn*). Above all, however, and to repeat: the treatise is speaking of one and the same Song, sung by Moses and the men and by Miriam and the women in unmixed choral groups. I suspect that Lauterbach was unwittingly affected by his *correct* observation on the proper vocalization of *m k y l t ʾ*, on which see below. (I want to thank my dear and erudite friend, Professor Franz Rosenthal, for the privilege to consult him on this problem, and for his good counsel.)

2. Cf. below, pp. 10 f. n. 9.

3. Note, indeed, that when the Mekilta speaks of the Song at the Sea, it does not even call it *Ha-Shirah*, "the song," with the definite

3

the song referred to is that preserved in Exodus 15, the
song which was sung by Moses and Miriam and the
Israelite men and women at the Sea of Reeds, after the
miraculous deliverance of Israel and the destruction of the
pursuing Egyptian hosts. As the nineteenth verse of that
chapter puts it: "For the horses of Pharaoh, with his
chariots and horsemen, went into the sea; and the Lord
turned back on them the waters of the sea; but the Israelites marched on dry ground in the midst of the sea."[4]
Almost a millenium later, the event was still recalled in
vocabulary borrowed from the Exodus chapter: "And You
divided the sea before [the Israelites], so that they went
through the midst of the sea on dry ground; and You cast
their pursuers into the depths, as a stone into mighty
waters" (Neh. 9:11). Or again, as one of the Psalmists
(Ps. 106:9–12) recited:

> He rebuked the Sea of Reeds, and it became dry;
> And He led them through the deeps as through a
>   desert.
> So He saved them from the hand of the foe,
> And delivered them from the hand of the enemy.
> And the waters covered their adversaries,
> Not one of them was left.
> Then they had faith in His words,
> They sang His praise.[5]

Shirta is the earliest complete commentary we have on
the Song at the Sea, word for word following the biblical
text and interpreting it. A number of comments on the
Song can be found in several treatises of Philo;[6] Josephus
too calls attention to it (with more enthusiasm than ac-
curacy: "they passed the whole night in melody and mirth,
Moses himself composing in hexameter verse a song to
God").[7] But as detailed exegesis of all the verses of the

---

article, but simply *Shirah*, as though the word were a proper noun, a
title.

4. Cf. Josh. 24:6 f.

5. Cf. I Enoch 89:21–27.

6. In Philo's *Questions and Answers on Exodus*, no discussion of
Exodus 15 is extant.

7. *Antiquities*, II, end (Loeb, IV, 317).

Song, nothing extant is earlier than Shirta—although of course one might say that since translation implies interpretation, the Septuagint is almost five hundred years earlier.[8] Shirta, however, is not a translation, not a Targum, nor is it an epitome;[9] it is outspokenly commentary; and hardly a word of the Song does it pass over in silence.

It takes ten chapters for Shirta to comment on the first twenty-one of the twenty-seven verses which in our Bibles constitute Exodus 15. The first two chapters are devoted to the first verse alone of that Exodus 15:1–21 unit; one chapter is devoted to Exodus 15:2; each of chapters 4, 5, 6, and 7 interprets two verses; Shirta 8 explains Exodus 15:11; verses 12–16 are covered by Shirta 9; and the final chapter, 10, covers verses 17–21. Clearly, therefore, the chapters of Shirta simply follow the order of the biblical verses and are not organized according to any arithmetical scheme—so many verses of the Song at the Sea to a chapter of commentary. Nor is the division of the chapters determined by some mechanical principle of size or dimensions;[10] if the Lauterbach edition, for example, may serve as a standard, chapters vary in length as follows:

I, 153 lines;
II, 139 lines;[11]
III, 101 lines;
IV, 101 lines;[12]
V, 73 lines;
VI, 147 lines;
VII, 78 lines;
VIII, 106 lines;
IX, 126 lines;
X, 91 lines.

8. "The Septuagint, the oldest of our preserved *Midrashim*": *HJP*, p. 50.

9. See, for example, *Sefer ha-Yashar* (Berlin, 1923), pp. 273 f.

10. On the number of *halakot* or paragraphs the Shirta chapters may once have been divided into, cf. Lauterbach, "The Arrangement and Division of the Mekilta," in *HUCA*, I, 460.

11. But before the copyists abbreviated, it was longer (see below, pp. 99, 100, 105).

12. Again, see below, p. 137.

The size of the chapters is evidently governed by the material available to the compiler of the treatise. Where he has much at his disposal, he generously furnishes that; where he has little, he offers that.[13]

It is by no means surprising that even in ancient times more comment was available on some phrases or clauses or verses than on others. Six interpretations, for example, are presented for the one word *we-ʾanwehu* (*wʾnwhw*, "And I will glorify / enshrine Him"). No wonder; the verbal root, *nwh*, is still on the agenda of the philologians, and one of the latest translations of the Bible finally decides, like Rabbi Yose son of the Damascene (and the Aramaic translator Onkelos as well as the King James Version), that the expression means, "And I will enshrine Him." [14] More than seven examples from the biblical past are drawn upon to illustrate a particular interpretation of the idiom *gʾh gʾh* (*gaʾoh gaʾah*), "He is highly exalted." If this does mean "He lords it over all those who act high and mighty," [15] then the impulse to teach a lesson or two—that in the end the arrogant always get what's coming to them, as Isaiah too predicted,[16] that measure-for-measure will it be meted out to the insufferably proud, as has happened more than once—can hardly resist accumulating case histories: one's hopes for the future need not remain groundless. If something over one-fourth of Shirta's present 1,115 lines, are devoted to the first verse of the Song at the Sea, doubtless

13. This is not to imply that the redactor was indifferent to the *form* of his materials, that he was merely a kind of insensitive amanuensis and no more. Notice (in Pt. II, throughout) how frequently comments or proof texts or illustrations come in threes or sevens, etc.; in other words, in stylized arrangements.

14. *The Torah, A New Translation* (JPS, Philadelphia, 1962). See also the *Commentary* of Jonah ibn Janah (in the edition of A. Z. Rabinowitz [Tel Aviv, 5696], p. 25), s.v. On the root *nwh*, cf. below, Pt. II, chap. 3, s.v. "And I will glorify Him;" also A. Malamat, "Mari and the Bible: Patterns of Tribal Organization" (Heb.), in *Studies in the Bible Presented to M. H. Segal* (Jerusalem, 1964), p. 27.

15. At least the Aramaic versions (Tg Onkelos no less than Tg Jonathan and Jerusalem) are prepared to adopt this view. On *gʾh*, see M. D. Cassuto, "Širat ha-ʿAlilah be-Yiśrael," in *Kneset*, viii (Tel Aviv, 5703–04), 130. See also Luzzatto, p. 275.

16. E.g. Isa. 2:12 ff.

it is because from earliest times the theme and exultant mood of the Song as a whole were recognized in that verse. *Victoriam deumque cano.*

Given a lot, then, the compiler in turn gives us a like amount; given a little (on the clause "The deeps were congealed" he offers no more than "He made them into a kind of cupola"),[17] he is not in a position to give us more. The ancient versions, the Septuagint and the Vulgate, were also apparently at a loss for words this time.[18] The verse reports that it was out of love that God led the Israelites, and either the compiler found nothing more in his source than an explanation of what the love consisted of, or he was in no mood for exegetical exercises on shorthand notes.[19] So—lest we should wonder, What is this suddenly about love; did not God promise long in advance [20] that after centuries of bondage Israel would be quit of Egypt, did He not promise that He would deliver the Israelites who had suffered so unjustly at the hand of the Egyptians and would lead them up to a goodly land; [21] lest we should wonder, What is this sudden special emphasis on love as the motive for His guidance—the Midrash reports, "It was an act of love Thou didst perform for us, for we had no works to our credit." The fact is (so the Midrash compiler's source went on, or perhaps so another source informed him), "From the very beginning the world was created only with love." [22] This is all he tells us here, albeit again and again in other connections in Shirta he is eloquent enough on the theme of God's love for Israel.

Although early editions did not always number the

17. I am not entirely sure of the meaning: Does the Midrash imply that the waters froze and the *ice* was shaped into a kind of "ice-palace," or, *mirabilius dictu,* the waters themselves were formed that way? Perhaps (my Yale Press editor, J. Alkire, has suggested) it means that God molded the waters into an "ice-palace" as they were in the process of freezing.

18. Cf. F. M. Cross, Jr., and D. N. Freedman, "The Song of Miriam" in *JNES,* XIV (1955), 246, n. 23.

19. Cf. *Tanḥuma Exod.,* ed. S. Buber, 31b.

20. Gen. 15:13 f.

21. Exod. 3:7–8.

22. Cf. below, Pt. II, chap. 9, and the notes, ad loc.

chapters the same way,[23] in the editions and surviving manuscripts the material in these chapters seems always to have been organized as it appears today in Shirta. Each chapter closes on a note or with an exposition that makes a reasonable conclusion. To say that no other chapter divisions would be possible is more, I believe, than should be said. On the other hand, a good case can be made for the way the verses are now distributed among the chapters.[24] For example, the way interpretation of 15:5 is made movingly transitional to interpretation of 15:6 [25] helps explain why commentary on these two verses constitutes one chapter, and perhaps some desire to limit the number of chapters to ten may explain why no new chapter begins with the commentary on 15:20.[26] To repeat, however, I do not say that the present chapter divisions are the only ones that could be justified; what can be said is that as the chapters conclude there is nothing offensive to good sense, indeed, they often reflect a fine feeling for style: the end of chapter 6 and the beginning of chapter 7 are just as we would want them. The beginning and end of chapter 9 can even be supported by an attempt to arrange the biblical verses of the Song at the Sea into strophes.[27]

23. Cf. Lauterbach in *HUCA*, I, 429 ff.

24. On the conclusion of chap. 1, see below, Pt. II, the last note of the chapter.

25. Cf. below, Pt. II, ad loc.

26. Is this perhaps a concession to the notion of Ten Songs (cf. Pt. II, chap. 1)?

27. For some recent attempts cf. F. Perles, "On the Strophic Form of Exodus 15," in *JQR*, XVII (1926–27), 403 f.; Cross and Freedman, in *JNES*, XIV, 241 ff.; M. D. Cassuto, *Commentary on the Book of Exodus* (Jerusalem, 1959), pp. 119 ff.; M. Rozelaar, "The Song of the Sea," in *VT*, II (1952), 221 ff.; J. D. W. Watts, "The Song of the Sea— Ex. XV," in *VT*, VII (1957), 371 ff. See also the arrangement in *RSV* and in *The Torah, A New Translation*. For earlier suggestions and literature, see the bibliography in Cross, *Studies*, pp. 340 ff.

2. Mekilta

"The name *Mekhilta, Mekhilata* (literally: measure, measures), for the *Tannaitic* treatises which interpret the Bible
corresponds exactly to [*kanón, kanónes*], the treatise, or
treatises, of logic." [1] Actually, the word "Mekilta" was not
originally [2] restricted to the tannaite Midrash on Exodus.
R. Saadia Gaon (882–942) seems to be the first to mention
specifically Mekilta to the Book of Exodus; [3] the first to
designate the work by the title "Mekilta de-Rabbi Ishmael" was apparently R. Nissim ben Jacob of Kairawan
(ca. 990–1062); [4] and though other tenth and eleventh
century and even later authorities still referred to the work
under other general terms, gradually the name Mekilta
(de-Rabbi Ishmael) became the current and universal one. [5]

1. *HJP*, pp. 78 f. (cf. nn. 250–52, ibid.).

2. For what follows see Lauterbach, "The Name of the Mekilta,"
in *JQR*, XI (1920–21), 169 ff.; J. N. Epstein, "Mechilta and Sifre in
the Works of Maimonides" (Heb.), in *Tarbiz*, VI (1934–35), 99 ff., and
in his *Mebo'ot*, pp. 545 ff.

3. Although apparently he could still speak of Mekiltas, in the
plural, referring to tannaite midrashim as a whole; cf. Epstein, in
Tarbiz, VI, 106 f. As to the consonants *m k y l t ʾ*, see below.

4. Cf. S. Abramson, *Rabbi Nissim Gaon* (Jerusalem, 1965), pp. 20 f.
(of the introduction). On this important work, see now the learned
review by I. Twersky in *Tarbiz*, XXXVII (1968), pp. 318 ff.

5. "From the twelfth century on we find an increasing number of
teachers applying the name 'Mekilta' or 'Mekilta de-Rabbi Ishmael'
as a specific designation for the Midrash to Exodus. However, even
then the older practice of considering this Midrash as a part of the
Sifre and designating it as such still continued. And up to the
close of the fourteenth century we find our Midrash called by both
its older name [*sifre*], as well as by its new name Mekilta. Only after

Perhaps it is as Lauterbach has explained: [6] "We find, indeed, that our Midrash possesses a peculiar characteristic or one special feature which distinguishes it from the other Midrashim of its class, especially from the Sifre to which it originally belonged. . . . This special feature of our Midrash consists of its peculiar arrangement according to tractates." [7]

In other words, the Mekilta is not really one treatise or tractate; [8] it is an assembly of treatises, Mekilata, to adopt for this once the correct vocalization of the Hebrew consonants *m k y l t ᵓ*.[9] A number of treatises or tractates have

---

that period the older mode of designating our Midrash by the name of Sifre was no more used, and the new name Mekilta, or Mekilta de-Rabbi Ishmael, became its sole name" (Lauterbach in *JQR*, XI, 179).

6. *JQR*, XI, 192; cf. *PAAJR*, IV (1933), 113.

7. Note Epstein's stricture in *Tarbiz*, VI, 356, n. 5. His argument from the Sifra, that it too is divided into *megillot* or *massektot*, seems to me no refutation at all; for it is clear from the evidence Epstein himself assembled in his *Tarbiz* article and in his *Meboᵓot* that the Midrash on Leviticus was all the while distinguished as *The* Book, in contrast with the other three books. Hence when the Midrash on Exodus came to be distinguished from the Midrashim on Numbers and Deuteronomy, the very feature Lauterbach describes might well have been the reason for the title Mekilta. On the division of Sifre Zuta into "pericopes," see now S. Lieberman, *Siphre Zutta* (New York, 1968), p. 4, nn. 6–7.

8. See further L. Finkelstein, "The Sources of the Tannaitic Midrashim," in *JQR*, XXXI (1940–41), 211 ff. and esp. 223 ff.

9. "The correct pronunciation of the name is . . . Mekilata and not . . . Mekilta. Not only do the plural forms [*mkyltyn, mkylty,*] and [*mkyltn*] point to such a pronunciation, but we have direct evidence from mediaeval authorities for the plural form. Narboni mentions our Midrash under the name of [*mkylᵓtᵓ*] in the plural form (see Brüll, *Jahrbücher*, IV, p. 164). The doubt raised by Ginzberg . . . on the ground that in Midrash Tehillim 36 (Buber, p. 252) the singular form [*bmdt rby šmᶜwn bn ywhᵓy*] occurs, can easily be removed. The reference there is to one collection of R. Simeon b. Johai, hence the singular is used. But the name of our Midrash given to it because it consists of many collections or tractates, hence it is to be pronounced in the plural form. In a letter Ginzberg calls my attention to the fact that Azobi in his [*Qaᶜrat Kesef*] also gives the name of our Midrash in the plural form. The expression [*hmkyltᵓ mgdt*] (Lekaḥ Tob to Exodus 16.1, Buber 52a) does not prove anything against the plural form of the name, for the reference there is to the one particular tractate of the Mekilta where the quoted saying

been assembled,[10] nine in all, each devoted to a special theme (embodied in specific chapters and verses) of the biblical book of Exodus. And Shirta is a whole tractate in itself, concerned, as I have said, with the Song at the Sea.

As scholars have observed, from the days of David Hoffmann (1843–1921) to the present, Mekilta de-Rabbi Ishmael does not mean that the second-century tanna Rabbi Ishmael was the author of this work. It may be that Rabbi Ishmael's name was attached to the title "Mekilta" because he is the first savant or sage quoted in the exegesis of Exodus 12:2,[11] the first Exodus verse which gets down to the concrete subject of Pisḥa, the first treatise of the Mekilta [12]—for midrashic sources were on occasion named after the first sage referred to in the work. So, for example, in the companion Midrash to our Mekilta, the Mekilta de-Rabbi Simeon, Rabbi Simeon ben Yoḥai is the first authority mentioned. Nevertheless, in our Mekilta the sources assembled do derive ultimately from the School of Rabbi Ishmael. This is principally true of the halakic material, the discussions and views connected with the legal substance.[13] Correspondingly, the Mekilta de-Rabbi Simeon derives from the

occurs. The expression [mah she-ʾomer ha-mekilta] (in ʾOr Zaruᶜa, Hilkot Tefillin, 531), is probably shortened from [mah she-ʾomer baᶜal ha-mekilta] or it should read [mah she-ʾomer bi-mekilta] as in the same paragraph, referring to the same quotation, Or Zarua actually uses the expression [de-ʾamar bi-mekilta]. It cannot be denied, however, that already at a very early time the name was erroneously pronounced in the singular. Thus in the colophon at the end of the Mekilta the name is evidently used in the singular form. In the editions the colophon begins with the words [ḥslt mkyltʾ], and in the manuscripts it begins with the words [slyq mkyltʾ] or [slyq mkyltʾ kwlh], all of them using the singular form of the verb, which shows that they read the name Mekilta in the singular. This may have been originally due to a mistake by the copyists. The mistake was then accepted by many so that it became customary to pronounce the name in the singular form, Mekilta" (Lauterbach, in JQR, XI, 194, n. 23). Cf. PAAJR, IV, 114, n. 6.

10. Cf. also Epstein, Meboʾot, p. 572.

11. In the edition of Lauterbach, I, 15, beginning of chap. 2 of Pisḥa, the first Mekilta treatise.

12. Cf. Lauterbach, in JQR, XI, 195 f.; PAAJR, IV, 115; and Epstein, in Meboʾot, p. 550.

13. For the most detailed and latest analysis, cf. Epstein, Meboʾot, pp. 550 et seq.

School of Rabbi Ishmael's countercolleague, Rabbi Akiba,
one of whose leading disciples was Rabbi Simeon ben
Yoḥai.[14] Differences between these two Schools, that of
Rabbi Ishmael and that of Rabbi Akiba, are reflected also
in the respective technical hermeneutic terminologies and
several exegetical principles adopted by these and the other
tannaite Midrashim.[15]

As regards nonlegal substance, the haggadic (aggadic)
contents, both Schools are more or less at one. Since Shirta
is haggadah from beginning to end, it is not strange that
on this Exodus chapter and theme there is so close an
agreement between Mekilta de-Rabbi Ishmael and Mekilta
de-Rabbi Simeon. Here the Schools of Rabbi Ishmael and
of Rabbi Akiba virtually see eye to eye.[16] This very agreement within the haggadic materials is particularly noteworthy. One is here in the presence of rabbinic *consensus:*
not unanimity, but a hospitality on the part of both
Schools to the same corpus of various teachings for further
study and reflection. Thus one need not hesitate to say
that, for an encounter with the overall tannaite understanding of the Song at the Sea, there is no more reliable
a source than Shirta. And since these representative tannaite teachings profoundly affected subsequent talmudic
interpretation of the Exodus theme, and posttalmudic ones
as well, it may not be unfair to put it this way: Is it your
wish to recognize the Jewish view of the deliverance from
Egyptian bondage? [17] Study Shirta: for thus you learn how
Israel understood slavery and redemption, and to whom
one should cleave.

14. See Epstein's Introduction to *MRS* (and his *Meboʾot*, pp. 725–
40), and E. Z. Melamed's Introduction to *MRS* (Jerusalem, 1955).

15. See on this, briefly, H. L. Strack, *Introduction to the Talmud
and Midrash* (Philadelphia, 1931), pp. 206 and 333.

16. Cf. Epstein's and Melamed's introductions to *MRS* (pp. 25 and
27). See also L. Finkelstein, "Studies in the Tannaitic Midrashim,"
in *PAAJR*, VI (1935), 201, and in *JQR*, XXXI, 215. I do not understand
what E. Z. Melamed, *Ha-Yaḥas* (Jerusalem, 5727), p. 105 (first paragraph) means: the very examples he lists on p. 96 (Exod. 15:1) and
p. 100 (15:8) occur not only in Mekilta de-Rabbi Simeon but in our
Mekilta too (the edition of Lauterbach, II, 1 and 53).

17. See also *Midrash Tannaim* (Berlin, 1909), p. 86, on Deut. 15:15.

3. The Past Made Present and Immediate

Chapter 15 of the Book of Exodus begins with the words, "Then sang Moses and the children of Israel." Shirta teaches us that in Scripture the word "then" sometimes refers to times past and sometimes to times in the future. Even though, in that particular comment, Shirta declares that the "then" of Exodus 15:1 refers to the occasion in the past when the Israelites miraculously escaped from their pursuing foes, no reader of Shirta's ten chapters can fail to recognize that what is astir in the minds of the tannaite savants is not only—one may dare to say, not mainly —the event in ancient history, but also the immediate and poignant reflections produced by historical reminiscence, itself recurringly revived by the experiences in their, the Sages', times. "Ah, take her as of yore," wrote Judah ha-Levi (ca. 1075–1141) [1] centuries later,

> And cast her forth no more;
> Let sunlight crown her day
> And shadows flee away.
> > *Then a new song*
> > *Sang Thy redeemèd throng.*

> For Thy belovèd throng
> Still come to Thee with song,

1. For these dates cf. Ḥ. Shirman, "The Life of Jehuda Ha-Levi" (Heb.), in *Tarbiz*, ix (1937), 36 f.; and Professor Shalom Spiegel called my attention to the studies by S. D. Goitein, "Rabbi Yehuda Hallevi in Spain in the Light of the Geniza Papers" (Heb.), in *Tarbiz*, xxiv (1954), 21 ff. (specifically, p. 33) and "The Biography of Rabbi Judah Ha-Levi in the Light of the Cairo Geniza Documents," in *PAAJR*, xxviii (1959), 41 ff. (specifically, pp. 42 and 56, n. 40).

Singing with one accord:
Now who is like Thee 'mid the gods, O Lord!
Still Thy redeemèd throng
Sing a new song.[2]

Such immediacy in the Song at the Sea Shirta had already
discovered, and it elevated to the contemporary and prophetic and ultimate almost every single word of the 224
Hebrew words in Exodus 15:1–21. A very early reader [3] of
the Mekilta once observed: The Song at the Sea was only
one of ten songs sung by Israel, the tenth being that to be
sung in the Age to Come, when deliverance will be everlasting. Not only long ago was the Lord highly exalted:
His exalted reality will be manifest again when all the
high and mighty are finally cut down to size. Once upon a
time, before the Holy One, blessed be He, brought low the
worldly and world empires, He first brought their Guardian Princes to account; it will be no different in the Future.
God was Israel's salvation in the past, and *that* He will be
again.[4] And why, in the Song at the Sea, did the Israelites
say "My father's God, and I will exalt Him?" Because what
they meant was: "It is not only for the miracles Thou hast
wrought for me that I recite songs and hymns before Thee,
but for the miracles which Thou hast wrought for my
fathers and for me, and continuest to perform for me in
every single generation." Clearly, for the Tannaim history
is a preview of that future which arrives with the End of
time.

God, to be sure, is called "The Warrior," and has all the
military equipment the engagements demand. But He is
in need of none of it, for He battles by means of His Name:

2. This is from the rhymed version of Shirah Ḥadashah ("A New
Song") by Nina Salamon in *Selected Poems of Jehudah Halevi*
(Philadelphia, 1928), p. 171. For the combination of the Egyptian
experience in the past with the yearning for ultimate redemption,
see also the poem in the *Passover Haggadah*, ed. E. D. Goldschmidt
(Jerusalem, 1960), p. 104. For poetry contrasting Exodus and Exile,
departure from Egypt and departure from Jerusalem, see A. Mirsky,
"From Midrash to Piyyut to Jewish Poetry" (Heb.), in *Lešonenu*,
XXXII (1968), 129 ff.

3. See J. Goldin, "This Song" in the (forthcoming) *Salo W. Baron
Jubilee Volume*.

4. See also *Mid. Tan.*, p. 118, and cf. *Sifre Deut.*, 190, p. 232.

"And woe to the Nations of the World at what they hear with their own ears!"—when in the Future the Creator engages them in battle.

There is nothing tautologous about repetition of God's Name, for He was the God in the beginning and He will be the same in the end; He reveals Himself one way and another way and still other ways, to suit the variety of occasions; but it is always He and none other. Verbs in the Song reporting the acts of God appear in the future (imperfect) tense rather than the perfect, for good reason: they announce what is yet to happen. Of course, the tyrants and the insolent can imitate the literary style appropriate only for deity, but they are simply full of bombast, and the moment God blows with His wind, they are proved to be windbags. As once long ago the Nations of the World were forced to admit that among their gods there is none like God, so in the end too they will abandon their idolatry. As He worked wonders with the early generations, so He alone will work wonders with the later ones, for an enduring mercy is His mercy:

> Blessed be the Lord, the God of Israel,
> Who alone doth wondrous things,
> And blessed be His glorious Name forever;
> And let the whole earth be filled with His Glory!
> Amen, and Amen.

By virtue of the Torah and of the royal house of David they were later to accept, and of the Temple that they were going to build in the future, did God guide this people. Like the Egyptians at the time of the exodus, so subsequently all the Canaanite monarchs were reduced to stone-like lifelessness. Even the older generation of Israelites unwittingly prophesied and never guessed that they were uttering a prophecy, as coming events established; by the same token they foretold that the day would come when Israel would be resettled permanently on their Land, never again to be uprooted from it.

> Come, O Israel, who were designated Very-Own,
> To the Land of Israel, which was designated Very-Own,

> And build the Temple, which was designated Very-
> Own,
> By virtue of the Torah, which was designated Very-
> Own!
> That is why it is said,
> "In Thy Very-Own mountain." [5]

When in the Future His hands reestablish His Sanctuary, His sovereignty will be accepted everywhere by everyman for all time.

How did the Tannaim feel about the biblical verses? That the ones describing the first redemption were drawing the design for the final redemption too.

Such being the principal mood of Shirta, even though its purpose is expository—to teach the meaning of the words and phrases and sentences of a text—the discussion is once and again suddenly lifted from the syntax of prose to joyous, lyrical, and poetic exclamation. Or, more exactly: since the treatise is commentary on a poem, and since its mood is as I have attempted to describe it by means of summary, Shirta statements on a number of occasions get infected by the quality of the very source being interpreted and its theme, and themselves become poetic expression. If the verse says, "I will sing unto the Lord, for He is highly exalted," the commentator can hardly refrain from striking the chord,

> In the Lord greatness is comely,
> In the Lord power is comely,
> In the Lord glory, victory, and majesty are comely;
>> exactly as David says, "Thine, O Lord, is the great-
>> ness, and the power, and the glory, and the
>> victory, and the majesty."

"I will sing unto the Lord," Moses and the Israelites sang; and the commentator is swept by a waterfall of verses from the Psalms and a Deuteronomic song and lines from the Song of Songs. Not only adults sang the Song at the Sea, but infants too; and not only the infants, but those unborn still in their mothers' wombs; [6] and not only

5. Cf. below, pp. 19 f.
6. See also Ba-Ḥodesh, III, end (II, 220): " 'For sweet is thy voice'

humans but angels too: "O Lord, our Lord, how glorious
is Thy Name in all the earth! Whose majesty is rehearsed
above in the heavens." Is that all? No. For the heavens also
rejoiced at the redemption of Israel, and along with the
heavens the mountains "and all the hills, fruit trees and
every cedar, as it is said, 'Sing, O ye heavens, for the Lord
hath done it; shout, ye lowest parts of the earth; break forth
into singing, ye mountains, O forest, and every tree therein.'
And why? 'For the Lord hath redeemed Jacob, and doth
glorify Himself in Israel'; and it says, 'Sing, O heavens, and
be joyful, O earth.' "

The Shirah is the song that Israel sang. But do not all
the nations really proclaim the praises of the Creator?
Indeed they do, but Israel's praises are the sweetest before
Him. Listen to the litany:

1

Israel: "Hear O Israel: the Lord our God, the Lord is
     One."

The Holy Spirit: "And who is like Thy people Israel,
          a nation one in the earth."

2

Israel: "Who is like unto Thee among the mighty?"

The Holy Spirit: "Happy art thou, O Israel, who is
          like unto thee."

3

Israel: "(What great nation is there with a god so nigh)
     as the Lord our God is whensoever we call upon
     Him."

The Holy Spirit: "And what great nation is there that
          hath statutes and ordinances so
          righteous . . ."

4

Israel: "For Thou art the glory of their strength."

The Holy Spirit: "O Israel, in whom I am glorified."

(Cant. 2:14) at the Sea, (when thou didst say,) 'I will sing unto the
Lord, for He is highly exalted'; 'Thine appearance is comely' (Cant.,
ibid.), (when) 'From the mouths of babes and sucklings, Thou hast
founded strength' (Ps. 8:3)," that is, there was then sung the song
with the word ʿz (the Lord is my *strength*).

What prompts Israel to refer to their Redeemer as "my father's God"? The deep consciousness that

> A queen, the daughter of queens am I,
> Beloved, the daughter of beloved ones,
> Holy, the daughter of holy ones,
> Pure, the daughter of the pure.

No one would be tempted to forget origins like these. More important however, one now understands why Canticles is the love song of God's relations with Israel.

It is not superfluous to add "The Lord is His Name" after the words "The Lord is a man of war," for the repetition underscores that He is

> The same in Egypt, the same at the Sea,
> The same in the past, the same in the Age to Come,
> The same in this world, the same in the World to Come.

A similar impulse very probably led George Frideric Handel in the eighteenth century to repeat "The Lord shall reign for ever and ever" several times in his oratorio "Israel in Egypt."

Measure for measure is one of the principles making intelligible God's governance of the universe, and Shirta repeatedly refers to and enlarges on this. But even in the midst of a perfectly prosaic observation thereof, Shirta will suddenly be inspired. The Egyptians sank in the depths of the sea like a stone because they hardened their hearts like stone; "but as for Thee,

> Thy goodness, Thy manifold mercies, and Thy compassion
> are upon us,
> And Thy right hand is extended
> to all the inhabitants of the world,

as it is said, 'Thy right hand, O Lord . . . Thy right hand, O Lord'—(not once, but) two times!" Commentary is approaching the idiom of liturgy. And this will happen again: would that at the Sea Israel had declared not "The Lord *will* be King for ever and ever," but instead had used the present tense, as does the Aramaic version. That slip of the tongue, a Galilean sage felt, has been responsible for a severely long and trying interregnum.

> But verily over Thy people,
> Thy flock, Thy sheep,
> The sheep of Thy pasture,
> The seed of Abraham who loved Thee,
> The children of Isaac Thy favorite,
> The community of Jacob Thy firstborn son,
> The vine Thou didst pluck out of Egypt
> And the stock which Thy right hand hath planted,
> "May the Lord reign for ever and ever."

Adjectives and figures of speech become poetry's hints and code and "say something to us we can learn / By heart and when alone repeat." For example, Scripture speaks of the heart of the sea, of the heart of the terebinth, of the heart of heaven. This is instructive:

> (At first) the Sea
> Had had no heart, and then was given a heart . . .
> (At first) the Terebinth
> Had had no heart, and then was given a heart . . .
> (At first) the Heavens
> Had had no heart, and then were given a heart . . .

> Come, O Sea . . .
> Punish the Egyptians
> Who had a heart (at first)
> But enslaved the Israelites
> In all calamitous ways . . .[7]

> Come, Terebinth . . .
> Punish Absalom
> Who had a heart (at first)
> But stole—three thefts!—
> His father's heart,
>   the supreme court's heart,
>   the heart of Israel's men . . .

> Come, Heavens . . .
> Shower manna like dew for Israel

7. Cf. Origen's lovely comment on Exod. 15:5, where he says, "Peccatores graves sunt" (Migne, *PG*, XII, 334).

Who had a heart (at first)
Received the Torah
And served the Name (Lord)
   with all their heart
   and all their soul . . .

Or, consider the following: "Four were called majestic,"
the Holy One, blessed be He, Israel, Egypt, and the waters.

The Holy One appeared, who is majestic,
To Israel, who were called majestic,
To punish Egypt, which was called majestic,
By waters, which were called majestic,
   as it is said, "They sank like lead in majestic waters."

Or again: "Four were designated Masterpiece," Israel, the
Land of Israel, the Temple, and the Torah.

Come, O Israel, who were designated Masterpiece,
To the Land, which was designated Masterpiece,
And build the Temple, which was designated Master-
   piece,
By virtue of the Torah, which was designated Master-
   piece!
   That is why it is said,
   "This people Thou didst produce." [8]

8. Cf. above, p. 15 f. In connection with poetic expression in midrash,
one more feature deserves to be noted, though it is not confined to
commentary on poetry and appears therefore in all exegetical and
homiletical Midrashim. When a string of statements on a verse or
on some general proposition is offered, the Midrash may put the
statements into a fixed, stylized formulary, the repetition of which
produces an incantation effect. See, for example, the block of statements in chapter 6 introduced by "The same you have to say of"
and closing with "But Scripture resorts to euphemism"; or, again in
the same chapter, the section beginning with "Mightily dost Thou
exalt Thyself," or the beginning of chapter 7, and so on. While it is
probably true that such verbal recapitulations were intended as aids
to memorization, always important where Oral Torah is cultivated,
it may also be that either the homilists or the redactors or both were
aware of the poetic element in such word-by-word repetition. Note
the effect, for example, of the sevenfold repetition of an epigrammatic
formula in the *Mishnah*—in other words, in a halakic connection—
Parah 8:2–7.

4. The Relevance of Nonliteral Exegesis

Shirta, then, is indebted to the nature of the text it is elucidating for its own fairly frequent outbursts into song. But let me return for a moment to the matter of mood. "What is astir in the minds of the tannaite Sages is not only . . . the event in ancient history, but also the immediate and poignant reflections produced by historical reminiscence, itself recurringly revived by the experiences in their, the Sages', times." As we read some of the comments in Shirta, the preoccupations of the tannaite centuries, the first two centuries of our era, are projected so distinctly that the feeling is inescapable that something foreign is being forced into the original. According to Rabbi (Judah the Prince), the reason the verse reads "Then *yashir* Moses and the children of Israel," with the verb "sang" in the future (imperfect), rather than "Then *shar* Moses and the children of Israel," with the verb in the perfect tense, is to teach that the doctrine of Resurrection of the dead is based on a Pentateuch passage. The foe shattered by the Lord's right hand is, according to one interpretation, Esau, which is of course Rome.[1] Though Rabbi (Judah the Prince) is careful not to give reckless reassurances to Antoninus, who is contemplating a campaign against Alexandria, the saintly rabbi feels that a reliable intelligence report is available in

---

1. Cf. Ginzberg, *Legends*, v, 116, 271 ff., 278, 280, 294, 309; and vi, 68. Cf. A. Bender, "Das Lied Exodus 15," in *ZAW*, XXIII (1903), 24 f.: "dies Wort [ᵓoyeb, enemy], welches im Psalter immer ohne Artikel steht, bezeichnet abgesehen von [Psalm] 106, 10 den Feind katexochen, die heidnische Weltmacht, unter der die Gemeinde des zweiten Tempels seufzt."

an Ezekiel passage; and for the compiler of Shirta this is further evidence that the Egyptians may appropriately be compared with chaff (and with lead, rather than silver or gold; and with little foxes, rather than lions or bears or leopards). When Pharaoh wishes to inflame his own people with warlike passions, he promises to open up to them his *thesauroi* of silver and gold and other treasures. As the Israelites are to advance toward the Promised Land, what the Moabites fear is being subjected to annonary imposts. In their Song at the Sea Moses and the children of Israel sing of "the exact location of Thine abode," because "the terrestrial Throne faces over against the celestial Throne." [2]

We describe such interpretations as anachronistic and homiletical, which they plainly are, and forthwith dismiss them from serious consideration because they are not literal exegesis. They are certainly not to be treated as literal exegesis. Yet it would be a mistake to deny them all exegetical value. For, specifically in the case of Shirta, something of the primary source—the Song of Exodus 15—is preserved perhaps just because of the homiletical nature of the commentary. How so? Well, regardless of the number of strophes one divides the poem into, or the lines where presumably new strophes begin,[3] regardless too of the genuinely archaic character of some of the biblical expressions, what is perfectly clear is that the Song begins with God's triumph and moves in a prophetic forward direction, finally to a climax in an accomplishment long after the miracle in the Sea.[4] In other words, a cue for prophetic

2. On this notion, cf. *Legends,* VI, p. 74 (and also below, Pt. II, chap. 10, and notes, ad loc.). Of course the idea of such correspondence may be quite ancient (cf. the notes in V. Aptowitzer, "The Heavenly Temple in the Agada" (Heb.), in *Tarbiz,* II [1930–31], 140–45), but the exegetical statement that *makon = mekuwwan* (for both the consonants would be *mkwn*), is tannaite.

3. Cf. above, p. 8, n. 27.

4. Note even Cross and Freedman, in *JNES,* XIV, 240a: "There can be little doubt that the poet in vs. 16b anticipates the entry into the land of Canaan. The point of view is that of the Israelite host poised on the far side of the Jordan for conquest, or looking toward the consummation of the Conquest, being already engaged in the preliminary phases of it. It is difficult to decide whether the poet

interpretation of the Song is already in the Song itself.[5]
If now Shirta proceeds to refer terms in the Song to times
and situations in the future, or to interpret certain verbs as
predictive because several of them (not just one or two) are
in the future tense, though (prosaically at least) an ordinary
past would be expected, it is not altogether inimical to the
predisposition of the original biblical text. Shirta may thus
be reminding us that the Song at the Sea itself was intended
to convey more than the miracle at the *Sea*. Say what one
will, therefore, of the substantive content of Shirta, it is
a disclosing commentary: because in addition to the hortatory and haggadic approach it adopts in general, it does
not neglect to seek explanation for what often remains
difficult even for the literal commentator;[6] because it takes
hints from the biblical text it interprets; and, above all,
because it is responsive to the mood and melodiousness of
the original text. Whatever else they may have been, the
Tannaim were not naive in their understanding of the
Song at the Sea, and in Shirta they were not telling Tales
of the Ḥasidim.[7]

This direct response to the text of Exodus 15 can help
to explain the presence of still other elements in Shirta.
Measure for measure were the Egyptians punished; measure for measure were other wicked ones in history punished; a kind of measure for measure governs the dialogue and conduct of Israel with and toward God. Shirta

---

actually is in that situation, or has adopted that perspective, though
living at a somewhat later time. The writers [Cross and Freedman]
are inclined to the latter position." Cf. S. R. Driver, *Commentary on
Exodus* (Cambridge, 1911), p. 129; and Loewenstamm, pp. 15 and
114.

5. Observe how a "modern" scholar, A. Bender (in his study in
ZAW, xxiii, 1903), finds messianic signs everywhere in the Song.

6. The form for *ᶜzy* (*ᶜozzi*, with a *qameṣ* under the *ᶜ*) is still a
problem; so too *ʾnwhw* of v. 2, *yksymw* of v. 5, *nʾdry* of v. 6, *ʾymth*
of v. 16, and so on, let alone archaic forms like *yʾklmw*, *tmlʾmw*,
ksmw, etc., or the MT reading of *ydmw* (v. 16, on which, e.g., see
recently M. Dahood, in *Biblica*, xliii [1962], 248 f.; cf. below, Pt. II,
chap. 9, ad loc.).

7. The sermon of Rabbi (Judah the Prince) in chapter 10 is no
refutation of what I say here; cf. the note, ad loc., s.v. "On one occasion."

seems never to weary of this *talio* theme, and in this instance too it is the biblical text which has furnished if not
the model then at least the encouragement. Perhaps those
biblical critics are right who say that in the Song of Exodus
15 there is nothing to indicate what is reported in Exodus
14: [8] "Then Moses held out his arm over the sea and the
Lord drove back the sea with a strong east wind all that
night, and turned the sea into dry ground. The waters were
split, and the Israelites went into the sea on dry ground,
the waters forming a wall for them on their right and on
their left. The Egyptians came in pursuit after them into
the sea, all of Pharaoh's horses, chariots, and horsemen.
. . . [The Lord] locked the wheels of their chariots so that
they moved forward with difficulty. . . . Then the Lord
said to Moses, 'Hold out your arm over the sea, that the
waters may come back upon the Egyptians and upon their
chariots and upon their horsemen.' Moses held out his arm
over the sea, and at daybreak the sea returned to its normal
state, and the Egyptians fled at its approach. But the Lord
hurled the Egyptians into the sea. The waters turned back

8. Even Cross and Freedman, who part company with those insist-
ing on a late date of composition for the Song because "the song
is vague with regard to the miraculous events and . . . must be
further removed from the historical scene!", write (*JNES*, xiv, 238b):
"The poem itself, if read with an appreciation of hyperbolic Semitic
imagery and figurative language, tells no explicit narrative. So far as
the action is concerned, it describes only the destruction of the
Egyptians, with an allusion to the safe transit of the Israelites.
Nothing is related, however, of the manner of the Israelite crossing.
Vss. 8 and 10 describe in highly colored terms the wind and waves
of a tempest at sea. The Egyptians were drowned in a storm sent by
Yahweh. They were hurled into the sea (vss. 1b, 4) and sank under
the waters (vss. 5, 10). It is a mistake to see in the phrases, 'the waters
are heaped up' and 'the swells mount as a wall' (vs. 8), a description
of a path miraculously appearing between two walls of water." (On
this last sentence, however, contrast Loewenstamm, pp. 117 f.) Or
Cross again (in "The Divine Warrior," in *Biblical Motifs*, ed. A. Alt-
mann [Cambridge, Mass., 1966], p. 27, n. 58), "there is no hint of the
sea drying up, or of a path through the sea, in Exodus 15. These are
later accretions, probably arising precisely from the ritual crossing
of Jordan." Cf. M. Noth, *Das zweite Buch Mose, Exodus* (Göttingen,
1959), p. 96.

and covered the chariots and the horsemen—Pharaoh's entire army that had followed after them—into the sea; not one of them remained. But the Israelites marched through the sea on dry ground, the waters forming for them a wall on their right and on their left." [9]

There is no gainsaying that if only the first eighteen verses of the fifteenth chapter of Exodus had survived, we would not know that the sea turned into dry ground; that on it the Israelites passed through; that in the waters which turned back suddenly after they had been split to make way for the Israelites' crossing, Pharaoh's entire host were drowned. Perhaps the description of "the wind and waves of a tempest at sea" would have suggested no more to us than that the earth trembled at the presence of the Lord, at the presence of the God of Jacob, when Israel went out of Egypt. But the fifteenth chapter inherited by the Tannaim, and before them by the Psalmists and others, was already attached to the larger narrative framework. Who, reading the unit as a whole, and then meeting in the Song at the Sea vocabulary like "Horse and driver He has hurled into the sea," "Pharaoh's chariots and his army He has cast into the sea; and the pick of his officers are drowned in the Sea of Reeds"; "At the blast of Your nostrils the waters piled up, the floods stood straight like a wall"; "The foe said, I will pursue, I will overtake"; "You made Your wind blow, the sea covered them"; "You put out Your right hand"—who, reading the prose narrative of the flight from Egypt and then meeting such expressions and images in the Song, could have doubted that the two were intimately interconnected? And if so, in its essentials the Song does celebrate the justice meted out: it was measure for measure. Not only had the Egyptians, preferring to forget Joseph's services to them, drowned the newborn male children of the Hebrews long before, but in the present instance the pursuing Egyptians with their chariots and their horsemen were prepared to push Israel into the sea, if need be.[10] There is nothing extravagant, therefore, about

9. *The Torah: A New Translation*, p. 124.
10. Cf. Mekilta, Be-Shallaḥ, III (I, 205, 211), IV (I, 216, line 5).

a measure-for-measure interpretation of the theme of drowning and punishment in the Song: [11]

> Horse and his rider hath He thrown into the sea . . .
> Pharaoh's chariots and his host He hath cast into the
> sea:
> His chosen captains also are drowned in the Reed Sea.
> The depths have covered them:
> They sank into the bottom . . .
> Thou didst blow with Thy wind, the sea covered them:
> They sank . . . in the mighty waters.

11. Note a biblical expression like that in I Sam. 15:33, also Est. 7:9 f. On the "universality" of the measure-for-measure principle, cf. S. Lieberman in *LGJV* (Hebrew vol.), p. 255, n. 56.

5. Haggadic Interpretation

To call attention to the noteworthy compatibility of Shirta with the Song of Exodus 15 is in no way to suggest that Shirta confines its exegesis to the near-fetched and shuns the familiar devices of haggadic Midrash, such as word plays, free association, exaggeration, imaginative dramatization and overdramatization. Some aspects of Shirta's haggadah we have observed above, but it will not be superfluous to consider the following.

Since no word in Scripture is redundant,[1] certain grammatical constructions are bound to be provocative. For example, "He is highly exalted" equals $g^{\jmath}h \; g^{\jmath}h$ (ga*oh ga*ah) in the Hebrew; that is, the conjugated verb is accompanied by the infinitive absolute. And in the present case, one may add, infinitive absolute and conjugated form appear with identical consonants. This must be purposeful, and one authority in Shirta does not find it unreasonable that action and corresponding reaction are being suggested here: "He exalted me," Israel declares, "and I exalted Him. In Egypt He exalted me . . . so too in Egypt I exalted Him. . . . At the Sea He exalted me . . . so too at the Sea I exalted Him." [2]

Similarly, stylistic peculiarities are not the result of ac-

---

1. Cf. *Mid. Tan.*, pp. 205 and 262 (last line). See also E. J. Bickerman, in *PAAJR*, XXVIII, 36. For the Christian attitude, see de Lubac, IV, 61 f.

2. Such grammatical constructions can be of halakic significance also; cf., e.g., M. Baba Meṣiaᶜ 2:9 (and Albeck's supplementary note on IV, p. 419 of the Albeck-Yalon edition [Jerusalem-Tel Aviv, 1952–58]), M. Ḥullin 12:3.

cident. If there is anything in an odd verbal root, and its
letters can be manipulated to intimate that I stand in some
relationship to Him, Abba Saul can tell me what *imitatio
dei* really means; hence, *w'nwhw (we-'anwehu)* may be a
prod that *'ani,* I, ought to be like *hu',* like Him. Repetitions of clauses and phrases? We have already seen above
what significance there is to a sentence like "The Lord is
a man of war, the Lord is His Name." [3] But there are
others. "Thy right hand, O Lord . . . Thy right hand, O
Lord," we read in Exodus 15:6, and once again in verse 12
it says, "Thy right hand." One interpretation has it that
since there is a left hand as well as a right hand, this
refrain of "right hand, right hand," reveals something
about God's relation to Israel: "When Israel do the will
of God, they make His left hand into a right hand . . . But
when Israel do not do the will of God, they make His right
hand into a left hand . . ." And what in turn does that
mean? The Lord neither slumbers nor sleeps, Scripture
reassures us. On the other hand, it also reports cries to
Him, "Wake up!" Is this a case of Scripture contradicting
itself? Not at all, for now we know why at times even God
nods. Thus we know also why sometimes this merciful God
is shaken with fury, why sometimes this Defender of Israel
leaves Israel in the lurch.

Not for nothing is the clause "Till (Thy) people pass
over" repeated, for even in the Song at the Sea, more than
the crossing at the Sea of Reeds was celebrated.

Given the right ambiguous verbal root, heaps of water
can be made cunning. Paronomasia will convert what may
be a heap or a hill or a wall into a water bottle. An unusual
spelling may lead one to contemplate not only celestials or
mighty ones, but what extraordinary powers are necessary
to keep one's peace under certain provocations.

Though the Egyptians were drowned in the Sea, they
were spared the horror of remaining *insepulti.* So say the
words of the Song, "the earth swallowed them." [4] The
reason nations like the Philistines, Edomites, Moabites, and
others inside the boundaries of Canaan trembled at the

3. Cf. above, p. 14 f.
4. Note also Exod. 14:30b.

news of Israel's sensational progress is that they now
remembered in their past what they wished had never
happened. That Miriam and the Israelite women had taken
along musical instruments for a journey through the desert
only goes to show what confidence is possessed by those
who are righteous.

A parable can make you see not only how two things
resemble each other, but also how they differ. Compare the
publicity broadcast about the virtues of flesh-and-blood
sovereigns and of the Sovereign over all! Watch a military
parade and every squadron leader is the image of a major
general, and the general is often indistinguishable from the
brass surrounding him; yet at the miracle in the Sea, even
a handmaid could tell at a glance who was the Com-
mander-in-chief. No father accompanied his restless son
with greater solicitude than God did Israel. Consider men
who have been famous as soldiers and field marshals, and
recall their incompetence; then think of Him who is hailed
in the Song at the Sea as Man of War. If you want to know
what Pharaoh sounded like as he ranted and vowed what
he would do with Israel once he got to them, think of pre-
campaign and campaign promises, or of some gangster (or
zealot) eyeing the royal palace with envy and sedition in
his heart.[5] How can you possibly compare God's handiwork
with human craftsmanship! To God what is humanly impossible is possible.[6] When do we generally recognize that
the monarch's reign has begun? Obviously when he's taken
over occupancy of the royal palace and settled down in it.

In other words, Shirta, like the other haggadic sections
in the Mekilta and its kindred tannaite Midrashim, is not
without its fair share of homiletical flourishes and con-

5. For a contrast between king and *lestés*, see also John 18:39–40.
I am unable to make up my mind about the *lestés* in this parable
(hence my hedging in the parenthesis). The term may well be a
reference to insurrectionists or even more specifically to Zealots (with
a capital Z). According to Hengel, p. 25, *lestés* and *lestai* are the
most common expression for Zealots in Josephus; cf. his whole second
chapter. His remarks on p. 233 would certainly add to the pointed-
ness of the parable of the monarch's reign beginning on taking occupancy of the royal palace, in Shirta, 10, p. 238 f.

6. See also Pisḥa, VII (1, 55), the first comment on "I am the Lord."

ceits and elaborations. Nevertheless, in my opinion it would
be pedantry of the most unimaginative kind to regard its
exegesis—*taken as a whole* [7]—condescendingly. There is (to
speak for the time being only of Shirta, for that is the
treatise we are concerned with) a remarkable confluence of
the forthright explanatory with the hortatory and expan-
sive, of the commonsensical with the passionate, which en-
dows Shirta with the seriousness of Exodus 15 itself,[8] and
saves the treatise on the one hand from pettiness and on
the other from flamboyance.

7. I mean by this, not lifting one or two passages and picking away
at them without considering the whole accumulation of commentary
and the relationship between the literal and the haggadic explanations. Contrast Shirta, for example, with Origen's Homily VI (in his
"Homilies on Exodus," in Migne, *PG,* XII, 331–40) or with the Midrash
Wa-Yosha ᶜ (in A. Jellinek, *Bet ha-Midrasch,* I [Jerusalem, 1938], 35–
37).

8. Cf. H. de Lubac, *Exégèse médiévale,* 4 vols. (Aubier, 1959), I, 665
(although his remarks are in an entirely different context): "L'intérêt
porté à la lettre, et le goût dominant de l'esprit ne sont pas forcément
voués au divorce; le sens de l'histoire et l'élan mystique ne sont nul-
lement incompatibles. En revanche,—la chose aussi n'est que trop
certaine, et l'histoire de l'exégèse moderne dans l'Église avant le
renouveau scientifique de la fin du xixᵉ siècle n'en offrirait égale-
ment que trop d'attestations,—le littéralisme est tout autre chose que
la critique, le rejet de toute 'allégorie' n'est pas une garantie de
sérieux dans l'histoire, et l'on peut être aussi piètre érudit que maigre
spirituel."

But perhaps even more to the point here is what E. J. Bickerman
once put beautifully in discussing "The Septuagint as a Translation" (*PAAJR,* XXVIII, 34 f.): "The spirit of the age blew in Jerusalem
as well as in Alexandria. . . . The 'Seventy' approached the Torah
with . . . present-mindedness. As Philo later aptly remarks, when the
Scripture tells us that Terah left Chaldea and migrated to Haran,
the sacred author intends not to state a historical fact, but to give
a lesson of great service to our life. In their much maligned and
rarely understood exegesis of the Bible the rabbis followed the same
principle of living interpretation. For them, as for the 'Seventy,' as
for Philo, as for the sectarians of the Dead Sea, as later for church
fathers, the Scripture was not a monument of the dead past but a
way of their own life."

6. The Theme of the Song

For the Song at the Sea is serious in the extreme, and there is no mistaking what this ode proclaims: the triumph is God's triumph, from beginning to end. He is the truly exalted, and to Him even horses and chariots and top-flight officers are as nothing! He is my strength (and the theme of my song); [1] He is my salvation; He is my God and not just recently acknowledged by me; He is the Warrior responsible for the present victory; it is His right hand that crushed the enemy, His wrath that consumed them as though they were no more than stubble, His breath that mobilized the waters of the Sea. Who is like Him anywhere, who with His abilities? What He can bring about by just stretching forth His right hand! He redeemed and led this people to the appointed destination, to the dismay and terror of a number of powers, this one and that one and the third and others. All this was accomplished with His right hand, His mighty arm, and like stone were the hostile nations all around stilled. The ones He loved He brought to the holy habitation which was of His doing and making. It is He who reigns *in saecula saeculorum,* or, as the Vulgate (15:18) says, *in aeternum et ultra.* No one else redeemed Israel, no one else brought the astonishing deliverance, no one else led them to and into the country which was His own high range. As a later prophet said, "He divided the waters before them to make for Himself an everlasting name." [2]

This is the theme of the Song and Shirta never for a moment forgets it. That is why it spells out: "It was in

1. So the Midrash interprets the word *zmrt.*
2. Isa. 63:12b. Cf. *Sifre Deut.,* 306, p. 343; *Mid. Tan.,* p. 186 bottom.

praise of the Lord they recited it, and they did not recite it in praise of flesh and blood." This time even the women knew better than they were to know at a later triumph; [3] hence they too struck up with "Sing ye to the *Lord.*" Such praises and acclamations as are met with in Exodus 15 belong properly only to the Lord, and David knew it too. There is no denying that the vocabulary of high praise is employed even for those who are not divine; but this very fact exposes the preposterousness of flattery. No, the Lord alone is deserving of a te deum, not even His angels merit it. Repeatedly in history [4] there have been high-and-mighty ones, and to hear their boastings, you would think that theirs was the kingdom and power and glory. Idiots, that's what they were, wrecked in the end by the very resources on which they built their false sense of security and omnipotence.

The whole experience of Israel, at the Sea and elsewhere, says Shirta, is not to be explained in natural terms. What took place at the exodus (and what will in the end take place again) can be understood only as a supernatural, miraculous activity and event. You might legitimately ask of course, *Everything* a supernatural feat? What, for instance, is out of the ordinary in a horse and its rider drowning in the sea? [5] Does it take a god to get rid of a cavalry-

3. See on that eulogy, Gevirtz, pp. 15–24: it's almost as though Shirta would bear him out. Note, however, S. E. Loewenstamm, "Remarks on Stylistic Patterns in Biblical and Ugaritic Literatures" (Heb.), in *Lešonenu,* XXXII (1968), 33 f.

4. You'd think that by now criminals might have learned the lesson. I believe this is in part the intent of these summaries of biblical events (already a feature in some Psalms; see, e.g., Ps. 106); cf., for example, below, Shirta, 8, pp. 193 f. On reviewing biblical history with a particular theme in mind, cf. also Heb. 11.

5. On horse and rider, cf. Cassuto in his *Commentary on Exodus,* pp. 124 f. (and his study, "Širat ha-ʿAlilah be-Yisrael," in *Kneset,* VIII, 121 ff.). On this image of horse and rider, see also some interesting observations by Sister M. U. Vogel, Some Aspects of the Horse and Rider in *The Debate between the Body and the Soul* (Washington, D.C., 1948), pp. 31–37. And my colleague Professor Joel Kraemer calls to my attention the study by R. W. Ackerman, "*The Debate of the Body and the Soul* and Parochial Christianity," in *Speculum,* XXXVII (1962), 541–65.

man? So Shirta explains that "the horse and its rider" did not meet a natural drowning; the way man and beast were hurled this time was no human achievement. Indeed, the language of the biblical song is deliberately chosen to inform us how a whole army can be made to appear and to be as ineffective as one soldier. Or consider the deeps congealing or freezing: [6] even this was unlike some winter scene on a pond or a lake or a river.[7] And shallows can be as calamitous as the fathomless deep.

On the other hand, one sometimes wonders, how trustworthy is the biblical report? For example: here are the Israelites at the Sea, but they know what Pharaoh, back in Egypt, is planning; which only goes to prove that we are dealing with a supernatural phenomenon! [8] This makes it possible for us to understand how Moses *and* the children of Israel together could spontaneously sing the same Song at one and the same time.[9] So too we can appreciate that a man will sometimes say something, say it even with a lot of feeling, and not grasp what he himself is saying.

The commentary and the text, in short, teach the same primary lesson, and the commentary has recognized the chief objective of the text. This is not to say that they are both the same. "Shirta" is not Exodus 15 and Exodus 15 is not "Shirta": it is disastrous to confuse text and commentary, regardless of the latter's fidelity. But both move in the same orbit.

6. However, see also above, p. 7 and n. 18.

7. I think that this is in part the implication; cf. below, Pt. II, chap. 6, and the notes s.v. "He made . . . cupola" and "In the heart of the Sea."

8. On the other hand, see Be-Shallaḥ, II (I, 194), for the way the king of Egypt discovers Israel's plans!

9. This is not necessarily a universal view; see below, Pt. II.

7. Who Wrote the Song at the Sea: Speculation and a Proposal

Because the main lessons of Exodus 15 are not lost on Shirta, the biblical text makes it possible for us to understand the even more-than-literal, the haggadic, interpretations of this Midrash: since Scripture makes it plain that this triumph is God's triumph, Shirta underscores that too, by saying so outright, by satire against human potentates, by enlarging on the miraculousness of specific details in the Song. In other words, the biblical text makes the Midrash intelligible. Inevitably a question now forces itself upon us. Is it possible that the Midrash in turn, reciprocally, may illuminate something of the biblical text that we have not yet noted?

For the students and critics of biblical literature still have their problems with Exodus 15,[1] a principal one being that of date of composition. Whether or not the Israelites sang a song at the time of the reported miracle is of course not our question, simply because there is no way for the historian to answer such a question. But the text of the Song was composed once, and we do have in our hands a specific text. Is there anything in that text which can be of help to us?

Let us start with a somewhat antiquated view, for in part it is still attractive to some scholars:

> The ringing invitation of Miriam, "Sing unto Jehovah, for he has triumphed gloriously!" (Ex. 15:21) was taken

1. For a bibliography of the older literature, see the reference to Cross, *Studies*, above, p. 8, n. 27. See also Cross, "SSCM," pp. 1–25 (bibliog., pp. 9 f., n. 27).

up *more than seven centuries later* [2] by a well-intentioned *versifier* who composed the *prolix expansion* of
her song which we read in Ex. 15:1–18 (irregular 3:3
meter). This pious Jew of the *second half of the fifth
century* begins boldly, "Let me sing unto Jehovah, for
he has triumphed gloriously." But being a peace-loving
soul utterly devoid of martial fire, a townsman who
had never seen a battle, he chose a model that he could
not emulate and wrote not a miniature epic, like
Miriam, but a homiletic and devout paraphrase
thereof. Imitating the historical psalms, without succeeding in carrying out the correct meter, this *pseudo
poet* praises the Lord for his glorious deeds but, *for-
getting that his poem was supposed to have been sung
at the Exodus from Egypt,* he also summarizes the conquest of Canaan (15:13–18) and even refers to the
Temple in Jerusalem (15:17)—*not Solomon's but the
Second Temple, completed in 516.* About 250 B.C. the
Chronicler placed an echo of this poem in the mouth
of Ezra (Neh. 9:11). From a careful examination of
thought and language, A. Bender (*ZAW* 23 [1903] 1 ff.)
has *proved* its post-exilic origin.[3]

"Well-intentioned versifier", "prolix expansion", "pseudo
poet", within a few lines forgets the subject he had in mind
at first—all this and "a townsman who had never seen a
battle" too! What more, or less, would a bellicose townsman have said, or a pacifist suburbanite? Presumably the
invocation of Bender is intended as an unqualified en-
dorsement of the decision, "Das Lied Ex. 15, 1b–18 ist nach
jeder Hinsicht ein Psalm. Schon allein diese Thatsache
verweist es in die nachexilische Zeit." [4] Neither "diese
Thatsache" nor others about Aramaisms [5] and archaizings [6]
have *proven* a postexilic origin, as quite a number of
leading biblical scholars have demonstrated, especially in
the last thirty years.

2. All italics in this quotation are mine.
3. Pfeiffer, p. 281.
4. In *ZAW*, XXIII, 45. Cf. also Rozelaar, in *VT*, II, 226, n. 2.
5. Cf. Bender, *"Das Lied,"* pp. 11, 20.
6. Cf. Bender, ibid., pp. 17, 40.

That a "thoroughgoing study of the poem" would be "made since Canaanite poetic materials have become generally available," [7] was almost to be expected, particularly after 1944, when W. F. Albright published his study and rendition of the oracles of Balaam [8] in the light of "epigraphically known history of spelling in Hebrew." As Albright's students, F. M. Cross, Jr., and D. N. Freedman, said in 1950,[9] "Recent advances in our knowledge of the historical grammar and lexicography of Hebrew have changed the picture completely. Much of the evidence of supposedly 'late' language and style actually points to an early date. . . . The poem is not archaizing but archaic." [10] Neither is the Song at the Sea in an irregular 3:3 meter, nor are the first eighteen verses of Exodus 15 a homiletic and devout paraphrase.[11]

Over and above a number of archaic (or, in the opinion of late daters, archaizing) forms which Exodus 15 employs, several expressions in particular—hitherto assumed to clinch the matter of late dating—may indeed, as Cross and Freedman write,[12] reflect very early times: "*har naḥalateka* (*hr nḥltk*), Your own mountain, *makon le-shibteka* (*mkwn lšbtk*), the place You made Your abode."

> These phrases, however, are much older than the time of Solomon, and were current in Canaanite long before the Israelite conquest. The poems of Ras Shamrah,

7. Cross and Freedman, in *JNES*, xiv, 237a, and see again Cross, "SSCM."

8. In *JBL*, lxiii. Albright's views about the Song in Exodus 15, however, he had already expressed in his *Archaeology of Palestine and the Bible* (New York and London, 1932), 145 f. See further, below.

9. In the dissertation, *Studies*, p. 88, and in *JNES*, xiv (1955), 238b.

10. See also the unpublished dissertation (Yale University, 1966) by D. A. Robertson, "Linguistic Evidence in Dating Hebrew Poetry."

11. A fair case can be made for several of the proposals, though I like best the one in *The Torah, A New Translation*. See the arrangement recommended by Cross and Freedman, and now (1969) by Cross, "SSCM," pp. 12 ff. Noth, p. 98, writes, "Die Form des Hymnus ist nicht sehr streng." See the sobering remarks of Gevirtz, pp. 12 f.

12. In *JNES*, xiv, 250. On the word *hr* (mountain), see the explanation offered by Noth, p. 100; cf. Cassuto in his *Commentary*, p. 122. For the expression "crag of inheritance" and its association with *qdš* in Ugaritic poetry, cf. the quotation in Gevirtz, p. 57.

from the fourteenth century B.C., supply striking parallels . . . This mountain imagery was naturally applicable to Baal, god of Ṣapon; but it was also appropriate for Yahweh, whose close association with mountains is attested in the earliest sources . . . These expressions, then, could have been used by the Israelite poet at any time, and do not in themselves point to a Solomonic (much less a post-Solomonic) date for the poem.[13]

Thoughts of this kind lead Albright to the conclusion that, while the Song may in its present state contain some later accretions, "it is substantially Mosaic in date, that is, it probably goes back to the thirteenth century B.C." [14] Cross and Freedman, more cautiously (because of the "anachronistic" mention of Philistia, because of "the significant omission of Ammon"),[15] subscribe to a date of not earlier than the twelfth and not later than the eleventh century; [16] and they are speaking, as they italicize, of the poem "in its present form." These are not the only recent views, of course. One scholar in 1952 recommended a date at the earliest in the time of David and at the latest from the end of the seventh to the beginning of the sixth century.[17] In 1957 another scholar, who descries in the poem a combina-

13. They continue: "Later, of course, the phrases in question would be connected with Zion and the Temple at Jerusalem; and this interpretation, read back into the ancient ode, would give special weight to the words of vs. 17." Cf. Gevirtz, pp. 6–14 (an excellent discussion of tradition in poetry).

14. "The Psalm of Habakkuk," in H. H. Rowley, ed., *Studies in Old Testament Prophecy* (New York, 1950), p. 5, and cf. n. 22. Cassuto too accepts the Mosaic period as the date of composition (see his *Commentary*).

15. On the other hand, note their careful qualification (*JNES*, xiv, 239b–40a): "Neither the mention of Philistia (which may be the result of modernizing tendencies of oral tradition), however, nor the omission of Ammon (admittedly an argument from silence) are decisive means of dating." But see now Cross, "SSCM," p. 12, nn. 38–39.

16. Note also Cross in "SSCM," p. 11; and on p. 20 he writes, "the Song of the Sea cannot be fitted into the history of the prose and poetic traditions of the Exodus, except at the beginning of the development in the period of the Judges."

17. M. Rozelaar, in *VT*, II, 221–28.

tion of "two originally separate compositions," proposed still other dates.[18]

We have arrived on the island of speculation and even Shirta, as we shall see, invites us to linger here awhile. To get our bearings, let us first reexamine the text of Exodus 15 as prosaically as possible. What does that text say? That "when Israel saw the wondrous power which the Lord had wielded against the Egyptians" (Exodus 14:31), Moses and they sang the following song to the Lord:

God has triumphed gloriously, into the sea He has hurled horse and its driver.[19] My strength and song (or, might) are *yh* (the Lord); He has become (or, He is) my salvation. This God is my God and I will glorify (or, enshrine) Him; He is also the God of my father and I exalt Him. The Lord (is) a Warrior, His Name is YHWH (the Lord). He cast Pharaoh's chariots and his army into the sea, and the pick of Pharaoh's officers were drowned in the Sea of Reeds. They were covered by the deeps and like a stone they went down into the depths. —Now in direct discourse an exclamation to God: Your right hand glorious (or, is glorious) in power, Your right hand shatters the foe. You break up Your opponents in Your great triumph, You send forth Your fury and it consumes them like chaff. Waters piled up at the

18. J. D. W. Watts, in *VT*, vii (1957), 371 et seq. For still further dating suggestions of earlier modern scholars, cf. in Watts, p. 379, n. 4, and also S. R. Driver, *Introduction to the Literature of the Old Testament* (New York, 1925), p. 30, and E. Kautzsch, *Die Heilige Schrift* (Tübingen, 1922), pp. 118 f. Noth, p. 98: "Das grosse 'Schilf-meerlied' in 15, 1–19 ist ein verhältnismässig junges Stück, ohne dass doch die Zeit seiner Abfassung genauer zu bestimmen wäre. Es ist in seiner Gattung schon nicht mehr einheitlich." Note also how he goes on.

On the other hand, Loewenstamm (1965) accepts the time of the United Monarchy as the date of composition, and sees the Song as an integrated whole, as a meaningful unit (pp. 113 f.). In *Eretz-Israel*, ix (Jerusalem, 1969), 45, n. 4, H. L. Ginsberg writes: "But one has a feeling . . . that either the author [of the song] or a later hand has adapted the formula [*mkwn lšbtk*] with which Solomon inaugurated the temple (1 Kings 8:13). In the former event, the poem is most probably of Solomonic or early post-Solomonic authorship, in the latter it more probably antedates the building of the temple."

19. Or, maybe, "chariot"; cf. W. F. Albright, *Archaeology of Palestine and the Bible* (New York and London, 1932), p. 213, n. 55.

blast of Your nostrils, the floods stood up straight like a wall, and the deeps froze in the heart of the sea.

The poet now contemplates the difference between the enemy's rodomontade and God's actual "response" thereto —that is, His performance. Here is what the enemy said: "I'll pursue, overtake, divide the spoil, my appetite (desire) shall have its fill of them, I'll unsheathe my sword and my hand will subdue them."

Here is God's response to that "I'll do this, I'll do that, I'll do the other, I'll I'll, I'll": You blew [20] with Your wind, the sea covered them up, and down into the mighty waters they sank like lead. —Hence again an exclamation: Who even among the celestials (or, the mighty) is like You, Lord, who is like You majestic in holiness,[21] awesome in splendor (praises),[22] working wonders! You put forth Your right hand,[23] whereupon the earth [24] swallowed them up.

The account of the *gesta dei* is not yet done, but the scene shifts now from the sea and the enemy vanquished there to the progress of those for whose benefit God had acted as He did.

This people You redeemed, You led (or, You lead) in Your love, by Your strength You guided them to Your holy

20. The meaning is, With a mere puff, glug they were gone. See the way the verb *nashaf* (*nšp*) is used in Isa. 40:24b, where the meaning is clearly, At a mere puff of His they wither, while when there is a whirlwind, they are swept up and blown away like stubble. *LXX*, Isa. 40:24b., says lovelily *épneusen*, though it misses the point in Exod. 15:10 (and therefore the *Versio Antiqua* of the Latin did too; note, incidentally, Tg on Isa. 40:24); but the Vulgate, both in Exodus and Isaiah, reads "flavit." See indeed *Meṣudat Dawid* on the Isaiah verse, and cf. Rashi on Exod. 15:10 (and Naḥmanides's reaction to it).

21. Or, possibly, "majestic among the holy ones"; cf. Cross, "The Divine Warrior," p. 26, n. 49; "SSCM," p. 14, n. 49.

22. Cf. A. B. Ehrlich, *Mikra ki-Pheshuto* (New York, 1969), p. 165 (ad 15:11).

23. As though to say, All You have to do is lift Your hand, and it's all over with them. Note, by the way, in Exod. 14 (vv. 16, 21, 26, 27), how this "image" is employed, and for that matter observe the way the verb *nṭh* is used earlier in Exodus in the account of the plagues.

24. On "earth," cf. Cross and Freedman, in *JNES*, XIV, 247, n. 39. See also Bender, "Das Lied", pp. 32 f.; Noth, p. 99; Loewenstamm, p. 117, n. 31.

abode. At the news of this, the nations roundabout tremble
and shiver: the Philistines, the chiefs (or, clans) of Edom,
the mighty (or, tribes) of Moab, all the inhabitants of
Canaan. Gripped by terror because of Your mighty arm,
they are silenced like stone—until Your people, Lord, this
people You created (or, ransomed) pass over, over.[25] Them
You bring (or, will bring) and plant in Your own mountain,
the place You set for Your abode, the sanctuary, Lord,
Your hands established. —And so again and finally an
acclamation, that the Lord reign forever and ever.

It is certainly possible to divide the *stichoi* of the poem
behind the paraphrase just offered into a number of
stanzas or strophes, and there is some justification for each
of the suggested divisions.[26] One thing however is clear and
universally acknowledged: the substance of the poem is
divisible in two. Whereas in the first part—through verse
12—God's vanquishing of the foe is celebrated, in the
second part—verses 13-18, the culmination of the first
part—the theme is God's leading His whole people [27] with
love to His favorite location and settling them there.
Speaking still as a historian, one would have to say that
such lines are the product of a period after the Israelites
are *settled* (*tt'mw*) in the place to which they have been
conducted; as the prophet Nathan reported to David (II
Sam. 7:10),[28] "And I will appoint a place for My people,
for Israel, and will plant (settle, *wnt'tyw*) them," [29] and so
on. Interestingly enough, the author of the Book of Joshua
records (21:41–43) that "the Lord gave to Israel all the
land which He swore to give to their fathers; and having
taken possession of it, they settled (*wyšbw!*) there. And the
Lord gave them rest (*wynh*) on every side just as He had

25. Cf. Ehrlich ad Exod. 15:16.

26. Cf. above, p. 36, n. 11.

27. From this poem, "prophetic" as the latter half may appear,
you would never know that a split in the Kingdom had ever taken
place.

28. Cf. I Chron. 17:9.

29. Cf. the idiom in Jer. 24:6, 32:41; Amos 9, end; Ps. 80:9, 15 f.;
and see also the possible meaning in the Dead Sea fragment in
M. Baillet, J. T. Milik, and R. de Vaux, O. P., *Discoveries in the
Judaean Desert of Jordan*, III (Oxford, 1962), 125, and notes on 126.

sworn to their fathers; not one of all their enemies had withstood them, for the Lord had given all their enemies into their hands. Not one of all the good promises which the Lord had made to the house of Israel had failed; all came to pass." Yet even though he reports such successful occupation, not once does that author say that the tribes or the Israelites were *neṭuʿim* in their land.[30] We must therefore look for a time when it might be said with more or less justice that they were *neṭuʿim,* planted firmly, in their Land, although there is no such thing as absolute and unconditional security.

That to us, and to the author of the closing chapters of Judges, *that* period was hardly tranquil or reassuring, is not decisive. Despite its limitations, there may have been in Samuel's circle [31] those who regarded the days when the Judges judged as ideal.[32] But Israel *neṭuʿim* then?—in the

30. As for the one occurrence of the verb *nṭʿ* in the Book of Joshua (24:13), observe its completely neutral and plain meaning there. Cf. Deut. 6:11. In the Book of Judges, the verb does not appear at all. That the verb *nṭʿ* is to be taken seriously, can be seen also in the Sabbath Musaf (Additional) prayer, *Tikkanta Shabbat* (Baer, p. 238): *yehi raṣon . . . she-taʿalenu be-śimḥah le-ʾarṣenu, we-tiṭaʿenu bi-gebulenu;* only then, *we-sham naʿaśeh le-paneka ʾet qorbenot ḥobotenu,* etc. Cf. again Amos 9:15. Now see below, Pt. II, chap. 10, p. 232 f.! Note also how *Pesikta R.* 8a goes to the trouble to explain why the verse speaks of nails as *neṭuʿim.*

31. Cf. I Sam. 8:6 f.

32. There is a streak of antimonarchism running through Israelite and Jewish history which should not be ignored. In addition to the tradition embodied in the famous passage in I Sam. 8, note that in the literature (thus far) from the Dead Sea sectarians, apparently only God is referred to as King (except for allusions to Gentile kings and mention of biblical kings of Israel); even the eschatological Davidic messiah is called *naśi* (prince), but not *melek* (king). (Note the picture of the future in Ezekiel too: for example, 34:22–24.) In this connection, the antisectarian polemic in *ARNA,* p. 100, top of the page, becomes intelligible. And note too passages like that in Josephus, *Antiquities,* XVIII, 1:6 (Loeb, IX, 21), and *ARNA,* XX, p. 72; cf. G. Alon, *"Gaʾon, Geʾim,"* in Tarbiz, XXI, (1950) 106 ff. In my opinion the rather ample formula in the eleventh benediction of the ʿAmidah, u-melok ʿalenu ʾattah lebadeka (occurring in almost every one of the rites with that fulness; cf. L. Finkelstein, "Development of the Amidah," *JQR,* XVI [1925], 154–55) is making the same point. Cf. the petition of "the nation" to Pompey, in Josephus, *Antiquities,* XIV, 3:2

midst of those nations "which the Lord left to test Israel by them"? What about the eighty or so years of the United Monarchy (ca. 1000–922)? I Kings 5:5 (4:25) obscures more than it reveals: "And Judah and Israel dwelt in safety, from Dan even to Beersheba, every man under his vine and under his fig tree, all the days of Solomon." Whoever wrote this verse—it always comes as a shock that the Chronicler did not write it; maybe he knew better—was either on the staff of Solomon's publicity department [33] or was manifestly indulging in a hankering that even prophets [34] could not suppress.

However, let us return to the text of Exodus 15, for it had spoken of God bringing His people into His very own mountain and planting them there. Perhaps this text may help us: after all, it is the first time in Scripture where the planting of the people Israel is being referred to.

The poet declares,

> The place You made Your abode, O Lord,
> The sanctuary, O Lord, which Your hands established.

Cross and Freedman may be perfectly right that an expression like *mkwn lšbtk*, "the dais of Thy throne" (as they translate the words, or, the "place for Your abode") was much older than Solomon's time.[35] But even they admit that such an expression "could have been used by the Israelite poet at any time."

(Loeb, VII, 469). And that the prophet Samuel was not just a crank or merely the mouthpiece of *late* opponents of monarchy, can be seen in I. Mendelsohn's study in *BASOR*, No. 143 (1956), pp. 17 ff.

Professor Shalom Spiegel further calls my attention to M. Buber's discussion of "The Books of Judges and the Book of Judges," in his *Kingship of God* (New York, 1967), pp. 66–84: The Book of Judges "is composed of two books . . . Each of the two books is edited from a biased viewpoint, the first from an anti-monarchical, the second from a monarchical" (p. 68).

33. And in that case he talked exactly like an Assyrian Rabshakeh; cf. II Kings 18:21.

34. Cf. Mic. 4:4, Zech. 3:10.

35. In *JNES*, XIV, 250a, n. 59, they refer to Albright's note mm of his "Psalm of Habakkuk" study, but nothing in that note fixes the provenance of the specific phrase *mkwn lšbtk;* nor does Cross in "SSCM," p. 23, n. 74, provide an exact parallel (despite the Ugaritic "cliché," *ksᵓu tbt,* which he mentions).

In fact, it was used in Solomon's prayer when he had finished building the Temple; it may even have occurred in an earlier source, the Book of the Song.[36] But it occurs in Solomon's prayer of dedication.[37] At least that is something fixed. Needless to say, the commonly accepted dating for that prayer is also late, reflecting (it is argued) deuteronomistic style, and even a later one, or at least later notions, according to a number of scholars.[38] However, even if one were to concede that in its present form the prayer —even all of it—were no earlier than the seventh century, quite a number of its leading notions and ways of expression are far from being compellingly late, as Montgomery has demonstrated in his Commentary.[39] Enough remains in the core of verses 22-43, plus what may be learned legitimately from verses 12 and 13,[40] which is not irrelevant to a study of frames of mind and thought during the eight decades of the United Monarchy.

To begin with the building operation: "Built indeed have I," Solomon said (I Kings 8:13), "an exalted house for Thee,[41] a place for Thy dwelling forever (*mkwn lšbtk ʿwlmym*)," as the Hebrew reads. And even as he offers up prayer in behalf of the foreigner, he says: "Hear Thou in heaven Thy dwelling place (*mkwn šbtk*), and do according to all for which the foreigner calls to Thee; in order that

36. May, but not necessarily. What in the Hebrew Bible of I Kings 8 appears as vv. 12 and 13, occurs in the Greek version (*LXX*) after v. 53—though not quite, for where we would expect *mkwn lšbtk* (*hétoimon katoiketérion sou*: cf., e.g., vv. 39, 43, 49; Ps. 32:14; *LXX*), we get (*oikon ekprepé sautó*) *tou katoikein epi kainótetos*.

37. J. A. Montgomery's note in his (ICC) *Commentary on the Books of Kings* (Edinburgh, 1960), p. 202 (in connection with v. 30), is not relevant to our present problem or discussion. See also Loewenstamm, p. 15, and several times throughout his volume, who sees a connection between the exodus and the period of David and Solomon.

38. See Montgomery, pp. 193 ff.

39. See Montgomery, ibid., even as regards a fairly sophisticated idea like that of the celestial abode of a high god. (Correct the typographical error there, p. 193, line 4 from bottom, to read Isa. 66:1.)

40. On these verses, cf. Montgomery, pp. 189-91.

41. Cf. Montgomery in his Commentary, ad loc., for the exegetical details (I have deliberately helped myself to Montgomery's translation on p. 189). And in II Chron. 6:2, the pleonastic construction, *wa-ʾani baniti,* speaks volumes.

all the people of the earth may know Thy name and fear
Thee, as do Thy people Israel, and that they may know
that called by Thy name is *this house which I have built*"
(verse 43).

It is not only the biblical historians and editors, therefore, who record that Solomon was to build and built the
Temple.[42] The author of the prayer puts those very words
into Solomon's mouth: *I* built the house for Thee. The
gods have been known to give instructions for the building of their houses. After the gods Ninzagga and Ninsikila
had given Gudea the pertinent orders, Gudea proceeded to
build the temple of Ningirsu, whose *en*-priest he was.[43]
Something similar may have been the case with Solomon
too, if the Chronicler (I, 28:11–19, particularly verse 19)
can be depended on: "Then David gave Solomon his son
the plan of the Temple-vestibule . . . and the plan of all
that he had in mind for the courts of the house of the
Lord," and so forth; "All this in writing, from the hand
of the Lord; He hath made me wise, even all the works of
the pattern." [44] Be this as it may, "Solomon built the house
and finished it" (I Kings 6:14) and was not in the least
self-effacing about what he had done.[45]

42. Cf. II Sam. 7:13, I Kings 5:19, 6:1 and 2, 7:51, 9:1, etc., let
alone the passages in Chronicles. In our present discussion, I shall
not draw on verses 14–21 and 44–53 of I Kings 8—not because I
necessarily accept the generally current views, but because in this
connection nothing is to be gained by argument: even though late
postscripts and late formulations may well preserve reliable and
valuable traditions.

43. See the account in *ANET*, pp. 268b–69a. Cf. M. Haran, "Shiloh
and Jerusalem," in *JBL*, LXXXI (1962), 21 and n. 12.

44. I have adopted neither the *JPS* translation nor that of the
RSV for this very difficult verse. And on the theme it seems to express,
see provisionally what Y. Yadin reports in *Biblical Archaeologist*,
xxx (Dec. 1967), 138. And see now the dissertation by S. Z. Leiman,
"The Talmudic and Midrashic Evidence for the Canonization of
Hebrew Scripture" (University of Pennsylvania, 1970), p. 220, and n.
73 ibid.

45. Nor should it be overlooked that he spent on it six years less
than he spent on building his own palatial quarters: I Kings 6:38
and 7:1. Note how Josephus rationalizes in *Antiquities*, VIII, 5:1
(Loeb, v, 641), "for [his own palace] was not built with the same
industry as the Temple had been." Note too how Josephus goes on.

The point is that when Solomon said "I built this house," like many other builders of temples he meant the fact to be noted; [46] even as he conceded that there was something eccentric about putting up a house for Him whom not even the heavens and the heavens beyond the heavens could contain, he did not just say, "this house," but "this house which I have built." [47] It was no anonymous gift.

But if you read only the Song at the Sea you would never guess that. The *mkwn lšbt* the Song does honor to is the one "You made, O Lord, the sanctuary, *mqdš*, O Lord,[48] Your hands established."

46. Cf., for example, the text of the stela reporting Tut-ankh-Amon's restoration (*ANET*, p. 252a); Ramses III, on his building a temple of Amon (*ANET*, pp. 260b f.). For a limestone plaque *possibly* representing celebration at a temple dedication, cf. *ANEP*, number 427.
It may be asked: But do not all builders underscore that they have built the house (= temple) they built? My distinguished colleague, Professor Albrecht Goetze, calls my attention, therefore, to the following ritual (*ANET*, p. 356), where, although we are told (line 10) that the name of the sacrificer is to be mentioned, as the builder makes a number of prescribed deposits, he recites: "it is not we who have (really) built it, all the gods have built it. The gods—those (who are) craftsmen—have built it. Telepinus has laid the foundations. The walls above them, Ea, the king of wisdom has built (them). . . . But the mortar, the goddesses have brought it. They have laid the foundations of silver and gold; the gold they brought from Birunduma . . . The lapis they brought from Mount Takniyara. The marble they brought from the country of Kanisha. The jasper they brought from the country of Elam. The diorite they brought from the earth. The black iron of heaven they brought from heaven. Copper (and) bronze they brought from Mount Taggata in Alasiya. See! beneath the foundations they have deposited gold for (firm) founding."
47. V. 27. Of course this is not meant to deny that Solomon also speaks several times of "this house."
48. What a duplication! Cf. the other occurrence in v. 6 of Exodus 15, and possibly too the one in v. 3. That 86 MSS and the Samaritan version read YHWH where MT today reads ʾdny (cf. Cross and Freedman, in *JNES*, XIV, 250, n. 61), may be well and good. But that would still leave the question, Why did anybody change the consonantal text? And I believe there is an answer: If you count the number of times the name YHWH (not *yh* or ʾl, etc.) appears from v. 1 through v. 18, you find that it is 10! YHWH was certainly re-

Modern scholars disagree. Some interpret the *mkwn lšbt* and *mqdš* of Exodus 15:17 as references to some "temple," perhaps to one of the pre-Solomonic central sanctuaries,[49] perhaps to some future edifice anticipated by those redeemed from bondage,[50] perhaps to Solomon's temple.[51] Others see in these terms a reference to the Holy Land itself.[52] In either case, however, according to the Song at the Sea, if one is to speak of a *mkwn lšbt*, of a *mqdš*, there is no mistaking the hands which made and established it: *mkwn lšbtk* You made, O Lord, *mqdš*, O Lord, Your hands established. The poet clearly knows that there is a *mkwn lšbt*, a *mqdš*, not of Solomon's making. And it was toward that non-Solomonic sanctuary that God had in love led the people He redeemed.[53]

---

quired for the closing exclamation (let there be no ambiguity here when we say, Lord!); hence the ninth occurrence was written out *ʾdny*. Of course the arrangers of the text of Exod. 15:1–18 realized that the text of the Song began with 1b, but 1a was of great significance to them. Note that of the present 153 lines of Shirta Chapter I, 99 are devoted to Exod. 15:1a. Cf. above, 3, n. 3.

49. For example, Cross, "SSCM," pp. 21 ff. and 24; or cf. BDB (1907), s.v. *mqdš*, 874a.

50. Cf. Cassuto, *Commentary on Exodus*, p. 122.

51. Cf. Loewenstamm, pp. 113 f.

52. Cf. Y. Kaufmann, *Religion of Israel*, trans. M. Greenberg (Chicago, 1960), p. 241. See recently H. L. Ginsberg, in *Eretz-Israel*, IX, 45, n. 4 ("In Ex. 15:17, lines b and c can only be taken in apposition to the end of line a, with the entire verse referring to the Holy Land that YHWH made, not to the temple that Solomon built"), though, in addition, he observes (ibid.) that the present reading of lines b and c leaves something to be desired.

53. Perhaps that is why Shirta senses that in the words *mkwn lšbtk* there is a signal skyward. Interestingly enough, Josephus (*Antiquities*, VIII, 8:4 [Loeb, V, 695]) puts these words into Jeroboam's mouth as he discourages the population of the Ten Tribes from going to Jerusalem: "For it was a man that built that temple." Is something of this mood registered in Mark 14:58, "this temple made with (human) hands?" See also Stephen's speech in Acts 7:48 (and cf. the Jackson and Lake commentary, ad loc.).

It *may* be that Sirach calls Jerusalem *mkwn šbtyk;* cf. *Sefer Ben-Sira ha-Shalem*, ed. M. Z. Segal (Jerusalem, 1958), p. 225; in the Greek (36:12 in ed. Rahlfs) we read, however, *tópon* (variant, *pólin*) *katapaúmatós sou*. For the expression *mkwn šbt* not as a place for God's abode, cf. the prayer *Ha-Kol Yoduka* (Baer, p. 210): *moṣiʾ ḥammah mi-meqomah, u-lebanah mi-mekon shibtah.*

Hence we can understand the resounding exclamation which is the last line of the Song, *YHWH yimlok le-ʿolam waʿed,* which even the most recent English translations [54] render, "The Lord will reign for ever and ever." But how would one normally say in biblical Hebrew, The Lord will reign forever? Surely, *yimlok YHWH le-ʿolam!* How does the Psalmist (146:10) put it? *"Yimlok YHWH le-ʿolam,* The Lord will reign for ever, thy God, O Zion, to all generations." How, on the other hand, did Gideon put it when they offered him the rulership? "It is not I who will rule over you,[55] nor will my son rule over you; *YHWH yimshol bakem,* it is the Lord who will rule over you." [56] Or, how did the resentful Samuel repeat to the people their demand for a king? "You said to me, No, *ki melek yimlok ʿalenu,* but it is a king who shall rule us." [57]

What is the closing line of the Song at the Sea? "It is the Lord who will reign for ever and ever!" [58]

54. Cf. *RSV,* the Torah (JPS). And now see also *The New English Bible* (Oxford and Cambridge, 1970).

55. The pleonasm and its meaning are unmistakable: ל ʾmšl ʾny bkm! Cf. Jephthah in Judg. 11:9b. Although I do not want to say that the verb *mlk* in Exod. 15:18 *proves* that the Song could not originate before the period of the monarchy (cf. Cross, "Divine Warrior," p. 24, n. 43), I think it is worth noting that Gideon still speaks of *mšl;* even Abimelech talks that way to begin with (Judg. 9:2)! After the bloody purge, his true colors are visible (v. 6).

56. Judg. 8:23.

57. I Sam. 12:12. Note also, for example, the construction of the clause in Exod. 16:6b. On the other hand see Luzzatto, p. 291.

58. I think this may be partly what Abarbanel has in mind when he says (*Commentary,* ed. Warsaw [1862], p. 26b), *raʾuy she-ha-Shem yihyeh molek ʿalenu la-neṣaḥ.* (On my spelling of the name Abarbanel, cf. S. Z. Leiman in *Journal of Jewish Studies,* XIX [1968], 49, n. 1.) And, in my opinion, it is almost certainly what is being emphasized by that nonbiblical "verse" in the prayer *Yehi Kevod* (Baer, p. 68; cf. also the paragraph *Yirʾu ʿEnenu,* p. 169, and *Soferim* [ed. Higger], 257), YHWH melek, YHWH malak, *YHWH yimlok leʿolam waʿed,* our verse! It is the Lord who is King, has been King, and will be King forever and ever. On that problematic "verse," see Baer's comment, ad loc., and also the commentators in *Siddur ʾOṣar ha-Tefillot* (New York, 1946) ad *Yehi Kevod;* the reading in *Seder R. Amram Gaon,* ed. Hedegård (Lund, 1951), Hebrew text, p. 13 (but that may be dittography), and p. 73; *Siddur R. Saadia Gaon* (Jerusalem, 1941), p. 33; cf. *Maḥzor Vitry,* p. 79; and note the reading of Maimonides (according to the Oxford MS), D. Goldschmidt, in *Studies of the*

And nobody talks this way unless he means, It is the Lord who will reign for ever and ever, and not So-and-so (maybe even, not that So-and-so).[59] Partisans of the House of David and later Judaean historians might declare, "I will raise up your son after you . . . and I will establish the throne of his kingdom for ever"; [60] or again, "And your house and your kingdom shall be made sure for ever before Me; your throne shall be established for ever"; [61] or in sweet song David might sing, "For He has made with me an everlasting covenant"; [62] or Solomon might assert, "To David, and to his descendants, and to his house, and to his throne, there shall be peace for evermore"; [63] or, though Solomon had failed to behave as he should have, even God might still be quoted to the effect, "Yet to his son I will give one tribe, that David My servant may always have a lamp before Me in Jerusalem . . . I will for this [misconduct] afflict the descendants of David, but not forever." [64] Despite the volume of this support, there were other voices and other sentiments, if one takes the trouble to listen to whispers.

Those who were loyal to Saul and his household surely did not join the chorus, May the House of David rule for ever.[65] But who knows? In time [66] or in self interest [67] or in change of mind they might gradually have been won over.

Research Institute for Hebrew Poetry in Jerusalem, VII (Jerusalem-Tel-Aviv, 1958), p. 190! (Is Maimonides objecting to the mystics? But on p. 195 he does make use of the full formula!)

59. Exod. 15:18 does *not* mean, It's YHWH who will reign forever but not any of the ꜤElim. That the latter are nothing, or that compared to YHWH they don't amount to anything, the poet has already stated in verse 11. No emphasis is required that *they* won't reign forever.

60. II Sam. 7:12 f.

61. Ibid.: 16; note also vv. 25 and 29. See further, Ps. 89:4 f.

62. II Sam. 23:5.

63. I Kings 2:33; note also v. 45.

64. I Kings 11:36, 39.

65. There were plenty such; for example, cf. II Sam. 16:5 ff.; see also 20:1 ff.

66. See below, in connection with Jeremiah.

67. See, for example, the story of Abner in the early chapters of II Sam.

Even an American may gradually become a classicist in literature, royalist in politics, and anglo-catholic in religion. Perhaps Adonijah's followers might also have come to terms with the successful regime.[68] But to drive off Abiathar the priest to Anathoth and leave him there to smolder was to invite the formation of a colony of malcontents, to encourage embittered and (relatively speaking) learned [69] men and their families to brood over their displacement and, in frequent get-togethers, stimulate each other against the regime in savage outbursts or underground "publications." As much as three centuries later, a priest of Anathoth [70]

68. Although one cannot say who *all* were Adonijah's guests, note that when they got frightened, they left him and went each his own way (I Kings 1:49).

Solomon may not have been the wisest of all men, but he was not the stupidest either. His liquidation of Adonijah reveals that he understood only too well what was in Adonijah's mind when the latter asked for Abishag (I Kings 2:22), for to inherit or take possession of the father's concubines is a declaration that one has succeeded the father: note esp. II Sam. 16:21 and 22 ("in the sight of all Israel!").

Poor Reuben—cf. Gen. 35:22 (Bilhah, no less, Rachel's handmaid)! He saw himself unfairly displaced by the father's pet (Gen. 37:3), and apparently made up his mind not to delay any longer and to take matters into his own hands. But the attempt was evidently premature. In this business, however, one cannot afford to fail; and all Reuben's later attempts to make up for that rash act (note his conduct in Gen. 37)—so that no doubt he might thereafter say to his father: Here! If it had not been for me, you wouldn't have your darling any longer—all his efforts at making amends, were in vain. No wonder he cried out as he did (Gen. 37:30) when Joseph had been disposed of. God help you when your allies are fools.

69. Priests; see, e.g., Jer. 18:18, Ezek. 7:26. Cf. M. L. Margolis, *The Hebrew Scriptures in the Making* (Philadelphia, 1922), pp. 54–57. Among the Shilohnites were also prophets (I Kings 11:29, 14:2).

70. Observe how in Jer. 11:21–23 the citizens of Anathoth are ready to kill Jeremiah for prophesying. Have they forgotten their grudges? Perhaps, knowing that in the capital they are always regarded with suspicion, they fear that one of their own may get them into further trouble. Significantly, they tell Jeremiah simply, *We'll* kill you if you don't stop prophesying in the name of the Lord! Jer. 12:6 must be taken literally. Of the prophets, only Jeremiah was threatened in the words of Jer. 11:21b. Even Amos, who reports (2:12) the language used against the prophets and was himself denounced by Amaziah (7:16), was not told, Shut up or we'll kill you (cf. Amos

to whom God gave no peace would still remember the fate
of Shiloh; [71] and although of course by that time the
Temple in Jerusalem was for him too "the house which is
called by My name," he could not help reporting that
God planned to do to it "as I did to Shiloh." [72] And he
too was not indifferent to publication.[73]

Shilohnites must have been especially furious with all
that fanfare about the new eternal *mkwn lšbt* [74] in Jerusalem. A Shilohnite must have been delighted, at least at
first, to find an ambitious and capable administrator in
Jerusalem who could embarrass the family of Solomon.[75]
And who built this new temple? The man who not only
removed Abiathar from office, but himself provided high
places for every one of his foreign wives, so that they
could burn incense and sacrifice to their gods.[76] With
typical near-eastern ravenousness for magnificence, he
taxes and taxes.[77] Why, the numbers [78] in that harem itself! And listen to the sanctimony in that prayer of his, at
the dedication of the royal chapel, almost within earshot
of the *bamah* he put up to Kemosh, and to Molech.[79] Can
you even count the number of gods he's worshiping? [80] He

7:12 f.). On the other hand, cf. the experience of Uriah the son of
Shemaiah (Jer. 26:20 ff.), and note on the map the location of Kirjath-
jearim (compare its geographical position relative to Jerusalem with
that of the position of Anathoth relative to Jerusalem—in G. E. Wright
and F. V. Filson, *Westminster Historical Atlas to the Bible* [Phila-
delphia, 1956], Pl. IX): the range east and west just north of Jerusalem must have been a nest of anti-Establishment fanatics. Note
also the location of Gibeath Saul. (On the ancient location of
Anathoth, cf. E. G. Kraeling, *Rand McNally Bible Atlas* [New York,
1956], p. 308.)

71. Cf. Jer. 7:12.
72. V. 14. See also 26:6, 9.
73. Cf. Jer. 36.
74. I Kings 8:13.
75. I Kings 11:29.
76. I Kings 11:7–8.
77. I Kings 5:27 ff., 12:3. Cf. I. Mendelsohn, in *BASOR*, No. 85
(1942), pp. 14–17; No. 167 (1962), pp. 31–35.
78. I Kings 11:3.
79. I Kings 11:7.
80. I Kings 11:4–5, 7–8. And that Solomon was not doing this *pro
forma*, is candidly admitted; see the closing clause of I Kings 11:2,

dares to say, "There is no God like unto Thee"; [81] he sits
on "the throne of the Lord," if you please.[82] *He* built "this
house," did he? Indeed, *this* house he did: and everyone
knows what the prospects are for a house the Lord did not
build.[83] Maybe the onetime Shilohnites now dwelling in
Anathoth even said: A house [84] is not a sanctuary! [85]

---

and on the verb *dbq*, cf. J. Goldin, in *Harry A. Wolfson Jubilee
Volume* (in Hebrew; Jerusalem, 1965), p. 82. And what an infinitive
is that infinitive *lᵉhbh!* Exactly what Deuteronomy (e.g. 11:13) tells
me I must do as regards God! (Incidentally, cf. most recently A. Kohén,
in *Lešonenu*, xxxiii [1969], 238.)

81. I Kings 8:23. A cynic might have added: By George, he ought
to know, he's worshiped so many! A historian cannot fail to note
that the exclamation has already been put in the mouth of David:
II Sam. 7:22 (and note the context).

82. Cf. I Chron. 29:23 (but cf. *LXX* on the verse). Is Jer. 3:17 a
dig at the *notion behind* the expression in Chronicles?

83. Cf. Ps. 127:1 and note the heading of that Psalm.

84. But of this I'm not sure, although a Psalm (78:60), beholding
in David the chosen one, speaks of *mškn* of Shiloh and of a *tent;*
cf. I Sam. 2:22, II Sam. 7:6. The fact remains that *byt* is used in
connection with the Shiloh sanctuary (cf. I Sam. 1:7, 24, 3:15; in 1:9
and 3:3 see *hykl YHWH*), and *byt* is practically a commonplace for
temple in the ancient Near East. It is interesting nonetheless to
note how for its description of Shiloh the Mishnah, Zebaḥim 14:6
(cf. *Mid. Tan.*, p. 50), strives to suggest something substantial/not-so-
substantial.

It is difficult to shake off the feeling that the whole story (in II
Sam. 8 and I Kings 5:17–19; and see also I Kings 8:17 ff.) about David
wishing to build a temple, and being informed by a prophet of the
divine decree that not David but his successor was to build it (note
also in II Sam. 7:13 the promise that his rulership would be forever),
was part of the pro-Solomonic propaganda in behalf of the Temple:
to persuade everyone that such an unprecedented (in Israel) building
was not of Solomon's own and novel decision. There were surely many
even among the supporters of Solomon who wondered whether such
a temple was at all justified; what finer defense, therefore, than It's not
I who decided to build such a house; my father David was the
originator of the idea, but *God* said that only David's son was to do
it?

85. The word *mqdš* does not appear at all in Solomon's prayer
(though the verb *qdš* occurs in I Kings 9:3, 7); is this the reason the
Chronicler (I, 28:10) has David say to Solomon, "Take heed now,
for the Lord has chosen you to build a house for the *mqdš*, sanctuary?" The Lord does want a *mqdš*: Exod. 25:8. And the presence
of the word in the Song may therefore be particularly intentional

Doubtless, however, they did say other things, such as:
The painful irony of it! Wherever you turn, the place reeks
with Egyptian influence [86]—Egypt, the ʾoyeb, the foe [87]
from which we were delivered, is subtly recapturing us.
This passion for horses and stables and horsemen and
chariot cities [88] will be our undoing.[89] Look at what he's
making of our own people—men of war (ʾanshe ha-mil-
hamah), his servants, his commanders, his captains, his

(particularly, because a poet chooses every word intentionally),
whether Exod. 15:17c refers to a "temple" or to the Holy Land: what
God's hands establish is indeed a sanctuary, unlike any house
Solomon puts up.

86. Cf. briefly G. E. Wright, *Biblical Archeology* (London, 1962),
pp. 125–26 (and Professor Shalom Spiegel calls to my attention the
important studies by R. de Vaux, "Titres et Fonctionnaires égyptiens
à la Cour de David et de Salomon," in *RB*, XLVIII [1939], 394–405, and
J. Begrich, "Sofer und Mazkir," in *ZAW*, LVIII [1940–41], 1–29), and
more recently Y. Aharoni in *BASOR*, no. 84 (1966), pp. 13–19, and in
Biblical Archaeologist, XXXI (Feb. 1968), 15. Note that although
Josephus fails to grasp the meaning of some of the details he summarizes (see below, n. 92), he (unconsciously?) senses a kind of inva-
sion of Egyptian influence. Suddenly, after speaking of Solomon's
fortifications, in *Antiquities*, VIII, 6:2 (Loeb, V, 655 f.), he interrupts
his account of Solomon's accomplishments with a discussion of the
meaning of the name "Pharaoh" and reviews briefly some Egyptian
history. Only after this does he return to Solomon's exploits.
  In this connection, I believe it is worth observing that for a
long, long time there persisted a strong feeling that this affiliation
with Pharaoh's household on Solomon's part was the root cause of
major disasters in Jewish history. At the time Solomon married
Pharaoh's daughter, the Talmudic sources (B. Sanhedrin 21b [in the
name of R. Isaac], B. Shabbat 56b [in the name of Samuel, quoted by
R. Judah], P. ʿAbodah Zarah 1:2 [in the name of R. Levi], and Cant.
R. on 1:6, 9c [ditto]) state, the archangel Gabriel (or, Michael) came
down from heaven and thrust a reed into the sea. About this reed
more and more earth gathered, and on this spot Rome was built.
Cf. Ginzberg, *Legends*, VI, 280; Krauss, *Persia and Rome*, pp. 14 ff.;
P. Rieger, "The Foundation of Rome in the Talmud," in *JQR*, XVI
(1925–26), 227 ff. (That "Rome in the Talmud does not always designate the metropolis of the Roman empire" [p. 229] does not affect our
point here.) Cf. below, n. 96.

  87. Cf. Exod. 15:6, 9.

  88. I Kings 5:6; 10:26, 28 f. See also how Josephus (*Antiquities*,
VIII, 7:3 [Loeb, V, 671]) elaborates on this feature of Solomon's wealth.

  89. I Kings 5:6–8.

chariot commanders, and his horsemen (*shalishaw, śare rikbo, parashaw*).[90] No, Samuel did not exaggerate.[91] Even dates are reminiscent of Egypt,[92] though one would think these should serve to remind us of the influence we should *avoid*. Above all, mockery of mockeries which is Solomon's: When God led our ancestors out of Egypt, who was the prophet He put in change? The one whom Pharaoh's daughter raised, the man who left Pharaoh's household to bring God's message to Israel. Whom does Solomon in all his glory marry? Pharaoh's daughter,[93] whom he imports into the city where the house of the Lord is to be built,[94] whom he provides with extra elegant quarters,[95] and who turns her husband's mind to other gods.[96]

90. I Kings 9:22.
91. I Sam. 8:11 f.
92. Note I Kings 6:1. Cf. also Begrich, in *ZAW*, LVIII, 11. Regardless of when that chapter was written, it is clearly based on archival records, and some such dating must have been the case. Josephus completely misses the point here. The biblical verse expresses the chronology simply in terms of the time since the exodus from Egypt. Josephus, by correlating the date with still other dates and events (irrespective of the problems with his figures), has naively assumed that chronology as such was the biblical author's concern.

Observe also the Egyptian title, "Royal Friend," of one of Solomon's officers (I Kings 4:5b; Montgomery, p. 116); on the other hand, cf. de Vaux, in *RB*, XLVIII, 403 ff.

93. I Kings 3:1 f. and 11:1.
94. Note what the Chronicler does in II Chron. 8:11!
95. I Kings 7:8.
96. A. Malamat, "The Kingdom of David and Solomon in Its Contact with Aram Naharaim," in *Biblical Archaeologist*, XXI (1958), 97 ff., and even more fully in "Aspects of the Foreign Policies of David and Solomon," *JNES*, XXII (1963), 8 ff., pointed out the special significance of this particular marriage, for "From of old, a daughter of the king of Egypt has not been given to anyone," as an El-Amarna letter declares, which Malamat quotes. Thus one cannot dispute that "Solomon's marriage into the Egyptian royal house acquires extraordinary political significance." But I would like to suggest that this marriage must have been quite a shock even to Solomon's supporters; hence the several (rather than single) references to it and to her residence (I Kings 3:1, 7:8b, 9:24; on the last, cf. *LXX* 9:9, latter part: Is the Greek an echo of a tradition that Solomon wanted her especially close to him?). For the marriages of Solomon were long recalled with deep resentment (and the marriage to a Pharaoh's daughter especially; cf. *Sifre Deut.*, 52, p. 119). Note not only Deut.

It was not long before those who were repelled by the Egyptian vogue were able to say, There you have the outcome of all this! [97]

What is the point? That in Anathoth and the surrounding area were reflective and articulate men, once prominent but now deprived of all status and royal favor, who perhaps recalled the times in Shiloh when their families amounted to something, who must have been in a rage as they witnessed what was being put up and were now subjected to propaganda about its preeminence and sanctity and ideal purposes. Meanwhile wherever they looked they beheld reminders of Egypt. They were clearly powerless to use force to alter this situation, to prevent the building operations, to denounce Solomon publicly. See how far Adonijah and his party got, what Jeroboam had to do to save his skin. So they used "the pen." And in a poem, whose opening line they took over from a song which must long have been a favorite with the people,[98] they

---

17:16–17 (and the outspoken association of horses and Egypt in verse 16!), but also Nehem. 13:26 (cf. II Sam. 12:24). This resentment did not die out completely even in "Talmudic" times: cf. the note by L. Ginzberg, in J. Goldin, *Fathers According to Rabbi Nathan* (New Haven, 1955), p. 220, n. 46; cf. *Midrash Mishle* 22:28, 47a. (See now, however, S. Z. Leiman in his dissertation, n. 71, bottom of p. 166.) See also above, n. 86. The very protestation in B. Shabbat 56b, that only he who is mistaken says that Solomon sinned at all is the best proof of the hard time Solomon's reputation had for the longest time. In Christian tradition too there are "late" defenses of Solomon; cf. de Lubac, *Exégèse médiévale*, I, 287; cf. II, 164. See also now S. Lieberman, in *Meḥqarim be-Qabbalah u-be-Toledot ha-Datot* (Jerusalem, 1968), pp. 163 ff.

Sometimes I can't help wondering if the attributions of Proverbs, Canticles, and, later, Qohelet—yes, Qohelet too, particularly with its pious codicil—to Solomon may not be late propaganda to rehabilitate Solomon's reputation.

97. I Kings 14:25 ff.

98. It is more than likely that there was a tradition going back, perhaps as far back as the Mosaic period, that at the miraculous deliverance Miriam and the women sang a song with music and dance. Cf. Noth, p. 96: "Das älteste Element in diesem Abschnitt ist der kurze Passus V. 20–21." (On women as dancers in songs of triumph, cf. Driver in his Exodus commentary on Exod. 15:20, and H. P. Smith's reference in his ICC commentary on Samuel, p. 168; Gevirtz, p. 15.) Miriam *began* her song with a call to the women,

gave their version of the significance of the exodus from
Egypt (down with everything Pharaohnic!), of who was
and is verily the deliverer who rules over Israel forever,
what is the fate of braggarts, of what value were horses and
horsemen and chariots, and what was the destined climax
of that exodus: The place You made Your abode, O Lord,
the sanctuary, O Lord, which Your hands established. O
Lord, do *Thou* rule over us for ever and ever.

And if our speculations have not led us astray,[99] two
problems which keep bothering biblical students and critics
virtually disappear. One: the reference to the inhabitants
of Philistia in Exodus 15:14, which has been called an
anachronism.[1] It is anything but that, in the days when the
career and accomplishments of Solomon's father were still
fresh in everyone's mind, the days when one might still
run into Cherethites and Pelethites [2] or relations of loyal
Gittites.[3] Philistines in the time of the Exodus would be
an anachronism, I suppose, possibly, if the archeologists
insist; Philistines in the minds of those in Anathoth reflecting on their own times and the significance of the

---

"Sing (imperative plural) unto the Lord." "I will sing" (or, for those
who still prefer the *LXX* version and the versions dependent on it,
"We will sing") "unto the Lord," was the response composed by the
anti-Solomonic camp: beginning with the opening words of Miriam's
song. To Exod. 15:21b we are indebted for the title, the beginning of
Miriam's song; the titles of ancient texts and ancient poems were
their opening words or phrases or first line (cf. briefly, A. E. Speiser,
Anchor Bible, Genesis [New York, 1964], p. xvii). Loewenstamm,
p. 112, regards the Miriam song as the Song given in extenso in
Exodus 15, and so too does Cross, "SSCM," p. 11. I too accept that
what we have in Exod. 15:21b is the *incipit* of Miriam's song, but
what her full song was, I do not know.

99. See also M. A. Cohen, "The Role of the Shilonite Priesthood
in the United Monarchy of Ancient Israel," *HUCA*, xxxvi (1965),
59–99.

1. Cf. Cross and Freedman, in *JNES*, xiv, 239, and Albright cited
by them (with his suggested emendation), p. 249a. See Cross again,
however, in "SSCM," p. 12; and see now provisionally *Newsletter* No.
5 (Jan. 1970), American Schools of Oriental Research.

2. Cf. II Sam. 8:18 and 20:23. Note incidentally the way II Chron.
9:26 describes the extent of Solomon's rulership. Note too I Kings
2:39 f., where Shimei's two slaves fled to.

3. II Sam. 15:18 ff., 18:2.

historical Exodus would be an almost "natural" anachronism. How orderly indeed is the mind of the poet:

> Pangs have taken hold on the inhabitants of *Philistia*.
> Then were the chiefs (or, clans) of *Edom* affrighted;
> The mighty men (or, tribes) of *Moab*, trembling taketh
>   hold upon them;
> All the inhabitants of *Canaan* are melted away.

A perfect arc or circle has been described: since they are now *neṭuᶜim* in the Land, begin with the west, on the Mediterranean coast, move south, continue east, and then in a westerly direction enter the Promised Land. That is how the poet imagines the terror traveling.

But there is a second problem: Why in this catalogue of nations is not Ammon included?[4] In the first place, had the text ever either referred to or wished to refer to Ammon, it would have read not "Ammon" but something like "bands" or "princes" of *Bne Ammon* (*bny ᶜmwn*).[5] In the second place, note attentively the language of the Song at the Sea: the poet does not speak of Philistia, of Edom, of Moab, of Canaan, or of Philistines, Edomites, Moabites, Canaanites. He speaks of *yšby plšt, ʾlwpy ʾdwm, ʾyly mwʾb, yšby knᶜn*. In each case two words are required, and while *bny ᶜmwn* will give us two words, Ammonites (in this form —i.e. not as ᶜmwnym or ᶜmnym) would not be parallel to the other expressions; and (*pace* Pfeiffer) a real sense of style is one of the chief distinctions of the author of Exodus 15:1–18. Finally, even though the Midrash too does it, it would not be amiss if we stopped regarding Ammon and Moab as the biblical Bonnie and Clyde, in that every time the one appears, the other can't be far behind. By the time Joab finished with the Ammonites,[6] a Hebrew in Anathoth

---

4. Cf. Cross and Freedman, in *JNES*, xiv, 248, n. 44. Observe how Loewenstamm, pp. 113 f., tries to solve this problem.

5. See H. L. Ginsberg, *Koheleth* (Tel Aviv and Jerusalem, 1961), p. 35. Note the *LXX* reading of the so-called exception in I Sam. 11; on the other hand, see Ps. 83:8. On "bands of Bne Ammon," cf. II Kings 24:2; "princes," I Chron. 19:3.

6. Cf. II Sam. 12:26–31. It is possible to argue that reference to Ammonites would be risky because of Solomon's marriage to Naamah, the mother of Rehoboam. But I do not believe this argument is

or elsewhere in the Land had few occasions to think vividly
of them, and for him (as for us) anachronistic omission
would come as automatically as anachronistic inclusion.
But Moab and Edom and Philistia, and the inhabitants of
Canaan, would remain in the Hebrew mind for a long time
to come.[7]

No, the text of the Song at the Sea is in order, and the
song is indeed epochal. But it is, as Shirta recognizes in a
number of its comments, strongly polemical [8] and mocking
in flavor and purpose. Of course this is not intended even
remotely to imply that, for the tannaite savants whose
teachings the compiler of Shirta assembled, the Song at the
Sea was the workmanship of Anathothites or ex-Shilohnites.
Despite the persistence through and beyond the tannaite
centuries of memories of resentment against Solomon for
his lapses,[9] nothing preserved in the talmudic sources (to
the best of my knowledge and searching) would justify the
view that the talmudic teachers regarded Exodus 15 as an
attack upon him. Shirta has others in mind. If, says Shirta,
Exodus 15 states that Moses and the Israelites sang their
song to the Lord, then it is asserting that they did not sing
it to flesh-and-blood, even to conquering heroes; if it states
that the Lord is exalted, then it is asserting that only He
is genuinely exalted, not those flesh-and-blood monarchs
whom everyone flatters preposterously; if at the Sea one
could, so to speak, "point" to God and exclaim *"This* is
my God," then manifestly even those without special gifts
could recognize Him, while among human beings it often
happens that a king can't be told apart from the guards
around him; if the one who is the Lord may be called a

valid. Solomon was married also to a Moabitess, yet Exod. 15 refers
to Moab.

7. As for Moab, cf., e.g., II Kings 1:1; for Edom, II Kings 8:20 ff.;
Philistia, II Kings 18:8, and cf. Malamat, in *JNES*, XXII, 12 et seq.
See also I Kings 9:20 f. in regard to the inhabitants of Canaan.

8. And it would not surprise me in the least if the opening of
Exod. 15, *"Then* sang *Moses and the children of Israel,"* were a
counterretort to *"Then* said *Solomon"* (alone), of I Kings 8:12 (II
Chron. 6:1). (On the term "then," cf. Montgomery, p. 188.) But I don't
want to press the point.

9. See above, n. 86 and 96.

Warrior, note nevertheless that no warrior you might mention is like Him; note too, O Nations of the World, whom you will have to contend with in the Future; once you have heard what "the foe said," you will understand not only how frenetic were his promises but how disgusting were his ambitions and desires; to cry out, "Who is like unto Thee among the 'Elim," means (among other things) that none who were or are ever hailed as divine can be compared to Him, or can do what He does; if God is "awesome in praises," this is not of recent happening but from time out of mind (unlike johnny-come-lately gods who have become popular?); though in all crafts and arts there may be something wonderful, can any artisan or artist perform as wondrously as He? Such are the protesting sounds the Tannaim overheard in the Song at the Sea as they read it and thought about it and about their own times. But it is significant that in the Song they did overhear protest, that to them rumblings and grumblings were audible in that biblical ode. If not for Shirta, who knows if we would have become aware of these sounds.

8. God's Love and He Alone Is King

Shirta discovers moral topicality and emphasis in the Song at the Sea. No less does the Midrash express the conviction of God's extraordinary love for Israel. Purely out of love did He do for them what He did, for they had no special merit—acquired through good works—to their credit. Hence He is ever-attentive to their needs. Is it, however, only to Israel that He is attentive? What an idea! [1] He is the help and sustainer of all the world's inhabitants; so too He is the salvation of all, He nourishes and feeds all His creatures, is compassionate toward them, and when any of them cry out in distress He is attentive, for all the inhabitants of the world are His, and all souls are in His hand. In truth, He is even the theme for song for all the inhabitants of the world, they all proclaim His praises; and when they behold His mighty acts, they too recite *Shirah,* "Who is like unto Thee, O Lord, among the gods!" Nevertheless, His favorite songs are the ones Israel sing to Him, and He is their salvation especially; all the peoples are His, yet He has no chosen people for Himself other than Israel. Which means what? The prophetic proof-text (Isa. 43:21) explains, "This people (*'am zu;* cf. Exodus 15:13a, 16b–end)

1. This is almost surely the force behind the expression, *whry kl 'wmwt h'wlm* etc. (chap. 3, p. 110). Note too at the beginning of chapter 8, "And it was not Israel alone that recited the Song, but the Nations of the World too." Cf. Solomon ibn Gabirol, "The Royal Crown," VIII (in *Selected Religious Poems of Solomon ibn Gabirol* [Philadelphia, 1923], pp. 86 f.).

In my opinion this attitude is not rejected by Akiba in his comment on "And I will glorify Him." I hope to write this up in a special paper.

I formed for Myself that they might declare My praise."

It is perhaps this feeling on the part of the Tannaim—
that God's special love for Israel coexists with His love for
all men without inconsistency [2]—that accounts for the pro-
found sense of disappointment and pain expressed in a
number of exclamations inside Shirta: "And woe to the
Nations of the World at what they hear with their own
ears! For lo, it is He Who Spake and the World Came to
Be who will battle against them in the Future!" "(And)
woe to the Nations of the World at what they hear with
their own ears! For lo, the Temple is described as the product of labor on His part . . . yet they rose and destroyed
it. They cried: 'Rase it, rase it even to the foundations
thereof.' " For all the high and mighty are intolerable to
Him, from the Generation of the Flood to the latest speci-
mens of hybris and insolence: Idiots, by means of what I
lavish upon you, you become overbearing and arrogant!
Hence He rises against those who rise against Him; and
who are those who rise against Him? Those who rise
against Israel. Why did the very prophet who announced
the doom of this people and the Temple cry out, "Pour out
Thy wrath upon the nations that knew Thee not, and upon
the people that call not on Thy name?" Because "they have
devoured Jacob, they have devoured him and consumed
him, and have laid waste His [3] habitation." By contrast,
whenever anyone comes to Israel's assistance, it is as though
he came to the assistance of the Creator by divine fiat.

Even so, God does not punish His enemies because of an
uncontrollable temper. He granted them all an extension
of time, a grace period, to repent, and He never punished
any of them until after they had perpetrated the full measure of their wickedness. If His will is flouted by Israel, He
turns into their enemy the same way: the One who is
compassionate turns pitiless to them.

For alas, God's enemies turn out to be those who
abandon all sense of decency and restraint, as Suetonius

2. Cf. PA 3:14, and see the Bickerman reference in Pt. II, 9, s.v.
". . . (chosen) people other than Israel."

3. So the Midrash requires. Cf. also on 3 (p. 115) and 9 (p. 216).

too can bear witness.[4] And the amazing thing is that, for the realization of their ambitions, they are prepared to pervert and corrupt their own people. Perhaps that is why He will direct His evil decrees, once made, against the Nations of the World, His adversaries. Perhaps too that is why it is nothing less than a sign of God's omnipotence that He can be forbearing for so long. But His judgment will come. And when it does arrive at last, His singular sovereignty will be manifest in all the world.

For this is indeed the end of the matter: to the Lord alone belong kingship[5] and power and victory and glory forever, and to none other on high or below. In all the heavenly host none is His equal, and it is on earth as it is in heaven: no emperor or general even with a complete arsenal can achieve what He can with His Name only, and no Phidias or Praxiteles or Arcesilaus can measure up to Him. He, and He only, is truly exalted. As Handel perceived more than two centuries ago, "The horse and his rider, the horse and his rider, hath *He* thrown into the sea." Therefore, it is the Lord who shall reign for ever and ever. And because Israel had faith in this Lord and in His servant Moses, they were found worthy to sing the Song at the Sea, even as it is said.

4. One of the best auxiliary commentaries on the rabbinic view of the Nations of the World is *The Twelve Caesars*. The work should be read from beginning to end, for even when Suetonius may be passing on what is no more than gossip, he teaches us what gossipers delighted in circulating, then and in every age.

5. For several Targum renditions of Exod. 15:18, cf. M. McNamara, *The New Testament and the Palestinian Targum to the Pentateuch* (Rome, 1966), 206 ff.

Part II. Shirta: A New Translation, with Commentary

"As a reward for the faith that Israel had in the Lord, the Holy Spirit rested on them and they recited the Song, as it is said, 'They had faith in the Lord and in His servant Moses. Then Moses and the Israelites sang' . . ."

1. Then Sang Moses

THEN SANG MOSES: Sometimes "then" (ʾz) refers to what is past, and sometimes "then" refers to what will come in the future. "Then men began to call upon the name of the Lord" (Gen. 4:26); "Then she said: A bridegroom of blood"

THEN SANG MOSES: Sometimes . . . The same comment in *MRS*, pp. 70–71, except that it quotes five examples (rather than seven as in our Mekilta) for each category of ʾz, omitting in the first category Exod. 15:1 and Num. 21:17 (and instead of Josh. 10:12, it quotes Josh. 8:30—perhaps erroneously, the confusion due to the occurrence of the word ʾz); and in the second category omitting Isa. 58:8 and Jer. 31:12.

That ʾz would call attention to itself at this point is inevitable, for note its use later in the Shirah, Exod. 15:15, and here the verb is in the perfect tense. Note further below, 9, s.v. "Then were the chiefs of Edom affrighted."

On the idiom of our opening sentence, cf. also the expression in Pisḥa, xviii (I, 166).

For Samaritan commentary on the words "Then sang," cf. *Memar Marqah* 2:7 (ed. J. MacDonald, II, 56 f.).

to what is past *lšʿbr;* cf. also below, 3, p. 111.

will come in the future *lʿtyd lbʾ.* As a general rule (and observe also the statement by Rabbi below, on what the future tense of the verb suggests to him), this expression refers to the Age to Come (see, for example, PA 2:16, end, and frequently in talmudic literature). But the simple, literal meaning of "future" also occurs in early sources, for example, M. Berakot 9:4 or M. Ketubot 9:6. Note also the reading in *Sifre Deut.*, 309, p. 349. (See, by the way, the citation in connection with ʿtyd lbʾ in S. Lieberman, *Shkiin* [Jerusalem, 1939], p. 81.)

Interestingly enough, M. Rosh ha-Shanah 1:6 in ed. Lowe reads simply *lʿtyd;* and in *Tanḥuma Be-Shallaḥ* 10 our statement also appears simply as *lʿtyd.*

"Then men began to call . . ." It is worth observing that the verse chosen as proof-texts strike a festive or joyful note (for the

(Exod. 4:26); "Then sang Moses" (Exod. 15:1); "Then sang Israel" (Num. 21:17); "Then spoke Joshua" (Josh. 10:12); "Then David said" (I Chron. 15:2); "Then spoke Solomon" (I Kings 8:12)—now these refer to what is past.

Sometimes "then" refers to what will come in the future: "Then thou shalt see and be radiant" (Isa. 60:5); "Then shall thy light break forth as the morning" (Isa. 58:8); "Then shall the lame man leap as a hart" (Isa. 35:6); "Then the eyes of the blind shall be opened" (Isa. 35:5); "Then shall the virgin rejoice" (Jer. 31:12); "Then was our mouth filled with laughter" (Ps. 126:2); "Then said they among the nations: The Lord hath done great things" (Ps. 126:2) —now these refer to what will come in the future.

Rabbi says: ("Sang") is written here not as "Then *šr*

---

citation of I Chron. 15:2, cf. 16:7 ff.). Thus, not only the verses whose manifest context is festive but also Exod. 4:26 is apt, for it reports how Zipporah delivered Moses from death. Perhaps, therefore, it may be suggested that in our Midrash, Gen. 4:26 is interpreted positively, and not, as generally in other Midrashim, as proof-text for the introduction of idolatry (cf. *Tg Jon* on the verse, and *Gen. R.* 23:6–7, p. 227, and Theodor's note, ibid.). Cf. Jubilees 4:12, and Charles's note, ad loc. Note that *Memar Marqah* 2:6 (II, 56) also quotes this verse in a positive sense and in association with the Shirah (on which comment begins 2:7, immediately thereafter).

now these refer to what is past *MRS*, simply *lšʿbr* (the preceding verses refer) to what is past.

"Then thou shalt see . . ." Note the order in which the Isaiah verses are quoted here and also in *MRS!* It's almost as though the homilist were reading the book of Isaiah backward.

Now these . . . in the future For a partially similar idiom on the Song of Moses (Deut. 32), cf. *Sifre Deut.*, 333, p. 383.

In this instance too the *MRS* reading is briefer, simply *lʿtyd lbwʾ*.

Rabbi says Rabbi (Judah the Prince) is not necessarily in disagreement with the preceding view. It is simply that to him the "future" form of the verb suggests that an eschatological teaching is implied by the verse. Cf. G. Ṣorfati in *Lešonenu*, XXIX (1965), 238 f. In *Tanḥuma Exodus*, ed. Buber, 30b, the reading is: "It is not said, 'Then *šr*,' but, 'Then *yšyr*,' in the Age to Come—in the Age to Come Israel will recite Shirah to the Lord." Cf. Rev. 15:3. Presumably, therefore, according to Rabbi's view, *ʾz yšyr mšh* does not apply to the past alone. Cf. below, 3, s.v. "That He was."

The reading "Rabbi says," occurs also in *MRS*, p. 71; so too *Sekel Tob, Exod.*, p. 200. In B. Sanhedrin 91b the reading is, "Rabbi Meir says"; but cf. DS, ad loc.

It is doubtless the statement in our Midrash which led to the

Moses" but as "Then *yšyr* Moses"—thus from the Torah we derive the doctrine of Resurrection of the dead.

MOSES AND THE CHILDREN OF ISRAEL: When they recited the Song, Moses was on a par with Israel and Israel was on a par with Moses.

Another interpretation. MOSES AND THE CHILDREN OF ISRAEL declares that it was Moses who recited the Song, leading all Israel in it.

---

reading of the Mishnah, Sanhedrin 10:1, in the printed editions. On the original reading of the Mishnah, cf. *Mabo*, p. 229, the end paragraph of n. 5.

"Then šr Moses" MRS adds (from the verse), "and the children of Israel."

thus from the Torah we derive Cf. Melamed's n. 27a in his introduction to MRS, p. 30. Here the reference to the Torah, of course, is specifically to the Pentateuch.

Resurrection of *thyyt; MRS: lthyt.*

MOSES AND THE CHILDREN OF ISRAEL Before quoting this biblical clause, MRS reads: "Another interpretation"; and after the biblical quotation it reads: "The verse declares that Moses was on a par with . . ."—*mgyd hkt(wb) šhyh* . . .

Moses . . . with Moses Moses is, after all, one of the children of Israel, yet Scripture names him individually alongside them. It is this which provokes the midrashic comment. According to the present view (see further s.v. "Leading all Israel in it"), at the recitation of the Shirah, like Moses all the Israelites enjoyed the gift of the Holy Spirit, and this made the people and the prophet equals. For the expression "on a par with" (*šqwl k* . . .), see also Amalek, III (II, 166). Our Mekilta reads, *šqwl kyśr³l* (and *šqwlyn kmšh*), while MRS has *šqwl kngd yś(r³l)* (and *šqwlyn kngd mšh*).

declares MRS: "teaches."

the Song Our Mekilta reads *šyrh*, without the definite article and without the sign of the accusative (*³t*); MRS: *³t hšyrh* (but this may be either quotation of the biblical words, or "contamination" by the biblical words—for note MRS otherwise, e.g. p. 70, or critical apparatus to line 20, p. 71).

leading all Israel in it *kngd kl yśr³l;* cf. the reading in *Mid. Tan.*, p. 45. But none of them, not even all of them together, were his equals. According to this view, the biblical idiom, mentioning Moses first and then the children of Israel, implies that in recitation of the Shirah, Moses first recited (or began) each verse, and Israel repeated (or repeated and completed) it after him, only after he had given them the cue; see further, below, pp. 78 f. At all events, here we have a view disagreeing with the preceding statement, that at the recitation of the Shirah Israel were the equals of Moses. Our present

THIS SONG (*'t hšyrh hz't*): Now then, does *šyrh* occur only once, (here)? Does not indeed the word *šyrh* occur ten times (in Scripture)?—

The first was the one recited in Egypt, as it is said, "Ye shall have a song like unto the one sung in the night when the feast was hallowed" (Isa. 30:29).

The second was the one recited at the Sea, as it is said, "Then sang Moses" (Exod. 15:1).

---

statement emphasizes that even at the Shirah recitation Moses retained his prophetic preeminence.

On the expression *šqwl kngd,* see also below, 9, pp. 214 f., and *Mid. Tan.,* p. 45; and note indeed the reading in *Yalkut Shimeoni,* 241 (Salonica, 1526, 27c), where, from the way the passages are quoted, the view stands out clearly. Note too the reading in *Sifre Num.,* 157, p. 210, on Phineas (where the text clearly implies that no less than the whole army together was the equal of Phineas, *šqwl kpnḥs,* but that Phineas alone was equal to the whole army, *šqwl kngd kwlm*). Cf. *Sifre Deut.,* 52, pp. 118 f.

The reading in *Tanḥuma Be-Shallaḥ* 10 seems to me to blur what is involved in the two points of view registered by our Mekilta; observe that Tanḥuma does not include the clause "and Israel *šqwlyn kmšh.*"

does **šyrh** occur only once . . . For this translation and the interpretation of the following long, poorly preserved section, see J. Goldin, "This Song" in the (forthcoming) *Salo W. Baron Jubilee Volume.*

šyrh occur ten times Exod. 15:1; Num. 21:17; Deut. 31:19 (twice), 21, 22, 30; 32:44; II Sam. 22:1; Ps. 18:1.

On the subject of the Ten Songs see Kasher, XIV, 289 f., and Ginzberg, *Legends,* VI, 11, n. 59. On the notion of ten songs cf. *Origen's Commentary on Song of Songs* (trans. and annot. by R. P. Lawson, London, 1957), pp. 47 ff., 266 f., and see also S. Lieberman, *Yemenite Midrashim* (in Hebrew; Jerusalem, 1940), p. 14.

The first Here and in the following ordinals *MRS* does not have the definite article; it reads here, *r'šwnh,* and so correspondingly for all the rest.

as it is said Not in *MRS* either here or in the remainder of the proof-texts for the Ten Songs.

"a song . . . hallowed" See also below, 2, p. 88. Literally: "Ye shall have a song as in the night when a feast is hallowed." According to the Midrash, the song spoken of in Isa. 30:29 will be like the Song sung by Israel in Egypt during the festival on the night before they were delivered from Egypt. Cf. B. Pesaḥim 95b and Rashi, ad loc.

"Then sang Moses" *MRS,* quoting "This is my God, and I will glorify Him," is referring to the same thing as our Mekilta.

The third was the one recited at the Well, as it is said, "Then sang Israel" (Num. 21:17).

The fourth was the one Moses recited, as it is said, "And it came to pass, when Moses had made an end of writing" etc. (Deut. 31:24 ff.).

The fifth was the one Joshua recited, as it is said, "Then spoke Joshua to the Lord" etc. (Josh. 10:12 f.).

The sixth was the one Deborah and Barak recited, as it is said, "Then sang Deborah and Barak the son of Abinoam" (Judg. 5:1 ff.).

The seventh was the one David recited, as it is said, "And David spoke unto the Lord the words of this song" (II Sam. 22:1 ff.).

The eighth was the one Solomon recited, as it is said, "A Psalm; a song at the dedication of the House of David" (Ps. 30:1).—

Was it then David who built it? On the contrary, was it not Solomon who built it, as it is said, "So Solomon built the House, and finished it" (I Kings 6:14)? Why, then, does Scripture say, "A Psalm; a song at the dedication of the House of David?" Only because David gave over his

"had made an end of writing" Deut. 31:30 reads, "And Moses spoke . . . the words of this *song* (šyrh)." Note the *MRS* reading.

"Then spoke Joshua . . ." In this instance the word "song" does not appear, but Joshua's exclamation is plainly a poem, a song; and the Midrash indeed may be suggesting that *spr hyšr* (Josh. 10:13) is to be explained as Book of the Song. Cf. Peshitta (and contrast Vulgate, ad loc.; cf. *LXX* ad II Sam. 1:18).

and Barak Not in *MRS*.

"So Solomon built" Note the *MRS* reading and cf. the critical apparatus, ibid., to line 4, p. 71.

Why, then . . . House of David Not in *MRS*.

Only because אp *lpy; MRS*: אp. On David "building," cf. I Chron. 22:2–5; 28:11 ff.

David In reality, however, says the Midrash, it was Solomon who sang the song. Note by the way that *MhG, Exod.*, p. 285, adds: "Another interpretation: The Song of Solomon, as it is written, 'The song of songs, which is Solomon's'" (Cant. 1:1), on which cf. Tg, ad loc. (and the reference above, s.v. "Does šyrh occur . . . once").

gave over his life According to W. A. Meeks, *The Prophet-King* (Leiden, 1967), p. 312, the expression *ntn npš ʿl* "is the precise equivalent to *tén psychén tithénai*" of John 10:11 (the end of Meeks' n. 5 I do not understand).

life to it, to have it built; that is why it goes by his name.

And so too it says, "Lord, remember unto David all his affliction; how he swore unto the Lord, and vowed unto the Mighty One of Jacob: Surely I will not come into the tent of my house . . . until I find out a place for the Lord . . . Lo, we heard of it as being in Ephrath" etc. (Ps. 132:1 ff.). Hence, how does Scripture put it? "Now see to thy House, David" (I Kings 12:16). Lo then, because David gave over his life to it, it goes by his name.

You will find the same true of every man, that whatever he gives over his life to, goes by his name.

To three things Moses gave over his life, and they go by his name:

> **to have it built** *lbnwtw; not* in *MRS.*
>
> **goes by his name** *MRS* continues: "And where do we hear of David giving over his life for the house (= Temple)? For it is said, 'Lord, remember unto David,' and the whole passage" (lit., the matter, *ʿnyynʾ*).
>
> **how does Scripture put it** *MRS:* "What is said of him (by Scripture)."
>
> **"see to thy House, David"** Note that in I Kings 12:16 it is not said, *Son of* David, although that cry was aimed at Rehoboam (Landau), and the Midrash interprets "thy house" as "thy House"— i.e. thy Temple, the Temple to which you gave over your life.
>
> **Lo then . . . You will find . . . by his name** *MRS:* "Lo, every single thing that a man gives over . . . by his name." In our Mekilta, apparently, the sentence "You will find the same true of every man . . ." is intended to serve as an introduction to the discussion which follows.
>
> The subject of the Songs will be resumed below, p. 73. The long interpolation—a feature to be observed in all midrashic compilations—is introduced because of the comment on David, that *he gave his life* for the Temple and therefore *his name came to be associated* with it. (It might be interesting to note that *MhG, Exod.*, does not continue with the passage on Moses at this point.) On those giving their lives for Israel, see also Pisḥa, 1 (I, 10 f.); on other examples of giving one's life for someone or something, see further below, 10, p. 245 f.
>
> It is obvious that the Midrash is trying to underscore the importance of the theme of giving one's life for Israel and for the basic institutions and ideals of Israel. On a related idea, cf. Shabbata, 1 (III, 204 f.).
>
> **To three things . . . by his name** On this statement cf. *Deut. R.*, ed. Lieberman, p. 61, n. 5. Cf. L. Finkelstein, in *JQR*, XXXI (1940–41), 223 ff. See also Rabinowitz, *Halakah we-Aggadah* (in Yannai's poetry), p. 36.

He gave over his life to the Torah and it goes by his name, as it is said, "Remember ye the Torah of Moses My servant" (Mal. 3:22). But is it not on the contrary God's Torah, as it is said, "The Lord's Torah is perfect, restoring the soul" (Ps. 19:8)? Lo then, why does Scripture say, "The Torah of Moses My servant?" Only because he gave over his life to it; that is why it goes by his name. Where, however, do we find that he gave over his life to the Torah? In the passage, "And he was with the Lord" etc. (Exod. 34:28); it also says, "Then I abode in the mount forty days" etc. (Deut. 9:9). Lo then, because he gave over his life to the Torah, it goes by his name.

He gave over his life to Israel and they go by his name, as it is said, "Go, get thee down, for thy people have dealt corruptly" (Exod. 32:7). But are they not on the contrary the Lord's people, as it is said, "Yet they are Thy people and Thine inheritance" (Deut. 9:29), and it says, "In that men said of them: These are the people of the Lord" etc. (Ezek. 36:20)? Why, then, does Scripture say, "Go, get thee down, for thy people have dealt corruptly?" Only because he gave over his life to Israel; that is why they go by his name. Where, however, do we find that he gave over his life to Israel? In the passage, "And it came to pass in those days, when Moses was grown up, that he went out unto his brethren, and looked on their burdens" (Exod. 2:11);

"the Torah of Moses My Servant" Note also how on the day of Atonement the high priest expressed himself in his confession (e.g. M. Yoma 3:8), "As it is written in the Torah of Thy Servant Moses."

But . . . God's Torah MRS: "But is it the Torah of Moses? (Is it) not on the contrary the Lord's Torah?"

Lo then . . . "The Torah of Moses My servant" Not in MRS.

Where . . . that he MRS: "And where (do we find that) Moses"; and note this idiom, ibid., right through the passage.

In the passage Lit., "as it is said"; and MRS omits the expression here as well as below.

Lo then . . . to the Torah . . . his name Not in MRS, and so too in the following section.

to Israel In other sources (e.g. Pesikta R. 14b) instead of "Israel," the text speaks of "the Tabernacle." Cf. S. Lieberman, in Sinai, IV (Jerusalem, 5699), 239.

But . . . the Lord's people Note how the Mekilta appropriates the language of Ezek. 36:20. MRS reads: "Are they then the people of Moses? But are they not" etc.

Why then . . . "corruptly" Not in MRS.

and it goes on, "And he looked this way and that way" etc.
(Exod. 2:12). Lo then, because he gave over his life to
Israel, they go by his name.

He gave over his life to the pursuit of justice and the
judges therefore go by his name, as it is said, "Judges and
officers shalt thou appoint of thine" etc. (Deut. 16:18). But
is not justice, on the contrary, God's, as it is said, "For
justice is God's" (Deut. 1:17)? Why, then, does Scripture
say, "Shalt thou appoint of thine?" Only because he gave
over his life to the pursuit of justice; that is why the judges
go by his name. Where, however, do we find that he gave
over his life to the pursuit of justice? In the passage, "And
he went out on the second day" etc. (Exod. 2:13); and it
continues, "And he said: Who made thee a ruler and a
judge over us" (Exod. 2:14); and it goes on, "Now when
Pharaoh heard" etc. (Exod. 2:15). And it is written, "Now

and it goes on Lit., "and it is written."

"And . . . that way" "And he smote the Egyptian."

He gave . . . justice Although it is not clear whether the reading
should be *dinin* (justice) or *dayyanin* (judges; see also ed. HR, p. 117,
and the critical apparatus, ad loc.; MS Vatican 299 also reads *dyynyn*),
the basic idea is perfectly clear, that Moses gave his life for the institutions and maintenance of justice everywhere. See also the *Deut. R.*,
ed. Lieberman, reference, cited above, s.v. "To three things . . . by
his name." *MRS* reads here: "He gave over his life to the *dynyn* and
they go by his name." Cf. also Rabinowitz, *Halakah we-Aggadah*, p.
36, n. 36, and Lieberman, in *Sinai*, IV.

"shalt thou appoint of thine" *ttn lk*—that is, note the emphasis on
lk, thine, though the verse might easily and idiomatically have read,
"Shalt thou appoint in all thy gates" (*ttn bkl š'ryk*).

etc. *MRS* continues: "Are they then Moses's? Was it not said indeed
(*kbr*) . . ."

But is . . . God's Note again (cf. above, s.v. "But . . . the Lord's
people") how the Midrash adopts the biblical idiom of Deut. 1:17 (cf.
also below, p. 83). At this point *MRS*, p. 72, cites in addition Isa.
30:18 and Ps. 82:1.

Why then . . . "of thine" Not in *MRS*.

because . . . of justice *MRS:* "Because he surrendered (*msr*) his life
to them."

the judges go by *MRS:* "They go by."

In the passage Lit., "as it is said"; *MRS:* "Lo, it says."

a ruler and a judge Evidently, then, Moses had taken it upon himself to act as a defender of justice.

"Now when Pharaoh heard" Moses had to flee for his life. In

the priest of Midian had seven daughters" etc. (Exod. 2:16), and it goes on, "And the shepherds came and drove them away" (etc.) (Exod. 2:17). From strife he fled to return to strife, (everywhere) "executing the righteousness of the Lord and His ordinances with Israel" (Deut. 33:21). Lo then, because he gave over his life to the pursuit of justice, the judges go by his name.—

The ninth was the one Jehoshaphat recited, as it is said, "And when he had taken counsel with the people, he appointed them that should sing unto the Lord, and praise in the beauty of holiness" etc. (II Chron. 20:21); and it continues, "Give thanks unto the Lord, for His mercy endureth for ever" (II Chron. 20:21).—

MRS, p. 72, Deut. 33:21 is quoted at this point, and the comment on Moses in Midian, which follows in our Mekilta, is omitted, very likely by accident; for *MRS* adds the sentence, "from strife he went off to return to strife," which clearly belongs to the comment on Midian. Note how our Mekilta also treats Deut. 33:21.

"Now the priest . . ." etc. Having spoken of Moses giving his life to see justice carried out, and having cited the story in Exod. 2, of the flight of Moses, the Mekilta continues with commentary on Exod. 2: 16 ff., which reports another instance of Moses coming to the defense of those victimized by injustice. It is also likely that the Midrash is here calling attention to a play on the words *mdyn* (Midian) and *mdynyn* (from strife; reading as does ed. HR). Thus we see Moses everywhere giving his life for the establishment of justice and righteousness.

From strife . . . to strife Reading as does ed. HR (and so too *MRS*, p. 72, and MS Vatican 299), while ed. Lauterbach reads, *mdyynyn brḥ wldyynyn ḥzr* (note also Lauterbach's translation). See also D. Hoffmann, *Liquṭe batar Liquṭe* (Berlin, 1897), p. 13. The sentence has an epigrammatic flavor. On the nature of the injustice in Midian and Moses's conduct, see also *ARNA*, p. 72.

executing the righteousness of the Lord The verse speaks of "a ruler" (*mḥqq*) and "heads of the people," terms easily applicable to Moses; cf. Tg Onkelos and Tg Jonathan, ad loc. Note also how *Sifre Deut.*, 355, pp. 418 f., treats this verse in relation to Moses.

Lo then . . . his name *MRS* reads instead: "Lo, whatsoever a man gives over his life to, goes by his name."

The ninth Resuming the principal discussion of the Ten Songs.

with (the people) ʿl; MT: ʾl.

in the beauty of *bhdrt*; MT: *lhdrt*.

and it continues Lit., "and it says," *wʾwmr*, but note MT, ad loc., *wʾmrym*. However, perhaps the Mekilta is not quoting the biblical

Now then, why does this thanksgiving formula differ from all the other thanksgiving formulas in the Torah, in that all the other thanksgiving formulas in the Torah read, "Give thanks unto the Lord, for He is good, for His mercy endureth for ever," while here it reads, "Give thanks unto the Lord, for His mercy endureth for ever?" Only because, as it were, at the destruction of the wicked there was no joy in Him on high. If at the death of the wicked there was no joy in Him on high, a fortiori at that of the righteous, one of whom is the equal of the whole wide world, as it is

---

word here, but instead using the typical formula for "and it says." The discussion of the ninth song in *MRS*, p. 72, is in essence the same as in our Mekilta, but the sentences are arranged somewhat differently.

Now then *wmh; MRS: wky mh.*

why does this thanksgiving formula . . . A supplementary or parenthetical comment on the particular form or formula of this song. Note that *MhG, Exod.*, p. 285, does not include it. For the idiom of the question, cf. also the idiom of M. Pesaḥim 10:4, Wa-Yassaᶜ, v (II, 117), Pisḥa, I (I, 14), XI (I, 82), etc.

thanksgiving formulas in the Torah Torah here in the sense of Scripture as a whole, not just the Pentateuch.

"Give thanks . . . is good" For example, Ps. 118:1; see also Ps. 106:1, 107:1, 118:29, 136:1, I Chron. 16:34.

while here . . . "for ever" This sentence does not appear in *MRS*.

Only because *ᵓlᵓ;* not in *MRS*.

at the destruction of the wicked See the story in II Chron. 20:1–30 and cf. Ezek. 18:23. And that is why the full formula, with the clause "for He is good" = merciful, is not employed. Cf. Heinemann, p. 92. And yet in *Sifre Num.*, 117, p. 134, R. Ishmael tells his disciples that when the wicked are destroyed God does rejoice. On the fact that our Mekilta contains views not in accordance with R. Ishmael's personal view, see Epstein, *Meboᵓot*, III, 537 ff., 562 ff. In B. Megillah 10b, where the view of our Mekilta is cited, it is given in the name of R. Yoḥanan.

Where our Mekilta reads ᶜl ᵓbdn ("at the destruction"), *MRS* reads *bᵓbdn.*

there was no joy in Him (lit., before Him) on high *MRS:* "There is no joy before God (*hmqwm*)."

If . . . on high This clause is not in *MRS*.

a fortiori . . . righteous *MRS:* "A fortiori at the destruction of that righteous man"! Cf. M. Sanhedrin 6:5.

One of whom . . . world *MRS:* "who was the equal of all" (*šqwl kngd hkl*). One righteous man is the equivalent of a whole world.

said, "But the righteous is the foundation of the world"
(Prov. 10:25).—

The tenth is the one for the Age to Come, as it is said,
"Sing unto the Lord a new song, and His praise from the
end of the earth" (Isa. 42:10); it also says, "Sing unto the
Lord a new song, and His praise in the assembly of the
saints" (Ps. 149:1).—

For all the songs referring to past events the noun used is
in the feminine, (because) even as a female brings to birth,
so the triumphs in the past were succeeded by subjugation;
but the triumph which is yet to be will not be succeeded
by subjugation. That is why the noun used for it is in the
masculine, as it is said, "Ask ye now, and see whether a
man doth travail with child" (Jer. 30:6): (for) just as no
male gives birth, so the triumph which is yet to come will

One soul (= individual) *is* a whole world; cf. M. Sanhedrin 4:5. On
the righteous and the whole world, see further below, 9, p. 214 f., and
cf. also *Sifre Deut.*, 47, p. 106; 306, p. 333. On this theme and related aspects, see R. Mach, *Der Zaddik in Talmud und Midrash*
(Leiden, 1957), pp. 108 ff. ("Das Wirken des Zaddik").

"a new song" An entirely new song. Note indeed the tenor of the
passages in Isa. 42:10–13 and Ps. 149. See Mann, *Bible as Read*, p.
229, and with this compare *Yannai*, p. 263, line 35.

all the songs MRS: "all (the) salvations (triumphs)" (*tšwᶜwt*). See
further next note.

the noun . . . feminine *qrwᵓwt blšwn nqbh;* MRS: *nqrᵓw ᶜl šm
nqbh.* As the text stands, the statement is difficult, and it may well be
that the MRS reading *tšwᶜwt* (cf. preceding note) is an attempt to
get around the difficulty. For the meaning of our text, see the reference
given above, s.v. "Does *šyrh* occur only once."

the triumphs MRS reads without the definite article.

were succeeded *hyw ᵓhryhn;* MRS: *yš ᵓhryhn.*

but the triumph which is yet to be MRS: "But (the) triumph
coming in the Age to Come."

will not be succeeded by subjugation Not in MRS.

That is why . . . masculine Note the slightly different reading and
arrangement of clauses in MRS. But the sense is the same: both
Isa. 42:10 and Ps. 149:1 use the word *šyr* (masc.). On this notion of
šyrh, feminine, and *šyr*, masculine, see also the view of R. Samuel
bar Naḥmani in *Cant. R.* 1:5, 8d.

"whether . . . child" Note indeed that Jer. 30 speaks of the redemption of Israel and Judah.

not be succeeded by subjugation, as it is said, "O Israel, that art saved by the Lord with an everlasting salvation" (Isa. 45:17).

UNTO THE LORD: It was in praise of the Lord they recited it, and they did not recite it in praise of flesh and blood, as in the other passage, "And the women came out of all the cities of Israel, singing and dancing to meet Saul" etc. (I Sam. 18:6), and it continues, "And the lighthearted women struck up the song" etc. (I Sam. 18:7). In the present instance, however, it was in praise of the Lord they recited it, and they did not recite it in praise of flesh and blood.

will not be succeeded *P yh⁾ ⁾ḥryh; MRS: ⁾yn ⁾ḥryh.*

"an everlasting salvation" And never again shall they be reduced to shame or confounded, as the verse concludes.

and they did not recite it Neither here nor at the end of the paragraph does *MRS* repeat the verb "recite it."

It was . . . flesh and blood That is, not in praise of Moses. See also *Tanḥuma Be-Shallaḥ 11,* beginning, and *Tanḥuma Exodus,* ed. Buber, 30b. The wholly miraculous deliverance is here being underscored (nothing less would have saved them from the Egyptians), and the homilist insists on God alone as redeemer: on the later occasion the *women* did hail Saul and David as their redeemers (now contrast Exod. 15:20–21); but Moses was not so hailed.

On the tendency of the folk to hail Moses and attribute to him what should be attributed to God, cf. John 6:32, and see *MMKJV* (English vol.), pp. 278 ff. Note incidentally how the biblical narrator, as he describes the people (*ha-ʿam*) about to make the golden calf, has them say (Exod. 32:1), "For that man Moses"—N.B. "that man" and not only "Moses"—"who brought us up from the land of Egypt." On the other hand, at the Schechem covenant in Josh. 24:16 f., *ha-ʿam* declares: "For the Lord our God, He it is that brought us and our fathers up out of the Land of Egypt, from the house of bondage." See further below, s.v. "In the Lord greatness is comely."

"Flesh and blood" is the characteristic rabbinic way of referring to a human being, particularly in contrast with God. I believe it has not yet appeared in the Dead Sea literature, which still prefers the biblical expression of *bśr,* flesh. See also below, 8, p. 197 f.

as in the other passage *kmw šn⁾mr lhln; MRS: P kʿnyn šn⁾(mr).*

"And the lighthearted women" The Midrash is surely struck by the expression *hmšhqwt,* which it understands as "giddy, silly, frivolous," and possibly worse (cf., e.g., *Gen. R.* 53:11, pp. 567 f.); of these women too it is said (I Sam. 18:6) that they came with *mhlwt* and *tpym:* but how different from those at the Song at the Sea; cf. below, 10, end.

AND THEY SPOKE, SAYING: Rabbi Nehemiah says: The Holy
Spirit came to rest on Israel, and they recited the Song like
people reciting the Shema.

Rabbi Akiba says: The Holy Spirit came to rest upon
them, and they recited the Song like people reciting the
Hallel.

AND THEY SPOKE, SAYING The comments which follow, by
R. Nehemiah (note the name in *AhB*, I, 6) and the others, are an
answer to the question, What purpose is served by the addition of
the infinitive *l'mr*, "saying," to the verb? Cf. M. Soṭah 5:4 and Rashi
in B. Soṭah 27b, s.v., *'yn tlmwd lwmr*. And the very addition of the
word *l'mr*, in other words, the very *repetition* of the verb *'mr*, suggests to the sages that some kind of responsive (or even unison, i.e.,
not a "reading" on the part of one person where the congregation
listens only; see now J. Heinemann, in *Bar-Ilan Annual* VI [5728—
1968], 39–41), recitation took place when the Shirah was recited.
While in the Mekilta (and Tosefta and in both P. and B. Soṭah)
three views are offered, in the Mishnah only two authorities, Akiba
and Nehemiah, are cited.

Rabbi Nehemiah Cf. his view in Be-Shallaḥ, VII (I, 252 f.).

And they recited *whyw 'wmrym*; MRS: *w'm(rw)*—and so too in
the Akiba statement below.

Like people reciting the Shema According to T. Soṭah 6:3, this was
a responsive, antiphonal recitation; Moses would recite the beginning
of a verse or one verse, and Israel (by virtue of the Holy Spirit, as
the Mekilta puts it; see also above, s.v. "Moses . . . with Moses" and
"Leading all Israel in it") would know on their own how to complete
the verse properly or how the following verse continued—as the
Shema was presumably recited in the synagogue (and note also *TK*
ad T. Shabbat 1:12 on the teaching of children, Long Commentary,
pp. 10 f.). In B. Soṭah 30b Rashi says of the Shema recitation that it
was in unison. See further, below.

"Reciting" in the original is *šhn qwryn*; in MRS, *šqwr'yn*—and cf.
the reading in the Akiba statement also.

On the Shema see *JE*, XI, 266 f.; Elbogen, pp. 16–26, 496 f.; see also
Levi, *Yesodot ha-Tefillah*, pp. 65–68; L. Finkelstein, in *JQR*, XXXII
(1941–42), 387–400.

Rabbi Akiba says . . . Hallel The statement is far from clear, and
the difficulties are made vivid by reference to the parallel passages
(M. Soṭah 5:4; T. Soṭah 6:2–3; B. Soṭah 30b; P. Soṭah 5:4). First, however, note that MRS, p. 72, omits the clause "the Holy Spirit rested
upon them" (see also *AhB*, I, 6; *Yalkut Shimeoni*, 242, 27d; *Sekel Tob*,
p. 191) and reads Akiba's statement as follows: "Moses opened his
recitation with 'I will sing unto the Lord,' and Israel responded after
him and with him finished (the verse?), like (people) reciting the
Hallel in the synagogue." (Or does the latter clause mean: And

Rabbi Eliezer ben Taddai says: First Moses would begin a sentence and then Israel would repeat after him and with him conclude. Moses would begin to recite, "I will sing unto the Lord, for He is highly exalted" (Exod. 15:1), and Israel would repeat after him and with him conclude, "I will sing unto the Lord, for He is highly exalted; the horse and his rider hath He thrown into the sea" (Exod. 15:1);

Israel responded after him by *reciting* as he finished each verse, the way people do when they recite the Hallel in the synagogue?)

According to the Tosefta and P. Soṭah, Akiba maintains that the Shirah was recited as the Hallel is recited by a minor at school; that is, he is taught verse by verse, and he repeats each verse verbatim after it is read to him. (When, at a *service*, a minor acts as the reader of the Hallel, everything he recites must be repeated in full; cf. M. Sukkah 3:10.)

According to B. Soṭah, Akiba maintains that the Shirah was recited as the Hallel is recited by an adult; that is, after each verse which he recites, the congregation responds by repeating the (exclamatory) chapter heading (cf. M. Sukkah 3:10, loc. cit., and see *Talmudic Encyclopedia*, ix, 410 f.)—so that, in the case of the Shirah, as Moses finished a verse, each time Israel responded with "I will sing unto the Lord."

And this seems to me to be the meaning of M. Soṭah, as recorded in the Kaufmann Codex (note also ed. Lowe, 103a): "for like (people) reciting the Hallel, Israel responded after every single statement of Moses, 'I will sing unto the Lord for He is highly exalted.' " Cf. in this connection G. Șorfati, in *Tarbiz*, xxxii (1963), 139 f.

If the (Mekilta and Tosefta) clause in Akiba's statement, that the Holy Spirit rested on Israel, is authentic, perhaps the meaning may be this: that by virtue of the Holy Spirit resting on them, Israel knew how properly to respond to each verse recited by Moses—that they knew they should respond as the Hallel is responded to.

On a mystical Midrash quoting Akiba, that when Israel recited the Shirah, God put on a mantle of magnificence on which was engraved every ʾz ("then") occurring in the Torah, see the citation in Scholem, *Gnosticism*, p. 64.

On the Hallel, see *JE*, vi, 176 f.; L. Finkelstein, in *HUCA*, xxiii (1950–51), Pt. 2, pp. 319 ff.

Rabbi Eliezer ben Taddai MRS: "Eleazar ben Taddai" (and no "rabbi").

First Moses . . . and with him conclude Not in MRS.

Moses would begin *hyh pwtḥ;* MRS: *pwtḥ,* and so throughout the statement.

and Israel would repeat . . . and . . . conclude, "I will sing . . . He is highly exalted; the horse and his rider hath He thrown into the sea" MRS: "and Israel would repeat . . . and . . . conclude,

Moses would begin to recite, "The Lord is my strength and song" (Exod. 15:2), and Israel would repeat after him and with him conclude, "The Lord is my strength and song, and He is become my salvation" (Exod. 15:2); Moses would begin to recite, "The Lord is a man of war" (Exod. 15:3), and Israel would repeat after him and with him conclude, "The Lord is a man of war, the Lord is His Name" (Exod. 15:3).

'The horse and his rider . . . into the sea.'" This however need not represent a variant at all; *MRS* may be elliptical, and as often in midrashic texts quote only part of the relevant verse. See also next note.

and Israel would repeat . . . and . . . conclude, "The Lord is my strength . . . my salvation" *MRS:* "And Israel would repeat . . . and . . . conclude, 'This is my God and I will glorify Him.'" See preceding note.

"the Lord is His Name" As the Mekilta reads, it appears that according to Eliezer ben Taddai, Israel repeated that which Moses had already declared, and then, on their own, they would know how to complete the remainder of the verse along with him.

Behind the three opinions recorded by the Mekilta there may be echoes of an actual problem: How is the Shirah to be recited when it is read in the public service (see also Levi, pp. 136–38). And the problem itself may possibly reflect three different orientations, as it were, toward the Shirah: for R. Nehemiah, on the occasion when the Shirah was recited, Israel acknowledged the sovereignty of God (cf. Exod. 15:8 and R. Joshua ben Korḥa in M. Berakot 2:2; and for R. Nehemiah's view on why Israel merited the Holy Spirit at the Shirah recitation, cf. Be-Shallaḥ, VII [1, 252 f.]); for R. Akiba, on that occasion Israel witnessed God's especial greatness and might (cf. B. Berakot 58a, bottom, and note the following passage in the Mekilta), and hence recited a doxology; for at the miraculous deliverance from Egypt, God Himself, as it were, was redeemed (cf. *Sifre Num.*, 84, pp. 82 f.; and see below, 3, p. 115 f., for Akiba's view on how Israel proclaims God's glory before the Nations). Finally, perhaps for R. Eliezer ben Taddai, at the miracle at the Sea Israel was in its youth, and like children at their Scripture lessons, they recited the verses; that is, after the master began the verse, they repeated what he said and concluded it on their own.

Note also *Memar Marqah* 2:7 (II, pp. 57 f.): "The prophet Moses sang the Song in sections. When he finished each section, he would fall silent and all the Elders would respond with the verse, 'I will sing to the Lord, for He has triumphed gloriously: the horse and his rider He has thrown into the sea.' Then all Israel would say '(The Lord is) my strength and my song, and He has become my salvation' up to 'The Lord is a man of war; the Lord is His name.' They

I WILL SING UNTO THE LORD, FOR HE IS EXALTED:

> In-the-Lord   greatness   is-comely
> In-the-Lord   power   is-comely
> In-the-Lord   glory, victory, and majesty   are-comely;

exactly as David says, "Thine, O Lord, is the greatness, and
the power, and the glory, and the victory, and the majesty"
(I Chron. 29:11).

I WILL SING UNTO THE LORD, FOR HE IS HIGHLY EXALTED: A
king of flesh and blood enters a province, and everyone
acclaims him

---

would then fall silent and the prophet Moses would begin to sing."
On the procedure when Miriam sang, see ibid., p. 58 (cf. also ibid.,
2:11, II, 80). See further below, 10, p. 248, s.v. "Miriam . . . among
the women."

**I WILL SING UNTO THE LORD, FOR HE IS (EXALTED)
HIGHLY** Not in *MRS*.

greatness *gdwlh; MRS: hgdwlh.*

In-the-Lord greatness is-comely The Mekilta statement has the
quality of an acclamation (cf. Lake and Cadbury in their Commentary
on Acts 19:28, in *Beginnings of Christianity*, IV, 247), in the form
of a poetic doxology based on the idiom of I Chron. 29:11, and what
we have here is a three-line stanza with three words to the line.
MRS, p. 73, reads the same way except that in the third line it has
"His (are) glory and victory and majesty." With the reading in ed.
HR, cf. *Tanḥuma, Be-Shallaḥ,* 11. See further below, p. 84.

greatness . . . power . . . glory . . . These are the ingredients of
genuine exaltation ($g^{y}h$). It may well be that in these terms is expressed also a protest against the deified abstractions whose cults were
especially associated with the Roman emperor. Cf. L. R. Taylor, *The
Divinity of the Roman Emperor* (Middletown, Conn., 1931), pp. 153,
161, 181, 199, 225, 227, 245, and the reference to K. Scott, below,
s.v. "A king of flesh and blood."

I WILL SING . . . FOR HE IS HIGHLY EXALTED . . . *MRS*
omits the verse quotation and plunges at once into the parable with
the introductory formula, "A parable is told, to what may this be
likened."

A king of flesh and blood . . . Note also the reading in *AhB*, I,
149.

What we have here is, of course, a take-off on imperial eulogies
and panegyrics (cf. below, s.v. "Everyone flatters him"). Compare
Panegyricus of Plinius Secundus, 3:4 (Loeb, II, 329; my italics): "There
is no danger that in my references to [the Emperor's] *humanity* he
will see a reproach for *arrogance;* that he will suppose I mean *extrav-
agance* by *modest expenditure,* and *cruelty* by *forbearance;* that I

that-he-is	mighty	but-he-is	only	(a) weakling
that-he-is	rich	but-he-is	only	(a) pauper
that-he-is	wise	but-he-is	only	(a) fool

think him *covetous* and *capricious* when I call him *generous* and *kind, profligate* and *idle* instead of *self-controlled* and *active,* or that I judge him a *coward* when I speak of him as a *brave man."* (I owe this reference to Ziegler, p. 58.) Cf. also Dio Chrysostom, *Third Discourse on Kingship,* 2–5 (Loeb, I, 105 f.). See also K. Scott, *The Imperial Cult under the Flavians* (Stuttgart and Berlin, 1936), pp. 25 ff.

everyone acclaims him Cf. S. Lieberman, in *AA,* pp. 75–81. Everyone—*hkl;* neither here nor in the clause "everyone flatters him" does *MRS* read *hkl.*

Mighty . . . rich . . . wise Cf. the idiom in Jer. 9:22 and PA 4:1; see also Ba-Ḥodesh, VI (II, 245), but note the order in B. ᶜAbodah Zarah 55a. The order in *MRS,* p. 73, is "mighty, wise, rich." For these epithets in exclamation, see also *Lev. R.* 5:3, p. 104.

Note that no contrast is furnished for "just" and "trustworthy," and the same is true of the reading in *MRS.* On the term "trustworthy," cf. *GJP,* pp. 75 ff.

Here too, however, we seem to have a fragment of some "hymn" which read more or less like this:

I will sing unto the Lord for He is highly exalted

I-will-sing	unto-the-Lord	for-He-is	mighty
I-will-sing	unto-the-Lord	for-He-is	rich
I-will-sing	unto-the-Lord	for-He-is	wise
I-will-sing	unto-the-Lord	for-He-is	merciful
I-will-sing	unto-the-Lord	for-he-is	just
I-will-sing	unto-the-Lord	for-He-is	trustworthy

and as the text on p. 84 suggests,

I-will-sing	unto-the-Lord	for-He-is	comely
I-will-sing	unto-the-Lord	for-He-is	splendid
I-will-sing	unto-the-Lord	for-He-is	glorious
		and-there-is-none	His-equal.

As a little reflection will reveal, this poem breaks up naturally into three stanzas of three lines each, four words to the line. For fixed patterns in hymns, see Scholem, *Gnosticism,* chap. 4.

In the second stanza God's mercy is mentioned before His justice— i.e. his role as judge which would require Him to be severe. By His trustworthiness is understood that He can always be depended on and that He is unlike fickle human monarchs.

What we have here, then, is a hymn on the true exaltation and simultaneously a sideswipe at imperial flattery.

As to some minor textual variants:

"Merciful"—*rḥmny; MRS: rḥmn.*

"For He is (trustworthy)"—*šhwᵓ; MRS: whwᵓ.*

"Of all these virtues"—*mkl hmdwt hllw; MRS: mkl ᵓlw hmdwt.*

that-he-is merciful   but-he-is only (a) savage
that-he-is just
that-he-is trustworthy

and in him there's not one of all these virtues, but everyone flatters him. But that is not the case with Him that
Spake and the World Came to Be! On the contrary:

I-will-sing unto-the-Lord for-He-is mighty

as it is said, "The great God, the mighty, and the awesome"
etc. (Deut. 10:17); and it says, "The Lord strong and
mighty, the Lord mighty in battle" (Ps. 24:8); and it says,
"The Lord will go forth as a mighty one" etc. (Isa. 42:13);
and it says, "There is none like unto Thee, O Lord; Thou
art great, and Thy name is great in might" (Jer. 10:6).

I-will-sing unto-the-Lord for-He-is rich

as it is said, "Behold, unto the Lord thy God belongeth the
heaven" etc. (Deut. 10:14); and it says, "The earth is the
Lord's, and the fulness thereof" etc. (Ps. 24:1); and it says,
"The sea is His" etc. (Ps. 95:5); and it says, "Mine is the
silver, and Mine the gold" etc. (Mal. 2:8); and it says, "Behold, all souls are Mine" etc. (Ezek. 18:4).

I-will-sing unto-the-Lord for-He-is wise

as it is said, "The Lord by wisdom founded the earth"
(Prov. 3:19); and it says, "With Him is wisdom and might"

Everyone flatters him On the other hand, the prophets know, says
R. Isaac ben Eleazar, "that their God insists upon the truth, and
therefore they do not flatter Him," P. Berakot 7:3, end, and cf.
S. Lieberman in Tarbiz, xxvii (1957–58), 186. On rhetor's flattery, cf.
Sifre Deut., 343, p. 394 (Mid. Tan., pp. 208 f.). Cf. Tacitus, History
(Modern Library, 1942) 5:5: "Their (i.e. the Jews') flattery is not paid
to their kings, nor this honour to our Emperors."
    "The Lord . . . as a mighty one" Note the next clauses in the verse.
    At this point MRS cites also Ps. 86:10 (but note critical apparatus,
MRS, p. 73). Perhaps this should be added to our Mekilta, for in the
next two stanzas five proof-texts are furnished for each category.
    "There is . . . O Lord" Note how these proof-texts reverberate
with echoes of the Shirah (in this instance, cf. Exod. 15:11, and with
the Ps. 24 verse, cf. Exod. 15:3). See also below the quotation from
Jer. 10:7.
    "The earth is . . . thereof" Not in MRS.

etc. (Job 12:13); and it says, "For the Lord giveth wisdom"
etc. (Prov. 2:6); and it says, "He giveth wisdom unto the
wise" etc. (Dan. 2:21); (and it says,) "Who would not fear
Thee, O King of the nations? . . . Forasmuch as among
all the wise men of the nations, and in all their royalty,
there is none like unto Thee" (Jer. 10:7).

I-will-sing   unto-the-Lord   for-He-is   merciful

as it is said, "The Lord, the Lord is a God merciful and
gracious" etc. (Exod. 34:6); and it says, "For the Lord (thy
God) is a merciful God" etc. (Deut. 4:31); and it says,
"Remember, O Lord, Thy compassions" etc. (Ps. 25:6);
and it says, "The Lord is good to all; and His tender
mercies" etc. (Ps. 145:9); and it says, "To the Lord our
God belong compassions and forgiveness" (Dan. 9:9).

I-will-sing   unto-the-Lord   for-He-is   just

as it is said, "For justice is God's" (Deut. 1:17); and it says,
"God standeth in the congregation of God; in the midst of
the judges He judgeth" (Ps. 82:1); and it says, "The Rock,
His work is perfect; for all His ways are justice" (Deut.
32:4).

I-will-sing   unto-the-Lord   for-He-is   trustworthy

as it is said, "The faithful God" etc. (Deut. 7:9); and it says,
"A God of faithfulness" etc. (Deut. 32:4).

"For the Lord giveth wisdom" MRS (ntn) should most likely be
corrected (to ytn).
   "He giveth wisdom unto the wise" Not in MRS.
   "there is none like unto Thee" Cf. above, s.v. "There is . . . O
Lord."
   "The Lord is good to all" MRS: Ps. 145:8; both Mekiltas, however,
may have the combination in mind.
   "To the Lord . . . forgiveness" Not in MRS.
   "For justice is God's" Cf. above, p. 72. At this point MRS cites also
Isa. 30:18 (cf. also above, p. 72).
   "The Rock . . . justice" This verse MRS quotes in connection with
"I will sing unto the Lord for He is trustworthy."
   "The faithful God" Note the reference to the redemption from
Egypt in Dan. 7:8.

Lo then, comely in the Lord are the power and the glory and the victory and the majesty!

I WILL SING UNTO THE LORD:

For-He-is   comely
For-He-is   splendid
For-He-is   glorious   and-there-is-none   His-equal

as it is said, "For who in the skies can be compared unto the Lord" etc. (Ps. 89:7), and it continues, "A God dreaded in the great council of the holy ones" (Ps. 89:8), and it continues, "O Lord God of hosts (*ṣbʾwt*), who, mighty, is like unto Thee, O Lord" (Ps. 89:9).—What is the meaning of *ṣbʾwt* (hosts)? Like an ensign (*ʾwt*) He stands out in the midst of His host (*ṣbʾ*). So too it says, "And He

Lo then, comely . . . the majesty Cf. above, p. 80. *MRS,* p. 73, does not bring this perorating sentence, but after the (abbreviated) homily which follows.

For-He-is comely . . . glorious See above, s.v. "Mighty . . . rich . . . wise." The expression *nʾh wmšwbḥ,* comely and glorious, occurs frequently in midrashic sources to describe human beings; see, for example, *Sifre Deut.,* 343, p. 398 (along with "mighty"); *Pesikta Kahana,* ed. Mandelbaum, p. 220; *Deut. R.,* ed. Lieberman, p. 14, n. 10; *ARN,* 9, p. 41 (of Moses); etc. (On *nyʾwtyw wšbḥw* of God, see below, 3, p. 115.) Observe, however, that the Mekilta, so too *MRS*) speaks of God as "comely, *splendid (hdwr),* and glorious," and this tripling of terms sounds like a poetic expression applied especially to God; cf. *Tanḥuma Naśo* 25, where we read that the day the Tabernacle was set up, Moses entered it and heard *qwl hdr, qwl nʾh, qwl mšwbḥ* (a splendid, comely, glorious voice, sound), where *qwl hdr* may be put first because of the idiom of Ps. 29:4; cf. *Tanḥuma Num.,* ed. Buber, IV, 19b, and n. 131. The formula "for He is comely . . . splendid . . . glorious" may well be an ecstatic exclamation in some old hymn; indeed, observe the mood of the passage as it continues.

and-there-is-none His-equal Not in *MRS.*

"For who in the skies . . ." In Ps. 89:2a note *ʾšyrh,* "I will sing," and in the proof-texts that follow note the echoes of the Shirah in terms like *bny ʾlym* (v. 7), *nwrʾ* (v. 8), *my kmwk* (v. 9). On this passage, see also below, 8, p. 193, and *MRS* reading, ad loc.

What is the meaning of *ṣbʾwt* Not in *MRS.*

Like an ensign (*ʾwt*) . . . host (*ṣbʾ*) God towers above all, He stands out aloft like a standard or ensign in the midst of a troop. God's hosts are the angelic beings who, though extraordinarily splendid, still cannot be compared to Him. Note that *MRS* quotes Exod. 15:11 immediately after this comment! *MRS,* by the way, reads: "Thou

ʾtʾ (came) in the midst of (m) the myriads holy" (Deut. 33:2),
(that is,) like an ensign (ʾwt) in their midst He towers
above His holy myriads.—

And David also says, "There is none like unto Thee
among the gods, O Lord" etc. (Ps. 86:8). So too it says, "My
Beloved is white and ruddy" etc. (Cant. 5:10), and it
continues, "His head is as the most fine gold" etc. (Cant.
5:11), and it continues, "His eyes are like doves" etc. (Cant.
5:12), and it continues, "His cheeks are as a bed of spices"
etc. (Cant. 5:13), and it continues, "His hands are as rods
of gold" etc. (Cant. 5:14), and it continues, "His legs are as
pillars of marble" etc. (Cant. 5:15).

Rabbi Yose the Galilean says: Lo, it says, "Out of the
mouth of babes and sucklings hast Thou founded strength"
(Ps. 8:3)—"Babes" is a reference to those as yet in their

---

art ʾwt in the midst of Thy host." ʾwt bṣbʾ, "ensign in the midst
of host," is of course a typical midrashic word play, on ṣbʾwt.
Cf. Blau, *Altjüdische Zauberwesen*, p. 105.

"ʾtʾ (came)" Our text reads wʾtʾ (see also *Sifre Deut.*, 343, p. 398),
but MT has wʾth.

And He ʾtʾ . . . His holy myriads Not in *MRS*. The Midrash
interprets wʾtʾ (or, wʾth) as ʾwt hwʾ, He is a standard, an ensign (cf.
above, s.v. "Like an ensign . . ."). The holy myriads are also angelic
beings; cf. *Sifre Deut.*, 343, p. 398; *Mid. Tan.*, p. 211 (see also *AhB*,
I, 11); note too how our Mekilta chapter concludes, below, p. 87.
There is no mistaking who God is even when He is surrounded by
His splendid hosts: He is always and immediately and distinctly
recognizable, for none can be compared with Him. I intend "towers
above" to convey the force of the midrashic interpretation of the
prefix m in the word mrbbwt ("in the midst of the myriads").

And David also . . . So too it says Not in *MRS*. With the style of
Ps. 86:8, cf. Exod. 15:11.

"My Beloved is white and ruddy" *MRS*: "My Beloved is white and
ruddy etc., and the rest of the theme. Lo then, in the Lord greatness
is comely, etc., as was written above."
The verse continues, "preeminent above ten thousand," dgwl mrbbh,
which is so apt for the Midrash here: a standard, we might say,
towering above His myriad. On these Canticles verses, see further
below, 3, 116 f. It may be that the Mekilta is here suggesting that at
the miracle at the Sea, the Song of Songs was sung. See S. Lieberman
apud Scholem, *Gnosticism*, pp. 118 ff.

"founded strength (ʿwz)" Note Exod. 15:2, "The Lord is my
strength," ʿzy. See also Ba-Ḥodesh, III, end (II, 220). Even the infants
then recited the Shirah, and even those not yet born. On such and

mothers' wombs, as it is said, "Or as a hidden untimely birth I had not been; as babes that never saw light" (Job 3:16). "Sucklings" is a reference to those who were taking suck at their mother's breast, as it is said, "Gather the children, and those that suck the breasts" (Joel 2:16): —Rabbi says: "Babes" is a reference to those already up and around, as it is said, "To cut off the babes up and around in the streets" (Jer. 9:20), and it says, "The babes ask for bread" (Lam. 4:4). "Sucklings" is a reference to those still at their mothers' breasts, as it is said, "Gather the children, and those that suck the breasts" (Joel 2:16)—both the former and the latter opened their mouths and recited the Song before the Omnipresent, as it is said, "I will sing unto the Lord" etc. (Exod. 15:1 f.).

Rabbi Meir says: (That) the unborn children while in their mothers' wombs also opened their mouths and recited the Song before the Omnipresent, (we learn) from the verse, "In choral assemblies, O ye to come out of the very fountainheads of Israel, bless ye God, even the Lord" (Ps. 68:27).

---

similar notions, cf. Luke 1:41 and Strack-Billerbeck, ad loc.; Augustine, City of God, III, 31 (Loeb, I, 396); also G. Weil, *Biblical Legends* (New York, 1846), p. 94.

In the Talmud (B. Soṭah 30b, P. Soṭah 5:4) it is stated that the infants then *beheld* the Shekinah and broke into song. On the reading of T. Soṭah 6:4, cf. *TR*, II, 61. Note also the reading in *Midrash Ps.* 8:5, 39a.

"Sucklings" is a reference to those who were taking suck *MRS:* "And 'sucklings' are none other than (those) at" (their mother's breast).

"Gather the children . . . breasts" Neither here nor in Rabbi's statement which follows does *MRS* quote Joel 2:16. Like our Mekilta (and *MRS* too) a few lines below, *MRS* reads here, "Both the former and the latter opened their mouths and recited the Song, 'I will sing unto the Lord' etc."

before the Omnipresent, as it is said Not in *MRS.*

Rabbi Meir says *MRS* (p. 74) does not give R. Meir's view. Cf. *AhB*, I, 7, and n. 14. On R. Meir's view, compared with that of R. Yose as it is given in B. Soṭah 30b, cf. Tosafot, ad loc., s.v. "R. Meir says."

"ye to come out of the very fountainheads" This is of course the midrashic understanding of the verse, those who were to come forth from the womb. Note the use of *mqwr* and other euphemisms in M. Niddah 2:5. According to the Mekilta reading, it would seem that

And it was not only Israel who recited the Song before the Omnipresent, but the ministering angels also, as it is said, "O Lord, our Lord, how glorious is Thy name in all the earth! Whose majesty is rehearsed above in the heavens" (Ps. 8:2).

R. Meir and R. Yose do not disagree, but furnish different proof-texts for their view (cf. the Tosafot referred to in the preceding note).

not only Israel who recited the Song MRS continues: "Sing unto the Lord, for He is highly exalted"; and it does not have the words "before the Omnipresent." See also the reading in *AhB*, I, 31.

but . . . also ʾP ʾp; *MRS:* ʾP. On the angels at the redemption from Egyptian bondage, cf. Pisḥa, IX (I, 74) and XIV (I, 113).

"how glorious is Thy name" Cf. Exod. 15:3b and 11a. On other occasions when the angels recited this psalm, see *Midrash Ps.* 8:2, 37a ff.

"Whose majesty is rehearsed above in the heavens" Where the angels abide. And that this psalm is related to the exodus has already been noted above in the midrashic interpretation of its third verse.

It is perhaps not superfluous to observe that this chapter closes with a kind of crescendo of choral volume: all Israel, even the unborn children, and not only Israel but the ministering angels, have burst forth in song, each group singing the paean of God's praises. (For a somewhat similar exultant note at the close of a chapter, compare below, end of 6.) For note too that the redactor has deliberately ignored the logical verse division and has brought together commentary enlarging on "I will sing unto the Lord," which is of course "this song" of the opening half of verse 1. Chapter 2, then, begins with, "For He is highly exalted" (and therefore Friedmann's hesitations, expressed in his note in his Mekilta edition, are unnecessary).

2. For He Is Highly Exalted

FOR HE IS HIGHLY EXALTED: He exalted me and I exalted Him. He exalted me in Egypt, as it is said, "And thou shalt say unto Pharaoh: Thus saith the Lord: Israel is My son, My first-born" (Exod. 4:22); so too in Egypt I exalted Him, as it is said, "Ye shall have a song like unto the one sung (by you) in the night when the feast was hallowed" (Isa. 30:29).

Another interpretation of FOR HE IS HIGHLY EXALTED: He exalted me and I exalted Him. He exalted me at the Sea, as it is said, "And the angel of God now moved" etc.

He exalted me and I exalted Him *g꜄ny wg꜄ytyw; MRS: hg꜄ny whg꜄ytyw* (and so too below; but note *AhB*, 1, 9). The comment is typically midrashic: the infinitive absolute accompanying the verb in conjugated form is made to release special meaning. In the first two interpretations, the idea of correspondence is suggested: as He exalts Israel, Israel exalts Him.

as it is said Not in *MRS*.

"My son, My first-born" This was God's exaltation of Israel.

So too in Egypt I exalted Him, as it is said, "Ye shall . . ." *MRS:* "So too I exalted Him (*hg꜄ytyw*), and recited Shirah before Him, 'Ye shall . . .'"

"Ye shall have a song . . . hallowed" Cf. above, 1, p. 68, and n. Note, however, *Sekel Tob*, p. 201.

Another interpretation These two words do not occur here in *MRS*.

"And the angel of God now moved" Since an angel of God walked at the head (in front) of the camp of Israel, this was a special distinction. On the other hand, Landau suggests that since Exod. 14:19 reports that this angel moved from *before* Israel as they approached the Sea, and took up his station *behind* them, this was a sign (the cloud pillar) that God was personally, without intermediaries, going to perform the miracle for Israel, and *this* was the special exaltation.

(Exod. 14:19); so too at the Sea I exalted Him and recited the Song before Him, as it is said, "I will sing unto the Lord, for He is highly exalted."

Another interpretation of FOR HE IS HIGHLY EXALTED: He is exalted and in the Future will affirm His exaltedness, as it is said, "For the Lord of hosts hath a day upon all that is proud" etc. (Isa. 2:12); and it continues, "And upon all the cedars of Lebanon . . . and upon all the high mountains . . . and upon every lofty tower . . . and upon all the ships of Tarshish . . . and the loftiness of man shall be bowed down" etc. (Isa. 2:13–17); and it continues, "And the idols shall utterly pass away" (Isa. 2:18).

Another interpretation of FOR HE IS HIGHLY EXALTED: He lords it over all those who act the high and mighty—for in the very ways the Nations of the World adopt to act the high and mighty before Him, He brings them to account: For thus it says of the Flood Generation, "Their bull

so too at the Sea I exalted Him *MRS* does not repeat "at the Sea."

"I will sing unto the Lord, for He is highly exalted" *MRS* quotes instead, "This is my God and I will glorify Him," but essentially the same song is intended.

He is exalted . . . exaltedness In this interpretation both forms of the verb are applied to God and an eschatological note is struck: also typically midrashic. Note the abbreviated text in *MRS*.

"man" ʾdm; MT: hʾdm.

"idols shall utterly pass away" *The* climax of God's affirmation of His exaltedness; cf. the second paragraph of the ʿAlenu prayer (Baer, p. 132).

He lords it over all those . . . Cf. *AhB*, I, 9. Note that the Mekilta offers four interpretations for "For He is highly exalted," and now we have the fourth, whose mood has been well set by the Isaiah passage in the third interpretation. The verb forms gʾh gʾh (gaʾoh gaʾah) are understood to say: Against those who exalt themselves He comes exaltedly, triumphantly. See also Tg Onkelos and Jonathan on the verse. Cf. also below, 6, p. 152.

act the high and mighty hmtgʾym; MRS: hgʾym.

for in the šbmh; MRS: bmh.

very ways . . . account Measure for measure. See Moore, II, 249, n. 10; 251 f.; III, 193; Heinemann, pp. 64–69; and S. Lieberman in *LGJV* (Hebrew vol.), pp. 255 ff. and nn. 56, 106. See the speech of Artabanus at the beginning of Herodotus VII (trans. A. de Selincourt [Edinburgh, 1954], pp. 419 f.). Cf. below, 4, p. 135, s.v. "Whatever the measure."

For thus it says *MRS* begins with "And so we find," and makes no reference to the Flood Generation, but at once goes on to refer most

gendereth . . . they send forth their little ones like a flock
. . . they sing to the timbrel and harp, and rejoice" etc.
(Job 21:10–12 f.). But what else is reported in that very
place? "Yet they said unto God: Depart from us . . . What
is the Almighty, that we should serve Him" etc. (Job
21:14–15). They said: Is it not after all a matter of rain
drops (He sends down to us)? We don't need Him, for "a
flow will well up from the ground and water the whole
surface of the earth" (Gen. 2:6)!

Said the Holy One, blessed be He, to them: Idiots! By
means of the prosperity I lavish upon you, you act the
high and mighty? By your life! By means of that very thing
I will bring you to account, as it is said, "And the rain was
upon the earth" etc. (Gen. 7:12).

Rabbi Yose son of the Damascene says: To satisfy their

---

briefly to the Tower Folk and the Sodomites, and preserves a frag-
mentary reference to an anecdote about Rabban Gamaliel (presumably
the story in *Sifre Deut.*, 43, pp. 94 f.; note critical apparatus, ad loc.,
and the reference to B. Makkot should be 24a).

"Their bull gendereth . . ." The association of these verses with
the Flood Generation (who rebelled against God out of the super-
fluity of their prosperity; cf. *Sifre Deut.*, 43, pp. 92 f., and the references
furnished by Finkelstein, ad loc.) is suggested by Job 21:18b ("the
storm"), and cf. *Gen. R.* 30:1, p. 270, for the comment on Prov. 10:25.
Cf. Ginzberg, *Legends*, v, 173, n. 15.

(He sends down to us) Cf. Melamed in *Tarbiz*, vi (1934–35), 122.
Rabbi Yose son of the Damascene . . . On "son of the Damascene",
cf. Kutscher, pp. 96 f.; Ginzberg, *Legends*, v, 139, n. 19.

The translation of R. Yose's statement is an attempt to render the
text in accordance with the view of a number of commentators (cf.
Finkelstein's note to line 3 of his edition of *Sifre Deut.*, 43, p. 93)
who, following the suggestion of T. Soṭah 3:9 and *Gen. R.* 32:7,
p. 294, take our Mekilta text to mean: They set their eye on (= they
lusted after; note also *kdy l*ʿ*śwt tʾwtm*) the "daughters of men"
(Gen. 6:2). Thus, the expression ʿ*yn* ʿ*lywnh* (the upper eye, the eye in
the face) invites a play on ʿ*yn* (eye, fountainhead, maidenhead) and
*m*ʿ*yn;* and ʿ*yn tḥtwnh* would be a euphemism. (On a similar word
play with ʿ*yn,* cf. J. Goldin, *Fathers According to Rabbi Nathan*
[New Haven, 1955], p. 180, n. 48.)

Unfortunately, the reading of R. Yose's statement is not only very
difficult but uncertain, and to make different readings in different
sources say the same thing is hazardous in the extreme.

Lauterbach (in *Klausner*, pp. 181–84) suggests that in the Mekilta
R. Yose's statement makes no reference at all to unchaste conduct, but

lust they kept eyeing what's low lying; so, to destroy them, the Holy One, blessed be He, opened on them streams from top to bottom, as it is said, "On the same day were all the fountains of the great deep burst apart, and the floodgates of the sky broke open" (Gen. 7:11).

You find the same true of the Tower Folk, that by the very way they adopted to act the high and mighty before Him, He brought them to account; for it is said: "And they said: Let us build us a city" etc. (Gen. 11:4); and what is written after that? "So the Lord scattered them abroad from thence" etc. (Gen. 11:8).

You find the same true of the Sodomites, that by the very thing they adopted to act the high and mighty before Him, He brought them to account. For it is said, "The land out of which cometh bread . . . the stones thereof are the place of sapphires . . . the path unknown to bird of prey . . . untrod by wild beasts" etc. (Job 28:5–8). Said the Sodomites: We don't need people coming here to us. Lo,

---

is simply another way of saying that the Flood Generation refused to acknowledge that their prosperity was a gift from God: they regarded the waters from "the upper fountain" (rains) as dispensable, because after all they had waters rising from "the lower fountains" (note Gen. 2:6 cited above), and they could flourish on these alone. Hence God brought a flood of waters from on high and from below, for all sources of water are His.

Whatever the exact meaning of the words in the Mekilta, R. Yose's notion is also intended as an example of measure for measure.

On their unchastity as a final cause for the punishment of the Flood Generation, cf. Ginzberg, *Legends*, v, 173, n. 17.

To satisfy their lust If Lauterbach is right, then perhaps: "To satisfy their (insatiable) appetite" for huge prosperity and a carefree life.

streams from top to bottom Lit., fountains from on high and from below.

"build us a city" As the verse goes on to say, "lest we be scattered abroad" etc. On the other hand, cf. Mirsky, pp. 63 f. (and the version he cites also from Tanḥuma).

"land out of which cometh bread" The verse continues, "and underneath it is *turned up* as it were *by fire*," descriptive of the way Sodom was destroyed, Gen. 19:24–25.

We don't need . . . us. Cf. Philo, *On Abraham*, XXVI (Loeb, VI, 69 f.) and Josephus, *Antiquities*, I, 11:1 (Loeb, IV, 95 f.). See also *PRE*, chap. 25.

food supplies come from us, silver and gold and precious
stones and pearls come from us. Let's put out of mind all
thought of visitors!

Said the Holy One, blessed be He, to them: Idiots! By
means of the prosperity I lavish upon you, you act the high
and mighty and say, Let's put out of mind all thought of
visitors? I will leave no remembrance of you in the world!
As it is said, "He broke loose (against them) a stream from
its source, so that they are forgotten of passersby, they are
utterly reduced and removed from human contact" (Job
28:4); and it says, "(Let there be) a brand and contempt
against those with their smug thoughts . . . let those so
complacent in their tents be surrendered to plunderers"
etc. (Job 12:5–6). What brought all this upon them? "The

(Food supplies) come from us *ywṣ* *mᵓṣlnw*. Lauterbach translates,
"Behold, food is *taken from us*," evidently understanding, if visitors
come to us, our own possessions are diminished, are taken away from
us. But I believe the expression is to be taken as "has its source in
our midst"; that is, the Sodomites said, We need no visitors in our
midst: food supplies come from us, good things come from us (because of the superabundance we enjoy), we are well off as we are,
and we are in no need of outsiders. Note the use of *yṣᵓ* in the very
Job verse quoted. The reading of *Sifre Num.*, 139, p. 185, lines 5–6,
literally, "Scripture declares that it is only from before Him that all
spirits come forth," *ywṣᵓwt . . . mlpnyw*, seems to support the translation adopted. See especially *Sifre Deut.*, 259, p. 282: *bmqwm ṣprnstw
ywṣᵓh*.

silver . . . pearls A midrashic-talmudic cliché for fabulous wealth;
cf. *ARNB*, p. 5, and frequently; see also below, 7, p. 179.

Let's put . . . visitors For this vivid expression, cf. Job 28:4a
(latter half), quoted below in the text. On the variant reading, *twrt
hrgl*, see Yalon, *Bulletin*, I, 38 f.

"He broke loose . . . a stream" Of fire and brimstone; see Isa.
30:33, and cf. Rashi in B. Sanhedrin 109a, s.v. *paraṣ*.

"from its source . . . contact" The translation is an attempt to
suggest the midrashic interpretation of the verse, which departs
radically from the (difficult) literal rendering; cf. JPS, ad loc. The
original reads *mᶜm gr* (*meᶜim gar*), and cf. Rashi in B. Sanhedrin 109a,
s.v. Is it, perhaps, possible that instead of reading the consonants as
meᶜim gar, the Midrash reads them as *meᶜam ger*, and understands
the words of the clause to mean, He causes a stream of fire and brimstone to burst forth against the Sodomites out of their very midst,
out of the midst of a *people* that makes itself *stranger* to all?

"a brand" Associated with Sodom because it was destroyed by fire.

result of all that God had put into their possession" (Job 12:6b).

So too it says, "And they were haughty and committed abomination before Me" (Ezek. 16:50). And what did this bring upon them? "Therefore I removed them even as I saw it" (ibid.).

So too it says, "Behold, this was the iniquity of thy sister Sodom" etc. (Ezek. 16:49). What brought all this upon them? "She did not strengthen the hand of the poor and needy" (ibid.).

So too it says, "Before the Lord destroyed Sodom and Gomorrah they were like the garden of the Lord, like the land of Egypt" (Gen. 13:10). Then what else is written? "And they made their father drink wine" etc. (Gen. 19:33). — Now, where in that cave could they get wine? But it was the Holy One, blessed be He, who provided them with wine, even as it is said, "And it shall come to pass in that day, that the mountains shall drop down sweet wine" (Joel 4:18): If this is how the Holy One, blessed be He, provides

So too it says Note that *three* more passages are now to be explained as illustrative of the measure-for-measure principle (though actually two of the passages, the Ezekiel verses, refer to the same subject; cf. the reading in *Sifre Deut.*, 43, p. 94). Ezekiel's reference to Sodom would naturally recall verses from that book in the present context.

"even as" Measure for measure.

"iniquity of . . . Sodom" Note how the verse continues.

"Before the Lord destroyed . . . Egypt" Just before this the verse says that "it was well watered," *mšqh*, rich in drink, which the Midrash connects with the verb of Gen. 19:32 ff., and they gave their father to drink: the very wine which the region was rich in was the cause of Lot's undoing. See also Ginzberg, *Legends*, v, 243, n. 188 (on Lot, by the way, cf. *TK* ad T. Megillah 3:31, Long Commentary, 1214).

Then what else is written *wᵓḥryw*, that is, although what is reported in Gen. 19:25 overtook these once prosperous cities.

where in that cave . . . wine After so thorough a devastation as Gen. 19:25 reports; even for the night's lodging all they could find was a cave.

the Holy One . . . provided That is, "miracles never cease." See further next note.

"the mountains shall drop . . . wine" The very mountains can be made to release wine when God wills it, and note Gen. 19:30 for the location of that cave. Cf. R. Judah ben Simon's statement in *Gen. R.* 51:8, p. 538.

for those who infuriate Him, a fortiori for those who carry out His will!

You find the same true of the Egyptians, that by the very means they adopted to act the high and mighty before Him, He brought them to account. For it is said, "And (Pharaoh) took six hundred chosen chariots" etc. (Exod. 14:7), and it is written subsequently, "Pharaoh's chariots and his host hath He cast into the sea" etc. (Exod. 15:4).

You find the same true of Sisera, that by the very way he adopted to act the high and mighty before Him, He brought him to account. For it is said, "And Sisera gathered

If this is how . . . will A parenthetical observation on the last passage, not germane to our discussion, and in effect a stereotypical clause; see, for example, Wa-Yassaᶜ, IV (II, 110). Cf. Finkelstein in his edition of *Sifre Deut.*, p. 94.

You find the same true of . . . We return to our principal discussion after the brief digression. *MRS,* p. 74, once again runs parallel.

the Egyptians . . . account See also below, 6, p. 158, and note how T. Soṭah 3:13 describes the arrogance of the Egyptians.

and it is written subsequently *MRS:* "What does it say," and so throughout this section.

of Sisera See again below, 6, p. 158, and note how T. Soṭah 3:14 describes this example. What the measure for measure involved here is, is not altogether clear (the suggestion in ed. HR and in some commentators, that our text is to be understood in the light of B. Pesaḥim 118b, seems forced to me). If the brief statement in the Mekilta intends to express what the Tosefta says, then the proof-texts teach this: the stars (God's hosts) opposed Sisera's hosts, who were eager volunteers (cf. Judg. 5: 19b), and such of course would be God's hosts, the stars.

Perhaps, however, the Midrash in the Mekilta has something else in mind. In the proof-text of Judg. 4:13, which the Mekilta quotes, it is said that Sisera gathered together his huge army "from Harosheth-goiim, *unto the brook Kishon,*" and at the latter place presumably hoped to crush Israel. The quotation now of Judg. 5:20, which is supposed to demonstrate measure for measure, is not intended to stop at verse 20, but is the introduction to verse 21, which can indeed be regarded as proving the measure-for-measure principle: *"The brook Kishon* swept them away": the very place which was to have witnessed Israel's downfall was the scene and instrument of Sisera's defeat. (As Pharaoh's hosts and chariotry were overcome by a body of water, so Sisera's hosts and chariotry were overcome by a body of water, "the brook Kishon swept them away.") That in our midrashic texts, sometimes the key words of the biblical proof-text do not appear, is not at all uncommon.

together all his chariots, even nine hundred chariots of
iron" (Judg. 4:13); what is written subsequently? "They
fought from heaven, the stars in their courses fought
against Sisera" (Judg. 5:20).

You find the same true of Samson, that by the very thing
he adopted to act the high and mighty, He brought him to
account. For it is said, "And Samson said unto his father:
Get her for me, for in my eyes she is pleasing" (Judg. 14:3);
what is written subsequently? "And the Philistines laid
hold on him, and put out his eyes; and they brought him
down to Gaza" (Judg. 16:21). —Rabbi Judah says: His
deterioration began in Gaza; that's why his punishment
took place in Gaza.

Of Samson He is included also in the list of *MRS*, p. 74, but how
can Samson fit into a list of "the Nations of the World"? Note that
in *MhG, Exod.*, p. 288, neither he nor Absalom (see further below)
is included. Samson (Absalom too) is part of the T. Soṭah 3 list, but
there the discussion is of the general measure-for-measure principle,
and there is no word of Nations of the World. It would seem, therefore, that the Mekilta redactors have simply helped themselves to
the whole block of material which underlies the Tosefta source. Note
indeed that in the series (from "the Egyptians" on), only in the
examples of Samson and Absalom does the Mekilta give "further matter" in regard to the subject. It might be added that in M. Soṭah 1:8
Samson and Absalom represent a unit, as it were.

Finally, only in the loosest way can the expression "he acted high
and mighty" be applied to Samson: his eyes may have led him astray
(hence he was subsequently blinded), but we are not told that he
"acted high and mighty"; note indeed the reading in the Mishnah
and Tosefta Soṭah, T. Soṭah 3, M. Soṭah 1:8. It may be, however, that
the Mekilta is taking strong exception to Samson's way of speaking to
his father.

to act the high and mighty *MRS* adds here (and so too in the
passages on Absalom, Sennacherib, etc.), "before Him."

Rabbi Judah *MRS:* "Rabbi," and so too the Tosefta (and both
Talmuds). Note also *TR*, II, 59 (to lines 13–14). See further below, in
the discussion of Absalom, s.v. "Rabbi Judah."

His deterioration . . . took place in Gaza Literally, the beginning
of his deterioration was in Gaza, and *MRS* does not read "was."

Cf. Judg. 16:1. See B. Soṭah 9b and Rashi, ad loc. (the woman at
Timnah, Judg. 14:1, he married; but with the woman at Gaza—note
the explicit term in Judg. 16:1—his relationship was altogether
different).

R. Judah is also calling attention to the operation of the measure-
for-measure principle.

You find the same true of Absalom, that by the very thing he took pride in, He brought him to account. For it is said, "Now in all Israel there was none to be so much praised as Absalom for his beauty . . . And when he polled his head" etc. (II Sam. 14:25–26).—

Rabbi Judah says: He was a lifelong Nazirite and he would poll his head once a twelvemonth, as it is said, "And it came to pass at the end of forty years, that Absalom said" etc. (II Sam. 15:7).

Rabbi Yose says: He was a temporary Nazirite, for a fixed number of days, and he would poll his head once in thirty

of Absalom Cf. above, s.v. "Of Samson," and below, s.v. "Of the Prince of Tyre." On Absalom, see further below, 6, p. 171.

took pride in The expression in the text (*bmh šntgᵓh*) is the same as in all the other examples, which we have translated "act the high and mighty." The Midrash is suggesting (and so too the Mishnah, loc. cit.) that conscious of his good looks and aware of his popularity, Absalom was led on to encourage and organize revolt against his father.

"And when he polled his head" The conclusion of the thought will be brought below, p. 97, l. 7; in *MRS* (note too T. Soṭah 3:16) the conclusion is provided at once. Since the polling of his head has been referred to, the Midrash brings the various views regarding Absalom's Naziriteship. On Absalom as Nazirite, cf. Ginzberg, *Legends*, IV, 105; VI, 266, n. 98.

Rabbi Judah says *MRS* (and so too T. Soṭah, 3:16), "R. Judah the Prince"; but cf. *TR*, II, 59.

He was a lifelong Nazirite *MRS* does not have this clause. On the concept of a lifelong Nazirite, cf. M. Nazir 1:2 and 4, and on Absalom, cf. B. Nazir 4b–5a and the last Tosafot at the bottom of 4b.

he would poll his head once a twelvemonth *MRS:* "Every twelvemonth he would poll his head"; and so too this idiom ("Every thirty days") below.

"at the end of forty years . . . etc." From this verse we learn that Absalom had made a vow, equated by the Midrash with the Nazirite vow (see the Tosafot referred to above), and thus connected by the Midrash with Absalom's long hair. Since his hair was of extraordinary length (as would be more than implied by II Sam. 14:26; and see ibid., 18:10 f.), his was not a Nazirate of ordinary (thirty day) duration. By relating the expression *ymym lymym*, "at every year's (end)," of II Sam. 14:26 to *ymym*, "for a full year," of Lev. 25:29, the Talmud (Nazir, 4b–5a) derives that once a year, once in twelve months, Absalom had his hair lightly polled. That a lifelong Nazirite may have this done, cf. M. Nazir 1:2 and 4.

a temporary Nazirite . . . days Neither in *MRS* nor in the Tosefta

days, as it is said, "Now this would come to pass at the end of those days when he was permitted to poll his head" etc. (II Sam. 14:26).

Rabbi says: Every Sabbath eve he would poll his head, for that is the way of royal persons, to be polling their heads every Sabbath eve.—

What is written subsequently? "And Absalom chanced to meet the servants of David. And Absalom was riding upon his mule . . . and his head caught hold of the terebinth" etc. (II Sam. 18:9).

You find the same true of Sennacherib, that by the very way he adopted to act the high and mighty, He brought

---

(loc. cit.) does this clause occur. See further below, s.v. "Now this would come to pass."

once in thirty days On the undefined Nazirite vow, see M. Nazir 1:3, 6:3, and *Semahot* 7:8 and 20 (ed. Zlotnick [New Haven, 1966], pp. 53 and 56, and notes, ad loc.); *Sifre Zuta*, 241, and *MhG, Num.*, p. 132 (and n. 52 ad loc.); cf. Josephus, *War*, II, 15:1, Loeb, II, 445).

"Now this would come to pass . . . etc." So too *MRS* (and the Tosefta), although it is not clear how this verse serves as proof-text: note that neither the Palestinian nor the Babylonian Talmud nor *Num. R.* 9:24 nor 10:17 quotes this verse for the Nazirite who may poll his head once in thirty days. The translation adopted is an attempt to suggest that, perhaps, acccording to R. Yose this is how the verse should be understood: Now it was at the end of the days, those days when *ordinarily* a Nazirite polls his head. Or perhaps (so ʿEṣ Yosef ad *Tanḥuma Be-Shallaḥ* 12; cf. also *ZY* on our Mekilta passage), the word "days" of II Sam. 14:26 is associated by R. Yose with the expression "a whole month of *days*" of Num. 11:20, 21; cf. B. Nazir 5a.

Rabbi So too *MRS*, but cf. T. Soṭah 3:16 and note the reading in B. Soṭah 5a.

Every Sabbath eve Cf. Josephus, *Antiquities*, VII, 8:5 (Loeb, v, 461).

for that is the way of But note B. Sanhedrin 22b and B. Taʿanit 17a.

royal persons Lit., sons of kings; *MRS:* "kings" (and note the orthography on p. 75, plus the critical apparatus, ad loc.).

On what distinguished Absalom, therefore, from other members of the royal family, if these at all events polled their heads once a week, cf. B. Nazir, loc. cit.

What is written subsequently . . . Resuming and completing the original thought on Absalom. On the *MRS* reading, cf. above, s.v. "And when he polled his head."

of Sennacherib Cf. below, 6, p. 158 f.

him to account. For it is said, "By thy messengers thou hast
taunted the Lord . . . I have digged and drunk waters"
etc. (II Kings 19:23-24); and what is written subsequently?
"And it came to pass that night, that the angel of the Lord
went forth, and smote in the camp of the Assyrians a
hundred fourscore and five thousand" (II Kings 19:35).
—It is said: The highest of their officers was in charge
of one hundred and eighty-five thousand, and under their
lowest ones there were no less than two thousand, as it is
said, "How then canst thou turn away the face of one
captain, even of the least of my master's servants" etc.
(II Kings 18:24)?— "This is the word that the Lord hath
spoken concerning him: The virgin daughter of Zion hath
despised thee . . . Whom hast thou taunted" etc. (II Kings
19:21-22), and it is written, "This very day shall he halt at
Nob" etc. (Isa. 10:32).

You find the same true of Nebuchadnezzar, that by the
very way he adopted to act the high and mighty, He
brought him to account, as it is said, "And thou saidst in
thy heart: I will ascend into heaven . . . I will ascend
above the heights of the clouds" etc. (Isa. 14:13-14); what
is written thereafter? "Yet thou shalt be brought down to
the netherworld" etc. (Isa. 14:15).

He brought him to account *MRS:* "he was punished" (*lqh*).

"By thy messengers" Now note verse 35, "the angel (= messenger) of
the Lord . . . smote" etc. Cf. clearly B. Sanhedrin 94a-b.

"and smote" Note the orthography in *MRS* and contrast with MT.

"and five" Compare the MT reading.

"of the least . . . servants" In the verse immediately preceding (II
Kings 18:20) it is said, "Now therefore . . . make a wager with my
master the king of Assyria, and I will give thee *two thousand horses*"
etc. *MRS* actually cites this verse. The Midrash thus makes of the
Rabshakeh one of the *least* of Sennacherib's hosts. On the size of
Sennacherib's army, see further, Ginzberg, *Legends*, IV, 267.

"This is the word . . . taunted" Another conclusion or retort to
the arrogance of Sennacherib and Rabshakeh. *MRS* introduces this
proof-text with the formula, "What (else) does it say, '*And* (this is
the word' etc.)."

"This very day . . . at Nob" Compare the verses in Isa. 10:32 ff.
with II Kings 19:22 f., and see Tg on Isa. 10:32 ff. *MRS* does not cite
Isa. 10:32.

of Nebuchadnezzar Cf. below, 6, p. 159 f. Note the subject of Isa. 14:
14 et seq. On Nebuchadnezzar, cf. Ginzberg, *Legends*, VI, 422 (bottom)
and ff.

You find the same true of Tyre, that by the very way it adopted to act the high and mighty, [He brought it to account,] as it is said, "Thou, O Tyre, hast said: I am of perfect beauty" etc. (Ezek. 27:3), and it is written, "Behold, I am against thee, O Tyre, and will cause many nations to come up against thee" etc. (Ezek. 26:3).

You find the same true of the Prince of Tyre, that by the very way he adopted to act the high and mighty, [He brought him to account,] as it is said, "Son of man, say unto the prince of Tyre: Thus saith the Lord God: Because thy heart is lifted up, and thou hast said: I am a god" etc. (Ezek. 28:2); and how does it go on? "Thou shalt die the deaths of the uncircumcised by the hand of strangers" (Ezek. 28:10).

of Tyre . . . the high and mighty Observe that our text does not complete the sentence, but simply says, "etc." (As to the fact that for "etc." our text here uses the abbreviation *wgw* [= *we-gomer*] and not *wkw* [= *we-kuleh*], see *Lešonenu la-ʿAm*, xix [1968], 191 f., in reply to the observations in the same publication, pp. 115–20. See now S. Abramson, ibid., xx [1969], 103–05, 191 f.) The same feature occurs in the following passage on the Prince of Tyre.

Further, *MRS* has no section on "Tyre," although it does have one on the Prince of Tyre. See further, below.

Note the mechanical repetition ("way it adopted to act the high-and-mighty") of *šntgᵓh* (not *šntgᵓth, šntgᵓt,* fem.); yet observe the gender used in the verse cited.

of the Prince of Tyre See the comment above on "Tyre."

The two paragraphs, on Tyre and the Prince of Tyre, seem to be actually alternative versions of one homily. Note indeed that as our Mekilta text reads, eleven examples are furnished for the proposition, "In the very ways the Nations of the World adopt to act the high and mighty before Him, He brings them to account." If the last two paragraphs, however, are really variants of one example, then our list would consist of *ten* examples.

Further, if we recall that the Samson and Absalom sections do not really apply to our principle here (cf. above), we would have eight (i.e. twice four) examples of the Nations of the World being punished according to the measure-for-measure formula. And perhaps this was what the original Mekilta list was like. But some redactor, possibly, observing that the list of examples for R. Meir's general statement on measure for measure in the Tosefta numbered ten (the *soṭah* plus the nine "historic" examples), simply helped himself to the Samson and Absalom illustrations to round out *his* number of examples to ten, and either ignored (or failed to observe) the difficulties he was creating.

Lo then, in the very ways the Nations of the World adopt to act the high and mighty before Him, He brings them to account, as it is said, "For He is highly exalted."

THE HORSE AND HIS RIDER: What now? Was there only one horse and was there only one rider? Was it not said, "And he took six hundred chosen chariots" etc. (Exod. 14:7), "Pharaoh's chariots" etc. (Exod. 15:4)? However, when Israel do the will of God, before them their enemies are like no more than one horse and his rider.

The same thing is to be said of "When thou goest forth to battle against thine enemies, and seest a horse and a chariot" (Deut. 20:1). What now? Was there only one horse and was there only one chariot? Does it not say, "A people more than thou" (Deut 20:1)? However, when Israel do the will of God, [before them their enemies are like no more than one horse and one chariot.]

THE HORSE AND HIS RIDER: This reports that the horse was strapped to his rider and the rider was strapped to his horse, up on high rising together, down to the deep de-

---

Lo then . . . For a similar stylistic formulation at the end of a section, cf. Pisḥa, I, end (I, 15), or Be-Shallaḥ, VI, end (I, 243), or Be-Shallaḥ, VII, end (I, 254).

as it is said MRS: "Therefore it is said."

Was there . . . was there MRS does not duplicate the verb *hyh*.

"Pharaoh's chariots" etc. MRS does not quote this verse.

However, when Israel do the will of God . . . one horse and his rider MRS: "However, this teaches that in the presence of God they were no more than one horse and one chariot" (*rkb;* but it is possible that this last word equals *rokeb*, hence "rider"; cf. p. 76, top line). Cf. Heinemann, p. 118.

Does it not say, "A people more than thou" Not in MRS.

[Before them . . . one chariot] Note once again that our text abbreviates; MRS does not. It is perhaps worthy of notice that Deut. 20:1 concludes with an allusion to the deliverance from Egypt.

THE HORSE AND HIS RIDER MRS introduces this passage with the formula, "Another interpretation."

reports MRS: "teaches."

the horse was strapped . . . horse The comment is suggested by the clause "the horse and his rider hath He thrown" (*rmh*); that is (as the passage continues), normally when one hurls two objects upward (a play on the words *rmh* and *mrwm*), they would come apart.

scending together, neither separating from the other! When a person throws two objects up in the air, is it not a fact that one gets detached from the other? Here, however, "the horse and his rider" together "hath He thrown," "hath He cast down": "hath He thrown," for up on high they rose (together); "hath He cast down," for down to the deep they descended (together), neither separating from the other!

One verse (15:1) reads, "He hath thrown into the sea," and another verse (15:4) reads, "He hath cast down into the sea": How preserve both these readings? "He hath

---

But God can fling horse and rider up on high, and they do not detach one from the other. Cf. Ginzberg, *Legends*, III, 28.

However, what is the point of such a comment altogether? To underscore not only God's greatness but the supernatural character of the deliverance and of what happened at the Sea. Throughout the Shirah commentary the miraculous character of the redemption is being emphasized. See further below, 5, s.v. "Up surged the lower deeps . . . ," and 9 s.v. "Because they trespassed . . . the oath."

The parallel *MRS* passage for this and the next few lines reads as follows: "the horse was (*hyh*) strapped to his rider and the rider was strapped to his horse. 'Hath He thrown': One verse reads, 'He hath thrown,' and another verse reads, 'He hath cast down': how preserve both readings? 'He hath thrown,' for up on high they rose; 'He hath cast down,' for down to the deep they descended, and they did not separate from each other. In the world, ordinarily when a person throws two objects up in the air, is it not a fact that one gets detached from the other? Here, however, 'He hath thrown' and 'He hath cast down,' (that is,) 'He hath thrown,' for up on high they rose (together); 'He hath cast down,' for down to the deep they descended (together), and they did not separate from each other."

"hath He thrown," "hath He cast down" In Exod. 15:1 the verb *rmh* is used, and in 15:4 the verb *yrh,* as the Mekilta goes on to explain. The homilist is playing on the words *rmh-mrwm* and *yrh-yrd.* Cf. below, 4, p. 135 f. Perhaps, however, no play on *yrh-yrd* is involved. As Rashi says (Exod. 15:1 at the end of the comment on *rmh*), *yrh* means to throw down from above.

How preserve both these readings A characteristic exegetical formula in Midrashim from the School of R. Ishmael (cf. Bacher, *EM*, p. 117). There is nothing superfluous in Scripture, and furthermore, Scripture surely knows precisely what it wants to say; why, then, two different terms?

On such close attention to style, see also, for example, Quintilian, VIII, 3:83 f. (Loeb, III, 259): "There are two kinds of *emphasis:* the one means more than it says . . . An example of the former is found in Homer, when he makes Menelaus say that the Greeks

thrown," for up on high they rose; "He hath cast down,"
for down to the deep they descended.

Another interpretation of "He hath thrown" (*rmh*):
When Israel beheld the Prince of the Empire fall, they
began to proclaim (God's) praises. That is why it is said,
rmh.

You find the same true of the Age to Come, that not
until the Holy One, blessed be He, first brings their Princes
to account, will He bring the empires to account, as it is
said, "And it shall come to pass in that day, that the Lord
will (first) punish the host of the high heaven on high," and

---

descended into the Wooden Horse, indicating its size by a single verb.
Or again, there is the following example by Virgil: 'Descending by a
rope let down,' a phrase which in a similar manner indicates the
height of the horse."

Prince of the Empire MRS: "Prince of Egypt."

fall On the notion of the guardian angels of the Nations, cf.
Moore, I, 403 f.; III, 62; Ginzberg, *Legends,* VII, 197, col. b; Bamberger,
Fallen Angels, pp. 108 ff. See also Ginzberg, *Legends,* V, 205.

The notion is associated with our verse because of the word *rmh,*
the one to be thrown down from on high. But very likely there is
also some connection with the singular, "its rider"; cf. indeed
Exod. R. 23:15: "It is not said, 'Their horses and their riders' (in the
plural) but 'the horse and its rider' (in the singular)—this teaches that
the Holy One, blessed be He, first took and cast their Prince into the
Sea." See also Ginzberg, *Legends,* VI, 4, n. 21.

It is very likely not mere coincidence that our passage closes with
the citation of the verse against Edom (= Rome). And perhaps there
is an onomatopoetic play on the words Rome, *rmh, mrwm.*

proclaim (God's) praises MRS adds, "before Him," and reads,
ᵓ*t hšbḥ* (not just *šbḥ*).

That is why it is said, *rmh* That is, the homilist is summing up
associations with the word "exalt" (cf., for example, Ps. 99:5, 9, or
see I Sam. 2:1).

**You find the same true of the Age to Come, that not until the
Holy One, blessed be He, first brings their Princes to account, will
He bring the empires to account** MRS: "You find the same true, that
God (*hmqwm*) does not bring the empires to account before first
casting down (= defeating) their Princes."

Again the exodus from Egypt suggests the theme of ultimate
triumph. In this connection, see the Midrash published by Mann in
The Bible as Read, I, 227–30 (of the Hebrew section).

"shall come to pass . . . on high" Note (and so too MRS) that Isa.
24 is quoted before Isa. 14 (and such is the order too, for example, in

only thereafter, "the kings of the earth upon the earth" (Isa. 24:21). It also says: (First,) "How art thou fallen from heaven, O daystar, son of the morning!" And only thereafter, "How art thou cut down to the ground, that didst cast lots over the nations" (Isa. 14:12)! It also says: (First,) "For My sword hath drunk its fill in heaven," and only thereafter, "Behold, it shall come down upon Edom" (Isa. 34:5).

THE HORSE AND HIS RIDER: Both the horse and his rider the Holy One, blessed be He, brings to trial. He says to the horse: "Why did you pursue My children?" And the horse replies: "It was the Egyptian, he drove me on against my will" —as it is said, "And it was the Egyptians who pursued after them" etc. (Exod. 14:9). Then He says to the Egyptian: "Why did you pursue My children?" And he says: "It was the horse, he made me give chase against my will"—as it is said, "For it was the horses of Pharaoh that went in"

Cant. R. 8, 42a). Isa. 24:21 states the general prediction of what will happen in the end; then come the verses specifically on Babylon (the past) and Edom (the future).

"upon the earth" Our text, *bᵓdmh;* contrast MT. But note also *Deut. R.,* ed. Lieberman, p. 29.

It also says Neither here nor before citation of Isa. 34:5 does *MRS* read this formula.

"upon Edom" It may be that the Midrash is in part drawn to suggest a play on the words Edom (ᵓdwm) and ᵓdmh (earth) of Isa. 24:21.

The horse and his rider *MRS* introduces this comment with the formula, "Another interpretation."

the Holy One . . . brings *MRS:* "would bring," or perhaps better translate *hyh mbyᵓ,* "brought." Note this construction with *hyh* in *MRS* right through the comment.

to trial The Midrash is answering the question, Why should the horse, the beast, be made to suffer punishment? For the attitude reflected, cf. M. Sanhedrin 7:4, "Granted the human being sinned, but how can the beast be held to sin?" See also Pisḥa, XIII (I, 99). Note too *MhG, Exod.,* p. 132 (on Exod. 9:10, end). As regards the view of Josephus, cf. Loewenstamm, pp. 46 f. And cf. V. Aptowitzer, in *HUCA,* III, 135.

Why *lmh; MRS: mpny mh* ("for what reason"), and so too below.

And the horse replies Lit., "and he replies"; *MRS* does not read the pronoun.

etc. (Exod. 15:19). What does God do? He mounts the man
on the horse and passes sentence on both together, as it is
said, "The horse and his rider hath He thrown into the
sea."

Antoninus asked our sainted Rabbi: "After a person dies,
his body perishes. How can the Holy One, blessed be He,
summon it to trial?"

Said Rabbi to him: "Why ask me only about the unclean
body? Ask me about the pure soul! (But) there is a parable

"**For it was the horses of Pharaoh . . .**" So the Midrash interprets the verse, as though the horse had a will of its own and acted
on its own initiative.

What does God (*hmqwm*) . . . **"into the sea"** *MRS:* "And the
Holy One, blessed be He, brought the horse and his rider and
sentenced them together" (*kʾḥd*).

Antoninus asked . . . trial On Antoninus and R. Judah the Prince,
cf. L. Wallach, in *JQR*, XXXI (1940–41), 259–86, and M. Avi-Yonah,
Bime Roma u-Bizantiyon (Jerusalem, 1946), pp. 28 ff. See also *GJP*,
pp. 78 ff., and *Deut. R.*, ed. Lieberman, p. 64, n. 14.

Another exchange between Antoninus and R. Judah the Prince
occurs in our treatise, below, 6, p. 165. And for statements about
Antoninus by Rabbi, see Be-Shallaḥ, I (I, 185), II (I, 202).

Presumably, "our sainted Rabbi" is Rabbi Judah the Prince. *MRS*
reads simply, "Rabbi" (the more frequent way of referring to Rabbi
Judah the Prince, the compiler of the Mishnah). Cf. L. Finkelstein,
in *JQR*, XXXI, 225 ff.

This sentence, in the *MRS*, translates literally: "This (is the question
which) Antoninus asked Rabbi; he said to him: Since after (*wmʾḥr*)
this human being dies his body perishes, in what possible way (*klwm*)
can the Holy One, blessed be He, bring it (*mbyʾw*) to trial? He said
to him: Before you (*ʿdth*) ask me about (the) unclean body" etc. On
the subject of resurrection, cf. Marmorstein, *Studies in Jewish
Theology*, pp. 145–61.

"**the unclean body**" The expression (though it does not occur in the
parallel passages of B. Sanhedrin 99a-b and *Lev. R.* 4:5, 88 f.) is
doubtless intended to serve as contrast to the following "pure soul";
in *Sifre Deut.*, 306, p. 341, it is said of man simply that "his soul is
from the heavens and his body is from the earth." But the notion of
"the unclean body" may well have been current; cf. *ARNB*, p. 69, last
two lines. Cf. Philo, *Allegorical Interpretation*, III, 69 (Loeb, I, 347).
However, it may also be that the expression "unclean body" really
means the dead body, the corpse, which is a source of uncleanness.

"**the pure soul**" Cf. the prayer on waking, B. Berakot 60b and Baer,
p. 39 (and his note, ad loc.).

which is told; to what may this be likened? To a king of flesh and blood who had a flourishing orchard. The king set in it two watchmen, one of whom was lame and the other blind . . ."—up to "and thereafter 'to judge His people' " (Ps. 50:4).

Isi ben Shammai says: Here (Exod. 15:1) (the punish-

"a parable which is told . . ." Note that our text is abbreviated in the extreme (see further below, s.v. "up to, 'and thereafter' etc."), while *MRS* gives the parable in full. In *Lev. R.* 4:5, p. 88, this parable is introduced by "R. Ishmael taught." On the parable, cf. Ziegler, pp. 298 f.; Moore, I, 487 f.; II, 384; III, 148, 205. See also I. Goldziher, *Harṣaʾot ʿal ha-ʾIslam* (Jerusalem, 1951), pp. 37 f., 226, and above, Pt. I, chap. 6, n. 5.

"two watchmen" Note the reading of our text, *šwmrym šnym*. (Does this reflect an old reading of a narrative, deliberately "literary" style of story telling?) *MRS*, simply: *šny šwmrym*.

up to . . . " 'His people' " The compiler cites here the conclusion of the source that had furnished the full parable as well as the interpretation of Ps. 50:4 which occurs in that connection. And the Midrash treats the word ʿmw (ʿammo, His people) as though it read ʿimmo (with Him). For another example of such word play on ʿam/ʿim, cf. the citation in Lieberman, *Yemenite Midrashim*, p. 17. (Cf. also above, p. 92, s.v. "From its source," *mʿm gr*.)

The full text of the parable, after the opening, reads more or less like this: In the garden were fine new fruits. Said the lame man to the blind: I see fine early fruits . . . Let me ride on your back and we will get the fruit. (This they did.) Some time thereafter the king appeared and asked, Where are the fine fruits? Said the blind man: Am I able to see? And the lame man said: Am I capable of getting about? But the king who was clever made the lame man mount the blind one and sentenced them together. So it is with the body and soul. At Judgment God says to the body, Why did you sin; and the body replies: Am I capable of sin? Lo, from the moment the soul quit me, I've been as immobile as stone. Then God says to the soul, Why did you sin; and the soul replies: Am I able to sin? It's the body's doings, for have I not been pure before Thee since I quit the body? Thereupon God puts the soul back into the body and judges them as one, "as it is said (Ps. 50:4), 'He calleth to the heavens above,' that's a reference to the soul (whose origin is heaven), 'and to the earth,' that's a reference to the body (whose origin is earth)—and then 'to be judged by Him' "; i.e. God then judges, sentences, the union of body and soul.

Isi ben Shammai This sage is cited again in the Mekilta, Wa-Yassaʿ, IV (II, 113 f.; but *MRS*, p. 111, for that passage, reads "Isi ben Akabya"; cf. Epstein, *Meboʾot*, p. 571, n. 188) to the effect that "When

ment of the) "horse" is spoken of in unspecified terms, but elsewhere (Zech. 12:4) (the punishment of the) "horse" is spoken of in specific terms, as it is said, "I will smite every horse with bewilderment, and his rider with madness; and I will open Mine eyes upon the house of Judah, and will smite every horse of the peoples with blindness"; and it says, "And this shall be the plague" etc. (Zech. 14:12), and it continues, "And so shall be the plague of the horse" etc. (Zech. 14:15): the specific serves to teach something about the unspecified—even as the specific was a punishment of five plagues, so the unspecified was of five plagues.

---

the manna came down for Israel, (it was in such huge quantities that) all the Nations of the World saw it, as it is said (Ps. 23:5), 'Thou preparest a table for me in the presence of mine enemies.' "

In our passage Isi's comment on the number of plagues (punishments) visited on the Egyptians' horses, has something of the flavor of the comments on the plagues visited on the Egyptians themselves, in Be-Shallaḥ, VII (I, 251), and the *Passover Haggadah* (cf. ed. Goldschmidt [Jerusalem, 1960], p. 123, and also pp. 47 f.).

(of the) horse . . . in specific terms Not in *MRS,* and note how it quotes Zech. 12:4.

and it says, "And this shall be the plague" *MRS* cites the verse without the introductory formula "and it says."

specific serves to teach . . . about the unspecified For this idiom, see also Neziqin, v (III, 47) and *Mid. Tan.,* p. 157; cf. *MRS,* p. 29.

a punishment *mkh;* this word is not in *MRS.*

of five plagues Half the number of plagues visited on the Egyptians. The five plagues seem to be (1) bewilderment, (2) madness, (3) blindness (Zech. 12:4), (4) flesh consumed, and (5) so their tongue (Zech. 14:12). Other commentators have other suggestions; cf. HR, p. 125. On the Zechariah verse in juxtaposition with Pharaoh's horses, see also Mann, *Bible as Read,* p. 230 (Hebrew section).

Note that in Isi's statement a detail of the eschaton is drawn upon to interpret a detail of the exodus from Egypt.

3. The Lord Is My Strength

THE LORD IS MY STRENGTH (ʿzy) AND SONG:"My strength" is nothing other than a reference to Torah, as it is said, "The Lord will give strength unto His people" etc. (Ps. 29:11), and it says, "The strength also of the King who loveth justice" (Ps. 99:4).

Another interpretation of MY STRENGTH: "My strength" is nothing other than a reference to the royal house (of David), as it is said, "O Lord, in Thy strength the king

nothing other than On this formula, cf. *HJP*, pp. 49, 51.

. . . a reference to Torah Cf. *AhB*, I, 10. In *MRS* (p. 74) this comment occurs as the second interpretation, and what in our Mekilta is third is there offered as the first interpretation.

as it is said . . . justice See also below, 9, p. 215; Amalek, III (II, 163); Ba-Ḥodesh, V (II, 234). This proof-text of the Lord *giving* strength *to His people* is intended to suggest God's *giving* of the Torah *to His people*. But the full significance of this verse in the present context emerges after the citation of Ps. 99:4 which now follows, and which should be seen especially in connection with 99:7, "He spoke unto them in the pillar of the cloud . . . and the statute that He gave them." Note, however, the citation of Job 12:16 in this connection in *Sifre Deut.,* 343, p. 398. By virtue of the Torah which He is to give to me, Israel sings to the Lord, has His salvation come to me.

Is this comment intended to suggest that the "strength" which God gives His people is one that leads to *peace* (note the end of Ps. 29:11), and is our comment, therefore, a discouragement of uprisings against the Roman powers? Cf. S. Spiegel, "On Medieval Hebrew Poetry," in Finkelstein, *The Jews* (3d ed.) I, 861 f.

the royal house That the reference is to the royal house of David is explicitly stated below, 9, p. 215 f.

rejoiceth" (Ps. 21:2), and it says, "And He will give strength unto His king" (I Sam. 2:10).

Another interpretation of *ᶜzy:* "*ᶜzy*" is nothing other than a reference to my All Mighty One, as it is said, "It is the Lord who is my strength and my stronghold" (Jer. 16:19), and it says, "It is the Lord who is my strength and my shield, in Him hath my heart trusted, and I am helped" (Ps. 28:7).

Another interpretation of MY STRENGTH (*ᶜzy*): Thou art the Helper (*ᶜwzr*) and Sustainer of all the inhabitants of the world, but mine above all! AND THE LORD IS MY SONG:

"in Thy strength . . . rejoiceth" Note latter half of this verse.

"And He will give strength unto His king" Note how this verse also concludes. Instead of this verse, *MRS* quotes Ps. 28:8, but note its idiom too. Cf. the reading in ed. HR, p. 126.

Again, is this comment intended to suggest, My real strength and salvation will come with the restoration of the Davidic house in the end of days?

nothing other than . . . my All Mighty One Cf. Tg Onkelos and Jonathan, and note also *LXX* on Ps. 118 (117):14. For God as *tqyp*, cf. *Sifre Deut.*, 307, pp. 344 f. (and note also Marmorstein, *Old Rabbinic Doctrine of God*, p. 107). Cf. *Lev. R.* 29:4, p. 673.

According to this third interpretation of *ᶜzy*, it seems that the Midrash wishes to say that the form of the word *ᶜozzi* in this verse is to be equated with the meaning of the word *ᶜzy* when it is vocalized *ᶜuzzi;* in other words, it is to be understood literally, not figuratively. Note, for instance, that in the three occurrences of our verse, here, Isa. 12:2, and Ps. 118 (117):14, the *LXX* translates the word in three different ways, and cf. also Rashi and Ibn Ezra ad Exod. 15:2 (with the Tg on Ps. 118:14, cf. Tg Jon ad Exod. 15:2). The Mekilta may be explaining that the word is to be understood as the corresponding term is understood in the Jer. and Ps. vv.

What may also be involved is this: no merely human or military undertaking is the source of my strength, and one must patiently await His ultimate deliverance; cf. the latter half of Jer. 16:19.

Incidentally, on *tqp* in the sense of superior strength, cf. *Sifre Deut.*, 323, p. 373.

"my heart . . . helped" Note conclusion of Ps. 28:7.

Thou art the Helper Play on *ᶜzy* and *ᶜzr;* note *LXX* on this verse. See again Ps. 28:7, "my strength . . . and I am helped." Cf. *Mid. Tan.*, p. 222.

of all the inhabitants of the world The emphasis is of particular significance in the present connection, lest one get the impression that by delivering Israel from bondage and punishing the Egyptians,

Thou art the theme for song for all the inhabitants of the world, but for me above all!

He has made me distinctive, and I have made (known) His distinctive (character):

"He has made me distinctive," as it is written, "And the Lord has this day made thee distinctive (as His treasured

---

God exhibits an indifference toward the wellbeing of those not Israel.

but mine above all In the original, "but mine" is ꜥbl ly; MRS: wly, and so too in the following.

The sense of the whole is "The Lord is *my* strength . . . and He is become *my* salvation." On this sense of special intimacy and love, see Kaspa, IV (III, 184 f.), and *Sifre Deut.*, 31, pp. 53 f.

A threefold comment grows out of the special style of the verse (and this sentence, as we have observed, occurs in Scripture three times; and in Isaiah note the reference to the exodus at the very end of chapter 11, while in Ps. 118:15b–16 observe the triplicated reference to the right hand of the Lord):

"My strength"—Thou art the helper and sustainer of all the inhabitants of the world, but mine above all.

"(My) song is the Lord"—Thou art the theme for song for all the inhabitants of the world, but mine above all.

"My salvation"—Thou art the salvation of all the inhabitants of the world, but mine above all.

Thou art the theme for song Cf. *AhB*, I, 10. The homilist is probably playing on the word zmrt as though it read or said, zimrah-ꜥatt(ah).

theme for song . . . above all In reality, and despite transitory appearances to the contrary, God is the object of the whole world's praises. See further, below, s.v. "All the Nations of the World proclaim."

At this point (note the order in our Mekilta) *MRS* puts the following: "For lo, the Nations of the World proclaim the beauty and praises of Him Who Spake and the World Came to Be; but mine is sweetest before Him, as it is said, 'And sweetest are the songs of Israel.'"

"He has made me distinctive" *MRS* actually supplies the pronoun "He," hwꜥ; so too in the following sentence.

As for "distinctive," Lauterbach reads ꜥmyrh, but I have adopted the reading ꜥymrh (cf. his critical apparatus), which is also the reading of Vatican MS 299 (note *MRS*, ꜥmrh).

For the meaning of ꜥymrh in "made . . . distinctive," cf. the discussion in Y. Yadin, *The Finds from the Bar Kokhba Period in the Cave of Letters* (Jerusalem, 1963), pp. 210, 211, and 231. See M. Negaꜥim 11:10, end.

people)" (Deut. 26:18). "And I have made (known) His distinctive (character)," as it is written, "You have this day affirmed the distinctive (character) of the Lord" (Deut. 26: 17).

But lo, do not all the Nations of the World proclaim the praises of Him Who Spake and the World Came to Be? To be sure, but mine are sweetest before Him, as it is said, "And sweetest are the songs of Israel" (II Sam. 23:1):

Israel declare: "Hear, O Israel: the Lord our God, the Lord is One" (Deut. 6:4), and from heaven the Holy Spirit calls aloud, saying, "And who is like Thy people Israel, a nation one in the earth" (I Chron. 17:21);

and I *MRS:* "and so too I"; and the same in the following sentence.

But lo, do not all the Nations . . . The arrangement of the text seems to be more logical in *MRS* (cf. above, s.v. "Theme for song . . . above all"). On the other hand, perhaps in our Mekilta the word for "distinctive" is intended also to stir up notions of "proclamation," hence the sentence here on the Nations' proclamation of God's praises.

At all events, the way in which Israel and God antiphonally proclaim each other's preeminence is now illustrated by four examples, becoming, as it were, four stanzas.

all the Nations of the World proclaim . . . Cf. above, s.v. "Theme for song . . . above all." The statement reflects an awareness of the fact that crude idol-worship does not really represent the fundamental belief of at least sophisticated Gentiles. See also below, 8, p. 190. Note too how this thought is expressed in the *Tanna debe Eliyahu* passage incorporated in *Lev. R.* 2:8, p. 47. Israel's uniqueness consists in the determined and exclusive attachment to the one God; note the tenor of the verses which form the responses between God and Israel. On the passage as a whole, cf. the view of Marmorstein in *HUCA*, vi (1929), 186 f.

Israel declare: "Hear, O Israel . . ." In addition to the four examples of this call and response in our Mekilta, *MRS* brings Israel: Cant. 2:3, and God: Cant. 2:2; Israel: Exod. 15:2b, and God: Isa. 43: 21. And what in our Mekilta comes first is third in *MRS*.

"Israel declare: 'Hear, O Israel . . .' " is clearly an allusion to the recitation of the Shema. On the Shema, see above, 1, s.v. "Like people reciting the Shema."

and from heaven the Holy Spirit calls aloud *MRS:* "And the Holy Spirit through them announces the tidings." The term "Holy Spirit" for God is very likely used here because biblical verses constitute God's proclamations.

"a nation one in the earth" Note the reference to the redemption

Israel declare: "Who is like unto Thee, O Lord, among the mighty" (Exod. 15:11), and from heaven the Holy Spirit calls aloud, saying, "Happy art thou, O Israel, who is like unto thee" (Deut. 33:29);

Israel declare: "(What great nation is there with a god nigh) as the Lord our God is whensoever we call upon Him" (Deut. 4:7), and from heaven the Holy Spirit calls aloud, saying, "And what great nation is there, that hath statutes and ordinances so righteous" etc. (Deut. 4:8);

Israel declare: "For Thou art the glory of their strength" (Ps. 89:18), and from heaven the Holy Spirit calls aloud, saying, "O Israel, in whom I am glorified" (Isa. 49:3)!

AND HE IS BECOME MY SALVATION: Thou art the salvation of all the inhabitants of the world, but mine above all!

Another interpretation of AND HE IS BECOME MY SALVATION: That He was and that He will be—"that He was," in times past; "and that He will be," in the Age to Come.

---

from Egypt in the latter part of the verse. As Israel uses the term "One" for God, so He uses the term "one" for them.

"O Israel, who is like unto thee" Even as they say of Him, "Who is like unto Thee." See the note of triumph in Deut. 33:29. Cf. Y. Yadin, *Scroll of the War of the Sons of Light against the Sons of Darkness* (Oxford, 1962), pp. 304 f. and notes, ad loc.

"as the Lord . . . Him . . ." Compare the idiom of *all* of Deut. 4:7 with Deut. 4:8, especially the words "what great nation is there" in verses 7 and 8. The Midrash, of course, takes the former verse as Israel's exclamation and the latter verse as God's response.

"the glory of their strength" Note here the reference to "strength" as well as to "glory."

Thou art the salvation See above, s.v. ". . . above all."

Another interpretation This formula does not appear here in *MRS*.

that He was and that He will be The verb in the verse is not *hyh* (the perfect tense) but *wyhy*, the future (imperfect) with the *waw* conversive. And in typical midrashic manner this is interpreted as a deliberate suggestion of past and future deliverances. Compare below, 8, p. 205 f., and how our treatise began with attention to the form *yšyr*.

At the end of the comment *MRS* quotes Isa. 45:17; and for "will be," where our text reads *yhyh*, it reads *hwwh*.

in times past *lš'br;* cf. the beginning of Shirta, s.v. "to what is past."

in the Age to Come Lauterbach translates: "future"; cf. the beginning of Shirta, s.v. "will come . . . future."

THIS IS MY GOD, AND I WILL GLORIFY HIM: Rabbi Eliezer says:
How can you tell that at the Sea a bondswoman could see
what neither Isaiah nor Ezekiel nor all the other prophets
ever saw? For of them it is said, "And in the ministry of
the prophets I appeared in likenesses (only)" (Hos. 12:11),
and it is written, "The heavens were opened and I saw
reflections of God" (Ezek. 1:1). A parable is told; to what
may this be likened? To a king of flesh and blood who
entered a province surrounded by his circle of guards, warriors to his right and left, his troops in front of him and
behind him, so that everyone had to ask, "Which one is

Rabbi Eliezer says . . . See also Ba-Ḥodesh, III (II, 212). *MRS* (p. 78)
spells the sage's name ʾlʿzr (note, however, critical apparatus, ad loc.,
and the reading on p. 154).

On R. Eliezer's view, see Lieberman, in Scholem, *Gnosticism*, pp.
119 ff.

can you tell ʾth ʾwmr; these two words are not in *MRS*.

Bondswoman I am inclined to think that the meaning is, even a
non-Jewish bondswoman (cf. *MhM*, III, 268 f.) in the service and
company of Israel (cf. Exod. 12:38), although the expression "Hebrew
šphh" does occur (e.g. Mishnah Baba Mesiaᶜ 1:5 or T. Pesaḥim 7:4,
etc.; perhaps because the word ʿbd, "male slave," occurs in the clause),
and although the reading in *MRS*, p. 154, is "bondswoman in Israel"
(where the reading can be justified, since the discussion is of the
Sinai revelation; here, however, the reading is as in our Mekilta);
and note the same reading in *ARNB*, p. 125, top, where the exodus
from Egypt is spoken of. See further below, s.v. "All . . . loudly
exclaimed."

neither Isaiah nor Ezekiel I.e. *even* these two, in connection with
whom Scripture reports extraordinary visions, Isa. 6 and Ezek. 1.

nor all the other prophets Not in *MRS*.

saw Note the spelling of the verb (and also of Isaiah's name) in
MRS, p. 78.

of them Not in *MRS*.

"I appeared in likenesses" The prophets were vouchsafed only
images, refractions, as it were, not the sight of the Reality itself.

and it is written *MRS:* "and it says."

A parable is told Cf. Ziegler, p. 70.

his circle of guards For this translation (and the reading underlying
it), cf. *MhG, Exod.*, p. 292, note to line 12 (and *MRS*, p. 78, line 9).
See also Krauss, *Persia and Rome*, p. 182.

warriors Lit., "his warriors"; *MRS*, simply "warriors." The two
clauses on "warriors" and "troops" *MRS* reverses.

the king?"—for like the others he is of flesh and blood. But
when the Holy One, blessed be He, revealed Himself at the
Sea, not one of them had to ask, "Which one is the King."
On the contrary, as soon as they saw Him, they recognized
Him, and all of them loudly exclaimed, "This is my God,
and I will glorify Him!"

AND I WILL GLORIFY HIM: Rabbi Ishmael says: Is it then
possible for flesh and blood to bestow glory on its Creator?

so that everyone . . . king *MRS*, lit.: "Everyone needs to ask concerning him to know, Which one is it."
    like the others *kmwtn; MRS: kywṣ bhn.*
    the Holy One, blessed be He *MRS:* "God" (*hmqwm*).
    not one of them had to ask Although at the miracle at the Sea,
when God manifested Himself, He was accompanied by hosts of angels
(cf. above, 1, p. 87, and *Sifre Deut.*, 343, p. 398); see Ginzberg, *Legends*,
VI, 9, n. 45. On the other hand, cf. *Sekel Tob, Exod.*, p. 192.
    "Which one is the King" Not in *MRS*.
    as soon as they saw Him they recognized Him *MRS:* "All of them
recognized (Him)."
    All . . . "my God" As the parable makes clear, R. Eliezer's point is
that at the miracle at the Sea, so visible, so clear, was the splendid
presence of God, that (1) no special individual talent was required to
be able to see Him, and (2) there was no mistaking anyone else for
Him. And that is why the verse reads, "*This* is my God."
    The words of the verse suggest to R. Eliezer, it seems to me (if
the parable is to have real point), not so much the remarkable
capacities of Israel as the extraordinary generosity of God's self-
revelation (on God's "descent" at this time, cf. *ARNB,* p. 96, last
line). And an irony of sorts is also being implied: this God who is
invisible, when He reveals Himself, is recognizable at a glance. On the
other hand, a creature of flesh and blood is certainly visible; yet
when an emperor or king makes his appearance, one cannot tell him
apart from his entourage (let alone that he has to be protected by so
many bodyguards).
    And I will glorify Him *wᵓnwhw*. Six different interpretations of
this word will now follow, for it is indeed a hapax. See BDB (1907),
p. 627, and F. M. Cross, Jr., and D. N. Freedman, in *JNES*, XIV (1955),
244, note referring to Albright.
    Is it then possible for flesh and blood to bestow glory Mekilta:
lhnwwt l . . . ; *MRS:* "But how is it possible for a human being to
glorify" (*lnᵓwt ᵓt*).
    its Creator *qwnw;* on this term see also Cross and Freedman, in
JNES, XIV, 249, n. 57, and further below, 9, end, s.v. "This people
Thou didst produce."

Yes indeed! I bestow glory on Him by means of the religious acts: I prepare for His sake a handsome *lulab*, a handsome *sukkah*, beautiful *ṣiṣit*, beautiful *tefillin*.

Abba Saul says: Do take after Him! Even as He is gracious and compassionate, so should you be gracious and compassionate.

Rabbi Yose says: Before all the Nations of the World I

I bestow glory on Him by means of the religious acts (*mṣwt*) Cf. *AhB*, I, 12. *MRS:* "Be comely before Him by means of religious acts" (*mṣwh*). According to either reading, the idea is that I make manifest God's splendor by performing His commandments beautifully; that is, when the commandment calls for the making or the use of some object or instrument, I do what I can to enhance its aesthetic appearance.

On *lulab*, cf. Lev. 23:40; *sukkah*, Lev. 23:42 f.; *ṣiṣit* (fringes), Num. 15:37 ff.; on *tefillin*, Deut. 6:8 and *JE*, X, 21 ff.

On *sukkah, lulab,* and *tefillin* as a kind of stock example, cf. the idiom in M. Nedarim 2:2 or M. Shabbat 3:8. It would be well to note, however, that each of these, as well as *ṣiṣit,* is what the individual Jew, personally, wears or uses for the performance of the relevant commandment. It is also interesting to note how in later sources this list of examples is enlarged; for the passages and discussion, cf. Kasher, XIV, 290 ff.

I prepare for His sake (*lpnw*) *MRS:* "Make (thou) for Him" (*lw*).

beautiful *tefillin* In our text in the singular, in *MRS* in the plural; cf. Kasher, XIV, 292.

Do take after Him *nᵓ dmh lw; MRS: hdmh lw.* Abba Saul looks upon the radicals *wᵓnwhw* as suggesting *ᵓny whwᵓ*, that I may be like Him.

gracious and compassionate Cf. the biblical idiom—e.g. Ps. 111:4; note also, e.g. Exod. 34:6.

you be *thᵓ; MRS: hyh.*

Note a fuller statement of this teaching (but no mention of Abba Saul) in *Sifre Deut.,* 49, p. 114, and Finkelstein's note, ad loc.; however, see also Abba Saul's statement in Sifra, 86c, bottom. On the idea of *imitatio dei,* cf. Schechter, *Aspects,* pp. 199 ff., and see also Epictetus, II, 14:11 ff. (Loeb, I, 309).

Rabbi Yose *MRS* (which brings this statement after that of R. Yose the son of the Damascene): "R. Yose the Galilean." Cf. also ed. HR, p. 127.

Before all the Nations of the World Not in *MRS*. Cf. R. Akiba's statement, below.

shall proclaim the beauties and the splendor of Him Who Spake and the World Came to Be!

Rabbi Yose the son of the Damascene says: For His sake I shall make a beautiful Temple—for *nwh* is nothing other than a reference to the Temple, as it is said, "And they have laid waste His *nwh* (habitation)" (Ps. 79:7), and it says, "Look upon Zion, the city of our solemn gatherings; thine eyes shall see Jerusalem a peaceful *nwh* (habitation)" (Isa. 33:20).

Rabbi Akiba says: Before all the Nations of the World I shall hold forth on the beauties and splendor of Him Who

I shall proclaim MRS, "speak" (*dybr;* and the same spelling in R. Akiba's statement, ibid.). Cf. the two different readings in *AhB*, I, 172, and III, 138.

the beauties *ny'wtyw;* MRS, *bny'wtw* (HR adopt the reading *nyynw*). The radicals of *w'nwhw* suggest *n'h* to the homilist—that which is beautiful, comely. See further, below, s.v. "Beauties," "and splendor."

Him Who Spake . . . to Be Cf. J. Z. Lauterbach, *Studies in Jewish Bibliography in Memory of A. S. Freidus* (New York, 1929), p. 146.

For His sake *lpnyw;* MRS, *lw.*

beautiful Temple Cf. Tg Onkelos, ad loc. At this point MRS (which reads *byt mqdš*) quotes Exod. 15:13; cf. below, 9, p. 216. See also below, 6, p. 162, and next note.

for *nwh* is . . . "(habitation)" R. Yose relates the word for "habitation" with the root of the verb "to glorify." Note indeed Aquila on Jer. 10:25 and Theodotian on Ps. 79:7 (cf. Field's n. 8, ad Ps 79:7).

Before all *bpny kl;* MRS: *lpny.*

I shall hold forth on Lit., "I shall speak" (*'dbr b* . . .); MRS: *dybr,* and the preposition *b* is omitted from the following words.

beauties and splendor Reading *n'wtyw* as "beauties" (cf. the critical apparatus in Lauterbach, and also Lieberman apud Scholem, *Gnosticism,* p. 123, n. 25). Lauterbach (the same is true of Vatican MS 299) adopts the reading *nbw'wtyw,* "His prophetic revelations" (?— however, this need not be the meaning, for *b* = *w* quite often; cf. recently Yalon, in *Lešonenu,* XXXI, [1967], 120, and n. 17, ibid., and M. Sokoloff [1968], in XXXIII, 30). Cf. *AhB*, I, 11 and n. 11, and III, 138; however, cf. III, 338, and see also *Sekel Tob, Exod.,* p. 192.

Although as our passage continues it is cryptic, it is clear that R. Akiba is speaking of visions of God's glory, of proclamation of God's *doxa,* to which the Canticles verses are said to refer. On this passage, see Lieberman, in Scholem, *Gnosticism,* pp. 118 ff., and Scholem himself, pp. 36–42.

As our Mekilta reads it is difficult to see what difference there is

Spake and the World Came to Be! For, lo, the Nations of
the World keep asking Israel, "What is thy Beloved more
than another beloved, that thou dost so adjure us" (Cant.
5:9), that for His sake you die, for His sake you let yourselves be slain, as it is said, "Therefore do the maidens
(ᶜlmwt) love Thee" (Cant. 1:3)—they love Thee to the
point of death (ᶜd mwt)!—and it is written, "Nay, but for
Thy sake are we killed" etc. (Ps. 44:23). Look you! You're
attractive, look you! you're brave. Come, merge with us!

But Israel reply to the Nations of the World: Have you
any notion of Him? Let us tell you a little bit of His
Glory: "My Beloved is white and ruddy" etc. (Cant.
5:10 ff.).

---

between the views of R. Yose and R. Akiba; but cf. above, s.v. "Before
all the Nations of the World."

keep asking Lit., "ask . . . to say"; MRS: "ask . . . and say to
them."

"What is . . . adjure us" Note how the Midrash amalgamates the
biblical statement with its own. On the give-and-take reported here,
cf. Y. Baer, in Zion, XXI (1956), 3, but see also Alon, Toledot, I, 327,
n. 25.

you die MRS: "you are put to death."

as it is said MRS: "even as it is said."

to the point of death A typically midrashic word play, taking the
one word ᶜlmwt as though it were two words, ᶜl mwt, and understanding by them ᶜd mwt. Cf. HJP, pp. 69, 75. On various kinds of
word-play for rhetorical effect, cf. Quintilian, IX, iii, 66 ff. (Loeb, III,
485 ff.).

Although MRS also quotes Cant. 1:2 here, it does not spell out
its midrashic interpretation as does our Mekilta. See in this connection R. Loewe, pp. 186–91.

Look you! You're attractive . . . Israel reply to . . . World Not in
MRS. On "merge with us," cf. the idiom in Ps. 106:35.

Have you any notion of Him? Let us tell you a little bit of His
Glory MRS: "Let us tell you a little bit of His Glory; you have no
notion of Him."

Concerning "a little bit of His Glory": No praise of God could ever
be full or completely adequate; see also the delightful anecdote in
B. Berakot 33b. Moreover, to those who are not initiates no complete account could be given of the extraordinary vision of God's
Glory. Cf. Lieberman, in Scholem, Gnosticism, pp. 123 ff. Note also
how Aknin, p. 283, expresses this.

"My Beloved . . . ruddy" Cf. above, 1, p. 85.

It is clear from the reading in MRS that the citation is intended

And when the Nations of the World hear but a little bit
of the Glory of Him Who Spake and the World Came to
Be, they say to Israel, Let us go along with you, as it is
said, "Whither is thy Beloved gone, O thou fairest among
women? Whither hath thy Beloved turned Him, that we
may seek Him with thee" (Cant. 6:1)?

But Israel reply to the Nations of the World: You have
no part of Him; on the contrary, "My Beloved is mine, and
I am His" (Cant. 2:16), "I am my Beloved's and my Beloved
is mine" etc. (Cant. 6:3).

And the Sages say: I shall be in His company until I arrive with Him at His Temple. This is like to a king whose

---

to extend right through Cant. 5:16; see also *Sifre Deut.*, 343, p. 399.
But *specifically* what the mystical interpretation of these verses was,
has obviously not been preserved by our sources. Cf. the references
to Lieberman and Scholem, above, s.v. ". . . and splendor."

Nations . . . hear but a little bit *MRS*, lit.: "Nations . . . heard
the beauty of" (cf. also the reading, ibid., p. 232, "His beauty and
His splendor/Glory").

Let us go along with you For the idiom, cf. Zech. 8:23. *MRS*, lit.:
"Let us come with you."

the Nations of the World Not in *MRS*.

You have no part of Him For the idiom, cf. Josh. 22:25, 27, etc.,
and see also Ba-Ḥodesh, 1 (II, 198).

on the contrary . . . As the proof-texts reveal, R. Akiba interprets
the radicals of *ʾnwhw* as though they represented the two words,
ʾny whwʾ ("I and He"); i.e. this is an exclusive relationship between
me and Him.

"My Beloved is mine and I am His" *MRS* does not quote this
verse.

I . . . in His company until I arrive with Him *MRS*: "*nyʾʾynw*
until we arrive with you" (pl.). Is the first word miswritten for
nlwwnw, "we shall be in His company"? Cf. critical apparatus, ibid.,
p. 79, and the reading on p. 232. For the reading of our Mekilta see
also *AhB*, 1, 12, and note the interpretation, ibid., p. 13.

The midrashic statement of the Sages seems to involve, first, an
equation of *ʾnwhw* with *ʾlwhw* ("I shall accompany Him"; cf. *TK* ad
Kil'aim 5, p. 658, n. 47) and, second, an association of the verb with
the noun *nwh*, habitation, as already suggested above in the statement of Yose the son of the Damascene. But the statement of the
Sages is not clear, and the translation is frankly conjectural; cf.
further below, s.v. "until with them" and "Scarce had I passed."

This is like to Lit., "a parable." *MRS*: "A parable is told; to what
may this be likened? To a king of flesh and blood who entered a

son had gone overseas and the king set out after him to
stand by him; then the son moved on to another province,
and the king set out after him to stand by him. So here:
when Israel went down to Egypt, the Shekinah went down
with them, as it is said, "I will go down with thee into
Egypt" (Gen. 46:4); when they went up out of it, the
Shekinah went up with them, as it is said, "And I will
bring thee up and also come up with thee again" (ibid.);
when they got down to the Sea, the Shekinah was with
them, as it is said, "And the angel of God moved along"
etc. (Exod. 14:19); when they set forth into the wilderness,
the Shekinah was with them, as it is said, "And the Lord
went before them by day" (etc.) (Exod. 13:21)—until with
them they had brought Him along (as it were) to His
Temple. And so too it says, "Scarce had I passed from
them" etc. (Cant. 3:4).

---

province, and was told: 'Lo, your son is in So-and-so's province.' (The
king thereupon) set out after him to stand by him. (The king) entered
a certain province; he was told, 'Lo, your son is in So-and-so's province.' (The king) set out after him to stand by him."

to stand by As a protector. On the parable, cf. Ziegler, p. 441.

So here . . . See also Pisḥa, xiv (i, 114 f.).

the Shekinah went down with them MRS omits the verb in this
clause as well as in the clause below, "the Shekinah went up with
them."

"I will go down with thee into Egypt" Note that in this verse
Jacob is referred to by his name Israel.

when they set forth into the wilderness MRS: "When they came
to the wilderness." See further, next note.

"And the Lord went before them by day" But this verse refers to
their presence in the wilderness *before* the event at the Reed Sea!
Note that MRS (pp. 79 f. and 233) quotes instead Deut. 1:31.

until with them they had brought Him along . . . to His Temple
MRS, p. 80: "until they came to the Temple"; p. 233 (and cf. critical
apparatus, p. 80): "until they came with Him to the Temple." Note
also the reading in Lauterbach, critical apparatus, "until I will come
with Him (him?) to His Temple."

The translation is an attempt to recover some sense and consistency
from the ambiguity in the statement of the Sages, an ambiguity especially underscored by the parable. See further below, s.v. "Scarce had
I passed."

And so too it says MRS: "as it is said."

"**Scarce had I passed**" The proof-text at this point is also difficult. By citing the parable plus its application, and then this Canticles verse, it may be that the Mekilta is ascribing the whole of Cant. 3:4 to God (in the dialogue between Israel and God which Canticles is supposed to represent), and interprets as follows: God says: Scarce, that is, never did I part from them; once I found those whom I loved, I never forsook them, right up to My arrival with them, "until I had brought him," Israel, to "the chamber from which decision and instruction" issue to all Israel—i.e. the Temple ("the chamber of *hwrty*"; the Midrash plays on the verbal roots of *hrh*, to conceive, and *yrh*, to teach, render decision; see, e.g., *Midrash Shir ha-Shirim*, ed. Grünhut [Jerusalem, 1897], p. 28a; note also *Lekah Tob* on this verse, p. 53; and cf. below the reading of *MRS*).

Note incidentally that in our Mekilta the Canticles verse is not introduced by the formula "as it is said" but by "And so too it says"; that is, the verse is apparently used merely as a further reinforcement of the idea expressed by the application of the parable, where the action of God is the theme.

However, in this interpretation the connection between (1) the parable, its application, and the midrashic understanding of Cant. 3:4, and (2) the statement of the Sages remains very awkward; for in that statement the theme is not God's action but Israel's exclamation ("I shall be in His company until I arrive with Him at His Temple") and—according to the Lauterbach text—it is of Israel that it is said, "until with them they had brought Him along to His Temple."

Perhaps another approach is possible. In *Midrash Shir ha-Shirim* R. Yohanan is quoted as saying that in the first half of Cant. 3:4 God is the speaker in the dialogue, but in the last half of the verse the speaker is Israel; so that the clause of the verse "until I had brought Him" etc. would be Israel's response. This can serve as a more logical proof-text for the statement, "until with them they had brought Him along to His Temple." But the *Midrash Shir ha-Shirim* passage is discussing the notion of God's attachment to Israel despite their provoking His wrath, a notion to which our Mekilta text here does not refer.

The text, therefore, remains difficult, and the ambiguities in our passage make it impossible to determine with precision the connection between the Sages' statement and all that follows. In a rough sense, however, the statement is understandable: Israel exclaims, *'nwhw*, I shall have Him in my midst at every step and He will never leave me, until with Him I arrive in His Temple where He will finally cause His Shekinah to rest.

In *MRS*, after the citation of Cant. 3:4, the text continues: "This is a reference to the Tent of Meeting, for from there Israel came under the obligations of the Law" (*hwr'h*, lit., the teaching). Cf. *Lev. R.* 1:10, p. 25, and *Cant. R.* 3:4, 19c. (Are Tent of Meeting and Temple being equated by *MRS*?)

MY GOD (*ʾly*): Me He treated with the attribute of Mercy, but my Fathers He treated with the attribute of Justice. And how do we know that *ʾly* is nothing other than a reference to the attribute of Mercy? For it is said, "My God, my God (*ʾly ʾly*), why hast Thou forsaken me" (Ps. 22:2), and it says, "Heal her now, O God (*ʾl*), I beseech Thee" (Num. 12:13), and it says, "The Lord is God (*ʾl*), and hath given us light" (Ps. 118:27).

MY FATHER'S GOD, AND I WILL EXALT HIM:

(A) queen,	the-daughter-of	queens	(am) I
Beloved,	the-daughter-of	beloved (ones)	
Holy,	the-daughter-of	holy (ones)	
Pure,	the-daughter-of	(the) pure.	

Me . . . with the attribute of Mercy *MRS* introduces this comment by quoting "My father's God."

On the equation of El (*ʾl*) with mercy, cf. A. Marmorstein, in *JQR*, n.s. XXII (1931–32), 295–306, and *Pesikta R.*, ed. Friedmann, 22a, n. 111.

But my Fathers . . . with the attribute of Justice The verse speaks of "my father's Elohim," and in rabbinic literature Elohim is said to suggest God as judge applying strict justice. Cf. Moore, I, 387 ff.; III, 120 f. Note also below, 5, p. 150; 4, p. 131. Contrast Philo, *Who Is the Heir*, sec. 166 (Loeb, IV, 367).

In effect Israel declares: Though I hardly deserved such miracles and deliverances, God in His mercy granted them to me; on the other hand, my Fathers who were exemplary God treated with strict justice: presumably, for the slightest misstep the Patriarchs were taken to task (see also *ZY* on this passage).

Incidentally, in *Sifre Deut.*, 311, p. 351, it is said that with the arrival of Abraham in the world, God ceased being merciless in punishing the world's sinners.

And how do we know that This formula is absent from *MRS*.

For it is said *MRS:* "So too it says."

and it says (bis) Not in *MRS*.

"The Lord is God (*ʾl*)" I.e., my El, and note that in this verse the term *ʾl* is joined with "the Lord," which in the rabbinic view represents God as merciful. Cf. above, s.v. "but my Fathers . . . with the attribute of Justice."

(A) queen . . . Manifestly another comment on the expression "my father's God"; indeed, *MRS* introduces it with the formula, "Another interpretation."

The comment grows out of the inflected forms, *my El, my father's*

A parable: When a man goes to betroth a woman, sometimes he is embarrassed by her, sometimes he is embarrassed
by her immediate family, sometimes he is embarrassed by
her relations. But of me that is not true! On the contrary,

(A) queen,	the-daughter-of	queens
Beloved,	the-daughter-of	beloved (ones)
Holy,	the-daughter-of	holy (ones)
Pure,	the-daughter-of	(the) pure.

Elohim, to which the Midrash is calling attention. And as the commentators put it (see also Rashi on this verse), since God is not only
my El but also the Elohim of my father, clearly I am not the first
generation of royal stock, my fathers were that already; hence a
queen, daughter of queens, etc.

Note incidentally that by adopting words like queen and daughter
in this comment, and by the parable which is then presented, the
Mekilta is reflecting the mood assumed by the midrashic interpretation
of Canticles, that it is an allegory of the relation between the Groom
and His bride, God and Israel. For in the vocabulary of Exod. 15:2
there is nothing necessarily to suggest a feminine gender.

the-daughter-of-queens . . . Note the poetic nature of the exclamation, four lines and three words to the line, and then after the parable
the recitation repeated. *MRS* has (essentially) the same text, except
that the order of the poetic lines is different:

Beloved, the daughter of beloved ones
A queen, the daughter of queens
Pure, the daughter of the pure
Holy, the daughter of holy ones.

A parable *MRS:* "A parable is told; to what may this be likened?
To a king of flesh and blood" etc.

a man goes to betroth a woman As *ZY* observes nicely, The Holy
One, blessed be He, betrothed Israel, cf. Hos. 2:21 f. *MRS:* "a king
. . . who wed a woman."

by her relations *MRS* (p. 80): "by her fathers" (ancestors); but note
the variant readings, ibid. and p. 233.

that is not true! On the contrary Not in *MRS.*

. . . (A) queen . . . The repetition, word for word, is surely intended as deliberate emphasis (was this a recitation, or some song?),
and perhaps its aim was to counteract the effect of slanderous remarks about Jews (e.g. cf. Josephus, *Against Apion*, II, 236 [Loeb, I,
389]). On "holy and pure," cf. Büchler, *Types*, p. 52, n. 2.

MY FATHER'S GOD, AND I WILL EXALT HIM: Rabbi Simeon ben Eleazar says: When Israel do the will of God, His Name is magnified in the world, as it is said, "And it came to pass, when the kings of the Amorites heard" etc. (Josh. 5:1); and Rahab the harlot said the same to Joshua's messengers: "For we have heard how the Lord dried up the water of the Reed Sea . . . And as soon as we had heard it, our hearts did melt" etc. (Josh. 2:10–11). But when Israel do not do the will of God, His Name is profaned in the world, as it is said, "And when they came unto the nations, whither they came, they profaned My holy Name" etc. (Ezek. 36:20), and it continues, "But I had pity for My

MY FATHER'S GOD, AND I WILL EXALT HIM Not quoted at this point by *MRS*. In any event, the comment which follows is on the verb and its object suffix, "and I will exalt Him." It may be worth noting that in the preceding two paragraphs and in the present one we have been offered commentary on each word of the clause—i.e. first on ᵓ*lhy,* then on ᵓ*by,* and now on *w*ᵓ*rmmnhw.*

When Israel do the will of God And thus bring it about that He rewards them; thus Israel exalts God by giving Him occasion to reward them. Now note the proof-texts adduced by the Mekilta.

His Name is magnified in the world As is evident from what follows, "magnified" (*mtgdl*) has the meaning also of "sanctified" (*mtqdš*); cf. Ezek. 38:23. The triumphs of Israel redound to God's credit; their defeats are a discrediting of God (note the Ezekiel verses quoted below) and thus His Name is profaned. Cf. also Wa-Yassaᶜ, VII (II, 129), and Be-Shallaḥ, II (I, 193), VII (I, 244). See also Yadin, *Scroll of the War* 11:13 ff. (pp. 312 f.). Cf. Bonsirven, I, 86–89; Moore, II, 104 f.

and Rahab . . . Joshua's messengers Not in *MRS;* but note ibid., p. 233.

The spies sent by Joshua (cf. 2:1) are referred to as "Joshua's messengers", and the same expression for them occurs below, 9, p. 225; note also T. Soṭah 8:4. Apparently the word *mrglym* ("spies") is reserved for the men Moses sent to spy out the land (Num. 13 f.). Cf. below, 9, s.v. "When the spies entered the Land."

"as soon as we had heard it . . . melt" Note the idiom in the two Joshua quotations, and particularly Josh. 2:11b. On these verses see also below, 9, p. 225.

But when *wbzmn* šᵓ*yn; MRS: wkš*ᵓ*yn.*

is profaned *mtḥll; MRS: mḥwll.*

"whither they came" Note the reading for "whither" in *MRS,* and cf. ibid., critical apparatus.

and it continues (*bis*) Not in *MRS.*

holy Name, which the house of Israel had profaned" (Ezek.
36:21), and it continues, "Therefore say unto the house of
Israel: Thus saith the Lord God: I do not this for your
sake . . . And I will sanctify My great Name, which hath
been profaned among the nations" etc. (Ezek. 36:22–23).

MY FATHER'S GOD, AND I WILL EXALT HIM: Said the Synagogue of Israel before the Holy One, blessed be He: Master
of the universe, It is not only for the miracles Thou hast
wrought for me that I recite songs and hymns before Thee,
but for the miracles which Thou hast wrought for my
Fathers and for me, and continuest to perform for me in
every single generation. That's why it is said, "My father's
God, and I will exalt Him."

MY FATHER'S GOD . . . HIM Another comment on the clause,
and it is intended to answer the question, Why should Israel at the
Sea suddenly see fit to speak of "my father's God"? The Midrash,
further, having observed that the verse speaks in the singular ("my
God, my father's God") falls into the same style and speaks of *knst
yśrʾl.*

Said the Synagogue of Israel . . . universe Not in *MRS.* I have
deliberately translated "Synagogue of Israel," for I feel that here *knst*
is meant to emphasize which is the true ecclesia.

It is not only . . . generation *MRS:* "It is not only for miracles
which He wrought for me that I express the Praise before Him"
(*ʾny nwtnt lpnyw ʾt hšbḥ;* note also ibid., p. 233), "but for miracles
which He wrought for my Fathers and will in the future perform for
me. That is why" etc. What our Mekilta calls "songs and hymns" *MRS*
calls *šbḥ.*

That's why . . . "Him" The Song is therefore a Thanksgiving
Hymn for God's bounties to Israel in every age. Cf. also M. Pesaḥim
10:5 and further, below, 8, pp. 205 ff.

4. The Lord Is a Man of War

THE LORD IS A MAN OF WAR, THE LORD IS HIS NAME: Rabbi
Judah says: Here is a verse made rich in meaning by many
passages, (for) it declares that He revealed Himself to them
with every manner of weapon:

He revealed Himself to them as a warrior girt with his
sword, as it is said, "Gird thy sword upon thy thigh, O
warrior" (Ps. 45:4);

He revealed Himself to them as a cavalry officer, as it is

Here is a verse . . . many passages Cf. Be-Shallaḥ, v (I, 224). The
formula means: the idiom and idea of this verse are made concrete and
are illuminated by a number of verses in other parts of Scripture.
See also Bacher, *Erke Midrash* (Tel Aviv, 5683), p. 80. Six examples
will now be given of how a warrior is equipped, and so when our
verse speaks of God as warrior, we are to understand how well
equipped He was. Since, however, the verse concludes with "the Lord
is His Name," says the Midrash, manifestly it is with His Name that
He will battle, and He does not really need the arms He bears. On
the reading of our passage, see also *AhB*, I, 13 f.

Revealed Himself to them *nglh ʿlyhm; MRS: nglh lhm.*

He revealed Himself . . . with His sword *MRS:* "He appeared
(*nrʾh*) to them as a warrior." The order of examples in *MRS* differs
slightly from that in our Mekilta: what is here listed first is in *MRS*
second, here second is there third, here third is there first, here fourth
is there sixth, here fifth is there fourth, here sixth is there fifth. And
where our Mekilta reads *nglh ʿlyhm, MRS* reads *nrʾh* ("appeared")
lhn; cf. also preceding note.

"Gird thy sword upon thy thigh" This is a proof-text not that God
so appeared but only that a "warrior" is so girded. On the Lord as
warrior (*gbwr mlḥmh*), however, see Ps. 24:8 (note also Yadin, *Scroll
of War* 12:8, p. 317), and cf. Isa. 42:13. Is the image in this statement
to suggest an infantryman in contrast with the following statement
in our text? On the various weapons mentioned, see Krauss, *Persia
and Rome*, pp. 209 ff.

said, "And He rode upon a cherub, and did fly" (Ps. 18:11);

He revealed Himself to them in coat of mail and helmet, as it is said, "And He put on righteousness as a coat of mail" (etc). (Isa. 59:17);

He revealed Himself to them with a spear, as it is said, "At the shining of Thy glittering spear" (Hab. 3:11), and it says, "Draw out also the spear, and the battle-ax" etc. (Ps. 35:3);

He revealed Himself to them with bow and arrows, as it is said, "Thy bow is made quite bare" etc. (Hab. 3:9), and it says, "And He sent out arrows, and scattered them" etc. (II Sam. 22:15);

He revealed Himself to them in buckler and shield, as it is said, "His truth is a shield and a buckler" etc. (Ps. 91:4), and it says, "Take hold of shield and buckler" etc. (Ps. 35:2).

Shall I deduce (from all this) that He is in need of any of these means? The verse says, "The Lord is a man of war, the Lord is His Name": by means of His Name He makes battle, and has no need of any one of these means! But if so, why does Scripture feel it necessary to itemize each and every single one of these? For this reason, that if Israel require it, God will make battle for them. And

"And He put on . . . coat of mail" Note how the verse continues.

and it says, "Draw . . . battle-ax" Note that for the imagery from this point on, two proof-texts are supplied for each instance (while up to this point, for each image there was only one proof-text).

bow and arrows *MRS* does not speak of arrows and therefore does not quote II Sam. 22:15.

that He is in need *šhw> sryk; MRS: šsryk.*

of any of these means *MRS:* "(of any) of all these means." And so too in the following line. Cf. Krauss, *Persia and Rome,* p. 218 (bottom).

by means of His Name He makes battle See below, p. 134, and note, ad loc., s.v. "The Lord is His Name . . . means." Cf. Blau, *Altjüdische Zauberwesen,* pp. 117 ff., and esp. p. 120. On the significance of the Name in biblical thought, see J. Pedersen, *Israel,* 2 vols. (London and Copenhagen, 1926), first vol.: I–II, 245 ff.: some of the observations there continue to apply to rabbinic thought.

every single one of these *MRS:* "all these verses."

For this reason *>P; MRS, lwmr* (to teach; lit., to say).

if Israel require . . . battle for them *MRS:* "If Israel require *(ystrkw)* any one of these, lo, He will make (battle) for them."

God requires no weapons or arms, but of course Israel may; and if

woe to the Nations of the World at what they hear with their own ears! For lo, it is He Who Spake and the World Came to Be who will battle against them in the Future!

THE LORD IS A MAN OF WAR. Why is it said, THE LORD IS HIS NAME? For at the Sea He revealed Himself as a warrior making battle, as it is said, "The Lord is a man of war," (while) at Sinai He revealed Himself as an elder full of compassion, as it is said, "And they saw the God of Israel" etc. (Exod. 24:10 f.). —As for the time when they were redeemed, what does it say? "And the like of the very

---

they do, God will furnish them with all the necessary arms. Perhaps the words ʿwśh lhm mlḥmh in our text should be understood as "provides them (with the arms for) war"; note the literal meaning of the MRS reading, ʿwśh lhn.

On our passage, cf. Marmorstein, in HUCA, VI, 180 f.

And woe to the Nations MRS: "Woe to the Nations . . . at what their ears hear, for He Who Spake . . . will in the Future Himself (hwʾ) battle . . ."

We have here doubtless a comforting on the part of the homilist to encourage his dispirited audience. See also below, 10, p. 236 f.

THE LORD IS A MAN OF WAR MRS introduces the quotation with the formula "Another interpretation."

Why is it said Not in MRS. The question means, What purpose is served by the clause "the Lord is His Name," after the verse had said that the Lord is a man of war?

For at the Sea . . . "man of war" The thought of the Midrash is clear enough: the different descriptions of God in Scripture are simply statements of His various self-manifestations, each appropriate to the individual occasion, but all statements of one God and in no way suggesting duality or plurality. Therefore, when the verse says, "the Lord is His Name," after having said, "the Lord is a man of war," it is affirming that at all times this is one and the same God (see also Bonsirven, I, 154 f.). There is difficulty here with several lines in the text that follows. See further, below.

MRS reads: "For when the Holy One, blessed be He, revealed Himself at the Sea, He appeared to them as a young man making battle (mlḥmh; our Mekilta reads, mlḥmwt, plural); (but) 'the Lord is His Name,' at Sinai He revealed Himself . . ." Cf. Midrash Shir ha-Shirim, ed. Grünhut, 51a.

an elder The sage who teaches, an image appropriate to the giving of the Torah at Sinai. In MhG, Exod., p. 295, the reading is simply, "an elder wrapped (in his cloak)," and the words "full of compassion" do not occur.

full of compassion He appeared not only as the teaching sage but in the character opposite to that of a warrior in battle.

heaven for clearness" (ibid.).— And it says, "I beheld till
thrones were placed, and One that was ancient of days did

as it is said . . . for clearness Not in *MRS*. Concerning "And they
saw the God of Israel" etc., see also Pisḥa, xiv (I, 113), and Ba-Ḥodesh,
v (II, 231).

As a proof-text this is very difficult (as observed in the preceding
note, it is not quoted by *MRS*), unless we are to assume that the
Midrash is referring not so much to Exod. 24:10 as to 24:11a, and
God's mercy would then be demonstrated by the fact that though they
had looked upon God, "upon the nobles of the children of Israel He
laid not His hand," but spared them.

On the relevance of **"As for the time . . . for clearness"**, I. Lewy,
Ein Wort über die Mechilta des R. Simon (Breslau, 1889), p. 9, n. 1,
suggests that this passage is mistakenly reproduced in Shirta from
Pisḥa, xiv (and HR apparently accepts this suggestion). There the
passage makes excellent sense: "Whenever Israel are in bondage, the
Shekinah is as it were in bondage with them; as it is said, 'And they
saw the God of Israel; and there was under His feet (the like of
brickwork)' etc."; i.e. even as they were engaged in making bricks
during their bondage, so He had at His feet the likeness of a brick,
symbolizing His sharing their fate. "But when they were redeemed,
it was as the verse says, 'The like of the very heaven for clearness' "—
i.e. the brightness of the skies symbolizing God's joy.

Although I find no support for the following in the relevant
parallel passages, I think the Mekilta text here may originally have
read as follows: ". . . (while) at Sinai He revealed Himself as an
elder full of compassion, as it is said, 'And they saw the God of
Israel' etc." (For the meaning of this proof-text, see preceding note.)
"Another interpretation of 'They saw the God of Israel' etc.: *Such
was (the view) until they were redeemed"* (cf. *Lev. R.* 23:8, p. 537—i.e.
the view of God with the brick at His feet); "but as for the time
when they were redeemed, what does it say? 'And like the very
heaven for clearness.' "

In other words, once Exod. 24:10 was quoted, the Midrash compiler
brings still another interpretation of the verse which he can use to
support his point; viz., during Israel's bondage God appears one way,
but He appears in another way when they are redeemed. And our
text, if I am right, has suffered from homoeoteleuton (what may have
fallen out, I have underlined).

For a somewhat similar interpretation by Lauterbach, see *Klausner*,
pp. 184 ff.; but he does not suggest reading "Another interpretation";
cf. his n. 4, p. 185.

With other preoccupations, Philo uses Exod. (the *LXX* version) 24:10
in connection with thoughts of God's immutability; cf. *On Dreams*,
II, 222 (Loeb, v, 543), and *Confusion of Tongues*, 96 (Loeb, IV, 61).
See also his *Questions and Answers on Exodus*, II (Loeb, Suppl. II,
79).

sit" (Dan. 7:9); but it also says, "A fiery stream" etc. (Dan. 7:10). Now, in order to give no opening to the Nations of the World to say, There are two Powers, Scripture reads, "The Lord is a man of war, the Lord is His Name,"

The same in Egypt, the same at the Sea,
The same in the past, the same in the Age to Come,
The same in this world, the same in the World to Come,

And it says . . . "A fiery stream" These verses will again serve to demonstrate that it is the same God who appears in different aspects, in one verse Daniel suggesting an elder (hence a merciful aspect), and in the following verse someone fiery (hence a militant aspect). *MRS* quotes only Dan. 7:9, apparently because this verse is intended as proof-text of God as merciful elder in contrast to Him as warrior, of which Exod. 15:3 speaks.

One final point. When the Mekilta here speaks of God's appearance at Sinai as "an elder full of compassion," it is focusing principally on the *compassion* aspect of God, in contrast to the militant aspect which is reflected by "The Lord is a man of war." While "elder" at Sinai is apt (cf. above, s.v. "an elder"), here really it is not the teaching which is of primary concern, but the compassion. When later Midrashim however (e.g. *Pesikta Kahana* 223 and *Pesikta R.* 100b) emphasize God's role as *teacher* at Sinai, they have shifted the emphasis. Note, by the way, the interesting reading in Maimonides' Code, Yesode ha-Torah I, 10: "Our master Moses himself saw Him at the Sea as a warrior making battle, and at Sinai *as the congregational emissary wrapped in his cloak* (for prayer)." See above, s.v. "an elder." On the latter image, cf. B. Rosh ha-Shanah 17b and *Eliyahu Zuta*, 42 (I owe the last reference to Professor Isadore Twersky).

to the Nations of the World Not in *MRS;* but cf., ibid., the variant reading, and also p. 233.

There are (hn) two Powers *MRS:* "There are (yš) two Powers in heaven." On the protest against dualism, see also Ba-Ḥodesh, v (II, 231 f.), and cf. Moore, I, 364 ff.; III, 115 ff.; *EJ*, VI, 93 f. Cf. also de Lubac, *Exégèse médiévale*, IV, 13 ff.

The same in Egypt . . . *MRS* introduces this statement with the formula "Another interpretation," and continues: " 'The Lord is a man of war,' He makes battle in Egypt; 'the Lord is His Name,' He makes battle at the Sea; / and the same at the Jordan, and the same at the Arnon streams; / the same in this world, and the same in the World to Come; / the same in the past, and the same in the Age to Come." Then follow the proof-texts as in our Mekilta, except that *MRS* quotes also Isa. 44:6 between the quotations of Deut. 32:39 and Isa. 4:14, and after the latter *MRS* quotes also Isa. 48:12. (Are these four proof-texts to correspond to the four lines of its comment?)

as it is said, "See now that I, even I, am the same" etc.
(Deut. 32:39), and it says, "Who hath wrought and done
it? He that called the generations from the beginning, I,
the Lord, who am the first, and with the last am the same"
(Isa. 41:4).

Sometimes in a country there is a warrior fully armed,
but he has no strength, no courage, no strategy, no war
experience. But it is not so with Him Who Spake and the
World Came to Be. On the contrary, He has strength and
courage and strategy and war experience, as it is said, "For
battle is the Lord's, and He will give you into our hand"

In Ba-Ḥodesh, v, where the comment is on "I am (ʔnky) the Lord
thy God," and seven statements are made ("It is I in Egypt, I at the
Sea, I at Sinai, I in the past, I in the Age to Come, I in this world,
I in the World to Come"), proof-texts are brought where together
the word "I" (ʔny) occurs seven times. Now, in our Mekilta here
we have six statements about God, and note that in the two proof-
texts adduced, the word ʔny ("I") occurs six times. (The additional
verses in ed. HR therefore seem to me superfluous.)

Concerning "in the Age to Come," the proof-text of Deut. 32:39,
"I kill, and I make alive," indicates that lʿtyd lbʔ should so be
translated here (and not simply as "future"). Cf. on this verse Sifre
Deut., 329, p. 379.

Sometimes . . . there is a warrior A series of comparisons, con-
stituting still "another comment" on the clause "The Lord is a man
of war"; indeed, MRS introduces its series with "Another interpretation of 'The Lord is a man of war, the Lord is His Name.'" In our
Mekilta we now get six comparisons, the first four of which begin,
"Sometimes in a country there is a warrior," and the last two, "When
a king of flesh and blood" is engaged in war (in this connection,
perhaps, there may once also have been what now occurs in Sifre
Num., 102, p. 100 [cf. Sifre Z., p. 249], which would make seven
comparisons; note Yalkut Shimeoni!). In MRS (see also notes, below)
all the comparisons are introduced by the formula "Sometimes there
is a warrior standing in battle" (once the participle ʿwmd is wanting);
the order also differs slightly from that in our Mekilta. At all events,
we seem to have before us some handy collection of comparisons,
with a stylized introductory formula. On the passage, cf. Krauss, Persia
and Rome, pp. 218 f.

Fully armed kl kly zyyn; MRS (p. 82) does not read kl.

but he has no strength MRS, lit.: "But he has no knowledge of
either (neither) strength" etc.

no strategy (ṭqsys), no war experience MRS: "No war strategy"
(ṭksysy mlḥmh). On the defective reading of the next line, 7, in MRS,
p. 82, see ibid., p. 251.

(I Sam. 17:47), and it is written, "A Psalm of David. Blessed be the Lord my Rock, who traineth my hands for war, and my fingers for battle" (Ps. 144:1).

Sometimes in a country there is a warrior in full possession of his strength, (but) a man of forty is not like a man of sixty, and a man of sixty is not like a man of seventy; rather, the longer he lives, the more his strength declines. But it is not so with Him Who Spake and the World Came to Be. On the contrary, "I the Lord change not" (Mal. 3:6).

Sometimes in a country there is a warrior who, once he's filled with passion and power, will charge furiously and attack even his father, even his mother, even his other relations. But it is not so with Him Who Spake and the World Came to Be. On the contrary, "The Lord is a man of war, but His Name remains the Lord": "The Lord is a man of war," for He makes battle against Egypt; "But

and it is written *wktwb* (which should perhaps be *wktyb;* nevertheless, cf. below, p. 133). *MRS:* "And it says."

(but) a man of forty . . . In English usage we would say, But a man of sixty is not like a man of forty, and a man of seventy is not like a man of sixty.

Forty is an age of both physical and intellectual maturity; cf. also PA 5:21. *MRS* (p. 81): "as a man of forty" (*kbn ʾrbʿym*).

MRS does have the word "but."

is not like a man of sixty, and a man of sixty is not like a man of seventy *MRS:* "Is not (ʾyn) like a man of sixty or a man of seventy."

the longer he lives *MRS:* "The longer the time he lives."

On the contrary, "I the Lord change not" *MRS:* "(But it's not so with Him . . . World Came to Be:) 'The Lord is a man of war' who battles against Egypt; 'the Lord is His Name,' the same in the past, the same in the Age to Come. And so too it says," and then the Malachi quotation follows.

"Change not"—i.e. at all times remain in full strength. From the way *MRS* uses the Malachi verse, it would seem to be interpreting the verb as "am not unfaithful, can always be depended on"; cf. *HJP,* pp. 49 f. and n. 26 (see also S. Lieberman, in *Lešonenu,* XXXII [1967–68], 92). And perhaps this too is what our Mekilta is driving at: I, the Lord, can always be depended on.

will charge furiously . . . relations . . . *MRS:* "Will make no distinctions, but charge furiously and attack . . ." See the story in Tacitus, *History* 3:25 and note Tacitus's closing sentence.

but His Name remains the Lord So the verse must be translated in the present context. See further below, s.v. "The Lord, the Lord."

"a man of war," for He makes battle (lit., He battles) **against Egypt** *MRS* (p. 82): "A man of war—He makes battle (ʿwśh mlḥmh), and

His Name remains the Lord," for He has compassion upon
His creatures, as it is said, "The Lord, the Lord is a God
merciful and gracious" etc. (Exod. 34:6).

In a country there may be a warrior; once his arrow has
flown from his hand, he cannot retrieve it, for it is out
of his hand now. But it is not so with Him Who Spake
and the World Came to Be. On the contrary, when Israel
do not do God's will, an evil decree goes forth, as it were,
from before Him, as it is said, "When I whet My glittering
sword" etc. (Deut. 32:41); the moment they repent He
retrieves it, as it is said, "But My hand holds onto the
punishment" (ibid.).— However, am I to conclude from
this that He brings it back unfulfilled? The verse says, "I
will render vengeance to Mine adversaries" (ibid.): Against

---

nevertheless 'the Lord is His Name,' He is compassionate toward all
His creatures."

as it is said, "The Lord, the Lord" *MRS:* "What is His Name? 'The
Lord, the Lord.' "

In addition to God's merciful character of which the verse speaks
specifically, His mercy is here implied by His Name YHWH, Adonai.
See above, 3, s.v. "But my fathers . . . with . . . Justice," and the
Moore references, ibid. Cf. below, 5, s.v. "They make a Compassionate
One pitiless."

for it is out of his hand now This sounds rather flat; the clause
does not occur in *MRS*. Note also the critical apparatus in Lauterbach.

On the other hand, the statement may reflect the following thought:
once a human being has fired his shot, the missile is completely *out of
his control,* and there is nothing he can do about it (and if he regrets
having fired, it's just too bad). God, however, never "loses His control"
over anything: even after He has issued His decree, "it is never too
late" and nothing is irreversible or irrevocable.

goes forth For the spelling *ywṣ* in *MRS,* cf. critical apparatus
and Melamed's Introduction, ibid., p. 41 (and n. 60).

as it were Not in *MRS.* Here, of course, the expression is meant to
ward off evil possibilities.

"When I whet My glittering sword" etc. The "etc." here refers
essentially to verse 41b.

the moment Not in *MRS.*

"But My hand . . . punishment" Instead of the parallelism in
Deut. 32:41a, the Midrash sets the two clauses in antithesis to each
other.

However Lit. "or"; not in *MRS.*

that He (šhwᵓ) . . . unfulfilled *MRS* omits the pronoun *hwᵓ.*
For the imagery see the expression in II Sam. 1:22b.

whom does He direct it? Against the Nations of the World,
as it is said, "And I will mete out to them that hate Me"
(ibid.).

When a king of flesh and blood sets out to war and
(citizens) of the provinces—(even) those close to him—
come with their requests to him, they are told: "He is
(now) in an ugly frame of mind, he is setting out to war;
when he has been victorious and returns, then come and
lay your requests before him." But it is not so with Him
Who Spake and the World Came to Be. On the contrary,
"The Lord is a man of war," for He makes battle against
Egypt; "But His Name remains the Lord," for (in the
same time) He gives ear to the cries of all the inhabitants
of the world, as it is said, "O Thou that hearest prayer,
unto Thee doth all flesh come" (Ps. 65:3).

(Sometimes) when a king of flesh and blood is engaged in
war, he is unable to feed his troops or to provide them with
their pay. But it is not so with Him Who Spake and the

Against whom does He direct it? *MRS:* "I direct it against."

as it is said, "And I will . . . Me" Not in *MRS.* On this passage,
see also *Mid. Tan.,* p. 203. Cf. E. Bickerman, *Four Strange Books* (New
York, 1967), 36 f.

When a king . . . sets out to war The same formula (except for a
minor change in the verb) will also be used in the following comparison; see above, s.v. "Sometimes . . . there is a warrior." On this
passage, cf. Ziegler, pp. 47 f.

provinces—(even) those close to him *MRS:* "(Citizens of) nearby
provinces come to him."

with their requests *wšw^ɔlwt; MRS: ltbw^ʕ* (lit., "to demand").

they are told *whn ^ɔmrym lhn; MRS: ^ɔm(r) lhn.*

"ugly frame of mind" *z^ʕwp; MRS, zw^ʕp.*

"when he has been victorious" *lkšynṣḥ; MRS, kšynṣḥ.*

"then come" *MRS* omits "come."

"lay your requests" *wšw^ɔlyn; MRS, mš^ɔlyn.*

"before him" *MRS* adds, "and he will fill them"—lit., "do."

On the contrary, "The Lord is a man of war" *MRS:* "On the
contrary, even if all the inhabitants of the world cry out before Him,
He hears the cry of them all, as it is said, 'O Thou that hearest' . . ."

"His Name remains the Lord" Again the Tetragrammaton emphasizing God's mercy. Cf. above, s.v. "as it is said, 'The Lord, the Lord.'"

as it is said So read (Lauterbach's text, p. 34, line 60, is a printer's
error). Cf. below, 8, p. 198.

a king . . . his troops Cf. *AhB,* I, 14. See Ziegler, p. 64.

or to provide . . . their pay See Liddel and Scott, s.v. *opsonion.*

World Came to Be. On the contrary, "The Lord is a man
of war," for He makes battle against Egypt; "But His Name
remains the Lord," for He feeds and sustains all His creatures, as it is said, "While He is still dividing the Reed
Sea in sunder" etc. (Ps. 136:13)—as is written thereafter—
"He gives food to all flesh" (Ps. 136:25).

THE LORD IS A MAN (³yš) OF WAR: How is it possible to speak
so, when it is plainly said, "Do not I fill heaven and earth?
saith the Lord" (Jer. 23:24), and it is written, "And one
called unto another, and said" etc. (Isa. 6:3), and it says,
"And, behold, the glory of the God of Israel came" etc.
(Ezek. 43:2)? Why, then, does Scripture say, "The Lord
is a *man* of war?" For this reason: Because of My love for
you and because of your holiness, I sanctify My Name in
your midst. And so too it says, "Indeed I am God; but am

Note the reading in *MRS* and in the critical apparatus, ibid. Our
Mekilta reads, *wlᵓ lspq; MRS* reads, *wlspq* (provide). For "their pay,"
note the slight variant in *MRS*.

"The Lord is a man of war" . . . **"His Name remains the Lord,"
for He** Not in *MRS*.

feeds and sustains all His creatures *MRS:* "Feeds and sustains all
the inhabitants of the world and all the work of His hands whom He
created in His world"; then it proceeds at once to quote Ps. 136:25,
147:9, and 145:9 (but not 136:13, as our Mekilta does).

For "feeds and sustains," see also the idiom in Baer, p. 555.

"dividing the Reed Sea in sunder" At which time He was making
war against the Egyptians. Cf. *Midrash Psalms* on Ps. 136:13, 261a.

How is it possible to speak so Cf. Be-Shallaḥ, I (I, 185), and see
also Ba-Ḥodesh, IV (II, 221). Comment is provoked by the very bold-
ness of the anthropomorphism, and especially that God should be
referred to as ³yš. Note Tg Onkelos and Tg Yerushalmi on the verse,
and also *LXX* reading.

"do I not . . . Lord." This verse is not quoted by *MRS.*

and it is written *wktwb;* cf. above, p. 130, s.v. "and it is written."
and it says *wᵓwmr* is not in *MRS.*

"And, behold, the glory . . . came" Note that our Mekilta has
apparently deliberately chosen a proof-text from each of the "major"
prophets.

Why, then . . . "The Lord is a *man* of war" Not in *MRS.*

**Because of My love for you and because of your holiness I sanc-
tify My Name in your midst** The *MRS* reading at this point is as
follows: "Because of My love for you and because of your holiness—
for My Name has been sanctified through you [šqdšw ³t šmy ᶜl

I, the Holy One, not also *man* in the midst of thee?" (Hos. 11:9)—My Name I sanctify in your midst.

THE LORD IS HIS NAME: By means of His Name He makes battle, and is in no need of any one of these (military) means! So David also says, "Thou comest to me with a

---

ydykn]; and so David says, 'Some trust in chariots, and some in horses,' etc.; 'They are bowed down and fallen,' etc.; 'Save, Lord,' etc. (Ps. 20:8–10)—it is that I shall sanctify My Name through you. [Therefore it is said, 'The Lord is a man of war.']" (On "Therefore it is said, . . . war,'" see critical note, ibid., p. 82, and reading, p. 234.). On the other hand, the *MRS* reading ʿl *ydykm* may mean, "for your sake"; cf. Ba-Ḥodesh, II (II, 202), ʿl *ydykm* with *MRS*, p. 138, *bšbylkm*. See further *MRS*, p. 141, and note to line 3, ibid.

The daring term *ʾyš*, the Mekilta says, is no qualification of God's divinity or omnipresence, but an expression of His love. Compare the comment on Jer. 23:24 by Ben Azzai in *Sifra* 4a. Even the whole world cannot, of course, contain God, as the biblical verses state; yet because God loves Israel and because of their holiness, He sanctifies His Name *in their midst* (*bkm*, and note the Hosea proof-text, *bqrbk*); i.e. He boldly manifests Himself as a warrior (*ʾyš mlḥmh*) fighting in the midst of Israel's ranks and bringing them triumph— thus His Name is sanctified. Nor will this extraordinary self mani- festation on His part lead to a wrong conception of His true being, for the Hosea verse reminds us that He is El (cf. the exclamation in the Shirah, "This is my El"); and when it continues (according to the present midrashic interpretation), "And am I not also man," it im- mediately explains what that means; i.e. *in your midst* I am *qdwš*, I bring about the sanctification of My Name. (Contrast Lauterbach's translation.)

Once having made this comment, the Mekilta proceeds with com- mentary on "The Lord is His Name" of the remainder of the verse.

The holiness of Israel referred to is obviously necessary if God is to appear in their midst.

For an early cabalistic interpretation of "The Lord is a *man* of war," see the quotation in Scholem, *RhK*, p. 40.

THE LORD IS HIS NAME . . . means Not in *MRS*. On this statement, cf. above, p. 125, and notes. See also Origen, *Contra Celsum*, v:45–46 (ed. H. Chadwick [Cambridge, 1953], pp. 299–301). Note *Memar Marqah* 2:9 (II, 69): "All the names of God are attributive except the name Lord (YHWH), which does not consist of any attribute. Hence the great prophet Moses said in this Song, 'The Lord is His name.' There is none like it." Cf. MacDonald's note, p. 111, ad loc. Is it possible that Marqah is misunderstanding the word *mdwt* here?

So David also says . . . On the association of the following verses with prayer, cf. Be-Shallaḥ, III (I, 208).

sword, and with a spear, and with a javelin; but I come to
thee in the Name of the Lord of hosts" (I Sam. 17:45); and
it is written, "Some trust in chariots, and some in horses,
but we in the Name of the Lord our God" (Ps. 20:8); so
Asa also says, "And Asa cried unto the Lord his God" etc.
(II Chron. 14:10).

PHARAOH'S CHARIOTS AND HIS HOST ETC.: Whatever the measures a man adopts, so is it meted out to him:
    They said, "Who is the Lord" (Exod. 5:2), and in like
measure Thou didst mete it out to them; that is why it is
said, "Pharaoh's chariots and his host hath He cast down
into the Sea."— One verse (15:4) reads, "He hath cast

"Thou comest to me . . . hosts" *MRS* does not quote this verse.
David comes with the very Name which the Philistine "has taunted."
    "trust in chariots . . . in horses" Exactly like Pharaoh! Cf. Exod. 14.
    "in the Name of the Lord our God" *MRS* continues to quote
v. 9–10, and then concludes, "for I will sanctify My Name through
you."
    so Asa also says . . . Not in *MRS;* instead, we get here the follow-
ing: "Another interpretation of 'The Lord is a man of war, the Lord
is His Name'—'Pharaoh's chariots and his host hath He cast into the
sea.' "
    Whatever the measures a man adopts, so is it meted out to him
MRS: Whatever the measures a man adopts, so hast Thou meted it
out to him." See also the following notes. On this idea of measure
for measure, see also below, 5, p. 143; 6, p. 165 f.; Amalek, II (II, 148);
and for a related notion, see above, 2, p. 94, and note, s.v. ". . . very
ways . . . account." Note also the formulation in Wisdom of Solomon
11:16. Cf. Be-Shallaḥ, VI (I, 241 f.).
    They said *MRS,* "he said." In our Mekilta, evidently, verses related
to Pharaoh are taken as representative of all Egypt.
    Note that in the course of the next several pages (right into chapter
5) we shall get six examples of this measure-for-measure principle,
and the formula is, "They said . . . and in like measure Thou" etc.
The seventh example will appear in 6, p. 165 f.
    and in like measure Thou . . . that is why it is said . . . "hath
He cast down ino the Sea" *MRS:* "In this measure Thou didst show
them Thy fear and Thine awe on the Sea. 'Pharaoh's chariots' etc."
According to *MRS,* therefore, the measure for measure consisted in
this: Pharaoh spoke scornfully of God ("Who is the Lord" etc.), and
as a result God so punished him that he might recognize the awesome
power of God.
    Presumably the same idea is being expressed by our Mekilta, but
the proof-text is far from clear, as all the commentators observe (cf.

down," and another verse (15:1) reads, "He hath thrown": how preserve both readings? "He hath cast down," for down to the deep they descended; "He hath thrown," for up on high they rose.

Another interpretation of PHARAOH'S CHARIOTS ETC.: In the very measure they adopted, Thou didst mete it out to them. They said, "Every son that is born, into the river" etc. (Exod. 1:22), and in like measure Thou didst mete it

---

ed. HR, ad loc., and also Kasher, XIV, 117, note to sec. 89)—for how do the words "Pharaoh's chariots" etc. demonstrate the principle of measure for measure in action? That other, later Midrashim had a problem with our passage is evident from the ingenious interpretations they provide for the word *my* (*who* is the Lord); cf. *Exod. R.* 5:14, 16b, and *Tanḥuma Wa-ʾera*, 5, end, where the suggestion is made that the consonants for "sea" (*ym*) are the reverse of the consonants for "who" (*my*), and that on this word-play the proof-text is based. See also next note.

One verse (15:4) . . . Cf. above, 2, p. 101. Note that all this is wanting in *MRS* (p. 83), and it does seem to be out of place here. Perhaps, however, for our Mekilta this too is part of our homily on measure for measure: Pharaoh had dared to say *my*, and so by *mem* (*m*) and *yod* (*y*) he had sinned; therefore by *mem* and *yod* he was punished. That is, by *mem* of *rmh* and *yod* of *yrh* he was hurled high and low. For note that the consonants of *yrh* and *rmh* are identical except for the *y* and the *m*. On *yrh* = descent and *rmh* = high up, see above, 2, p. 101 of translation, p. 101 of commentary. The sentence beginning with "One verse reads" would then be an explanation of the way the verse "Pharaoh's chariots hath He cast (*yrh*) into the sea" serves as proof-text.

"He hath thrown," for up on high they rose (1) Note that on this occasion the Mekilta first explains *yrh* and then *rmh*, for in the present verse the verb used is *yrh*. (2) Here the Mekilta does not add the phrase "neither separating from the other," for that is *not* the point here. Now contrast the reading above, 2, p. 101 of translation, p. 101 of commentary.

Another interpretation . . . CHARIOTS I wonder if the formula "Another interpretation" is really appropriate here; cf. the variant reading in Lauterbach's critical apparatus.

It is not clear if *MRS* is here repeating the verse "Pharaoh's chariots." If *MhG, Exod.*, p. 296, and *MRS*, p. 234, are any criterion, then MRS, p. 83, is not repeating the verse.

They said, "Every son . . ." MRS reads: "Pharaoh said." On this passage, cf. Jubilees 48:14, Wisdom 18:5.

out to them; that is why it is said, "Pharaoh's chariots and
his host hath He cast into the Sea."

Of them it is said, "And he took six hundred chariots"
(Exod. 14:7), and in like measure Thou didst mete it out
to them; that is why it is said, "Pharaoh's chariots" etc.

AND HIS CHOSEN CAPTAINS ARE SUNK IN THE REED SEA: In the
very measures they adopted, etc. Of them it is said, "And
captains over all of them" (Exod. 14:7), and in like measure
Thou didst mete it out to them, "And his chosen captains
are sunk" etc.

THEY ARE SUNK IN THE REED SEA: In the very measures they
adopted, etc. They: "And they made (the Israelites') lives
bitter with hard service, in mortar" (Exod. 1:14), and in
like measure Thou didst mete it out to them: for them
Thou madest the water like mire into which they sank;
that is why it is said, "They are *sunk* in the Reed Sea."
Now, "sinking" is nothing other than a reference to (sinking) in mire, as it is said, "And Jeremiah sank in the mire"

---

that is why it is said, "Pharaoh's chariots" *MRS* omits the formula,
"that is why it is said."

Of them it is said, "And he took . . ." *MRS:* "Of him it is said . . ."
On this instance of measure for measure, cf. above 2, p. 94.

AND HIS CHOSEN CAPTAINS . . . they adopted, etc. Note that
in the text of our Mekilta, the opening refrain is not concluded (and
all we get is *wkw*, "etc."); cf. above, 2, p. 99. *MRS* does not repeat it at
all. Cf. below, s.v. "sunk in the Reed Sea."

Of them it is said *MRS:* "Of him it is said."

SUNK IN THE REED SEA . . . they adopted, etc. Note again
that our Mekilta text does not conclude the opening refrain, and that
again *MRS* does not quote it at all.

They: "And they made . . . in mortar" *MRS:* "He made the
children of Israel serve with rigor" (cf. the idiom in Exod. 1:13); but
note the variant reading in *MRS,* ad loc.

**and in like measure Thou didst mete it out to them: for them (*lhm*)
Thou madest the water like mire into which (*bhm*) they sank** *MRS:*
"So too Thou didst harden" (*hqšyt;* cf. below, 5, s.v. "madest the
waters like stones") "the water for them (*ʿlyhn*) (so that it became)
like mire into which (*bw*) they sank." The mire corresponds to the
mortar spoken of in Exod. 1:14.

That is why . . . "*sunk* in the Reed Sea" Not in *MRS.*

Now, "sinking" *MRS:* "Sinking." Cf. Luzzatto, p. 280.

(Jer. 38:6), and it says, "I am sunk in deep mire" (Ps. 69:3). That is why it is said, "They are sunk in the Reed Sea."

in deep mire After this, *MRS* quotes Ps. 69:16 and apparently has in mind also the preceding verse (but note ibid., p. 234, which has only the two verses our Mekilta quotes).

That is why . . . "sunk in the Reed Sea" Not in *MRS*.

Thus far we have had five illustrations of the measure-for-measure principle; for the sixth, see below, 5, p. 143.

5. The Deeps Cover Them

THE DEEPS COVER THEM: But are there "deeps" there? Why, it's a swamp! Why then does Scripture say, "(The deeps) cover them?" However, this teaches that up surged the lower deeps and the upper deeps, and their waters inflicted upon the Egyptians all kinds of disasters. That is why it is said, "The deeps cover them."

are there "deeps" there? . . . What in our Mekilta is first comment, is second comment in *MRS*, and vice versa.

Why, it's a swamp I owe my understanding and explanation of this statement to Professor Saul Lieberman.

ʿšwnyt (in *MRS*, *šnyt*) is a swamp. Now, a swamp is a shallow place, and hence the question arises, How can one speak of "deeps" in connection with a swamp? The Mekilta asks: Is not this location an *ʿishunit* (*ʿšwnyt*)? For the very name of the sea, Sea of Suf, Sea of Reeds, suggests that we are speaking of a swamp: reeds grow in a swamp, not in deep waters! Note that *LXX* equates *thwmwt* with "open sea," *pontos.*

See further below, p. 142, the comment on "They went down into the depths." On *ʿšwnyt* (*šnyt*), cf. also P. Shekalim 7:5, 50c.

(In regard to the *MRS* reading referred to by Albeck on *ʾAhilot 7:1, p. 541, cf. A. Goldberg's edition [Jerusalem, 1955] of that treatise, p. 54, and note, ad loc.)

Why then does . . . "cover them" Not in *MRS.*

up surged (ʿlw) the lower deeps and the upper deeps, and their waters inflicted upon the Egyptians (lit., upon them) Cf. *Tanḥuma Be-Shallaḥ*, 14. *MRS*: "Up surged (ʿlh) the lower deeps and the upper ones, and they inflicted upon the Egyptians."

The reference to *thwmwt* by the verse suggests to the homilists that in the battle of God against the Egyptians, even the primordial abysses participated, for inevitably the word *thwmwt* would recall the *thwm* of Gen. 1:2. On the conception of these upper and lower abysses, cf. Ginzberg, *Legends*, v, 39. What we have here again, therefore, is

Another interpretation of THE DEEPS COVER THEM: But are there "deeps" there? Why, it's a swamp! Why then does Scriptures say, "The deeps cover them?" However, this teaches that the lower deeps rose to join with the upper deeps, covered up the sky over them, and darkened the light of the stars overhead, as it is said, "All the bright lights of heaven" etc. (Ezek. 32:8). And to what end? "So

---

an emphasis on the supernatural character of the deliverance from Egyptian bondage. Cf. above, 2, s.v. "The horse was strapped to his rider." Both upper and lower deeps or abysses may be spoken of here because the verse reads *thwmwt*, in the plural.

all kinds of disasters At this point *MRS* (pp. 83 f.) introduces the passage on Jonah (see below, s.v. "Jonah went down").

That is why . . . "cover them" Not in *MRS*.

Another interpretation In *MRS* this comment comes first.

Why, it's a swamp . . . "cover them" Not in *MRS*.

the lower deeps rose to join with the upper deeps *MRS*, more simply: "The lower deeps rose." Lauterbach translates our Mekilta sentence, "The lower depth rose above the upper depth," but I am not sure I understand his point. It seems to me that the meaning is, The lower depth (abyss) rose and mingled with the upper depth; and note Ginzberg, *Legends*, VI, 10, n. 52: ". . . the abyss ascended and united itself with the waters above in the heaven, so that the Egyptians met their death while engulfed in gloomy darkness." At all events, here too we are dealing with a kind of "eschatologic"-mythologic thought suggested to the homilist by the word *thwmwt*, and this time also providing an explanation of the verb "covered"—i.e. explaining specifically what it was that these abysses covered up.

covered up Cf. the reading *whykh* in *MRS* and the note in the critical apparatus, ibid.

darkened the light of the stars Note the idiom in Ezek. 32:7. Instead of "stars," *MRS* reads, "the luminaries" (*mᵓwrwt*).

as it is said *MRS:* "and so too it says."

"All the bright lights . . ." Note that Ezekiel is speaking of Egypt; cf. 32:2.

The verses which the Mekilta quotes here do not prove that these catastrophes took place at the Sea; the verses simply demonstrate that such cataclysms are spoken of by the prophets. Therefore we are not to doubt that the same could occur at the first redemption, which was of course preceded by disasters (plagues) visited on the Egyptians, one plague indeed being "darkness." See also *SY,* ad loc. Here, as it were, the nature of that first redemption is made vivid by features which will characterize the final redemption. (Sometimes, in reverse, the Midrash foretells the characteristics of the future age by referring

that I will set darkness upon thy land, saith the Lord God"
(ibid.).

So too it says, "For the stars of heaven and the constel-
lations thereof shall not give their light" (Isa. 13:10). How
so? "The sun shall be darkened in his going forth" etc.
(ibid.).

So too it says, "At Tehaphnehes also the day shall grow
dark" etc. (Ezek. 30:18). How so? "As for her, a cloud shall
cover her" (ibid.).— And it is written, "And I will visit
disaster upon the world" etc. (Isa. 13:11).

Jonah went down as far as one deep, as it is said, "The
deep was round about me" etc. (Jon. 2:6), but the Egyptians

---

to the miraculous character of events in the past; see, for example,
Sifra 110d–111a.)

Note, by the way, that three biblical proof-texts of the final
cataclysm are brought here.

And to what end Lit., "and why"—i.e. to what purpose will these
disasters be brought on? *MRS* does not have this interrogation.

"darkness upon thy land" Note also Ezek. 32:9, which *MRS* explicitly quotes.

So too it says *MRS:* "and it says."

"For the stars of heaven . . ." The verses from Isaiah also are merely
meant to illustrate what happens—the terrifying darkness—when
God in the end punishes Israel's enemies. Note that Isa. 13:9 speaks
of the coming Day of the Lord.

How so (*wlmh*)? **"The sun shall be darkened in his going forth"**
MRS: "Wherefore (*mpny mh*)? 'And I will visit . . . upon the world'
etc." (Isa. 13:11), which our Mekilta quotes after the next Ezekiel
citation. Having brought proof from Isaiah also that darkness equals
disaster, the homilist brings another quotation to the same effect from
Ezekiel, where again the reference is to Egypt.

In *MRS* the reading of Ezek. 30:18b is not in accord with MT.
Was the scribe writing from memory?

So too it says, "At Tehaphnehes" *MRS* does not quote the formula,
"So too it says."

"I will visit . . . world" This verse is an extension of the idea in
the other verses, for in the End it will be not only Egypt that is
affected, but all the arrogant and the proud (cf. Isa. 13:11b).

Jonah went down . . . This passage is introduced here as a kind
of further comment on the term *thwmwt*, in the plural. In Jonah 2:4,
6, note the occurrence of the terms *thwm*, *mṣwlh*, and *swp* (and on
this last term, cf. also Ginzberg, *Legends*, VI, 350, n. 31, end).

"The deep was round about me" The deep, in the singular; and observe that the latter half of the verse refers to *swp*.

went down two deeps, as it is said, "The deeps cover them." Jonah went down one fathom deep (*mṣwlh*), as it is said, "For Thou didst cast me into a *mṣwlh*" etc. (Jon. 2:4), but they went down two fathoms deep, as it is said, "They went down into *mṣwlwt*" (Exod. 15:5). And *mṣwlh* is nothing other than a reference to overpowering waters, as it is said, "For Thou didst cast me into a *mṣwlh*, in the heart of the seas" (Jon. 2:4.), and it is written, "And their pursuers Thou didst cast into *mṣwlwt*, as a stone into overpowering waters" (Neh. 9:11).

THEY WENT DOWN INTO THE DEPTHS (*mṣwlwt*): But are there "depths" there? Why, it's a swamp! Why then does Scripture say, "They went down into the depths?" However, this teaches that the Great Sea emptied into the Reed Sea, and

the deeps In the plural, and the minimum plural is two.

Jonah went down one fathom deep . . . In *MRS* this statement comes after the comment below on "They went down into the depths."

For the translation of *mṣwlh* as "fathom deep," cf. *OED*, p. 100, col. a, s.v. "Fathom," 3d and 6.

two fathoms deep Note our Mekilta reading *šny* (masculine) for "two." In *MRS*, on the other hand, earlier, *šty thwmwt*; but note the variant reading ibid. Cf. also below, s.v. "Thy right hand, O Lord . . . two times."

And *mṣwlh* is nothing other . . . seas None of this is in *MRS*; and as conclusion of the comment on Jonah, instead of quoting the Nehemiah verse, *MRS* simply quotes Exod. 15:5b.

Our Mekilta here, it seems to me, is trying to underscore the character of the miracle at the Sea: though Israel crossed dry-shod, do not think that the waters which miraculously returned to drown the Egyptians were just in ordinary quantities or force. On the contrary, they were, as the verse in Nehemiah puts it, in devastating amounts, as it would be in the depths of the deep seas. And all the more remarkable, therefore, was the passage through the region where such waters had been; cf. Isa. 43:16.

But are there "depths" . . . a swamp Cf. above, p. 139, and note, ad loc.

Why then does Scripture . . . "into the depths" *MRS* does not have this question.

the Great Sea . . . Reed Sea Thus, though the Reed Sea itself was a sea of reeds and hence presumably without large quantities of water, or without extraordinary depths, huge quantities of water were now let loose on the Egyptians. See incidentally Plate V in G. E. Wright and F. V. Filson, *The Westminster Historical Atlas to the Bible* (Philadelphia, 1956), where can be seen vividly the "proxim-

the waters inflicted upon the Egyptians all kinds of disasters. That is why it is said, "They went down into the depths."

LIKE A STONE (*ʾbn*): In the very measures they adopted, Thou didst mete it out to them. They said, "Ye shall look upon the birthstool (*ʾbnym*)" (etc.) (Exod. 1:16), and in turn for them Thou madest the waters like stones, and as such the waters kept striking them on (their) stones. That is why it is said, "Like a stone."

Another interpretation of LIKE A STONE: This was an

---

ity" of the Mediterranean to Lake Menzaleh and the body of water to its south over which the Israelites must have crossed at the exodus.

Our Mekilta passage, by the way, may help explain the dialogue in *ARNA*, p. 50, between the Angel of Death and the *Great Sea* ("Since Israel passed through me . . ."). To be sure, *ARNB*, p. 52, reads simply "Sea," and not "Great Sea"; but note also the reading in *Deut. R.*, ed. Lieberman, p. 40. Cf. J. A. Fitzmyer, *The Genesis Apocryphon* (Rome, 1966), pp. 136 f. See also Albeck ad M. Parah 8:8 (in his edition of the Mishnah, p. 564).

and the waters inflicted upon the Egyptians Cf. Ginzberg, *Legends*, VI, 10, n. 52. *MRS:* "And (the sea) inflicted . . ."

That is why . . . "into the depths" Not in *MRS*.

Like a stone: In the very measures . . . Cf. above, 4, pp. 135 ff. Here we have the sixth illustration of the action of measure for measure. In *MRS* this passage follows what in our Mekilta is brought as the next interpretation, and *MRS* does not have the sentence "In the very measures . . . mete it out to them."

They said *MRS*, "he said."

"birthstool" *ʾbnym;* stone = *ʾbn*.

in turn . . . Thou Correct the misprint in Lauterbach's text (p. 39, line 2) accordingly.

madest the waters like stones For the *MRS* reading, cf. above, 4, s.v. "and in like measure . . . water like mire . . ."—"Thou didst harden."

the waters kept . . . stones *MRS* does not repeat the subject, "the waters," and reads "their" explicitly.

We have here another aspect of the measure-for-measure principle: where they attacked is where they are now attacked, not only that they sank like stone.

That is why . . . "Like a stone" Not in *MRS*.

Another interpretation of LIKE A STONE In *MRS* (cf. above, s.v. "Like a stone") this is also introduced by the formula "Another interpretation," apparently because the statement "Jonah went down one fathom deep . . ." is taken as the first interpretation of "They went down into the depths like a stone."

intermediate punishment—the worst of them were tossed
about "like stubble" (Exod. 15:7), the moderate ones, "like

This was an intermediate punishment Cf. the reading in *AhB*, I,
17 (and see also next note). There is in this comment a play on the
words *ɔbn* (stone) and *bynwny* (intermediate); cf. also *SY*. But the
present comment is not part of the group above illustrating measure
for measure; see further below.

On the notion of the various grades among the Egyptians, see
Be-Shallaḥ, VI (I, 242), and below, 7, p. 183. Cf. Ginzberg, *Legends*, III,
27 f.; VI, 9 f., n. 51.

The idea that not all the Egyptians were guilty to the same degree
is suggested, needless to insist, by the different expressions for punishment in Exod. 15:5b, 7b, and 10b. But it seems to me that the Midrash is led to this observation not merely by the verses but by the
basic concern for justice; that is to say, since God is just, and since
it is unlikely that *all* the Egyptians entertained the identical views
toward Israel (cf. Exod. 14:25b and Be-Shallaḥ, VI, on this verse),
although all the Egyptians were hostile, the Mekilta calls attention to
the fact that three kinds of punishment are spoken of by the chapter,
to establish that God did not visit one and the same punishment on
all, but to each according to the degree of his guilt. This becomes
especially clear in the characterization of the different groups of
Egyptians in chapter 7, below.

For "intermediate punishment," *MRS* reads: "intermediate party
(*kt*) among them"; and note the comment on our Mekilta in ed. HR,
p. 133.

the worst of them . . . Lit., "the (thoroughly) wicked" in their
midst, etc. *MRS* reads: "The best (*kšryn*) of them were tossed about
like stubble, the intermediate ones (were sunk) like a stone, the worst
of them sank like lead in the mighty waters." See also Kasher, XIV, 119,
comment on no. 100. Apparently the ones our Mekilta calls *pqḥym*
(the best of them; lit., the wisest) are the *kšrym* of *MRS*. Note that
in Be-Shallaḥ, VI (I, 242), the *pqḥym* are contrasted with *ršͨym* and
ṭpšym, and note also the reading in *MRS*, p. 66, top two lines. In the
Passover Haggadah ḥkm (wise) and *ršͨ* (wicked) are also opposed to
each other.

tossed about "like stubble" If our Mekilta reading is the correct
one, we shall have to say that the punishment for the worst of them
was that, before they could sink (if ever! like chaff), they were tossed
about for a long time, made to suffer pain and anguish, and not put
out of their misery at once. The punishment of the moderate, or
intermediate, ones was that after some moderate tossing about, they
sank—as it is, let us say, when one throws a flat stone across a body of
water: it skims the water once or twice and then sinks; cf. *Sekel Tob*,
p. 193. (On such a game with stones being played by boys, see
Octavius of Minucius Felix 3:6 [Loeb, 319].)

a stone," the best of them "sank as lead in the mighty
waters" (Exod. 15:10).

Another interpretation: LIKE A STONE, for like stone they
hardened their hearts.— But as for Thee,

> Thy goodness, Thy manifold mercies, and Thy com-
> passion are upon us,
> And Thy right hand is extended to all the inhabitants
> of the world,

as it is said, "Thy right hand, O Lord . . . Thy right hand,

"sank as lead . . ." They sink at once and (according to our
Mekilta) escape excessive torment. See also Rashi on Exod. 15:5.

Another interpretation: LIKE A STONE *MRS*, "Another interpretation: Why like a stone?"

for (*ʿl*) like stone they hardened their hearts *MRS*, "For (*lpy*) like
stones they hardened their hearts." Cf. *AhB*, I, 17.

On the hardening of heart see Exod. 5; 7:3; 8:11, 15, 28; 9:34 f.;
10:20, 27; 13:15.

In this alternative interpretation of "Like a stone," what we have
is simply another explanation of the *sixth* example of the operation
of the measure-for-measure principle, not a seventh example of that
principle. That will be furnished below in 6, p. 165, on "And with the
blast of Thy nostrils the waters were piled up."

But as for Thee, Thy goodness, Thy manifold mercies . . . *MRS:*
"But us, by Thy mercy and by Thy goodness and by Thy great
compassion and by Thy right hand which is extended to all the inhabitants of the world." Cf. *AhB*, I, 17. See also *Sifre Num.*, 134,
p. 180.

There is a distinct "liturgical" flavor to the statement, and it may
also be compared with the passage below, 10, p. 240. The statement
seems to be a kind of bridge between commentary on "Like a stone"
and on "Thy right hand, O Lord" of the following verse. And perhaps it comes here because in a sense a new strophe of the Song
begins with "Thy right hand, O Lord"; for note that at this point
in the Song Israel begins to address God directly, in the second person.
As to the sense of the passage, see further, below.

"Thy goodness, Thy . . . mercies": for a combination of *twb* and
ḥsd, cf., e.g., Ps. 25:7. On "Thy manifold mercies," cf. *Maḥzor Vitry*,
p. 65. The biblical construction would be *rb ḥsdyk*; cf., e.g., Ps. 106:7.
On "Thy . . . mercies . . . Thy compassion," cf., e.g., Ps. 25:6. As
for "Thy compassion . . . upon us," for the construction *rḥmym ʿl*,
cf., e.g., Ps. 145:9.

And Thy right hand is extended Cf. the Neʿilah Prayer of the
Atonement Day (Baer, p. 436, top line), as well as the Taḥanun prayer
(ibid., p. 115).

O Lord" (Exod. 15:6)—(not once, but) two times! (It says also,) "But Thy right hand, and Thine arm, and the light of Thy countenance, because Thou wast favorable unto them" (Ps. 44:4); and it is written, "By Myself have I sworn, the word is gone forth from My mouth in charity, and shall not come back" (etc.) (Isa. 45:23).

MAJESTIC IN POWER: How comely Thou art, how majestic in power!

"Thy right hand, O Lord . . ." two times Not in *MRS*. Cf. *AhB*, I, 18. Note the reading *šny* in our text for "two," and see also above, s.v. "two fathoms deep," as well as below, p. 149 (cf. Wa-Yassa', I [II, 94]).

The duplication of "Thy right hand, O Lord" in Exod. 15:6 suggests to the homilist here that the very hand of God which punishes is nevertheless stretched forth in love to all men, and that the very right hand which delivers Israel is the right hand which is extended to all the world's inhabitants. See further, below.

"But Thy right hand . . . unto them" On the one hand, what Israel acquire is Thy doing (Thy right hand) because "Thou wast favorable unto them." On the other hand, God's word has gone forth in charity (in love), so that to Him every knee shall bend (Isa. 45:21–24; and in verse 24 note the reference to ꜥz).

and it is written In *MRS* only the verse, not this formula. (In line 13, ibid., the word *ṣdqh* should doubtless be added.)

"The word . . . in charity" *ṣdqh* in the rabbinic sense of charity, love. Note not only how this verse proceeds to express the idea that all peoples will acknowledge the Lord, but in the immediately preceding verse (Isa. 45:22) the prophet declares, "Look unto Me, and be ye saved, all the ends of the earth."

The homilist seems to be saying this: The Egyptians were punished, sunk like stone, because they hardened their hearts like stone. They, and above all Pharaoh (who is also their god!), have hearts of stone; but Thou God art full of love for all men even when Thou displayest special love to us. A contrast is therefore being drawn between Israel's God and the god of the Egyptians, a contrast particularly underscored by the proximity of "like a stone" to "Thy right hand, O Lord." And as the proof-texts from Psalms and Isaiah demonstrate, the notion the homilist is especially eager to emphasize here is that God's punishment of the Egyptians is *not* His rejection of "all the inhabitants of the world"; on the contrary, His right hand continues to be extended to them.

How comely . . . power Cf. *AhB*, I, 18. A play on the word *nꜣdry* as though it expressed *nꜣh* (comely) *wꜣdyr* (and majestic); see also below, 8, p. 197, and cf. above, 1, p. 84. Cf. *HJP*, pp. 69 f. The

For to the Flood Generation Thou gavest a grace period to repent, but they would not repent, as it is said, "And the Lord said: My spirit shall not pass sentence" etc. (Gen. 6:3), and Thou didst not condemn them to destruction until after they had perpetrated the full measure of their wickedness before Thee.

You find the same true with regard to the Tower Folk, that Thou gavest them a grace period to repent, but they would not, as it is said, "And the Lord said: Behold, they are one people, and they have all one language; and this is but the beginning of their activity; and now" etc. (Gen. 11:6)—for the expression "and now" is nothing other than a reference to time for repentance, as it is said, *"And now, Israel, what doth the Lord thy God require of thee"* etc. (Deut. 10:12)—and Thou didst not condemn them to

---

Mekilta now proceeds to show that God's majesty in *power* consists of His long-suffering. See also *Sifre Num.*, 134, p. 180, for the comment on "Thy *strong* hand."

Incidentally, note that in this interpretation of *nᵓdry* the Mekilta relates the word to YHWH and not to *ymynk* ("Thy right hand"); cf. also Ibn Ezra and Rashbam on the verse (and also Cross, *Studies,* pp. 112 f.; on the other hand, in *JNES,* xiv (1955), 241 and 245 f., that interpretation is abandoned).

to the Flood Generation . . . period See Ginzberg, *Legends,* I, 153 f.; v, 174 ff. In our Mekilta "Flood Generation" is *dwrw šl mbwl;* in *MRS, dwr hmbwl.*

to repent *MRS:* "in order that they might repent."

They would not repent *MRS:* "they would not."

"My spirit . . . sentence" This proof-text is to be understood as follows: God said, I shall not *judge,* pass sentence—i.e. *punish.* That is to say, God gave them time to repent because He did not want to punish. Indeed, this verse occurs just before the story of the Flood; and, as the Midrashim point out (in connection with the 120 years of Gen. 6:3), God waited 120 years, and then an additional 7 days, before He brought the Flood.

You find the same *MRS:* "We find the same," and so too below in the statement on Sodom.

Tower Folk (ᵓnšy hmgdl) **. . . period to repent** *MRS:* "ᵓnšy mgdl . . . perhaps they might repent."

"And now, Israel . . ." It is significant that the homilist sees in this verse the ideal of, or summons to, repentance, *tšwbh;* note that the verb *šwb* does *not* appear in Deut. 10:12! Cf. *Lekaḥ Tob* and Sforno on this verse.

destruction until after they had perpetrated the full measure of their wickedness before Thee.

You find the same true with regard to the Sodomites, that Thou gavest them a grace period to repent, but they would not, as it is said, "And the Lord said: Verily the cry of Sodom and Gomorrah . . . I will go down now, and see" etc. (Gen. 18:20–21). Now, what is reported in that section? "Then the Lord caused to *rain* upon Sodom" etc. (Gen. 19:24)—"rain," that is, if they repent; otherwise? Lo, "brimstone and fire" (ibid.)! Thou didst not condemn them to destruction until after they had perpetrated the full measure of their wickedness.

Ten plagues Thou didst bring upon the Egyptians in Egypt, and Thou didst not condemn them to destruction until after they had perpetrated the full measure of their wickedness.

Another interpretation of THY RIGHT HAND, O LORD,

didst not condemn . . . until Obviously a mechanical repetition of the formula, for God did not destroy the builders of the Babel Tower. In fact, rabbinic sources underscore that for good reasons the Tower Folk were not destroyed; cf. Ginzberg, *Legends,* I, 180 (and note, ad loc.). On their punishment after refusing to repent, see *Legends,* v, 204, n. 90 (end).

Sodomites These three groups (Flood generation, Builders of the Babel tower, and citizens of Sodom) are frequently brought together to illustrate God's actions (here His merciful ones) throughout early history. See also, for example, above, 2, pp. 89 ff.

"And the Lord said" . . . section Not in *MRS.*

"I will go down now, and see" Cf. *Gen. R.* 49:6, p. 504; *Legends,* v, 239, n. 167.

"rain" . . . if they repent; otherwise? Lo, "brimstone and fire" *MRS:* "Here rain is spoken of, and brimstone and fire are spoken of: if they repent, lo, rain; otherwise, brimstone and fire." According to the Mekilta, the use of the verb *hmṭyr* in the verse suggests that had the Sodomites repented, God would have been prepared to bring them the blessings of rain, *mṭr.*

Thou didst not condemn . . . wickedness Not in *MRS.*

Ten plagues . . . In this way God showed long-suffering toward the Egyptians, for not until after all these warnings and chastisements were they destroyed utterly in the Sea.

the full measure of their wickedness *MRS:* "the full measure of their wickedness before Thee,"

MAJESTIC IN POWER: When Israel do the will of God, they make His left into a right hand, as it is said, "Thy right hand, O Lord . . . Thy right hand, O Lord": (not once, but) two times! But when Israel do not do the will of God, they make His right into a left hand, as it is said, "He hath turned His right hand into its opposite" (Lam. 2:3).

When Israel do the will of God, sleep has no place in His presence, as it is said, "Behold, He neither slumbers nor sleeps" etc. (Ps. 121:4). But when Israel do not do the will of God, there is, as it were, need for Him to sleep, as it is said, "Then the Lord awaked as one who had been asleep" (Ps. 78:65).

When Israel do the will of God, wrath has no place in His presence, as it is said, "Fury is not in Me" (Isa. 27:4).

Another interpretation . . . When Israel The commentary is primarily on the duplication of "Thy right hand, O Lord," in the verse; and whereas the previous interpretation of "majestic in power" was on God's relationship with the Gentiles, now the interpretation is applied to Israel, making plain what happens especially when Israel do not do God's will. And note, once the principle (cf. the reading in *Sifre Num.*, 157, p. 211) of "When Israel do . . ." is stated, three additional applications of it are introduced (in *MRS*, two; see below).

they make Our Mekilta has the subject pronoun *hn*, but *MRS* omits it; and so too below.

His left into a right hand By repeating "Thy right hand, O Lord," the verse (says the homilist) suggests that God's left hand becomes a right hand, as it were. Left over against right signalizes misfortune; see, for example, Philo, *Embassy to Gaius*, 95 (Loeb, x, 47 f., and Colson's note b) and 104 f. (51 f.); cf. also *Cant. R.* 1:9, 10c, and the view of the Sages, ibid., 1:2, 4c; Matt. 25:31 et seq.

On the subject of right and left, cf. also M. Middot 2:2, and see *TK* on T. Shabbat 6:17, Long Commentary, pp. 89 f., and the illuminating references in the notes, ibid.; S. Lieberman, in *P'raqim*, I (Jerusalem, 1967–68), 98 ff. Cf. also Rashi on Gen. 1:26 and Aknin, *Divulgatio*, ed. Halkin, pp. 75, 409. See also, by the way, the citation and paraphrase in N. Cohn, *Pursuit of the Millenium* (London, 1962), pp. 213 f.

"Thy right hand" . . . two times Cf. above, p. 146, and note, ad loc., s.v. "Thy right hand, O Lord . . . two times." For "two" once again our Mekilta reads *šny* (see also above, s.v. "Two fathoms deep"). *MRS* does not read "two times."

When Israel do . . . sleep has no place . . . This example is not in *MRS;* but cf. the critical apparatus, ibid., 85.

But when they do not do the will of God, wrath is, as it were, in His presence, as it is said, "Then the anger of the Lord is kindled" (Deut. 11:17).

When Israel do the will of God, He makes battle for them, as it is said, "The Lord will fight for you" (Exod. 14:14). But when Israel do not do the will of God, He battles against them, as it is said, "Therefore He was turned to be their enemy, and Himself fought against them" (Isa. 63:10). And what is more, they make a Compassionate One pitiless, as it is said, "The Lord is become as an enemy" (Lam. 2:5)!

SHATTERS (*tr^cṣ*) THE FOE: It does not say "*r^cṣt* (hast shattered) the foe" but "*tr^cṣ* (wilt shatter) the foe"—in the Age to Come! As it is said, "Thou wilt march through the earth in indignation" etc. (Hab. 3:12).

But when they do not do *MRS:* "But when Israel do not do."

wrath is, as it were, in His presence *MRS* adopts a euphemistic expression: "He is filled with wrath against *the enemies of Israel.*"

He battles against them *MRS:* "He battles, as it were, against them." The exact idiom of the verse has been adopted by the Mekilta. Cf. *Sifre Num.,* 157, p. 211.

"and Himself" (Isa. 63:10) MT, "Himself."

they (*hn*) make a Compassionate One pitiless *MRS* omits the pronoun subject and speaks of "the Compassionate One."

The verse speaks of "the Lord," which points to God's attribute of mercy, and yet it says that the *Lord* has become an enemy. On the names of God and the attributes of justice and mercy, see also above, 3, p. 120, and the comments, ad loc., s.v. "Me . . . with the attribute of Mercy" and "But my fathers . . . with the attribute of Justice." Cf. also above, 4, p. 131, and the comment, s.v. "As it is said, The Lord, the Lord."

as it is said *MRS:* "even as it is said."

SHATTERS THE FOE *MRS* reverses the order of the two comments on this verse.

It does not say "*r^cṣt* (hast shattered)" . . . but "*tr^cṣ* (wilt shatter)" Cf. above, 1, p. 66 f. on *yšyr.* Verbs in the imperfect give the homilist his opportunity to suggest eschatological intentions. Note how frequently this note is struck in Shirta: see below, 6, p. 161; 8, p. 205.

As it is said *MRS:* "And so too it says."

"Thou wilt . . . in indignation" According to HR (p. 134, note to line 13), the verb *ṣ^cd* (march through) is being interpreted as though it were *r^cṣ* (shatter; in appearance, there is only a slight difference between the *d* and the *r* in Hebrew). On the other hand, perhaps the homilist is thinking of the latter half of verse 12, "Thou threshest the

SHATTERS THE FOE, to wit, Pharaoh, as it is said, "The foe
said" (Exod. 15:9).

According to another interpretation, it is Esau, as it is
said, "Because the foe hath said" (etc.) (Ezek. 36:2).

---

nations in anger" and also part of verse 13, "Thou woundest the head
out of the house of the wicked." Note verse 13a. Incidentally, on the
association of Hab. 3:14–15 with miracles at the Sea, see Be-Shallaḥ,
IV (I, 220); V (I, 223–24); and VII (I, 247).

to wit, Pharaoh Cf. below, 7, p. 177. According to this interpretation,
of course, "tr⁽ṣ the foe" is not to be referred to the Age to Come. Cf.
below, s.v. "Esau."

another interpretation MRS: "And some say."

Esau Of course, this is Rome; and to this interpretation one is to
apply the comment above that "tr⁽ṣ the foe" refers to the Age to
Come. Lauterbach calls attention to the fact that in Ezek. 36:5 it is
evident that Esau is meant, who is Edom.

"Because" MRS reads, y⁽n ky (cf. critical apparatus, ibid.).

6. And in Thy Mighty Exaltation

AND IN THY MIGHTY EXALTATION THOU OVERTHROWEST THEM
THAT RISE UP AGAINST THEE: Mightily dost Thou exalt Thyself against those who rise against Thee! And who are they
who rise against Thee? The ones who rise up against Thy
children. (For) it is not written here, "Thou overthrowest
them that rise up against *us*," but "Thou overthrowest them
that rise up against *Thee*": Scripture is declaring that
whenever anyone rises up against Israel, it is as though he
is rising up against Him Who Spake and the World Came
to Be.

So too it says, "Forget not the voice of Thine adversaries,

Mightily dost Thou exalt Thyself So the Midrash interprets the
expression "in Thy mighty exaltation" of the verse. Cf. also above,
2, p. 89, "He lords it over all those who act the high and mighty."
  against *ngd; MRS, kngd*.
  The ones who rise up *hm šqmw; MRS, my šqmw;* cf. below, s.v.
"The ones who."
  Thy children Cf. *AhB*, I, 19 f., on this passage. In *MRS* first the
comment on the ones "who rose up against Thy favorite" is given
(see further, below) and then the comment on those who rise "against
Thy children." But an exact parallel to these few lines is not in *MRS;*
cf. below, s.v. "So too it says, 'Forget not the voice,'" and "For, lo,
Thine enemies." Cf. Kasher, XIV, 122, note to no. 112 (end).
  What the Mekilta is here saying is that Israel's enemies are the
enemies of God, as the next lines spell out specifically. Cf. Tg Onkelos
and Jonathan on the verse.
  (For) it is not written . . . Came to Be Not in *MRS*. On this statement, cf. *Sifre Num.*, 84, p. 81: "Are there then those who rise up
against (lit., before) Him Who Spake and the World Came to Be?"
Observe, indeed, how the whole section continues.
  So too it says, "Forget not the voice of Thine adversaries" In *MRS*
(p. 86) this is introduced as follows: "It is not written here, 'Thou

152

the tumult of those that rise up against Thee which as-
cendeth continually" (Ps. 74:23); "For, lo, Thine enemies
are in an uproar" (Ps. 83:3). For what reason? "Against
Thy people they hold crafty converse" etc. (Ps. 74:4). It is
also written: "Do not I hate them, O Lord, that hate Thee"
etc. (Ps. 139:21). For what reason? "I hate them with utmost
hatred; (for) I count them mine enemies" (Ps. 139:22).—

So too it says, "Surely, he that toucheth you toucheth
the apple of *his* eye" (Zech. 2:12). Rabbi Judah says: The

---

hast broken down (*hrst*) them that rise up against Thee,' but, 'Thou
breakest down (= shalt break down, *thrws*) them that rise up against
Thee,' (that is,) in the Age to Come. So too it says, 'Forget not . . .'"
Cf. below, s.v. "Thou breakest down them . . ."

"For, lo, Thine enemies are in an uproar" Instead of this verse,
MRS quotes first Ps. 92:10 ("For, lo, Thine enemies, O Lord, for,
lo, Thine enemies shall perish") and immediately thereafter Ps. 73:27
(cf. *Sifre Num.*, 84, p. 81), apparently employing these verses to prove
that in the Future God will exterminate His enemies. As is evident,
at this point our Mekilta is concerned with something else, using
(other) verses to prove that Israel's enemies are God's enemies.

For what reason Not in MRS. Our Mekilta asks: What is the reason
for such an outcry as the Psalmist's in Ps. 83:2? And the answer is:
Taken together, Ps. 83:3 and 4 show that those called God's enemies
are the ones who take counsel against His people (see, indeed, the
verses that follow), and in Ps. 74:23 we learn that His enemies are
called those who rise up against Him.

"Do not I hate them" . . . **For what reason** Note first the idiom
of Ps. 139:21b, and then observe that in verse 22 the Psalmist says
that God's enemies are his enemies.

So too it says . . . **"of *his* eye"** We now get a whole section devoted
to the theme of "Scripture resorts to euphemism," but this whole section is wanting in MRS.

Once the subject of God's identification with Israel's plight has
been raised, a related illustration thereof is introduced. But this illustration (The one that toucheth you, toucheth the apple of *His* eye)
obviously comes from some source where a list of passages exemplify-
ing the tradition of "Scripture resorts to euphemism" was drawn up:
note how our Mekilta begins here with the comment on the Zechariah
verse and then at the end of the list (below, p. 155) repeats it all over
again; and observe the same in *Sifre Num.*, 84, p. 81.

After this particular section is disposed of, the Mekilta will return
(below, cf. p. 156) to the treatment of its own theme.

On the subject of "Scripture resorts to euphemism," cf. in addition
to *Sifre Num.*, 84, p. 81; *Tanḥuma Be-Shallaḥ*, 16; and see the important discussion in *HJP*, pp. 28 ff.

verse does not say, "the apple of *the* eye," but "the apple of *his* eye"—(in reality) aiming, as it were, at Him on high. But Scripture resorts to euphemism.

The same you have to say of, "Ye say also: Behold, what a weariness is it! And ye have snuffed at *it*" etc. (Mal. 1:13). But Scripture resorts to euphemism.

The same you have to say of, "For the iniquity, in that he knew that his sons did bring a curse *upon themselves*" etc. (I Sam. 3:13). But Scripture resorts to euphemism.

The same you have to say of, "Why hast Thou set me as a mark for Thee, so that I am a burden *to myself*" (Job 7:20)—Scripture resorts to euphemism.

The same you have to say of, "Art not Thou from everlasting, O Lord my God, my Holy One? *We* shall not die" (Hab. 1:12)—Scripture resorts to euphemism.

The same you have to say of, "Hath a nation changed its gods, which yet are no gods? But My people hath changed *its* glory" (Jer. 2:11)—Scripture resorts to euphemism.

Rabbi Judah says: The verse . . . R. Judah's point is this: The verse does not say, "the apple of *My* eye"; note, however, that even R. Judah is expressing himself euphemistically, speaking in general terms, "the apple of *the* eye." In the verse, according to the Midrash, God is really referring to Himself, to His own eye, as it were (cf. Vulgate, Zech. 2:8); but because that would be much too bold and irreverent a way of putting it, the pronominal suffix has been changed by Scripture from "My eye" to "his (own) eye." On R. Judah's statement, see *MRS*, p. 2.

The same *kywṣ² bw;* cf. Bacher, *ʿErke Midrash*, s.v. p. 52. Cf. below, 7, s.v. "It is the same with."

"ye have snuffed at it" Again, says the Midrash, what is really intended is "Ye have snuffed at *Me*," but the change has been made to avoid irreverence.

"a curse upon themselves" The verse presumably wants to say, "Because they curse *Me*." On the other hand, cf. *LXX*, and see Geiger, *Ha-Miqraʾ we-Targumaw*, p. 175; C. D. Ginsburg, *Introduction to the Massoretico-Critical Edition of the Hebrew Bible* (London, 1897), p. 354.

"a burden to myself" That is, instead of saying directly, "So that I am a burden to Thee." Cf. *LXX* and Ginsburg, pp. 360 f.

"We shall not die" Instead of saying, "Thou shalt not die."

"hath changed its glory" Instead of "Hath changed *My* glory." See also next note.

It is the same with "Thus they exchanged *their* glory for the likeness of an ox" (Ps. 106:20)—Scripture resorts to euphemism.

It is the same with "And if Thou deal thus with me . . . and let me not look upon *my* wretchedness" (Num. 11:15) —Scripture resorts to euphemism.

It is the same with "We have no portion in David . . . every man to *his tents,* O Israel" (II Sam. 20:1)—Scripture resorts to euphemism.

It is the same with "And, lo, they put the branch to *their* nose" (Ezek. 8:17)—Scripture resorts to euphemism.

It is the same with "When he cometh out of *his* mother's womb" (Num. 12:12): the verse should have said, "came out of *our* mother's womb"; but Scripture resorts to euphemism.

And so too here you have to say of "He that toucheth you toucheth the apple of *his* eye" (Zech. 2:12). Rabbi Judah says: The verse does not say, "the apple of the eye," but "the apple of his eye"—(in reality) the words of the verse are aiming at Him on high, as it were. But Scripture resorts to euphemism.—

"they exchanged *their* glory" Again instead of "My glory"; cf. Ginsburg, p. 360.

"let me not look upon *my* wretchedness" (*rᶜty*) Instead of reading, "upon *Thine* evil, *rᶜtk,*" in order to avoid ascribing evil action directly to God. Cf. Geiger, p. 215; Ginsburg, p. 353.

"every man to *his tents*" Cf. Geiger, p. 204; Ginsburg, pp. 355 f. Instead of reading "every man to *his gods, Plhyw,*" our biblical texts read *Phlyw* (to his tents). What is involved is a simple transposition of the two consonants *h* and *l*.

"their nose" Instead of "*My* nose"; cf. *HJP,* p. 33.

"came out of *our* mother's womb" Why such an expression should be offensive is explained in *HJP,* p. 32; see also pp. 33 f., on standards of taste. Note that this last example is the only one in our list where reverence for God is not at issue; cf. ibid.

While I do not understand why this is the particular order for the different passages which have been cited, it seems to me that the Num. 12:12 passage is put at the end of the list in the Mekilta (and the *Sifre Num.,* 84, p. 81) because unlike the other passages it does not have God as the subject.

And so too here . . . Thus by repeating the first example in the list of the scriptural euphemisms, we are brought back to the principal subject with which the Mekilta is dealing in its commentary on the verse. Cf. also *Sifre Num.,* 84, p. 81.

But whenever anyone comes to the assistance of Israel, it's as though he is coming to the assistance of Him Who Spake and the World Came to Be, as it is said, "Curse ye Meroz, said the angel of the Lord, curse ye bitterly the inhabitants thereof, because they came not to the help of the Lord, to the help of the Lord against the mighty" (Judg. 5:23).

Mightily dost Thou exalt Thyself against those who rise against Thee! And who are they who rise against Thee? The ones who rose up against Thy favorite. Meaning whom? "Chedorlaomer king of Elam," etc. (Gen. 14:9 ff.). "And at night (Abram) deployed against them" etc. (Gen. 14:15 f.). "Who was it that stirred one up from the East"

But whenever anyone comes . . . And so too *Sifre,* ibid. Note that what the proof-text demonstrates is that he who does *not* help Israel does not help God. *Tanḥuma Be-Shallaḥ,* 16, spells this out rather pedantically.

Mightily . . . Thy favorite Now a second comment on "And in Thy mighty exaltation Thou overthrowest them that rise up against Thee." In *MRS* (p. 85) this is the first of the comments on the verse; cf. above, s.v. "Thy children."

The reference "Thy favorite" is to Abraham (and on Abraham as *ydyd,* favorite, cf. *Sifre Deut.,* 352, p. 409; B. Menaḥot 53b; *ARNB,* p. 121). Although the consonants of our text (and so too *MRS*) read as though the word were in the plural, *ydydyk,* I believe the singular is intended, the third *y* in the word being a vowel letter (*segol*) and not a sign of the plural (cf. Epstein, *Mabo,* pp. 1240–43).

Meaning whom Lit., And what were they like—i.e. Who were they? These words are not in *MRS.*

"Chedorlaomer . . ." Although the quotation is from Gen. 14:9, the reference is actually to the whole section in Genesis. The war of the kings is interpreted by the Midrash as in reality a war against Abraham; cf. *Pesikta R.* 196b and Friedmann's n. 17, ad loc.; Ginzberg, *Legends,* I, 230, bottom line; v, 223, n. 84; 224, n. 88. Instead of quoting Gen. 14:9, *MRS* seems to be quoting 14:1, and then it reads, "(And) what does (Scripture) say?" Then, like our Mekilta, it quotes Gen. 14:15.

"And at night . . . against them" Although seriously outnumbered, Abram was able to defeat the kings because God personally engaged in this battle and thus brought victory to the patriarch. Cf. *Lev. R.* 1:4, pp. 13 f., and Margulies's note, ad loc. (particularly his quotation from Ḥizquni).

"Who was it that stirred one up . . ." *MRS* introduces this quotation by the formula, "And concerning him it is spoken clearly in the non Pentateuchal parts of Scripture," *wᶜlyw mprš bqblh* (cf. Bacher,

etc. (Isa. 41:2)? "It is He who maketh (the enemy's) sword
as the dust" etc. (ibid.). What else does it say? "He pursueth
them and passeth on safely" etc. (Isa. 41:3). So too it says,
"The Lord saith unto my lord . . . The rod of thy
strength the Lord will send out of Zion . . . Thy people

<hr>

Erke Midrash, pp. 105 f., 113). On the word *qblh,* see now the dissertation (University of Pennsylvania, 1970) by S. Z. Leiman, p. 114,
n. 16.

These verses from Isaiah, and the ones from Ps. 110 which follow
(on which see below), are applied by the Midrash to Abraham: Who
was it that stirred up that one—namely, Abraham—to quit the east,
Mesopotamia? *Ṣdq*—that is, the *Ṣdyq,* the Righteous One, the One
who accompanied Abraham when he set forth against the kings. (It is
also possible that the Mekilta is interpreting the verb *hⁿyr,* stirred
up, as *hⁿyr,* illuminated; and the meaning of the verse would then
be taken as, Who was it that illuminated [the course for Abram] that
he should quit the east, Mesopotamia? Cf. *Gen. R.* 42:3, p. 418, and
Theodor's note to line 1.) He (i.e. God) miraculously brought it about
that what was hurled at Abraham was reduced to dust and chaff,
unable to wound the patriarch; but the very dust and chaff *he*
hurled at his enemies became swords and bows (cf. *Gen. R.* 42:3,
R. Judah and R. Nehemiah). In miraculous strides Abraham was able
to pursue his enemies and himself arrive safe and sound ("in peace,"
probably involving also a play on the word Salem, *šlm,* of Gen. 14:18).

Note that the Mekilta simply quotes the Isaiah verses without providing the midrashic comment which would make this biblical quotation intelligible. In other words, our Midrash here is based on another
Midrash, whose explanation the Mekilta takes for granted!

What else does it say *MRS* does not have these words.

So too it says *MRS:* "And it says."

"The Lord saith unto my lord" Ps. 110 is applied to Abraham in
the Midrash (cf. Ginzberg, *Legends,* v, 224 f., n. 95); and again note
that the Mekilta quotes these verses as though their application to
Abraham were self evident. Significantly, *MRS* follows the quotations
from Ps. 110 with Gen. 15:1 (and adds thereafter II Sam. 22:3, 31,
because there God is spoken of as "shield").

It may be that the commentary on Abraham has been introduced
at this point because Exod. 15:7b speaks of the enemy being consumed like "stubble," and this served by association to recall the
Isaiah verse (41:2), whose closing words also refer to "stubble"; and
this verse, as we have seen, was midrashically connected with Abraham.
Once Abraham was brought into the discussion, Ps. 110 could easily
come to mind (moreover, Ps. 110:5a may be serving as an echo of
Exod. 15:6).

On this Midrash of the Mekilta (cf. also *Tanḥuma Be-Shallaḥ,* 16),
cf. Strack-Billerbeck, IV, 452 f. (citing Rashi) and 458–60.

offer themselves willingly in the day of thy warfare . . .
The Lord hath sworn and will not repent," etc. (Ps. 110:1–
4). And how does it continue? "The Lord is at thy right
hand" etc. (Ps. 110:5).

Mightily dost Thou exalt Thyself against those who rise
against Thee! And who are they who rise against Thee?
The ones who rose up against Thy children. Meaning
whom?

Pharaoh and all his host. For it is said, "And he took
six hundred chosen chariots" etc. (Exod. 14:7). What follows? "Pharaoh's chariots and his host hath He cast into
the sea" etc. (Exod. 15:4).

Sisera and all his chariots. For it is said, "And Sisera
gathered together all his chariots" etc. (Judg. 4:13). What
follows? "They fought from heaven" etc. (Judg. 5:20).

Sennacherib and all his hordes. For it is said, "By thy

Mightily dost Thou . . . Pharaoh . . . Essentially, this is like the
first interpretation (above, p. 152), except that this time, in a kind of
historical survey, the Midrash spells out who were the enemies of
Israel in the past. See also above, 2, pp. 89 ff. *MRS* introduces this comment with the formula "Another interpretation" and quotes Exod.
15:7a.

    against those *MRS:* "against all those."

    The ones who *hm; MRS, my;* cf. above, s.v. "The ones who rose
up."

    Meaning whom *kngd,* like the expression earlier in the section
on Abraham, *mh ṭybn,* also translated as "meaning whom." *MRS*
reads: "And who are they that rose? Pharaoh . . ." In our Mekilta
kngd is a kind of shorthand for the fuller clause, *hrbyt lhtgʾwt kngd
Prᶜh,* "Mightily didst Thou exalt Thyself against Pharaoh."

    Pharaoh and all his host Cf. the idiom of Exod. 15:4, and observe
how for stylistic effect each of the subjects is given its own expression.

    Sisera and all his chariots Cf. the idiom of Judg. 4:13. On the
formulas "Sisera and all his chariots, Sennacherib and all his hordes,
Nebuchadnezzar and all his mob," cf. *Mid. Tan.,* p. 200; see however
Sifre Deut., 324, p. 375.

    Sennacherib and all his hordes (*ʾgpyw*) Why *ʾgpyw?* Perhaps it
is used in connection with Sennacherib not only because of the vast
size of his army, but because, in the defiant response to him, it is
said (II Kings 19:28, Isa. 37:29), "I will put My hook in thy nose";
now a similar expression occurs, "I will put hooks into thy jaws" in
the prophecy against Gog (Ezek. 38:4), and in connection with Gog
"hordes" are indeed spoken of (v. 6 and 9). On Gog and Magog and

servants hast thou taunted" etc. (Isa. 37:4). What follows?
"And the Lord sent an angel, who cut off all the mighty
men of valor" etc. (II Chron. 32:21).

Nebuchadnezzar and all his mob. For it is said, "And thou
saidst in thy heart: I will ascend into heaven" etc. (Isa.
14:13)—Nebuchadnezzar said: "I will make me a small

---

their *'gp*, cf. *MRS*, p. 15. In Scripture *'gp*, horde, appears only in
Ezekiel. (For the term and its meaning in the Thanksgiving Scroll 3:29,
see ed. J. Licht [Jerusalem, 1957], p. 86 and note to line 29.)

"By thy servants . . ." *MRS* quotes instead II Kings 19:23.

"sent an angel . . ." After quoting II Chron. 32:21, *MRS* proceeds
to quote Isa. 10:32 and II Kings 19:21.

In our Mekilta the reading of II Chron. 32:21 has been confused
slightly with that of II Kings 19:35. Cf. above, 2, p. 98. (It is [re-
motely] possible that the reading *wyk* is an abbreviation of *wykḥd*,
thus, *wyk'*.)

Why, however, does the Mekilta quote as proof-text a verse from
II Chron. rather than one from either II Kings or Isaiah? Note above,
2, p. 98, for example.

It seems to me that the Midrash here is eager to underscore God's
triumph over *all* the forces of Sennacherib (as of Pharaoh and Sisera
and Nebuchadnezzar too), and this does not altogether emerge from
the reading of either the II Kings or the Isaiah verses. Even with
their clause, "behold, they were all dead corpses," all we learn is
that 185,000 *of* Sennacherib's army were killed. On the other hand,
in II Chron. 32:21–23 we read: "And the Lord sent an angel who
cut off *all the mighty men of valor, and the leaders and captains, in
the camp of the king of Assyria* . . . Thus the Lord saved Hezekiah
. . . from the hand of Sennacherib the king of Assyria, *and from the
hand of all.*"

Further, it may be worth observing that the clause "Thus the Lord
saved Hezekiah" is an echo of "Thus the Lord saved . . . Israel" of
Exod. 14:30.

Nebuchadnezzar and all his mob *MRS* reads, "Nebuchadnezzar and
all his host." Cf. II Kings 25:1; note too Ezek. 29:18. Perhaps our
Mekilta uses the expression *kl hmwnw* in order not to repeat the
terms it has used in the other connections. (Or is the word meant
also to suggest Nebuchadnezzar's blustering?) In ʿAmalek, II (II, 156;
cf. *Sifre Deut.*, 357, p. 427), *kl hmwnw* is used in connection with
Gog; cf. Ezek. 39:11.

At this point *MRS* continues: "He (i.e. Nebuchadnezzar) said: 'It
is impossible (ʾypšr = ʾy ʾpšr) (for me) to dwell with human beings;
I will make me a small cloud and dwell in it,' as it is said, 'I will
ascend above the heights of the clouds' etc. Said the Holy One,
blessed be He: 'You' etc."

cloud and dwell in it," as it is said, "I will ascend above the heights of the clouds" etc. (Isa. 14:14). Said the Holy One, blessed be He, to him: "Since you wanted to withdraw from human beings, human beings will withdraw from you in the end," as it is said, "At the end of twelve months . . . The king spoke and said: Is not this great Babylon . . . While the word was in the king's mouth . . . And thou shalt be driven from men . . . The same hour was the thing fulfilled upon Nebuchadnezzar" etc. (Dan. 4:26–30). How (else) does Scripture put it? "All this came upon the king Nebuchadnezzar" (Dan. 4:25).

"Belshazzar the king made a great feast . . . Belshazzar, while he tasted the wine, commanded . . . Then they brought the golden vessels . . . They drank wine . . . In the same hour came forth fingers . . . Then the king's countenance was changed" etc. (Dan. 5:1–6 ff.). Of him it says, "Woe unto him that giveth his neighbor drink . . . Thou art filled with shame instead of glory" (Hab. 2:15–16). And it says, "In that night Belshazzar was slain" (Dan. 5:30).

a small cloud ʿb qṭnh. ʿb may be masculine or feminine; cf. I Kings 18:44.

"Since you wanted . . . beings" Perhaps this is the idiom that lies *behind* the saying in PA 2:4b; cf. *ARN*, p. 86, ʾl tprwš ʿṣmk mn hṣbwr (see also Taylor ad PA 2:4b).

We have here one of the central protests of the Rabbis against all manifestations of that *hybris*, that sin of pride which is part of the imperial pretensions. The sin is not to acknowledge the *human* nature of oneself. Therefore, measure for measure—or perhaps we might almost say, more than measure for measure: the punishment is to become even less than human. And the Daniel verses are superb in this context.

How (else) does Scripture put it Lit., "What does it say"; in the earlier paragraph this was translated as "What follows."

"All this came upon" The emphasis is on "All this"; i.e. the whole battery of disgrace is let loose against him.

"Belshazzar the king . . ." This is very likely not to be taken as a fifth example, but simply as a continuation of the discussion of Nebuchadnezzar. Note that no formula is used to introduce Belshazzar (this is true also of the reading in *MRS*); rather the text plunges at once into the biblical verse. And in B. Shabbat 149b the Habakkuk proof-text is applied indeed to Nebuchadnezzar.

"Thou art filled with shame . . ." MRS introduces this verse by "and it says."

THOU BREAKEST DOWN (*thrws*) THEM THAT RISE UP AGAINST
THEE: It is not written here, "*hrst* (hast broken down)
them that rise up against Thee," but "*thrws* (Thou shalt
break down) them that rise up against Thee"—in the Age
to Come! As it is said, "Break their teeth in their mouth"
etc. (Ps. 58:7). Why so? "Because they give no heed to the
works of the Lord, nor to the operation of His hands. He
will break them down and not build them up" (Ps. 28:5):
"He will break them down," in this world; "And He will
not build them up," in the World to Come.

THOU SENDEST FORTH (*tšlḥ*) THY WRATH: It is not written
here, "*šlḥt* (hast sent forth) Thy wrath," but "*tšlḥ* (Thou
shalt send forth) Thy wrath"—in the Age to Come! As it
is said, "Pour out Thine indignation upon them" etc. (Ps.
69:25). It also says, "Pour out Thy wrath upon the na-

THOU BREAKEST DOWN THEM . . . On the *MRS* reading, see
above, s.v. "So too it says, 'Forget not the voice . . .'" The interpretation our Mekilta offers here appears in *MRS* (p. 86) as "Another interpretation."

It is not written here, "*hrst* (hast broken down)" See above, 5, p.
150, and the comment s.v. "It does not say '*r*ʿ*ṣt*' . . . but '*tr*ʿ*ṣ*'." These
comments are a good example of how the Rabbis see "prophecy" in
history; that is, events of the past are for them a foreshadowing also
of the future. And perhaps the same comment is made on *tr*ʿ*ṣ*
(shatter), *thrws* (break down), *tšlḥ* (send forth), *yʾklmw* (consume), to
serve as a fourfold affirmation.

As it is said *MRS:* "And so too it says."

Why so That is, why so harsh a penalty? Then comes the answer
from Ps. 28:5. But note also below on "Thou sendest forth Thy
wrath."

"He will break them down" . . . World to Come Not in *MRS*.
Having quoted Ps. 28:5, our Mekilta offers also, in typical midrashic
fashion, an interpretation thereof. Cf. also *ARNB*, end of chap. 32,
p. 71.

THOU SENDEST FORTH THY WRATH *MRS* does not quote
the verse, but begins immediately with "It is not written here, 'Thou
hast sent forth . . .'" Cf. below, s.v. "It consumeth them as stubble."

in the Age to Come Not in *MRS;* and instead of our Mekilta's "as
it is said," *MRS* continues with "and so too it says." Cf. below, s.v.
"in the Age to Come."

"Pour out Thine indignation . . ." Note the idiom in the latter
half of the verse.

It also says *MRS* quotes the following verse without this formula.

tions" etc. (Jer. 10:25). Why so? "For they have devoured Jacob" (etc.) (ibid.).

IT CONSUMETH THEM (*y*'*klmw*) AS STUBBLE: It is not written here, "'*klmw* (hath consumed them) as stubble," but "*y*'*klmw* (will consume them) as stubble"—in the Age to Come! As it is said, "And the house of Jacob shall be a fire" etc. (Obad. 18); it also says, "In that day will I make the chiefs of Judah like a pan of fire among wood, and like a torch of fire" etc. (Zech. 12:6):

When wood burns, it makes no sound; but when chaff burns, the noise travels! So did the voice of the Egyptians travel because of the punishment Thou didst bring upon them.

When wood burns, there is some substance to it; but of

"Pour out Thy wrath . . ." See also Ps. 79:6 and note the biblical reference given by the *MRS* editors to this verse.

Why so? "For . . . Jacob" (etc.) Not in *MRS*. Note how the verse in Jeremiah ends (and see too Ps. 79:7b). And on the word "habitation," see above, 3, p. 115, the view of Rabbi Yose son of the Damascene; and cf. Tg on Ps. 79:7 and David Qimḥi's alternative interpretation of the Jeremiah verse.

On the question "why so," see above, the note s.v. "Why so."

IT CONSUMETH THEM AS STUBBLE Here too *MRS* does not quote the verse but begins at once with the following comment. Cf. above, s.v. "Thou sendest forth Thy wrath."

in the Age to Come Cf. above, s.v. "in the Age to Come."

"the house of Jacob . . . a fire" Note how the verse continues. Esau = Edom = Rome. On the wicked being destroyed like straw, cf. also I Enoch 48:9.

When wood burns . . . The Mekilta now goes on to comment on the expression "as stubble" in the verse; indeed, *MRS* specifically quotes "as stubble" and then proceeds to comment. Cf. *AhB*, I, 20 f.

it makes no sound Lit., "their sound (noise) does not travel"; *MRS*: "they have no sound."

chaff Lit., "the chaff"; *MRS* does not read with the definite article, and so too in the following comment. On the burning of wood and chaff, cf. *Eccl. R.* on 7:6. Note also Tg Onkelos and Jon. on our verse.

So did the voice of the Egyptians *MRS:* "So were the Egyptians, their voice traveled . . ."

Because of the punishment Thou didst bring upon them *MRS:* "Because of the punishments that were coming upon them."

In this comment on the comparison of the Egyptians to stubble, the Mekilta speaks of the severity of punishment, which made the outcry of the Egyptians so loud. Note how *Sekel Tob*, p. 204, reads.

chaff when it burns, there is nothing substantial. Perhaps, however, since it is said (of the Egyptians), "And he took six hundred chosen chariots" etc. (Exod. 14:7), I might deduce that there was something substantial to them? Scripture says, "It consumeth them as stubble": even as of chaff when it burns, there is nothing substantial, so to the Egyptians there was nothing substantial because of the punishment Thou didst bring upon them—so too it says, "They lie down together, they shall not rise, they are extinct, they are quenched as a wick" (Isa. 43:17)—to teach you that there was no more abject a kingdom than Egypt; but for the glory of Israel, it attained temporary eminence:

but of chaff . . . nothing substantial At this point *MRS* adds: "So the Egyptians: there was nothing substantial to them because of the punishments."

Perhaps, however, since it is said Ed. Lauterbach reads merely *šnᵓmr*, but note the critical apparatus, ibid., and the reading in HR, p. 137: *lpy šnᵓmr*. The translation is based on this latter reading (contrast Lauterbach's translation), and note *MRS*, "Since it says." The point the Mekilta makes is this: since the verse, after all, reports that Pharaoh took along six hundred chariots, etc., it might seem that the Egyptians could hardly be regarded as insubstantial.

chosen chariots After this quotation from Exod. 14:7, ed. Lauterbach reads, "or." Note critical apparatus, ad loc.

chaff when it burns *MRS*, simply, "chaff" (and again without the definite article).

so *kk*; *MRS*: "(So) also," *ᵓp*.

the punishment Thou didst bring upon them *MRS*, simply, "the punishment."

In the present comment on the comparison of the Egyptians to stubble, the Mekilta speaks not so much (if at all) of the punishment of the Egyptians, as of their insignificance. The remark is patently intended as a disparagement of the Egyptians. Cf. also the exchange below, between Antoninus and Rabbi, and observe how *Sekel Tob*, p. 204, speaks in the present passage.

"quenched as a wick" Note indeed the whole context in Isaiah, ad loc., which fits admirably the description of exodus from Egypt.

to teach you that there was no more abject a kingdom than Egypt *MRS*: "So too you find that there is no kingdom more abject than the Egypt(ians)," *yrwdh ytyr mn ḥmṣᵓ*. This is the reason, says the Mekilta, the Egyptians were compared to chaff and stubble (cf. also *SY*, ad loc.).

for (*bšbyl*) the glory of Israel, it attained temporary eminence (*šrrh*) *MRS*: "Because of (*mpny*) the glory of Israel it attained temporary sovereignty (*mlkwt*)."

In describing other kingdoms, Scripture compares them only to cedars, as it is said, "Behold, the Assyrian was a cedar in Lebanon" etc. (Ezek. 31:3), and it says, "Yet destroyed I the Amorite before them, whose height was like the height of the cedars" (Amos 2:9), and it says, "The tree that thou sawest" etc. (Dan. 4:17); but in describing the Egyptians, Scripture compares them only to stubble, as it is said, "It consumeth them as stubble."

In describing other kingdoms, Scripture compares them only to silver and gold, as it is said, "As for that image, its head was of fine gold" (etc.) (Dan. 2:32); but in describing the Egyptians, Scripture compares them only to lead, as it is said, "They sank as lead" (Exod. 15:10).

In describing other kingdoms, Scripture compares them

With the Mekilta statement here cf. Be-Shallaḥ, II (I, 196 f.). In this Mekilta statement (as well as in similar ones elsewhere in the Midrash; cf., for example, *Lam. R.* on 1:5, ed. Buber, 33a), what we meet is the pathos of self comfort of a small and defeated people; not by mean or average powers is Israel overcome, only by world empires. "Temporary eminence" refers to the period while Israel was in bondage to Egypt. See also Ginzberg, *Legends*, VI, 3, n. 15.

in describing . . . The Mekilta now proceeds to amplify on the disparagement of the Egyptians—"no more abject a kingdom than Egypt"—by offering three (possibly four; see below, s.v. "Antoninus") examples of expressions which serve as comparisons of Egypt with other *world* powers.

In *MRS* the order is "lead," "foxes," "stubble." In *Cant. R.* 2:15, 18c, we get four comparisons, three of which are the same as those in the Mekilta, and the fourth being what is essentially the Mekilta comment with the Isaiah proof-text.

other kingdoms, Scripture compares them only ʾt hmlkywt ʾynw mwšln lP; MRS: mlkywt mwšln. Note also the reading in each of the following comparisons.

as it is said MRS quotes its proof-texts in this whole section without any introductory formula; moreover (p. 87), after the Ezekiel proof-text, it quotes first the Daniel verse and then the verse from Amos.

"The tree that thou sawest" etc. Though the verse does not literally and specifically mention the cedar, note the splendor of the description and compare this with the other proof-texts.

In describing MRS (p. 86), kšhwʾ, while our Mekilta reads, wkšhwʾ; and so too in the next comparison.

compares them only to lead And these were the best of them! Cf. above, 5, p. 145.

only to the mighty beasts, as it is said, "And four great beasts" etc. (Dan. 7:3); but in describing the Egyptians, Scripture compares them only to foxes, as it is said, "Take us the foxes" (Cant. 2:15).

Antoninus asked our sainted Rabbi: "I am eager to go down to Alexandria; but will it perhaps raise some monarch against me who will conquer me?"

Said Rabbi to him: "This I do not know. At all events, for us it is written that the land of Egypt will be unable to raise up either ruler or prince, as it is said, 'And there shall be no more a prince out of the land of Egypt' (Ezek. 30:13), 'It shall be the lowliest of the kingdoms' etc." (Ezek. 29:15).

AND AT THE BLAST OF THY NOSTRILS THE WATERS NᶜRMW (GREW CUNNING): In the very measure they adopted, Thou didst mete it out to them. They said, "Come now, let us

---

mighty beasts The beasts in Daniel!

"foxes" The *little* foxes (cf. Cant. 2:15, the verse quoted in text), and not just foxes!

For the equation of these foxes with Egypt, cf. B. Soṭah 12a; *Cant. R.*, 2:15, 18c; *Exod. R.* 22:1; *Seder Eliyahu R.*, ed. Friedmann (Jerusalem, 5720), p. 43; note also *Agadat Shir ha-Shirim,* ed. Schechter (Cambridge, 1896), p. 32, 108 f.; *Midrash Shir ha-Shirim,* ed. Grünhut, 25b; Rashi on the verse. But all these seem to me *attempts* to recapture some early midrashic notion, no longer evident; observe how *Lekaḥ Tob* (ed. Greenup [London, 1909], p. 46) tries to explain the comparison, ignoring the "explanation" of *Exod. R.* 22:1. Significantly, the Mekilta too (a tannaite midrash!) feels no need to explain the proof-text.

However, see *Yalkut* on Ps. 63:11, statement of R. Samuel bar Naḥmani and cf. R. Berekiah in *Exod. R.* 22:1. The vineyards of Cant. 2:15 are of course Israel; cf. Isa. 5:1 ff., and Pisḥa, 1 (I, 15).

Antoninus asked . . . This passage is not in *MRS*. Note that in *MhG, Exod.,* p. 299, where this story is repeated, the compiler seems no longer to get the point, for this is how he reproduces Antoninus's question: "If *someone* wishes to go down to Alexandria *of Egypt,* will some king rise and conquer him?"

In this exchange between Antoninus and Rabbi (Judah the Prince), once again we have a disparagement (the fourth? Cf. above, s.v. "in describing") and scorn of Egypt.

On Antoninus and Rabbi, cf. above, 2, p. 104 f. and notes, ad loc., s.v. "Antoninus" and "Our sainted Rabbi."

In the very measure . . . We have here finally the seventh example of the measure-for-measure discussion; see above, 5, p. 143, and 4, p. 135, s.v. "They said."

deal shrewdly with them" (Exod. 1:10); in turn Thou didst
put cunning into the waters, and the waters inflicted upon
them all kinds of disasters. That is why it is said, "And at
the blast of Thy nostrils the waters grew cunning."

Another interpretation of AND AT THE BLAST OF THY
NOSTRILS THE WATERS N῾RMW (PILED UP): He made them to
rise heaplike.

THEY STOOD UPRIGHT AS A WATER BOTTLE: Even as it is with
a water bottle, when it is tied tight, nothing escapes and

put cunning into the waters Cf. also Tg Onkelos on the verse.
Despite the homiletic interpretation, the problem before the Midrash
is a real one: What can n῾rmw mean in connection with water (note
indeed that in Scripture the *verb* seems to occur only here in the
sense of "heap up")? Hence the comment that a "pun" is intended,
and the verb is associated with ῾rwm, cunning. Cf. Ginzberg, *Legends,*
VI, 10, n. 52.

Our Mekilta reads *bmym* (into the waters), while *MRS* reads,
lmym.

and the waters inflicted . . . it is said None of this in *MRS,* though
it repeats the verse which follows.

There is a constant tradition to the effect that not only were the
Egyptians finally drowned in the sea, but first they were there subjected to all manner of torments; cf. *ARNA,* p. 95, and *ARNB,* p.
94. Note also *Memar Marqah* 1:11 (II, 43): "Ten times the Egyptians
were slain in the sea, because they did not believe in the ten miracles.
. . . Ten times they disbelieved in Egypt and ten times they were
slain in the sea . . ."

Another interpretation . . . heaplike Not in *MRS.* Cf. Tg Jon. on
the verse; see also Be-Shallaḥ, v (I, 224).

We might, I suppose, see in this comment a literal, as it were
natural, interpretation. On the other hand, it seems to me that the
point being made by the Midrash is akin to that expressed in *Memar
Marqah* 2:9 (II, 69): "God reversed the natural laws of the world in
all places for the sake of Israel. The natural flow of water is in a
downward direction, but in the Red Sea He made it go upward—*For
the waters piled up,* like a mountain of rivers, just like great mountains, to prepare a pathway for Israel to walk on." See also, ibid. 2:3
(II, 51) and 2:8 (II, 65). Note also the miraculous element spoken of
by *Sekel Tob,* p. 194.

THEY STOOD UPRIGHT AS A WATER BOTTLE The two
interpretations which follow are given in reverse order in *MRS.*

On "water bottle," see also Be-Shallaḥ, v (I, 224). On the biblical
word *nd,* cf. Cross and Freedman, in *JNES,* XIV, 246, n. 21. Note also
Barhebraeus, p. 121 (and p. 120 n.f.).

water bottle, when it is tied tight *nd ṣrwr; MRS, nd* (and note
vocalization, ibid.) *ṣrwr w῾wmd.* Observe that although the verse

nothing gets in, so was it with the appetite of the Egyptians,
it was tied up inside them; meanwhile Israel ate and drank
and rejoiced—for them, from the very midst of salt waters,
sources of sweet water issued forth, as it is said, "And He
brought forth flowing streams" (Ps. 78:16): for "flowing
streams" is nothing other than a reference to fresh water,
even as it is said, "A fountain of gardens, a well of fresh
water and flowing streams" (Cant. 4:15), and it says, "Drink

---

speaks of the *waters* standing like a *nd*, the Midrash makes the
Egyptians the subject. See further below, s.v. "it was tied up inside
them." *Sekel Tob,* p. 204, reads: " 'They stood upright as a *nd*,' that
is to say, they stood upright like a water bottle in (the midst of) flowing streams."

the appetite On *npš* = appetite, cf. Isa. 5:14 and Prov. 23:2; see
also below, 7, p. 181.

it was tied up inside them *ṣrwrh bhm; MRS, ṣrwrh wᶜwmdt,* and
adds after this, "and they could neither take in nor eliminate" (on
the spelling, cf. critical apparatus, ad loc.); see Lauterbach's critical
apparatus and cf. the reading in HR, p. 138.

The Mekilta is obviously commenting on the expression "standing
upright like a *nd*," and it equates *nd* (note how Tg Onkelos, Rashi,
Ibn Ezra, LXX, and the new JPS translation explain) with *nᵓd* (cf.
Tg Jon.) a wineskin, water bottle. Perhaps the Mekilta does not take
nd in the sense of "heap," or "wall," because that would be merely
a repetition of "At the breath of Thy nostrils the waters were piled
up." (For other midrashic interpretations of *nd-nᵓd* of this verse,
cf., e.g., *ARNA,* p. 97; *Midrash Psalms* 114, p. 237b, and see further
references in *Midrash Psalms.*)

The following seems to be the meaning of the present comment:
Like a water bottle or flask when it is tightly sealed and nothing
can come in or get out, so it was with the Egyptians: their appetite
was completely imprisoned in them; that is, though they might desire
to enjoy food, they were unable to (sickened by salt water?), in contrast to Israel, who could eat and drink with gusto.

sources *zkry; MRS, zkrwn.* Cf. Kasher, XIV, 126, note on no. 124.

issued forth *yṣᵓw; MRS, wywṣᵓ.*

as it is said *MRS:* "even as it is said."

"He brought forth flowing streams" Cf. Be-Shallaḥ, v (I, 224). Note
indeed that Ps. 78:16 is speaking of the exodus. Our Midrash therefore interprets the clause in Exod. 15:8 as follows: The Egyptians
were like a *nᵓd* in the very midst of flowing (= sweet) waters (which
only Israel could enjoy). See above, the *Sekel Tob* quotation, s.v.
"water bottle, when it is tied tight."

for . . . is nothing other than *wᵓyn; MRS, ᵓyn.*

even as it is said *MRS:* "as it is said."

and it says . . . *MRS* does not quote this verse; *Lekaḥ Tob* 48a

waters out of thine own cistern, and flowing streams out of
thine own well" (Prov. 5:15).

Another interpretation of THEY STOOD UPRIGHT AS A
WATER BOTTLE: Even as it is with a water bottle, when it is
full and tied tight, nothing escapes and nothing gets in,
so was it with the breathing of the Egyptians, it was tied
up inside them, and overcome by the stench of the Sea,
they could neither exhale nor inhale, as it is said, "He
maketh the deep to boil and stink" (Job 41:23); meanwhile,

---

does. On the verses cited by our Mekilta, see also Be-Shallaḥ, v (I,
225). What the Proverbs verse establishes is that "flowing streams"
equals drinkable water.

full and tied tight ṣrwr ʿwmd (cf. M. ʿEduyyot 5:1, end); MRS,
ṣrwr wʿmwd. See Albeck, in his edition of the Mishnah (Jerusalem-Tel
Aviv, 1953), pp. 304 and 482, as well as Hoffmann, in his edition
(Berlin, 1924), pp. 284 f.

nothing escapes . . . gets in Not in MRS. Cf. below, s.v. "they
could neither exhale nor inhale."

**so was it with the breathing of the Egyptians, it was tied up inside
them** MRS: "So were the Egyptians tied tight and ʿwmdyn (immov-
able?)."

The Hebrew term for "the breathing" is npš, which in the first
comment stood for "appetite." As the Midrash goes on to say, the
stench from (the salt waters of) the sea caused the Egyptians to pass
out. See further below, s.v. "He maketh the deep to . . . stink."

and overcome mʿwlpym; MRS, whyw mtʿlpyn.

they could neither exhale nor inhale Not in MRS; cf. above, s.v.
"Nothing escapes and nothing gets in."

"He maketh the deep to . . . stink" While for the Egyptians God
made the deep (cf. Exod. 15:5b, They went down into the depths) to
boil and set off bad smells (cf. Jastrow, p. 1026, s.v. sry II), for the
Hebrews He made the Sea like a pleasant ointment; note how the
Mekilta continues. Thus the first half of the proof-text is applied
to one group, and the second half to the other—again, typically midrashic.

The notion in our passage seems to belong to the view that for the
righteous there is available a sweet fragrance even in the midst of
badly smelling surroundings; see, for example, the observation in
regard to Joseph in Be-Shallaḥ, vi (I, 235), and cf. the statement in
the name of Abba bar Kahana in Gen. R. 84:17, p. 1021. Cf. the citation from Yalkut Maʿayan Gannim and comment in Kasher, vi, 1422,
to no. 151.

The picture of the Israelites now eating with gusto and inhaling
perfumes is intended to suggest how the former slaves now enjoy
masters' life, and how former masters are reduced to slavelike existence.

for Israel the Sea became like spices of all kinds, as it is said, "He maketh the Sea like unto a compound of spices" (Job 41:23); it says also, "Awake, O north wind; and come, thou south; blow upon My garden, that the spices thereof may flow out" (Cant. 4:16).

THE DEEPS WERE CONGEALED ($qp^{\jmath}w$): He made them into a kind of cupola ($qwph$).

IN THE HEART OF THE SEA: Where is a man's heart located? Two-thirds of the way up. So He congealed the Sea about them to two-thirds of its depth.

"that the spices . . . may flow out" Note the verb, associated of course with *nzlym*, "the floods, the flowing streams" of Exod. 15:8.

He made . . . cupola Cf. *AhB*, I, 21 f. This comment does not occur in *MRS*.

By condensing, congealing ($qp^{\jmath}$) the waters (note how *LXX* translates *thmt*) and forming them into a kind of dome or cupola ($qwph$; note also the reading *kyph* in Lauterbach's critical apparatus; cf. Be-Shallaḥ, v [I, 223]) over Israel's heads, God protected them from sunstroke. The view here is like that attributed to R. Eliezer in *ARNA*, p. 98, where one reads: "And the clouds of glory were over them, so that they would be unaffected by the sun; and so Israel passed through (the Sea) without distress. Rabbi Eliezer says: He formed the deep as a dome (*kph;* but cf. the reading in Schechter's n. 27, ibid.) on high over them, and under it Israel moved forward without distress." Contrast Rashi on our verse.

IN THE HEART OF THE SEA In the course of explaining the expression *heart* of the Sea (note, for example, the explanations of *LXX*, Tg Jonathan, Rashi), the Mekilta suggests still another interpretation of the congealing of the waters of the deep: that is, since a man's heart is located two-thirds of the way up his body from the soles of his feet, the Sea was congealed to that depth when the Egyptians stepped into the water, and this was one of the forms of punishment inflicted upon them. Indeed, *MRS* (p. 87) adds here, "in order to destroy them" (this does not occur ibid., p. 235). On the other hand, cf. *Sekel Tob*, p. 194, bottom line, which I do not entirely understand. The view expressed by the Mekilta here does not seem to me to be the same as in Be-Shallaḥ, v (I, 224). On the location of the heart, see also Wa-Yassaʿ, IV (II, 108).

Where is *hyʾk; MRS, hykn.*

Two thirds of the way up *mšny ḥlqym wlmʿln* (note the reading in *AhB*, I, 22, top line); *MRS, ʿl šny ḥlqym.*

So He congealed the Sea about them *MRS:* "So the waters of (the) Sea congealed about them."

to two-thirds of its depth *MRS* adds, "in order to destroy them"; cf. above, s.v. "In the heart of the Sea."

(At first) the Sea
Had had no heart, and then was given a heart,

as it is said, "In the heart of the Sea."

(At first) the Terebinth
Had had no heart, and then was given a heart,

as it is said, "While he was yet alive in the heart of the
terebinth" (II Sam. 18:14).

(At first) the Heavens
Had had no heart, and then were given a heart,

as it is said, "And the mountain burned with fire unto the
heart of heaven" (Deut. 4:11).

Come, O Sea
That (first) had had no heart, and to whom was given
a heart,
Punish the Egyptians
Who had a heart (at first)
But enslaved the Israelites
In all calamitous ways,

as it is said, "The Egyptians imposed tasks upon the Israelites ruthlessly" (etc.) (Exod. 1:13 f.).

(At first) the Sea . . . Now follows another comment on the expression "heart of the Sea," the Midrash being particularly impressed by
the figure of speech (heart, it should be recalled, is what we in our
idiom would refer to as mind). What we get now is a kind of poem
of three stanzas and two parts; cf. the similar pattern below, end of
7, p. 187 f.; end of 9, p. 228 ff.; 10, p. 233 f. On this poetic pattern see
also Mirsky, p. 44.

In MRS the words "Sea," "Terebinth," and "Heavens" appear
without the definite article.

In the poem manifestly an aspect of measure for measure is being
formulated.

the Terebinth Note the spelling אֵלָה in MRS.

Punish the Egyptians who had a heart (at first) But enslaved the
Israelites In all calamitous ways MRS: "Punish the Egyptians who
battled against Israel in all calamitous ways." (On the comments in
GS, I, 353, n. 26, cf. the variant reading in the critical apparatus of
MRS, p. 87.) See further, next note.

as it is said, "The Egyptians . . . ruthlessly" While the general
sense of this verse is of course appropriate to our subject, what has it

Come, Terebinth,
That (first) had had no heart, and to whom was given
    a heart,
    Punish Absalom
Who had a heart (at first)
But stole—three thefts!—
His father's heart,
        the supreme court's heart,
            the heart of Israel's men,

as it is said, "And Absalom stole the hearts of the men of
Israel" (II Sam. 15:6).

Come, Heavens,
That (first) had had no heart, and to whom was given
    a heart,
    Shower manna like dew for Israel
Who had a heart (at first),
Received the Torah
And served the Name

---

to do with *lb*, "heart"? The other examples of our Mekilta, as the
poem continues, are certainly more to the point. Note indeed that
MRS offers here no verse at all (nor in connection with Absalom).

It may be therefore that the proof-text lies not so much in Exod.
1:13 as in Exod. 1:14, "And they made their lives bitter with hard
service, in mortar and in brick (*lbnym*) . . . wherein they made them
serve with rigor (*bprk*)"; and the Midrash would then be indulging
in a play on the words *lb* and *lbnym* ("heart" and "bricks")—and
perhaps also there is a play on *bprk*, explained as *bkl . . . pwrᶜnywt*
("all calamitous ways").

Absalom Who had a heart *MRS* omits "who had a heart."

three thefts!—His father's . . . Cf. Neziqin, XIII (III, 105). On
Absalom's three thefts, cf. II Sam. 15 and Albeck's commentary on
M. Soṭah 1:8 (but perhaps in connection with the supreme court's
heart, II Sam. 15:4 is more apt; cf. *Num. R.* 9:24, 30b, and Rashi in
B. Soṭah 9b).

the heart of Israel's men Note the direct appropriation of the
biblical expression.

as it is said, "And Absalom . . ." *MRS* does not quote the verse;
cf. above, s.v. "as it is said, "The Egyptians . . . ruthlessly.""

like dew Not in *MRS;* the expression "like dew for Israel" is an
echo of Hos. 14:6.

with all their heart
and all their soul

as it is said, "And thou shalt love the Lord thy God with
all thy heart, and with all thy soul" etc. (Deut. 6:5).

And not only the heavens rejoiced at the redemption of
Israel, but the mountains too and all the hills, fruit trees,
and every cedar, as it is said, "Sing, O ye heavens, for the
Lord hath done it; shout, ye lowest parts of the earth;
break forth into singing, ye mountains, O forest, and every
tree therein" (Isa. 44:23). And why? "For the Lord hath
redeemed Jacob, and doth glorify Himself in Israel" (ibid.);

for Israel Who had a heart (at first), Received the Torah And
served the Name with all their heart and all their soul MRS: "For
Israel who received the (ʔt) Torah which was given to (ʕl) the heart."
In GS, I, 353, there is a reading "who heard the Torah," but I do not
find a record of this in any of the variant readings in MRS or in our
Mekilta, ed. Lauterbach, or HR.

On "And served the Name," note the variant readings in the
critical apparatus of ed. Lauterbach and HR; see also L. Finkelstein,
in Proceedings, AAJR, v (1934), 19. As already noted, the clause does
not occur in MRS, which also quotes Deut. 6:6 rather than 6:5 as
proof-text (6:6 obviously is apt for "given to [upon] the heart").

Is "Received the Torah And served the Name" an echo of the
phrase "For the Torah and for the Temple service" in, e.g., M. Yoma
7:1 or the blessing after the prophetic reading (cf. Baer, p. 228)?

as it is said MRS has no introductory formula for its proof-text,
Deut. 6:6; cf. preceding note.

And not only . . . This is really a supplementary statement (note,
for example, that MhG, Exod., p. 300, does not have it), a lyrical
exclamation brought on by the preceding statement on the heavens;
and the note of redemption it strikes makes a beautiful peroration to
the chapter. Cf. also end of chap. 1 (above, p. 86 f.) for a similar quality.
For a similar "note" of jubilation, cf. Sifre Deut. 333, p. 382, and at
greater length, Mid. Tan., pp. 203 f. Such a note at this point is
possibly not accidental. Exod. 15:1 had closed on the words "(Moses
and Israel) spoke, saying," and 15:2 began with "I will sing unto the
Lord." In Exod. 15:9, immediately after the verse we have now had
comment on, we read of what "the enemy said"; before we hear what
the foe had to say, the exclamation of joy at Israel's redemption is
sounded.

rejoiced śmḥym; MRS, hyw śmḥym.

but the mountains . . . and every cedar Note the appropriation of
the idiom of Ps. 148:9. MRS does not read "fruit trees and every
cedar"; for "all the hills" it reads wkl hgbʕwt.

and it says, "Sing, O heavens, and be joyful, O earth" (etc.) (Isa. 49:13).

And why I.e. why such "excessive" rejoicing? *MRS* does not have this interrogation.

"Sing, O heavens . . . O earth" Note indeed how Isa. 49:13 concludes: "For the Lord hath comforted His people, and hath compassion upon His afflicted"—the ultimate redemption! Cf. the reading in HR, ad loc.

7. The Enemy Said

THE ENEMY SAID: This should have been the beginning of the pericope; why then was it written at this point? For in the Torah there is no strict sequence of earlier and later.

This should have . . . pericope That is, since the preceding verses report that the Egyptians had already been drowned and destroyed, obviously what "the enemy said" or thought to do should have been put in the beginning. Note Naḥmanides on the verse who calls attention to the fact that Tg Onkelos (for that matter, cf. Tg Jon. as well) is sensitive to this and therefore translates the biblical clause with the pluperfect, "For the enemy had said . . ." Cf. *Memar Marqah* 2:7 (II, 57): "There is a problem involved here, about which we ask the Elders of the people who were gathered together to receive knowledge of the wonders which God did in Egypt through Moses His servant. These were prior to the wonders done in the Red Sea in Egypt in the presence of Israel. Why should the wonders done in the Red Sea precede the wonders done in Egypt in this Song?" See Macdonald's n. 51, ibid.

zh hyh tḥlt hprš does not mean that this actually was the beginning, but that logically this should have been the beginning; cf. the idiom in *Eccl. R.* 1:12 (5b), *zh hyh rᵓwy lhywt tḥlt hšyrh;* i.e. this should have come first in the Song.

why then . . . at this point MRS does not have the interrogation, neither at this point nor through the remainder of the comment.

For in the Torah . . . and later This seems to be a principle of R. Ishmael's; note the reading in *Eccl. R.* 1:12 (5b), and cf. Bacher, *EM*, pp. 114 f.; *AhT*, II, 7; Epstein, *Meboᵓot*, pp. 555 ff. (and spec. p. 557). R. Ishmael seems to hold that the order of biblical verses and sections is not a final criterion of the chronology, for the biblical material may have been arranged along other than chronological principles. And by bringing a number of examples here, seven of them including our verse, the Mekilta is in a sense demonstrating that the phenomenon is observable not only in our passage but throughout Scripture ("the Torah" here refers to all parts of Scripture, not

It is the same with "And it came to pass on the eighth day, that Moses called" etc. (Lev. 9:1): this should have been the beginning of "the book"; why then was it written at this point? For in the Torah there is no strict sequence of earlier and later.

It is the same with "In the year that king Uzziah died" etc. (Isa. 6:1): this should have been the beginning of the book; why then was it written at this point? Because in the Torah there is no strict sequence of earlier and later.

It is the same with "Son of man, stand upon thy feet" (Ezek. 2:1)— According to some: "Son of man, put forth a

---

just the Pentateuch). See also *Sifre Num.* 64, p. 61, and *Eccl. R.*, 1:12, for still other examples.

It is the same with Cf. above, 6, s.v. "the same." *MRS* reads throughout our passage, "You say the same."

"And it came to pass" . . . **"the book"** Lit., ". . . the beginning of the pericope," but *pršh* here surely stands for "the book," as *MRS* does read here and our Mekilta also in all the following examples.

Once the Tabernacle (the Tent of Meeting) had been set up, Aaron and his sons had to function there, not Moses. Now, according to Exod. 40:2 the Tabernacle was set up on the first day of the first month (of the second year), which would be taken to mean the first of Nisan. When Lev. 9:1 therefore speaks of the "eighth day," the Rabbis interpret this as the eighth day of "consecration" (equals Nisan 1). If then this is the beginning of activity in the Tabernacle, why should Lev. 1, which reports God's speaking to Moses from the Tabernacle, have been put before Lev. 9:1? Cf. Tg Jon on Lev. 9:1.

"In the year that king Uzziah died" From Isa. 6:1 one would get the impression that it was then that Isaiah's ministry began; why then should not this chapter open the Book? Interestingly, this view is shared by many modern critics; cf. Pfeiffer, p. 422; on the other hand, cf. J. Milgrom, "Did Isaiah Prophesy during the Reign of Uzziah," in *VT*, XIV (1964), 164–82.

"Son of man, stand upon thy feet" Note that the example from Ezekiel precedes the one from Jeremiah; but *MRS* cites the Jeremiah passage first, and the same is true in *Eccl. R.* 1:12. In B. Baba Batra 14b too, where the order of the prophetic books is given, Jeremiah precedes Ezekiel.

The assumption seems to be this: Ezek. 1:2 reports that the vision or message of chapter 1 came in the fifth year of king Jehoiachin's captivity. But Ezekiel began to prophesy before then. See also, next note.

According to some . . . "a riddle" Note that uncertainty is really reflected on how to date Ezekiel's prophecies. Presumably this

riddle" (Ezek. 17:2): this should have been the beginning of the book; why then was it written at this point? Because in the Torah there is no strict sequence of earlier and later.

It is the same with "Go and cry in the ears of Jerusalem" etc. (Jer. 2:2): this should have been the beginning of the book; why then was it written at this point? Because in the Torah there is no strict sequence of earlier and later.

It is the same with "Israel was a luxuriant vine" (Hos. 10:1): this should have been the beginning of the book; why then was it written at this point? Because in the Torah there is no strict sequence of earlier and later.

It is the same with "I Koheleth have been king" etc. (Eccl. 1:12): this should have been the beginning of the book; why then was it written at this point? Because in the Torah there is no strict sequence of earlier and later.

---

prophecy was delivered *immediately* after Jehoiachin's captivity; but the first chapter was in the *fifth year* of that captivity! (So Z. Einhorn —MHRZW—in *Eccl. R.*, 1:12, and cf. Qimḥi on Ezek. 17:12 f. and 17:4.)

Because in the Torah . . . and later Note that in its fourth, fifth, and sixth examples, *MRS* simply begins this formula but does not bother to complete it.

"Go and cry in the ears of Jerusalem . . ." Jeremiah was one of the Anatot priests (Jer. 1:1); hence first the book should have reported that he had been instructed to go to Jerusalem, and only then should his other prophecies appear (MHRZW in *Eccl. R.*). Perhaps there may be some significance to the fact that the opening clause of Jer. 2:2 is wanting in *LXX*.

"Israel was a luxuriant vine" Cf. Rashi and Qimḥi on Hos. 1:2. Why Hos. 10:1 should have been the beginning of the book is not clear to me. Is it because 10:3 reports, "Surely now shall they say: We have no king," and this would be taken to reflect premonarchic times? *ZY:* " 'Israel was a luxuriant vine' is the beginning of Hosea's prophecy because there (the prophet) reproves Israel for the idolatry of which they were guilty before they were exiled, and the remaining prophecies (were delivered) after they were exiled, (and they refer also) to the redemption."

"I Koheleth have been king" In the following verses Koheleth goes on to say that he began to explore and *then* found that everything was vanity; before he began to explore, how could he know this? Why then the first eleven verses of the book before what follows in the text (MHRZW)? *SY* suggests more or less the same thought. Perhaps in this context it might be better even to translate the verse, "I Koheleth *had* been king."

THE ENEMY SAID, to wit, Pharaoh. But how could Israel know what Pharaoh, in Egypt, was contemplating against them? However, it was by means of the Holy Spirit which came to rest upon them that they knew what Pharaoh, in Egypt, was contemplating against them:

When Pharaoh realized that Israel had gone off, he said: "It may not be worth our while to pursue Israel, but for the sake of the silver and gold they took from us, it certainly is worth it!"

When some of the populace, who had lost only a little

THE ENEMY SAID, To Wit, Pharaoh *MRS:* "Another interpretation: 'The enemy said': But how could Israel know . . ."—*wky mʾyn yśʾ . . . prʿh mḥšb . . .*

Cf. above, 5, s.v. "To wit, Pharaoh." The Midrash at this point is not so much concerned with the explanation of "enemy" = Pharaoh, as with the thought of how Israel could know what Pharaoh in Egypt was contemplating against them. Note indeed the reading of *MRS*. But obviously the present comment depends on the interpretation of enemy = Pharaoh, and not on enemy = Esau; cf. above, 5, loc. cit.

by means of the Holy Spirit which came to rest upon them *MRS* (p. 88) puts first the predicate and then the subject; cf. the reading in *AhB*, I, 22. In *MRS*, p. 235, we read: "But how did Israel know that Pharaoh was contemplating such things (*kk*) against them? However, they heard it from the mouth of the Almighty. This informs you (*lhwdyʿk*) that the Holy Spirit came to rest on all of them." On the Holy Spirit resting upon Israel at the Reed Sea, cf. Be-Shallaḥ, III (I, 210), and also above, 1, p. 77.

Since the Mekilta commentary on the Shirah is so constantly preoccupied with the ultimate redemption too, it may be that the thought here is subconsciously associated with Joel 3:1 ff.; and note Joel 3:3, which speaks of "blood, and fire, and pillars of smoke," with which compare the *Passover Haggadah* (ed. Goldschmidt [Jerusalem, 1960], p. 122).

Pharaoh . . . was contemplating Here too *MRS* reads *mḥšb* (where our Mekilta reads *ḥšb*).

When Pharaoh realized . . . "may not be worth our while" *MRS:* "What did Pharaoh say to his troops? He said to them: Even if we pursue Israel for no reason other than the (recovery of the) silver and gold they took away from us" (lit. "they made us lose"), "it is worth it to us."

The Mekilta and *MRS* are telling us what Pharaoh was contemplating in Egypt and what Israel perceived by means of the Holy Spirit. And the commentary will gradually move on to explain the remainder of the verse, "I will pursue, I will overtake, I will divide the spoil . . ."

wealth, realized it, they said: "Oh, let it go! Why pursue
Israel?"

When Pharaoh perceived this, he said: "It's share and

who had lost . . . wealth When they were stripped by the Israelites
(Exod. 12:35 f.). Our Midrash here describes the two different reactions in Egypt when the exodus occurred: Pharaoh reacted one way
(and presumably this was also true of his nobles); "some of" the
Egyptians (and presumably this is the mass of the poor) reacted
another way: they felt there was little to gain and much (their lives!)
to lose. In the touch of realism there is doubtless a good deal of
anachronism, the Rabbis reading back into the past the kind of
popular sentiments one might have encountered in Hellenistic times,
when plans for military campaigns were undertaken. That a king who
did not keep his forces happy could lose them, we see in I Mac. 11:38
and Josephus, *Antiquities*, XIII, 4:9 (Loeb, VII, 289 f.). Note E. Bickerman (Bikerman), *Institutions des Séleucides* (Paris, 1938), p. 73, "On
pouvait s'assurer les secours des villes et des dynastes et des peuples
indigènes au moyen de privilèges et d'exhortations." See further on
this subject, Bickerman, pp. 77 f. (I am indebted to my former colleague, the late Professor C. Bradford Welles, for the Bickerman reference, to which in turn I owe the reference to the I Mac. and *Antiquities* passages.)

When . . . populace . . . realized Lit., "saw," and so too above;
MRS: "heard."

Note by the way the reiteration of "when," *kywn*, for narrative
effect, in our passage.

As for "some of the populace," this seems to be an echo of the
notion that there were different groups and attitudes among the
Egyptians; cf. Be-Shallaḥ, VI (I, 242), and above, 5, p. 144, and the
note, ad loc., s.v. "This was an intermediate punishment." Our
Midrash is reporting here that those who were reluctant to pursue
Israel felt that the possible gain was hardly worth it. See further,
next note.

"Oh, let it go" *wwtrh* (cf. L. Finkelstein, in *Proceedings, AAJR*, V,
11); *MRS*, p. 89: *hꜣ ꜣtyrꜣ* (but cf. critical apparatus, ad loc.). This
seems to be a colloquial exclamation, something like the Americanism,
"Oh, to heck with it, it's hardly worth it." Note also the reading in
Sifre Deut., 1, p. 6. And see now S. Lieberman, in *TK*, VII, 588 (and
E. Y. Kutscher, in *Lešonenu*, XXXII [1967–68], 116 [suppl. note to
p. 106]).

Is there perhaps in the exclamation *wwtrh* something of an apolo-
getic note too, that Israel did not despoil the Egyptians of much after
all?

"Why pursue Israel" *MRS:* "Let's not pursue Israel."

When Pharaoh perceived this Instead of this clause, *MRS* reads,
"Another interpretation."

share alike in the loot!"—as it is said, "I will divide the
spoil" (Exod. 15:9). "And what's more, I shall open up to
you the treasury vaults of silver and gold, and distribute to
you precious stones and pearls."—

Another interpretation of THE ENEMY SAID: That is
Pharaoh, and he never grasped what he was saying! "The
designs of the heart are man's, but the slip of the tongue
is from the Lord" (Prov. 16:1). It is not written here, "We
will pursue, we will overtake, we will divide," but, "I will
pursue, I will overtake, I will divide," (that is,) I will be

"share . . . in the loot" Although normally the monarch takes the
lion's share. Cf. Be-Shallaḥ, II (I, 200).

The Midrash seems to reflect here on the conduct of tyrants. That
is to say, perhaps the Egyptian people would not have been hostile to
Israel if the Pharaoh had not goaded them on; and to have his way
the Pharaoh is even prepared to bribe his own people with all kinds
of excessive promises. In the end they suffer only because of him.
See also below, p. 186, s.v. "Oh! All those thousands . . ."

"I will divide the spoil" That is, not keep all of it myself. MRS puts
this proof-text at the end of Pharaoh's address.

"And what's more . . ." If sharing spoils is an insufficient induce-
ment, there are extra rewards, his own treasuries, which ordinarily he
keeps for himself.

"I shall open up . . ." MRS: "I shall open up to you the treasury
vaults and distribute to you silver . . . pearls, as it is said, 'I will
divide the spoil.' "

"silver . . . gold . . . precious stones . . . pearls" Cf. above, 2,
p. 92. Pharaoh's address to his troops is resumed below; see the
note s.v. "In the past when you plundered."

THE ENEMY SAID: . . . "Pharaoh" Not in MRS, which reads
simply, "Another interpretation: Pharaoh said . . ."

ENEMY SAID . . . what he was saying See this formula also in
Be-Shallaḥ, II (I, 191). Note the idiom below, at the beginning of 10,
p. 231, as well.

"the slip of the tongue . . . Lord" And the slip of the tongue often
foretells accurately what will happen. Cf. Heinemann, p. 130.

It is not written MRS: "He (or, it) did not say here, 'We will
pursue, we will overtake,' but 'I will pursue, I will overtake,' (that
is,) by them he shall be pursued, by their hand shall he be captured."

"We will pursue . . ." Had Pharaoh used the plural form, he
would have indicated that in truth he was going to share equally
with his troops. Instead, however, he used the verbs in the singular,
I will pursue, etc. The Midrash is calling attention, I believe, to the
accumulation of verbs all in the first person singular, and the hybris
this reflects. See further, next note.

pursued, I will be overtaken—by them I shall be pursued,

I will be pursued . . . overtaken I.e., instead of reading the consonants of these verbs (ʾrdp; ʾśyg) as imperfect active (ʾerdof; ʾassig), read them as imperfect passive (ʾeradef; ʾussag). Note the punctuation of the text in *Midrash Psalms* 27:3, 112b, and cf. Buber's n. 29.

What is not clear however is this: If by a slight vowel change the verbs in the first person singular active can be read as passive, why would not the same apply to the first person plural (reading, for instance, *neradef* instead of *nirdof*)?

(According to *SY*, the consonants of the verb in the singular, ʾrdp, can be read midrashically as "I will be *rdwp*"; but in the plural one would have to say, "We shall be *rdwpym*," and for that there are not enough consonants in ʾrdp.)

Despite the difficulty at this point, it seems to me that the Midrash is driving at the following: by a slip of the tongue Pharaoh kept speaking in the first person singular because subconsciously he recognized that despite his promises he would be unable to share booty with his troops, for he would be not a victor but a victim, he would have nothing to share. Moreover, he was probably a liar, he would probably never share a thing.

Philo too comments on the active-passive forms of the verb, and perhaps in some remote way our Midrash may be referring to the same thought. "We read of [Pharaoh] who crowns his self-love with madness, and declares that, though what I have be taken from me, I will contend for it as my own and win the victory. 'I will pursue,' he says, 'I will overtake, I will divide the spoil; I will satisfy my soul; I will destroy with my sword; my hand shall have the mastery.' To such a one I would say, 'Fool, is it hidden from you that every created being, who thinks he pursues, is pursued?' For maladies and old age and death, with all the other host of evils voluntary and involuntary, drive and hustle and pursue each one of us, and he who thinks to overtake and conquer is overtaken and conquered, and many a one who thinks to spoil and is already in his thoughts parcelling out the booty has fallen under the foot of victorious enemies. He receives into his soul emptiness for satisfaction, slavery for lordship, he is killed instead of killing, and all that he thought to do to others falls with full measure upon himself. For in very truth this man was the enemy of convincing reason and of nature herself, when he took to himself all active functions and forgot the passive, as though he was secure from the mass of calamities which these severally bring. For it was 'the enemy,' as we read, who said 'I will pursue and overtake.' What deadlier foe to the soul can there be than he who in his vainglory claims to himself that which belongs to God alone? For it belongs to God to act, and this we may not ascribe to any created being" (*On the Cherubim*, 74 ff.; Loeb, II, 53 f.).

by them I shall be pursued . . . An elaboration of the comment just made, in this instance presenting the passive in participial form (mwrdp; MRS, nrdp).

by them I shall be captured, by them shall my loot and my
wealth be divided!—It is not written here, *"tmlˀm,"* but
"tmlˀmw my appetite"* (Exod. 15:9), (that is,) their appetite
shall be satisfied at my expense. It does not say here, "my
hand *twryšm,"* but *"twryšmw* my hand" (Exod. 15:9), (that
is,) I shall be surrendering my riches and honors to them!—

"In the past when you plundered them, in accordance
with imperial law I used to call you to account; but now, 'I
myself shall distribute the loot.'

"In the past when you were guilty of murdering them,
in accordance with imperial law I used to call you to account; but now, 'I myself will draw the sword.'

be captured *mwtps;* MRS, *ntpš.*

by them shall my loot and my wealth be divided (mḥwlq) This is
commentary on "I will divide the spoil." MRS reads instead: "It is
not written here 'I will divide their spoil,' but 'I will divide the
spoil,' (that is,) the spoil will be divided (*mtḥlq*) by them."

not . . . *"tmlˀm,"* but *"tmlˀmw"* By noting that the form of the
verb is *tmlˀmw* (see also below, on *twryšmw*) rather than the usual
form *tmlˀm,* the Mekilta suggests that unwittingly Pharaoh predicted
not that his appetite would be satisfied at their expense, but that
they, Israel, would receive satisfaction at his expense.

It does not say here MRS: "It is not written here."

not . . . *"twryšm,"* but *"twryšmw"* Similar to the comment above
on *tmlˀmw.*

I shall be surrendering For the reading in MRS, *mwlšny,* cf. critical
apparatus, ibid.

"In the past when you plundered . . ." Resuming now Pharaoh's
address to the Egyptians, cf. above, p. 179. The three statements (in a
fixed pattern, "In the past when you . . . but now . . .") are commentary on the three clauses of the verse, "I will divide the spoil," "I
will draw my sword," "My hand shall surrender them." Pharaoh, says
the Midrash, was prepared to undermine the established law, the
nomos, of civilized government; note how he encourages robbery,
murder, rape.

plundered them MRS: "When you plundered (them of) their
possessions."

"in accordance with imperial law" *bnymwsy mlkwt;* MRS (in all
three sentences), *mpny nymws mlkwt.*

"I used to call you to account (twbᶜ mydkn)" MRS, in all three
sentences, *mmḥḥ bydkn.*

but now Lit., "but here." MRS, in all three sentences, "now," *ᶜkšw.*

"I myself shall distribute the loot" That is, I myself will set the
example, and you follow suit with impunity.

"I myself will draw the sword" MRS quotes instead, "My lust shall
be satisfied upon them," very likely in order to preserve the proper

"In the past when you wanted to violate their wives and sons and daughters, in accordance with imperial law I used to call you to account; but now, 'With my own hand I shall surrender them' (to you)."—

And some say: "I shall *wield* my sword" is not what the verse says, but "I will *bare* my sword": (that is,) he planned to force them into pederasty, even as it is said, "And they shall bare their swords against the beauty and thy wisdom" (etc.) (Ezek. 28:7): the verse does not say here, "And they shall *wield* their swords," but "And they shall

----

order of the clauses of the verse; note our Mekilta, below, p. 184. Cf. Be-Shallaḥ, II (I, 203, lines 217–18).

"when you wanted" *MRS,* "when you sought."

"their wives" Not in *MRS.*

"and sons" Note below, that Pharaoh planned to force them into pederasty.

"With my own hand I shall surrender them" That is, I personally will hand them over to you to do with as you please. *MRS* reads: "I will draw my sword, with my own hand . . ."

"*Wield* my sword" . . . **verse says** . . . This alternative interpretation *MRS* puts after the passage, below, on the three groups of Egyptians. In our Mekilta this alternative interpretation of "I will bare my sword" is offered here and not earlier, when that clause was quoted, in order not to interrupt the unit "In the past . . . but now."

he planned to force them into pederasty As Lauterbach says, " 'emptying the sword' is taken as a euphemistic expression of pederasty." Cf. *Gen. R.* 63:9, p. 693, in regard to Rome.

In our Mekilta this contemplated act is attributed to Pharaoh; in *MRS* there is ambiguity because this sentence occurs right after the characterization of the third group of Egyptians (see below), and the reading is, "And some say, *Also* to force them into pederasty." At all events, the Midrash is here saying that Pharaoh hoped once again to make slaves of the Israelites for pederastic purposes, and what the Midrash has in mind is practice in Hellenistic-Roman times. Cf., e.g., Seneca, *Epistle* 95:24 (Loeb, III, 73): "How many young fellows besiege the kitchens of their gluttonous friends! I shall not mention the troops catamites, rated according to nation and color, who must all have the same smooth skin, and the same amount of youthful down on their cheeks, and the same way of dressing the hair, so that no boy with straight locks may get among the curly-heads." See on this subject W. Kroll, in *Pauly-Wissowa,* s.v. *Knabenliebe,* pp. 898 ff. The statement in our Midrash of Pharaoh's plans implies also a kind of self-compliment on the physical attractiveness of the Israelites.

Even as it is said *MRS:* "even as it is said of the Prince of Tyre."

bare their swords against the beauty and thy wisdom."—
Because he was so arrogant and puffed up with pride,
God degraded him and all the Nations of the World de-
spised him.

At the Sea the Egyptians formed three different companies against Israel. One proposed: "Let's take their
wealth—it is really our wealth!—but not slay them." And

the verse does not say here, "And they shall *wield* their swords,"
but "And they shall *bare* their swords against (ᶜl) the beauty and
thy wisdom" MRS: "It is not written here, 'They shall wield their
swords against (*b* . . .) the beauty and thy wisdom,' but 'And they
shall bare their swords against (ᶜl) the beauty and thy wisdom.' "
It may be (as HR suggest) that the Mekilta is engaged in word play,
as though *ḥrbwtm* (their swords) equals *ḥrptm* (their shame). At all
events, the image of the sword in conjunction with the verb "and they
shall bare" could easily suggest the idea.

he was so arrogant *šgᵓh; MRS: šntgᵓh.*

and puffed up with pride . . . Note the idiom in Ezek. 28:2, 17.
This peroration has nothing to do with Pharaoh, but is part of commentary on the Ezekiel passage concerning the Prince of Tyre. However, once the Mekilta has drawn on Ezek. 28:7 to explain the expression "bare . . . sword," it has gone on with comment on the
arrogance of the Prince of Tyre, very likely because that arrogance is
reminiscent also of Pharaoh's arrogance.

God degraded him MRS: "So (*kk*) God degraded him."

all the Nations of the World despised him MRS: "The Nations of
the World plundered" (? *bzzw*, but note critical apparatus on p. 89
and the reading on p. 235; or does it equal *bzwⁱ*). On the Nations of
the World despising the Prince of Tyre, cf. Ezek. 28:7, 10, 17–19.

the Egyptians formed three different companies MRS: "In three
different companies the Egyptians came against Israel."
We have here still another comment on the expressions "I will
divide the spoils," etc.; this time, however, what Pharaoh is quoted as
having said is attributed to different groups of Egyptians: they are
the "enemy speaking" of the beginning of Exod. 15:9. And the reason
for the comment is this: no word in Scripture is superfluous; in what
way, then, do the expressions "*tmlᵓmw* my appetite, *twryšmw* my
hand" add to what is after all implied already by "I will divide the
spoil?"
On the three groups of Egyptians, see also above, 5, p. 143 ff.; cf.
Heinemann, pp. 131 ff.

"our wealth" Not in MRS. If the reading in our Mekilta is correct,
perhaps "(it is really) our wealth" is intended as an explanation of
"their wealth"; i.e. what the Hebrews have is what they took from
the Egyptians (cf. Exod. 12:36). Note that a few lines below even our
Mekilta does not repeat "our wealth."

one proposed: "Let's slay them and never mind their wealth." And one proposed: "Let's slay them and take their wealth."

To the one that said, "Let's take their wealth but not slay them," "I will divide the spoil" (applies). And "My desire shall be satisfied upon *them*" (applies) to the one that said, "Let's slay them and never mind their wealth." And "My hand shall dispossess them utterly" (applies) to the one that said, "Let's slay them and take their wealth."

Inside the land of Egypt Pharaoh stood mouthing five-fold blasphemies: "The enemy said: I-will-pursue, I-will-overtake; I-will-divide the-spoil; my-desire shall-be-satisfied-upon-them; I-will-bare my-sword; my-hand shall-dispossess-them." And corresponding to this fivefold speech, the Holy Spirit retorted as follows: "Thou didst blow with Thy

"**Let's slay them (and never mind their wealth)** *MRS:* "Let's slay (and never mind their wealth)."

"**I will divide the spoil**" That is, this was the group that said, "I will divide the spoil."

"**My desire . . . upon *them*"** Cf. Tg Jon. ad Exod. 15:9 ("And when my appetite shall be sated by the blood of their slain ones"), and the note above, s.v. "I myself will draw the sword." The Mekilta seems to be underscoring that the reading is *tml^Pmw* (and not *tml^Pm*); hence "upon *them*" shall my desire be satisfied.

"**My hand shall dispossess them utterly**" *MRS* quotes more fully: "I will bare my sword, my hand shall dispossess . . ." Our Mekilta is perhaps emphasizing the reading *twryšmw* (rather than the more regular *twryšm*), to suggest that the Egyptians were looking forward to dispossession affecting not only wealth but the very lives of the Israelites as well.

Inside the land of Egypt *MRS:* "In Egypt." Cf. below, s.v. "Inside the land of Egypt." That Israel would know what Pharaoh in Egypt was saying, the Mekilta has already explained, above, p. 177.

mouthing . . . blasphemies Perhaps it would be better to say, "snorting (grunting) . . . blasphemies"; cf. S. Lieberman, in *Lešonenu,* XXXII, 96, n. 29. On "fivefold blasphemies," cf. *AhB,* I, 23.

Still another commentary on that acccumulation of expressions in Pharaoh's defiant exclamation. Each of the five expressions is, in the Hebrew, made up of two words; hence the first contains the two verbs, "I will pursue, I will overtake."

And corresponding to this fivefold speech *MRS:* "And correspondingly."

retorted as follows *MRS:* "kept mocking them."

wind" etc. (Exod. 15:10); "Thy right hand, O Lord, shatters the foe" (Exod. 15:6); "And in Thy mighty exaltation Thou overthrowest them that rise up against Thee" (Exod. 15:7); "Thou sendest forth Thy wrath, it consumeth them as stubble" (ibid.); "Thou stretchest out Thy right hand" etc. (Exod. 15:12).

A parable is told; to what may this be likened? To a brigand who was standing behind the royal palace and blaspheming to this effect: "If I find the king's son, I'll seize and slay him! I'll crucify him! I'll put him to a most horrible death!"

"Thou didst blow with Thy wind" etc. *MRS:* "Thou didst blow with Thy wind, the sea covered them, etc." *MRS* continues at once with the parable, below.

. . . Thy right hand . . . The Mekilta now brings five quotations from the Shirah which speak of God's destruction of the enemy. It quotes first verse 10a because we are in the midst of commentary on verse 9, and have simultaneously moved on to interpretation of verse 10. Then in proper order the Mekilta quotes verse 6b and the two clauses of verse 7; finally it quotes verse 12, the very first verse (after this and verse 10a, which has already been quoted), speaking again of the destruction of the enemy by God. (This will answer the question raised by HR in their note, ad loc., p. 140.) The five quotations assembled by the Mekilta are indeed those verses of the Shirah which describe the direct punitive action of God.

A parable . . . Cf. Ziegler, p. 95; and see above, Pt. I, 5, n. 5.

a brigand *MRS:* "archilestes" (chief of brigands); cf. ibid., p. 251.

standing . . . and blaspheming *MRS,* simply "standing"; on the other hand, a few lines later (p. 90, line 10), "standing . . . and blaspheming," as in our Mekilta. On "blaspheming," cf. above, s.v. "mouthing . . . blasphemies."

For palace (*plṭryn*), *MRS* gives *plṭyrw*.

Obviously the brigand cannot even get into the king's palace, and thus the Midrash underscores the utter preposterousness of such defiance. So too Pharaoh, standing in Egypt, on the earth, outside God's habitation, which is the heavens, boasts preposterously of all the awful things he will do.

"If I find (ʾmṣʾ)" *MRS:* "(When) I find"—the participial form, *mwṣʾ*.

"the king's son (ʾt bn hmlk) *MRS: bnw šl mlk.*

"I'll seize" Not in *MRS.*

"I'll crucify him . . ." *MRS* repeats the subject pronoun ("I") with each participle and puts the pronoun after each participle.

"put him to a most horrible death" *MRS:* "and consign him to flames, (by) evil deaths I shall kill him," *mytwt rʿwt ʾny mmytw.*

So that villain Pharaoh stood inside the land of Egypt, blaspheming: "The enemy said: I'll pursue, I'll overtake" etc. But the Holy Spirit laughed him to scorn: "Thou didst blow with Thy wind" (etc.), and on to, "Thou stretchedst out Thy right hand" (etc.).

So too it says, "Why do the nations rage . . . Let us break . . . (But) He that sitteth in heaven laugheth" etc. (Ps. 2:1–4 ff.). So too, "Behold they belch out with their mouth" etc. (Ps. 59:8); but what is written immediately thereafter? "But Thou, O Lord, shalt laugh" etc. (Ps. 59:9). So too it says, "Sheba, and Dedan, and the merchants of Tarshish" etc. (Ezek. 38:13), but goes on to say, "And it shall come to pass in that day, on the day Gog comes . . . at My presence shall shake (etc.) (Ezek. 38:18 ff.).

—Oh! All those thousands and all those myriads "sank like lead" because of one man!

So that villain Pharaoh . . . Our Mekilta does not complete the parable; *MRS*, on the other hand, does in part, by adding before this, "(when) the king heard this, he was filled with fury against him." Even with this sentence, the parable is not quite completed, presumably because it is self-evident. For "that villain Pharaoh," *MRS* reads simply, "Pharaoh."

inside the land of Egypt *MRS*: "in Egypt"; cf. above, s.v. "Inside the land of Egypt."

But the Holy Spirit *MRS*: "And correspondingly the Holy Spirit."

laughed him to scorn Lit., "mocks at him and says" (*mlᶜgt . . . wᵓwmrt*); *MRS*: *hyth mlᶜgt*.

On to, "Thou . . . hand" Not quoted by *MRS*. Our Mekilta this time simply quotes the first and the last verses of the five relevant passages.

So too it says Now follow three examples to demonstrate God's destruction of those who defy Him, and as the passages make clear, it is God's ultimate triumph that is spoken of. Indeed, *MRS* introduces these examples with the formula, "So too you will find of the Age to Come." As so frequently, reflection on the redemption from Egypt leads to reflection on God's ultimate victory.

but what is written immediately thereafter *MRS*, simply "and it says."

"Sheba . . . shall shake" Chapter 38 of Ezekiel talks of the destruction of Gog in the end, Gog that had been so confident that he could devastate Israel. Note too the last verse (23) of the chapter, "Thus will I magnify Myself, and sanctify Myself, and I will make Myself known in the eyes of many nations; and they shall know that I am the Lord." Cf. also the language in verse 16.

Oh! All those thousands . . . one man Not in *MRS*.

Another interpretation of THEY SANK LIKE LEAD IN MA-
JESTIC WATERS:

Four   Were-Called   Majestic

The-Holy-One-blessed-be-He   was-called   majestic
as it is said, "The Lord on high is majestic" (Ps. 93:4).

Israel   were-called   majestic
as it is said, "And My majestic ones, in whom is all My
    delight" (Ps. 16:3).

Egypt   was-called   majestic
as it is said, "Her, yea offspring of majestic nations" (Ezek.
    32:18).

The-waters   were-called   majestic
as it is said, "Above the sounds of many, majestic waters"
    (Ps. 93:4).

The-Holy-One   appeared,   the-One-who-is   majestic,

As Lauterbach observes correctly, this exclamation refers not to
the immediately preceding passage but to the section earlier where
Pharaoh is described as influencing and persuading the Egyptians to
accompany him in his pursuit of Israel; cf. above, pp. 177–182. By
using the expression "Oh! All those thousands and all those myriads,"
the Midrash may be thinking of something like Exod. 14:28 and Ps.
106:11b.

Note how the idiom "sank like lead" is used in Hodayot 8:19 (ed.
Licht, p. 136), and see also I Enoch 48:9.

The translation "because of one man" follows Lauterbach; cf. above,
s.v. "Oh! All those thousands . . ." This sentence ("Sank like
lead . . . ,") has served at the same time as a comment on the clause
"They sank like lead in majestic waters"; that is why our Mekilta
now continues with "Another interpretation." *MRS*, however, does
not have this comment; therefore it proceeds directly without the
introductory formula, "Another interpretation."

Four . . . Majestic This sentence does not occur in *MRS*.

Cf. above, 6, p. 170 ff., and below 9, p. 228 ff., and 10, p. 233 f. See also
Mirsky, pp. 46 f.

The-Holy-One-blessed-be-He I am almost certain that the text here
read originally "The-Holy-One" (one word, *hqdwš*, and no more), for
the structure of the poem demands three words to each first line.
Note indeed below, last line of text on this page.

"And My majestic ones" The Midrash very likely reads *wᵓdyry*
(*we-ᵓaddire*) as *we-ᵓaddiray*.

"Her, yea . . . nations" The verse is speaking of "the multitude of
Egypt." Instead of this Ezekiel verse, *MRS* quotes Exod. 15:10, and
the same is true of the version in B. Menaḥot 53a.

The-Holy-One *MRS*, "The Holy One, blessed be He."

The-Holy-One appeared, the One-who-is majestic Note, not merely

To   Israel   who-were-called   majestic,
To-punish   Egypt   which-was-called   majestic,
By-waters   which-were-called   majestic,

as it is said, "They sank like lead in majestic waters."

"*called* majestic" but "*is* majestic" (I owe this observation to Professor Rowan Greer). But *MRS* reads here too, "who's called majestic." See further, next note.

The Holy One appeared . . . to (ᶜl) Israel Cf. *AhB*, 1, 23. *MRS*, p. 90, reads: "The Holy One, blessed be He, appeared through (ᶜl ydy) Israel" (and so too ibid., p. 236, except that here the reading is "The Holy One" and not "the Holy One, blessed be He"). Perhaps after all, then, the two Mekiltas are not making completely identical comments: Our Mekilta speaks of God as revealing Himself to Israel at the time of His punishing the Egyptians, whereas *MRS* may be trying to emphasize that by means of what He did for Israel did God reveal Himself. In B. Menaḥot 53a, revelation, strictly speaking, is not referred to, but simply God's coming to punish Israel's enemies.

Or, does ᶜl ydy equal bšbyl, for the sake of? Cf. above, pp. 133 f., s.v. "Because of My love . . ." And for the meaning "for," see, e.g. M. Yoma 3:4, M. Megillah 4:5.

To-punish *MRS:* "and let Him punish."

By-waters *bmym,* and so too *MRS.* But perhaps the reading should be *bmy hym* (two words rather than one word), "by the waters of the Sea"; thus, as in the other sentences, here too two words would appear at the beginning of the clause.

8. Who Is Like Unto Thee, O Lord?

WHO IS LIKE UNTO THEE, O LORD, AMONG THE ʼLYM (GODS):
When Israel saw that Pharaoh and his troops perished in
the Reed Sea, that the empire of the Egyptians was over
and done with, and that disasters were inflicted on their
idols, they all burst forth with the exclamation, "Who is
like unto Thee, O Lord, among the gods!"

WHO IS LIKE . . . (GODS) . . . Note how this verse is quoted in
Hodayot 7:28 (ed. Licht, p. 128).

When Israel saw *MRS:* "When they saw."

that Pharaoh and his troops perished . . . An echo in part of
Exod. 15:4. There are three elements in this triumph: (1) the punishment of the wicked, (2) the end of their dominion, and (3) the
disappearance of idolatry. Here, therefore, once again a projection
back to the triumph over Pharaoh of the features of the ultimate
triumph: note how the Mekilta continues. On punishment of the
idols, cf. *MRS,* p. 16; *Tanḥuma Deut.,* ed. Buber, 16b. See also
Ginzberg, *Legends,* II, 129, 250, 367; V, 435, n. 221; VI, 7 f., n. 41. On
punishment of the patron angels of the Nations, cf. above, 2, p. 102, s.v.
". . . fall."

**in the Reed Sea . . . the empire of the Egyptians was over and
done with, and that disasters were inflicted** *MRS:* "In the Sea, and
(that) the empire of the Egyptians perished, and the disasters, that
they were inflicted."

they all burst forth . . . *MRS* (p. 90): "They all burst forth and
thanked God, and exclaimed . . ."; note also the reading on p. 236.
On the expression "to burst forth with the exclamation," see also
above, 1, p. 86. With the language of the Mekilta, cf. also the liturgical
formula, "And in sanctity they all burst forth . . . and ascribe sovereignty to the Name of the divine King . . ." (Baer, p. 78); so too the
prayer, ". . . who made His children pass between the divisions of
the Reed Sea . . . When His children beheld His might, they praised
and gave thanks to His Name. Willingly they accepted His sovereignty . . . Who is like unto Thee, O Lord . . ." (Baer, p. 166).

And it was not Israel alone that recited the Song, but the Nations of the World too recited the Song. When the Nations of the World heard that Pharaoh and his troops had perished in the Sea, that the empire of the Egyptians was over and done with, and that disasters had been inflicted on their idols, all of them renounced their own idol worship and acknowledging God they all burst forth with the exclamation, "Who is like unto Thee, O Lord, among the gods!"

You will find the same true of the Nations, that in the Future they will renounce their idol worship, as it is said,

---

The Mekilta statement, however, is not entirely clear. Is the Mekilta suggesting that when Israel had passed through the Sea and saw that the Egyptians had been drowned, they began the Shirah, but that when Israel realized that this now marked the end of Egyptian dominion, Israel exclaimed, "Who is like unto Thee"? Cf. also the comment by Kasher, xiv, 133, note on no. 148.

And it was not Israel alone that recited the Song, but the Nations of the World too recited the Song MRS: "And it was not Israel alone, but also the Nations of the World"; note also the reading in AhB, I, 24 f.

On the idea that not only Israel but the Nations too recite God's praises, see also above, 3, p. 110. The Midrash seems here to be deriving the notion from the fact that the verse says, "Who is like unto Thee among the ʾElim, the gods," presumably assuming that such words would be spoken by those who had believed in (many) gods. SY calls attention to Rahab's exclamation in Josh. 2:11; possibly more germane is Jethro's exclamation in Exod. 18:10 f., and note especially verse 11a.

When the Nations of the World heard that Pharaoh and his troops had perished in the Sea . . . and that disasters had been inflicted on their idols MRS: "When they saw what had happened to Egypt and (to) their idols, all of them renounced . . ." Note also the reading, ibid., p. 236.

Cf. below, 9, p. 216, and the quotation from Memar Marqah, ad loc. There may also be some significance to the fact that according to the reading of our Mekilta, Israel saw, but the Nations heard, what God had done to the Egyptians.

all of them renounced . . . Thus foreshadowing what will come to pass in the End. Observe how the Mekilta proceeds.

You will find the same true MRS: "You will find the same true of the Age to Come."

the Nations MRS: "The nations of the world."

"O Lord, my strength and my stronghold, and my refuge, in the day of affliction, unto Thee shall the Nations come . . . Shall a man make unto himself gods" etc. (Jer. 16:19–20); and it says, "In that day a man shall cast away his idols of silver" etc. (Isa. 2:20), and it goes on, "To go into the cleft of the rocks" etc. (Isa. 2:21); and in the latter connection what else is written? "And the idols shall utterly pass away" (Isa. 2:18).

Another interpretation of WHO IS LIKE UNTO THEE, O LORD, AMONG THE ʾLYM: Note the spelling ʾlm: (That is to say,) Who among those capable of mighty deeds (ʾlmym) is like unto Thee, who can be the likes of Thee in the miracles and mighty deeds Thou didst perform at the Sea,

"O Lord, my strength . . ." MRS does not quote the Jeremiah proof-texts. Cf. the expression here, "O Lord, my strength," with Exod. 15:2 (beginning).

"a man (hʾdm) . . ." MRS reads ʾyš, and cf. critical apparatus, ibid.

and it goes on, "To go into" MRS here omits "and it goes on" (lit., "and it says"; but note critical apparatus, ibid., and p. 236); the formula really serves no particular purpose at this point. Cf. below, p. 206, and 9, p. 225, from which it would appear that wʾwmr has the force essentially of "etc."

and in the latter connection what else is written MRS: "what does it say." The Isaiah quotation at this point is from 2:18, thus preceding the question of 2:20–21; ʾhryw means no more, therefore, than "what else is written in that connection."

Note the spelling ʾlm That is, the word is written defective, without the yod. MRS does not have this clause. See further, next note.

Who among those capable of mighty deeds The spelling ʾlm suggests to the Midrash that we are dealing not with the plural of ʾEl but with a singular, meaning "strength"; the exclamation declares then, Who in strength, among strong ones, is like unto Thee. Note also the Judah ha-Levi, Kuzari, reference to which Kasher, XIV, 132, note on no. 141, calls attention. MRS, on the other hand, reads here, "Who is like unto Thee in the world" (bᶜwlm), apparently punning on the sound of ʾlm and ᶜwlm (note also the interesting reading, ibid., p. 236, and the note to line 37).

At all events, the Mekilta now proceeds to furnish five more interpretations of "Who is like unto Thee . . . ," and in these focuses on the word ʾlym (ʾlm).

the likes of Thee . . . deeds Not so much an additional notion as an explanation of the previous clause: in these miracles God's extra-

as it is said, ". . . Awesome things by the Reed Sea" etc.
(Ps. 106:22)—"And He rebuked the Reed Sea, and it was
dried up" (Ps. 106:9).

WHO IS LIKE UNTO THEE, O LORD, AMONG THE ʾLYM: Who
is like unto Thee, O Lord, among the mute ones (ʾylmym),
who can be the likes of Thee beholding Thy children disgraced and yet Thou keepest still, as it is said, "I have a
long time held My peace, I have been still, and restrained
Myself; now will I cry like a travailing woman, gasping and
panting at once" (Isa. 42:14).— In the past "I have been
still and restrained Myself"; henceforth, however, "I will

---

ordinary strength is manifested. On the expression "miracles and
mighty deeds," see also below, p. 206, and 10, p. 247; note further,
Be-Shallaḥ, I (I, 173 f.), III (I, 215); Wa-Yassaʿ, III (II, 105), VII (II, 129);
Amalek, III (II, 167) and so on.

Thou didst perform at the Sea MRS: "Thou didst perform for us
at the Sea."

as it is said MRS: "And so too it says." The Mekilta presumably
quotes Ps. 106:22 before 106:9 because in verse 22 the words
"Wondrous works . . . awesome things" appear; verse 9 tells, of
course, what these wondrous and awesome things were. The reading
wgw' ("etc.") in line 1, p. 192, seems to me mistaken; perhaps it is
dittography of the following word wygʿr ("and He rebuked"). MRS
does not read wgw'.

"And He rebuked" MRS introduces this text with "and it says."
In the preceding verse (106:8) God's might is referred to.

Who is like unto Thee . . . among the mute ones Cf. also ARNB,
p. 20. MRS does not have this sentence (but note the reading in its
critical apparatus and on p. 236). Cf. AhB, I, 26.

We have here another play on ʾlym, this time associated with
ʾlm = ʾillem (silent one, speechless, holding one's peace). On God's
long-suffering and putting up with the conduct of the wicked toward
Israel, and that this is a sign of His greatness and might, cf. also
B. Yoma 69b. See also S. Spiegel, The Last Trial (New York, 1967),
p. 94 and n. 68.

beholding Thy children disgraced MRS: "that beholds His children
disgraced."

as it is said, "I have a long time etc." MRS: "so too it says."

In the past "I have been still and restrained Myself" MRS: "I was
silent in the past." We have here a supplementary parenthetical
comment, brought on by the very proof-text cited. It strikes, of course,
a comforting note. See further, next note.

henceforth I.e. in the Future. Such exegesis is quite congenial to
much in the Mekilta on the Shirah. The Midrash may also be
attracted here by the very idiom of Isa. 42:13, "The Lord will go

cry like a travailing woman, gasping and panting at once
I shall lay waste" etc. (Isa. 42:14 f.).

Another interpretation of WHO IS LIKE UNTO THEE, O
LORD, AMONG THE ʾLYM: Who is like unto Thee among
those who minister before Thee on high, as it is said, "For
who in the skies can be compared . . . A God dreaded in
the great council of the holy ones . . . O Lord God of
hosts, who is a mighty one, like unto Thee, O Lord" (Ps.
89:7–9).

WHO IS LIKE UNTO THEE, O LORD, AMONG THE ʾLYM: Who
is like unto Thee among those who call themselves divine?
Pharaoh called himself divine, as it is said, "Because he
hath said: Mine is my river and I, I made it for myself"

---

forth as a mighty man, He will stir up jealousy like a man of
war . . .''

"gasping and panting at once" At this point *MRS* continues: "And
the rest" (lit., the whole) "of the matter up to 'I will not leave them
undone' " (i.e. up to Isa. 42:16).

like unto Thee among those who minister before Thee That is,
who even of the angelic beings, the celestials, may be compared to Thee!
Cf. also Scroll of the War 13:13 f. *MRS* reads here: "(Who is like
unto Thee, O Lord, among the ʾElim,) among those who stand before
Thee."

as it is said *MRS:* "and so too it says."

"For who in the skies . . . a mighty one, like unto Thee, O Lord"
MRS: " 'For who in the skies can be compared unto the Lord' and
so on, up to 'And Thy faithfulness is round about Thee' etc. (Ps.
89:9). ʾtʾ (= ʾt hwʾ, He is like an ensign? Cf. *MRS*, p. 236, and note,
ad loc.) in the midst of His host; 'There is none like unto Thee,
among the gods' (ʾlym; but MT, ʾlhym), 'O Lord; and there are no
works like Thine' (Ps. 86:8); 'My beloved is white and ruddy' and so
on, up to 'altogether lovely' (Cant. 5:10–16)." With this reading, cf.
above, 1, p. 84 f. and *MRS*, p. 73.

Who is like unto Thee among those who call themselves divine
Four examples will now be given, and the passage has all the ear-
marks of polemic against the cult of emperor worship. Cf. Suetonius,
The Twelve Caesars, Caligula, 22; Philo, *Embassy to Gaius*, 78–114
(Loeb, x, 39–57), and in the edition of E. M. Smallwood (Leiden,
1961), pp. 191 ff. See in this connection the important discussion in
A. Deissman, *Light from the Ancient East* (London, 1920), pp. 353 ff.

MRS reads: " 'Who is like unto Thee, O Lord, among the ʾElim,'
among those who called themselves divine."

"Because he hath said" yʿn ʾmr; *MRS:* yʿn ʾšr ʾmr. See the MT
readings of Ezek. 29:3 and 9, and cf. *MRS*, p. 236, note to line 9.

(Ezek. 29:3, 9). Sennacherib called himself divine, as it is said, "Who are they among all the gods of these countries" etc. (Isa. 36:20). Nebuchadnezzar called himself divine, as it is said, "I will ascend above the heights of the clouds" etc. (Isa. 14:14). The Prince of Tyre called himself divine, as it is said, "Son of man, say unto the Prince of Tyre: Thus saith the Lord God: Because thy heart is lifted up" etc. (Ezek. 28:2).

WHO IS LIKE UNTO THEE, O LORD, AMONG THE ʾLYM: Who is like unto Thee among those whom others call divine and there is absolutely nothing to them? It is of them that it is said, "They have mouths, but they speak not" etc.

"my river and I, I made it for myself" After quoting this verse, *MRS* continues: "So too it says, 'Behold, I am against thee, and against thy rivers' (Ezek. 29:10)." Indeed, in *MRS* each of the four examples includes the proof-text announcing God's punishment.

"among all the gods of these countries" *MRS* apparently quotes instead II Kings 18:35 (and doubtless read *hṣylw* instead of *hṣyl*), and then proceeds to quote II Kings 19:35.

"I will ascend . . ." *MRS* begins with Isa. 14:13 and then proceeds to quote Isa. 14:15.

Prince of Tyre *MRS:* "Hiram" (but note critical apparatus and p. 236). After quoting Ezek. 28:2, as does our Mekilta, *MRS* proceeds to quote Ezek. 28:10.

Who is like unto Thee among those whom others call divine . . . of them that it is said *MRS:* "Who is like unto Thee, O Lord, among the ʾElim, among those whom others call divine; what are they like? ('They have mouths') . . ."

"Others" is a reference to the Nations, those who are not Israel. On the meaning of "others" here, cf. *TK* on T. Shabbat 17:17, Long Commentary, p. 294 and n. 35.

"Whom others calls gods" seems to be an attack against the worship of idols, and the statement would be the counterpart of the previous "who call themselves divine." Hence, therefore, the Mekilta continues with reference to those who have mouths but cannot speak.

It may be, however, that, in addition, more than idols are intended. Cf. Philostratus, *Life of Appolonius* 8:5 (Loeb, II, 281): "The Emperor next asked the question: 'Why is it that men call you a god?' 'Because,' answered Appolonius, 'every man that is thought to be good, is honored by the title of god.'" In this connection see also the inscription recalled by Raubitschek to Goodenough, *Jewish Symbols*, x, 114. And it may be that this is what Jerome too has in mind when he says, "*Error gentilium qui omne quid super se est deos putant*" (cited by Bickerman [from the Commentary on Dan. 2:46] at the end of his *Institutions*, p. 257).

(Ps. 115:5 ff.)—these "have mouths but cannot speak." But
that is not the case with Him Who Spake and the World
Came to Be! On the contrary, in one utterance He says
two things, something impossible for flesh and blood to do,

The phrase "and there is absolutely nothing to them" possibly
represents a play on the word *ʾlym*, as though it were a plural of
the negative *ʾl* (*ʾalim*); cf. also *ZY*. Or again, this may be a play on
ʾlym = ʾlm, the mute ones, the ones unable to speak a word (cf. *SY*
and *ZY*).

But that is not the case . . . Came to Be Note how what follows
serves at the same time as an admirable transition to the passage on
"Who is like unto Thee majestic in holiness." The expression here
for God, "Him Who Spake and the World Came to Be," is very likely
deliberate, to underscore the contrast with those who have mouths
and cannot speak.

On the contrary . . . He says Although, properly speaking, He has
no mouth! Like the thought of Ps. 115:2–8, there is in this ridicule
of the idols the constant implication that they are given limbs and
organs and are thoroughly impotent, without substance, unreal; God,
on the other hand, cannot, strictly speaking, be said to have hands,
legs, and so on, and yet He does move about, He does act, He is the
height of potency and reality.

in one utterance He says two things *MRS:* "In one utterance He
said ten things, as it is said, 'And God spoke all these words, etc."
(Exod. 20:1); cf. also p. 237, ibid. (and in our Mekilta, Ba-Ḥodesh, IV
[II, 228]). *MRS* then quotes also Jer. 23:29; Ps. 62:12 does not seem to
be quoted; the verse from Job it quotes at the end of the long passage
MRS now introduces. See further, below.
On the statement of our Mekilta, cf. Ba-Ḥodesh, VII (II, 252), which
may indeed be the source for the expression "in one utterance two
things." In our passage, however, the phrase is already and very
likely a kind of stereotype (of course, note also Ps. 62:12); i.e. the
Midrash is contrasting God with flesh and blood: a human being
cannot say more than one thing at a time; on the other hand, God is
capable of saying "more than one thing at a time"; in other words,
"two *dbrym*" simply equals "more than one thing at a time."

something impossible for flesh and blood to do This statement is
not in *MRS*. Indeed, note that the passage in our Mekilta began with
a contrast between God and those entities others call gods, and
almost unobtrusively passed over to the contrast between God and
human beings. (See further, below.) Perhaps our Mekilta reading is
intended to serve as a transition to the first comment below, on "Who
is like unto Thee majestic in holiness." Or it may be that our
Mekilta reading here is "contaminated" by the reading of that first
comment on "Who . . . majestic in holiness."
After quoting Jer. 23:29, *MRS* continues at length as follows:

as it is said, "God hath spoken one word, but in this we have heard two" etc. (Ps. 62:12), "Is not My word like as

———

" 'They have eyes, but they see not' (Ps. 115:5); but He Who Spake and the World Came to Be is not like that; on the contrary, 'For the (eyes of the) Lord run to and fro' (II Chron. 16:9); and it says, 'The eyes of the Lord run to and fro' (Zech. 4:10); and it says, 'The eyes of the Lord are in every place,' etc. (Prov. 15:3).

" 'They have ears but they hear not' (Ps. 115:6); but He Who Spake and the World Came to Be is not like that; on the contrary, 'O Thou that hearest prayer, unto Thee doth all flesh come' (Ps. 65:3); and it says, 'Lord, Thou hast heard the desire of the humble' etc. (Ps. 10:17); and it says, 'Thou that dwellest in the gardens, the companions' etc. (Cant. 8:13); and it says, 'Then they that feared (the Lord) spoke' (*ndbrw* in MT; cf. *MRS, ydbrw,* and critical apparatus, ad loc.), etc. (Mal. 3:16); and it says, 'And it shall come to pass that before they call' etc. (Isa. 65:24).

" 'They have noses, but they smell not' (Ps. 115:6); but He Who Spake and the World Came to Be is not like that; on the contrary, 'An offering made by fire, of a sweet savor unto the Lord' (Lev. 1:9), 'And the Lord smelled the sweet savor' (Gen. 8:21).

" 'They have hands, but they handle not' (Ps. 115:7); but He Who Spake and the World Came to Be is not like that; on the contrary, 'Yea, My hand hath laid the foundation of the earth' etc. (Isa. 48:13); and also (cf. critical apparatus, ad loc.) 'I, even My hands, have stretched out the heavens' etc. (Isa. 45:12); and it says, 'Who hath measured the waters in the hollow of His hand' etc. (Isa. 40:12).

" 'They have feet, but they walk not' (Ps. 115:7); but He Who Spake and the World Came to Be is not like that; on the contrary, 'Then shall the Lord go forth, and fight against those nations' etc. (Zech. 14:3); and it says, 'The Lord will go forth as a mighty man' etc. (Isa. 42:13); and it says, 'And His feet shall stand in that day' etc. (Zech. 14:4).

" 'Neither speak they with their throat' (Ps. 115:7); but He Who Spake and the World Came to Be is not like that; on the contrary, 'His mouth is most sweet' etc. (Cant. 5:16); and it says, 'And speech goeth out of His mouth' (Job 37:2)."

Clearly, in *MRS* the long comment on the idols—what "others" designate as gods—is an opportunity for midrashic treatment of all the relevant verses of Ps. 115. When our Mekilta, however, speaks of "something impossible for flesh and blood to do," the contrast is between God and human beings (not God and the idols). See further below, s.v. "And speech goeth out of His mouth."

"God hath spoken one word . . . Note the reference to God's "strength" in this verse.

"we have heard" MT reads, "I have heard"; but note the reading "we have heard" in *MRS*, p. 237.

fire" etc. (Jer. 23:29); it is also written, ". . . And speech goeth out of His mouth" (etc.) (Job 37:2 ff.).

WHO IS LIKE UNTO THEE MAJESTIC IN HOLINESS: How comely Thou art, how majestic in holiness! For unlike the rule with flesh and blood is the rule of the Holy One, blessed

"Is not My word like as fire" The latter half of the verse reads, "And like a hammer that breaketh the rock in pieces"; now cf. B. Sanhedrin 34a: "In the School of Rabbi Ishmael it was taught (*tn*ᵃ): 'And like a hammer that breaketh the rock in pieces' (teaches that) even as a hammer (on a rock) produces many sparks, so one verse of Scripture releases many meanings."

Strictly speaking, this is not identical with what the Mekilta is discussing: the Sanhedrin context affirms that one verse—or, we might even say, one word of God—is capable of releasing many *meanings;* the Mekilta, on the other hand, states that God can utter two (more than one) things or commandments, in one breath as it were. But the Jeremiah verse is again and again cited in connection with the statement that God says two things in one breath; cf. Ba-Ḥodesh, VII (II, 252; note the parallel passages referred to by Lauterbach, Ba-Ḥodesh VII (II, 252); see also *Mid. Tan.*, p. 138; P. Nedarim 3:2, 37d; *Sifre Num.* 42, pp. 47 f., and the references supplied).

"And speech goeth out of His mouth" In *MRS* (cf. above, s.v. "something impossible . . .") this proof-text makes excellent sense: unlike the idols of whom it is said, "Neither *speak they* with their throat," of God it is said, "And *speech* goeth out of His mouth." Is this quotation of Job 37:2 in our Mekilta a sign that originally something like what is preserved in *MRS* was present in our Mekilta too, of which this verse is a remnant? Or perhaps in our Mekilta the Job proof-text is not intended to be limited to verse 2, but to point to all of Job 37 that speaks of the amazing effects of God's voice; thus we can see what God by His voice can accomplish.

How comely . . . in holiness Cf. *AhB*, I, 25. See above, 5, p. 146, and the comment, ad loc., s.v. "How comely . . . power".

"In holiness": Thou art revealed as comely and mighty on those occasions when Thy Name is sanctified, e.g., at the giving of the Commandments and when listening to the prayers of all men.

For unlike the rule with flesh . . . Now begins a section with the formula "the rule with flesh and blood . . . But He Who Spake and the World Came to Be." Ten such statements are made, two as comment on "Who is like unto Thee majestic in holiness" and eight more on the phrase "Awesome in praises." There is a doxological quality to this section, and it may even represent some kind of hymn of praise (*tehillah*); if so, perhaps each stanza originally repeated as a refrain, "For unlike the rule with flesh and blood is the rule of the Holy One, blessed be He." Note indeed the reading in *MRS*, pp. 93 f., as each "new interpretation" is presented.

be He. The rule with flesh and blood is that one cannot say two things simultaneously. But He Who Spake and the World Came to Be proclaimed the Ten Commandments in one utterance, something impossible for flesh and blood to do, as it is said, "And God spoke all these words in one utterance" (Exod. 20:1).

The rule with flesh and blood is that one cannot hear clearly when two people cry out simultaneously. But that is not the case with Him Who Spake and the World Came to Be! On the contrary, even when all the inhabitants of the world come and cry out before Him, He hears their cries clearly, as it is said, "O Thou that hearest prayer, unto Thee doth all flesh come" (Ps. 65:3).

the rule of the Holy One, blessed be He *MRS:* "the rule of God (*hmqwm*)" (and so right through the section).

The rule with flesh and blood is that one cannot *MRS,* simply "Flesh and blood cannot"; cf. below, s.v. "The rule with flesh and blood."

cannot say two things simultaneously Cf. Ba-Ḥodesh, IV (II, 228), and see also here at the end of the preceding section on "Who is like unto Thee, O Lord, among the *ᵓlym.*"

But He Who . . . Came to Be Cf. above, s.v. "But that is not the case . . . Spake and the World Came to Be."

the Ten Commandments (ᶜśrt hdbrwt) in one utterance *MRS:* "The Ten Commandments (ᶜśr dbrwt) in one utterance, even as it is said, 'And God spoke' (Exod. 20:1), as was written above." Cf. above, s.v. "in one utterance He says two things."

something impossible . . . to do Not in *MRS.*

"all these words" The Midrash is underscoring "all these" of the proof-text; cf. Ba-Ḥodesh, IV (II, 228–29). But note also *SY,* ad loc. Moreover, I feel that in addition to this emphasis, the Midrash is also interpreting the seemingly superfluous *ᵓmr* ("saying") as "in one utterance."

The rule with flesh and blood Cf. above, s.v. "The rule with flesh and blood is that one cannot." *MRS* introduces each "stanza" with "Another interpretation" and the repetition of the sentence (thus making it into a refrain), "For unlike the rule with flesh and blood is the rule of God"; cf. above, s.v. "For unlike the rule with flesh."

when two people cry out simultaneously Cf. above, 4, p. 132. *MRS:* "(cannot listen) to two people simultaneously." On this paragraph, cf. Ziegler, p. 158 f.

even when all the inhabitants . . . as it is said Not in *MRS.* See the whole lovely section in *Exod. R.* 21:4. Note that Midrash Psalms 65:2 speaks not merely of "flesh and blood" but of "a king of

AWESOME IN PRAISES: Not of recent vintage, but from all eternity "awesome in praises!"

Another interpretation of AWESOME IN PRAISES: The rule with flesh and blood is that one commands reverence toward himself from those far away more than from those nearby. But that is not the case with Him Who Spake and the World Came to Be! On the contrary, He commands reverence toward Himself from those who are near Him

---

flesh and blood"; cf. below, s.v. "The rule with flesh and blood . . . builds."

Not of recent vintage . . . "awesome in praises" Not in *MRS*.

In this comment of our Mekilta there may very well be a dig at contemporary fashions, the homilist implying that God is not like some lately deified emperor or *soter* because of his recent triumph or victory. On criticism of parvenu gods, see also Lucian, *Parliament of the Gods* (in Loeb, v, 421 ff.). According to *SY*, the proof-text lies in the word *nwrʾ* ("awesome"), because the participle form includes the meaning of past and future tenses. Perhaps, however, the proof-text is in the word "praises," the plural suggesting that from of old, from the very beginning, God's works of Creation praised Him; on this notion, cf. Ginzberg, *Legends*, I, 44, 83; VI, 61 f., 109 f., n. 100.

On the notion of gods of recent vintage, see also *Sifre Deut.*, 318, p. 364, and *Mid. Tan.*, p. 195. Cf. Ba-Ḥodesh, VI (II, 240), and *Mid. Tan.*, p. 20.

Another interpretation of AWESOME IN PRAISES . . . In *MRS* this appears as the only comment specifically attached to the phrase "Awesome in praises," and what our Mekilta (see below) has on "when a laborer is engaged . . ." *MRS* puts before the statement of "from . . . far away . . . nearby," and as part of the discussion of "Who is like unto Thee majestic in holiness."

reverence toward himself . . . nearby There may be in this comment an echo of the situation in regard to Augustus, who did not hesitate to encourage emperor worship in the provinces, but was careful not to emphasize this at Rome. Cf. Schürer, II (4th ed.), 33 f., and note, ad loc. On the policy with regard to Vespasian, cf. the opening pages of K. Scott, *The Imperial Cult under the Flavians* (Stuttgart and Berlin, 1936). In the present context, *nwrʾw* is surely not just plain "fear," but implies religious reverence and worship. On the idiom "far away and near by," see also below, 9, p. 224.

At all events the thought of the Mekilta seems to be this: in the case of a human being, the closer you get to him, the less you are inclined to attribute divinity to him; on the other hand, the closer you are to God, the more you are led to acknowledge His divine character.

reverence toward Himself from those who are near Him more than from those who are far from Him *MRS:* "reverence toward

more than from those who are far from Him, for it is said,
"Through them that are nigh unto Me I will be sanctified"
(Lev. 10:3); and it is written, "And round about Him it
stormeth mightily" (Ps. 50:3), and it says, "A God dreaded
in the great council of the holy ones and revered of all
them that are round about Him" (Ps. 89:8), and it continues, "O Lord God of hosts, who is a mighty one, like

---

Himself from those who are nearby more than from the ones far off."
The reference of "reverence . . . from those who are near" is to the
angels, those especially nigh to Him. Cf. indeed the proof-texts from
Psalms which follow.

"Through them . . . sanctified" MRS quotes this verse as the last
of the proof-texts. The purpose of this verse is simply to establish
that God is sanctified—i.e. revered and worshiped—by those who
are near to Him. The verses that follow, however, demonstrate that
those especially near to Him are the angels. See further below, s.v.
"and it continues, 'O Lord God of hosts.' "

"A God dreaded . . . the holy ones" Cf. also the verse immediately
preceding, "For who in the skies can be compared unto the Lord,
who among the sons of might can be likened unto the Lord"; and in
verse 9, note carefully, "Who is like unto Thee."

"revered of all them . . . round about Him" At this point MRS
quotes also Job 25:2.

and it continues, "O Lord God of hosts" Perhaps "and it continues" (w⁾wmr) is not altogether necessary (note incidentally Lauterbach's translation), but it is not necessarily impossible, for the homilist
may be impressed by the fact that verse 8 speaks of "them . . . round
about Him," and then verse 9 speaks of them "round about Thee."
Whether MRS also wants to refer to Ps. 89:9 is impossible to say.

(It seems to me that the parallel passages, listed by Lauterbach and
HR, are not really parallel to what our Mekilta is discussing.
B. Yebamot 121b, etc., while referring to Ps. 50:3 and Ps. 89:8 f., are
essentially concerned with the idea that God is strict and exacting
with the righteous, the ṣaddiqim, and this is already a midrashic
extension beyond what the Mekilta is talking about. The Mekilta is
not taking up the question of God's relations with the righteous, but
simply underscoring that even the angels, the beings in closest
proximity to the presence of God, are in utter awe of Him. Significantly enough, in none of the so-called parallels is Lev. 10:3 cited;
in B. Zebaḥim 115b where of course it is cited, the discussion is indeed devoted to Nadab and Abihu, and here Ps. 50:3 and Ps. 89:8 f.
are not quoted! Lekaḥ Tob on Exodus, p. 49a [cf. also Sekel Tob, p.
196] is also thinking principally of Nadab and Abihu; it quotes Ps.
50:3 because before speaking of "those round about Him," the verse
reads, "A fire devoureth before Him!")

unto Thee, O Lord? And Thy faithfulness is round about Thee" (Ps. 89:9).

The rule with flesh and blood is that when a laborer is engaged by a proprietor, whether he plows for him or sows for him or clears the land for him or hoes for him, it is always the same, with coin the proprietor keeps compensating him. But that is not the case with Him Who Spake and the World Came to Be! On the contrary, if a person craves sons, He gives them to him, as it is said, "Lo, children are a heritage of the Lord" etc. (Ps. 127:3); if he craves wisdom, He gives that to him, as it is said, "For the Lord giveth wisdom" (Prov. 2:6); if he craves possessions, He gives them to him, as it is said, "Both riches and honor come of Thee" (I Chron. 29:12).

The rule with flesh and blood is that whenever one

The rule with flesh and blood is that when a laborer is engaged . . . In *MRS* this is the third comment on "Who is like unto Thee majestic in holiness."

when a laborer is engaged . . . *MRS:* "When a laborer is engaged for work by a proprietor, whether he sows for him or plows for him or clears the land, it's always the same, with coin (he) compensates . . ."

the same, with coin Lit., "one coin," but the emphasis is of course not on *one* coin: the meaning is, Regardless of what the laborer does for his employer, the latter has *only* money to pay him; always remuneration is the same in kind, irrespective of what the laborer might really need.

keeps . . . *whwlk lw;* not in *MRS.*

If a person craves (tˀb) sons, He gives them to him . . . *MRS:* "If one craves (tˀwb) sons, sons He gives to him . . . if he craves wisdom, wisdom He gives to him . . . if he craves possessions, possessions He gives to him . . ."

sons . . . wisdom . . . possessions The typical desires of the civilized man. And, as the proof-texts declare, such rewards are only God's to give. The order in which these gifts are referred to, it seems to me, reflects not so much an idealized hierarchy of values (which may nevertheless be the case) as the order of the biblical books from which the proof-texts are drawn—i.e. Psalms first, then Proverbs, and finally Chronicles.

The rule with flesh and blood is that whenever one builds, he must first build . . . Again, *Midrash Ps.* 86:3 speaks of "a king of flesh and blood," and cf. *Gen. R.* 12:12, p. 110. Note above, s.v. "even when all the inhabitants . . . as it is said," and below, s.v. "He ceiled His universe . . ."

builds, he must first build the bottom part and only then
can he build the top one. But that is not the case with
Him Who Spake and the World Came to Be! He builds the
top and after that builds the bottom part, as it is said,
"In the beginning God created the heaven" and after that
"the earth" (Gen. 1:1).

The rule with flesh and blood is that when one puts up
a ceiling, to ceil he requires wood and stones and earth and
water. But that is not the case with Him Who Spake and
the World Came to Be! He ceiled His universe with water

MRS: "Flesh and blood must first build (the) bottom part and
only then can he build . . ." Moreover, *MRS* offers this as commentary on "Doing wonders."

In this and the following sections may well be preserved the
ancient Jewish response to the boast of the Nations of the World,
that their great architects and sculptors produced splendid structures
and works; yet even these great artists and craftsmen cannot do what
the God of Israel does. On the significance and high esteem of archi-
tecture (including also engineering) in Hellenistic-Roman times, see
Rostovtzeff, *SEHHW*, II, 1232 ff. For the appeal of sculpture, see, for
example, Lucian, *The Dream*, 7–8 (Loeb, III, 221 f.). To be sure, the
pagan philosophers might speak disparagingly of manual work (this
too is reflected in Lucian's *Dream*), but such views had little effect
on the public; in this connection see C. Dugas, in Daremberg and
Saglio, s.v. Sculptura, pp. 1151 ff.

But that is not the case . . . He builds the top *MRS:* "But that is
not the case . . . On the contrary, He builds (the) top . . ."

. . . and after that builds the bottom part . . . Contrast however
Pisḥa, I (I, 2). Landau (so too HR) observes that the Mekilta in our
present passage reflects the Shammaite view; cf. P. Ḥagigah 2, 77c,
and also Philo, *On the Creation*, 27 f. (Loeb, I, 23); see also Ginzberg,
Legends, V, 8, n. 17. The Mekilta adopts here the Shammaite view
because it is eager to emphasize in every way possible that God is
absolutely incomparable. See, however, L. Finkelstein, in *JQR*, XXXI,
221.

("God created the heaven") and after that ("the earth") In *MRS*,
" 'God created' etc."

and water Not in *MRS;* note also the critical apparatus in Lauterbach, ad loc., and cf. *AhB*, I, 25 f. On the expression "wood, stones,
and earth," cf. Lev. 14:45.

He ceiled His universe with water (only) *MRS:* "On the contrary, when He ceils His universe, He ceils with nothing other than
water."

In *Gen. R.* 4:1, p. 25, the reading is again, "a king of flesh and

(only), as it is said, "By water He ceils the tops of His chambers" (Ps. 104:3).

The rule with flesh and blood is that one is unable to mold a form in water. But that is not the case with Him Who Spake and the World Came to Be! On the contrary, in water He molded forms, as it is said, "And God said: Let the waters swarm with" etc. (Gen. 1:20).

The rule with flesh and blood is that one is unable to form anything in the dark recesses of the earth. But He Who Spake and the World Came to Be does fashion forms in the dark recesses of the earth, as it is said, "When I was made in secret, and curiously wrought in the lowest parts of the earth" (Ps. 139:15).

The rule with flesh and blood is that when one undertakes to form a figure, he must begin with its head or some

---

blood"; cf. above, s.v. ". . . flesh and blood . . . builds," and also below, next note.

to mold a form in water Cf. *AhB*, I, 166, and also *Gen. R.* 7:1, p. 50, again speaking of "a king of flesh and blood." In the very midst of the waters, the swarms of living creatures received their shape and form.

in the dark recesses of the earth Lit., "in the dust." *MRS:* "in the darkness" (*bᵓpylh*); *AhB*, I, 26: "in covert" (*bstr*). Is the point of the homilist that the artist requires strong light to make his statues or his structures—that underground, in complete darkness, the human being is unable to produce his work?

Despite the presence of this "stanza" in *MRS* also, I wonder if it is not after all a variant of the stanza on molding forms in water. Note in our Mekilta the slight departure from the regular refrain (observe the absence of "But that's not the case with Him Who Spake and the World Came to Be!"); and for the reading of *MRS*, see further, next note.

But He Who Spake . . . does fashion forms . . . *MRS:* "But God (*hmqwm!*) is not like that; on the contrary, He formed (*yṣr!*) forms in the darkness." However, cf. ibid., critical apparatus.

undertakes to form *MRS:* "forms."

must begin with its head At this point *MRS* adds, "or with its foot."

"There was no objection to piecing [statues]. Heads and outstretched arms were often made separately and attached with metal dowels and stone tenons, generally set in molten lead. Smaller pieces could be fastened with cement" (G. M. A. Richter, *A Handbook of Greek Art* [London, 1959], p. 46). It must have been the ambition of artists

one of its limbs and then gradually finish it. But that is
not the case with Him Who Spake and the World Came
to Be! He forms the whole figure at once, as it is said, "For
He forms the whole" (at once) (Jer. 10:16), and it says,
"Neither is there any ṣwr (Rock) like our God" (I Sam.
2:2), (that is,) "there is no ṣyyr (Artist) like our God."

The rule with flesh and blood is that when one goes to a
sculptor and says to him, "Make me a statue of Father,"
the sculptor says to him, "Let your father come and stand
before me, or bring me some representation of him, and I
will make his statue for you." But that is not the case with
Him Who Spake and the World Came to Be! On the contrary, out of a liquid drop He gives a child to a man, and
it's the image of its father!

---

to make their images appear as though of one block, with no joins;
cf. H. Stuart Jones, *Select Passages from Ancient Writers* (Chicago,
1966), p. 222: "The Laokoon is constructed of six blocks, but the
joins are so carefully concealed that even Michael Angelo could only
detect three."

and then gradually finish it Not in *MRS*.

But that is not the case with Him Who Spake . . . at once (kᵓḥt)
MRS: "But that's not the case with God (*hmqwm*), blessed be He. On
the contrary, when He forms a figure, He forms the whole (of it) at
once (*kᵓḥd*)."

"there is no ṣyyr (Artist)" A typical midrashic play on the words
ṣwr, ṣyyr, and yṣr. On related aspects of God as a unique artist, see
Sifre Deut., 307, p. 344 (*Mid. Tan.*, p. 187), and *Gen. R.* 1:9, p. 8.

"like our God" *MRS:* "like God."

"Father" Note the spelling ᵓbh in *MRS;* cf. also *Sifre Deut.* 352, p.
413, top line.

the sculptor Lit., that one, the latter. Not in *MRS*.

"Let your father come and stand" *MRS:* "Bring your father to me
and have him stand."

some representation of him ᵓqwnyn (icon) šlw; *MRS:* dywqnw. (Is
the word ᵓqwnyn used to emphasize the actual features? Cf. the passage of Pliny, *Natural History*, xxxiv, 16, in K. Jex-Blake and E. Sel-
lers, *The Elder Pliny's Chapters on the History of Art* [Chicago,
1968], p. 15, and note, ad loc. [as well as p. 233].)

"and I will make his statue for you" wᵓny ʿwśh lk ṣwrtw; *MRS:*
wᵓ ʿśh lk kṣwrth.

a liquid Lit., "water." And what is more, this happens in the dark!
Cf. above, s.v. "in the dark recesses" and "to mold a form in water."

a man lᵓdm; *MRS:* lᵓdm zh.

and it's the image *MRS,* "it's the image."

DOING WONDERS: Not "hath done wonders" is written here, but "doing wonders" in the Age to Come! As it is said, "Therefore, behold, the days come, saith the Lord, that it shall no more be said: As the Lord liveth, that *brought* up the children of Israel out of the land of Egypt, but: As the Lord liveth, that brought up the children of Israel" etc. (Jer. 16:14–15).

Another interpretation of DOING WONDERS: He hath wrought wondrous things for us and He performeth these for us in every single generation, as it is said, "Wonderful are Thy works, and that my soul knoweth right well (Ps. 139:14), and it says, "Many things hast Thou done, O Lord my God, even Thy wondrous works, and Thy thoughts toward us" (Ps. 40:6).

Another interpretation of DOING WONDERS: Doing wondrous things for the Fathers, and in the Future continuing

DOING WONDERS Since preceding statements had been given in *MRS* as comment on "doing wonders," it introduces what follows with the formula, "Another interpretation." The first comment now in our Mekilta comes as the second in *MRS*, and our second, there comes first.

Not "hath done wonders" is written here (Note indeed the MT *ketib;* the Midrash, however, is quite right about the vocalized text. Cf. *MRS*, p. 237.) For the idea, see also above, 1, p. 66 f., and 3, p. 111, as well as the comments on 5, p. 150, and 6, p. 161. The redemption in the Future will of course also be accompanied by miracles. See also *Mid. Tan.*, p. 119 (lines 5–6).

but "doing wonders" The participle form permitting the interpretation of Future.

As it is said *MRS:* "And so too it says" (similarly in the following comment). After quoting the Jeremiah proof-text, *MRS* proceeds with the two parables which occur in our Mekilta at Pisḥa, XVI (I, 133; on the second parable, ibid., cf. Lieberman, in *TK*, Long Commentary on T. Berakot 1:11, p. 14).

He hath wrought wondrous things for us *MRS:* "He hath wrought for (our) fathers." Our Mekilta is presumably saying, When God took us out of Egypt He performed miracles for us, but He continues thereafter to perform miracles in behalf of each and every generation. Note that the Psalms verses which are quoted speak of *my* soul knoweth, Thy thoughts toward *us*. This would suggest that the reading "for us" is perfectly legitimate. See further below, at the end of the chapter.

Doing wondrous things for the Fathers *MRS:* "He did for the Fathers." Cf. *AhB*, I, 27.

to do them for the sons, as it is said, "As in the days of thy
coming forth out of the land of Egypt will I show unto
him wondrous things" (Mic. 7:15): "I will show him" what
I never showed the Fathers—for lo, the miracles and mighty
deeds which in the Future I will perform for the sons will
exceed the "wonders" (at the Exodus), (they will be) "wondrous things" that I never performed for the Fathers! And

---

"of Egypt I will show" . . . **"wondrous things" that I never performed for the Fathers** Instead of this quite awkward and long reading, see the reading recommended by L. Finkelstein, in *PAAJR*, v,
11, literally as follows: "'. . . of Egypt will I show unto him wondrous things': In the future I will perform for the sons wondrous
things (the like of) which I did not perform for the Fathers."
For "I will show him" what I never showed the Fathers, *MRS*
reads, "I will show thee what I never . . ." Our Mekilta has simply
appropriated the expression "I will show him" from the Micah verse.
In making its statement, the Midrash is calling attention to the fact
that in the Shirah the word *pl'* (wonders), in the singular, is used,
whereas in Micah the word is *npl'wt*, in the plural; and thus the
descendants will be the beneficiaries of more abundant, greater,
miracles than those vouchsafed to the Fathers. Thus the midrashic
interpretation of the verse is, I believe, as follows: As it was when
you went out, I will show him wonders (greater) than (those at the
exodus from) the land of Egypt.
MRS continues after "never showed the Fathers": "Wonders which
I did not perform (*hpl'ty*) for the Fathers. For unlike the miracles
and mighty deeds which I performed (*š'šyty*) for the Fathers will I
perform for the sons in the Future—on the contrary, what I did not
perform (*hpl'ty*) for the Fathers (will I perform for the sons); and
so too it says, 'To Him who alone doeth wondrous things'—superbly
wondrous (*wnpl'y npl'ym*): what I did not do for the Fathers, as it
is said . . ." The expression "superbly wondrous" may be partially
indebted to the idiom of Ps. 139:14, *nplyty, npl'ym m'šyk* ("I am
wonderfully made, wonderful are Thy works"); at all events, for the
expression, cf. readings like those in *Sifra* 112a (e.g. *'yr 'ry 'rykm;
mqdš mqdšy mqdš(y)km*) or for that matter in the Mekilta itself
(e.g. Ba-Ḥodesh, III [II, 218], IX [II, 266]). And see now S. Lieberman,
Siphre Zutta (N.Y., 1968), pp. 89 f., n. 54.
"Miracles and mighty deeds" is a standard expression; cf. above, p.
191, and below, 10, p. 247.
On "will exceed the 'wonders'": i.e. the *pl'* at the exodus, the *pl'*
of our verse.
In "'wondrous things' (*npl'wt*) that I never performed," *npl'wt* is
again a quotation, the term occurring in the Micah verse.

so too it says, "To Him who alone doeth great wondrous things, for His mercy endureth forever" (Ps. 136:4).

> "Blessed be the Lord God, the God of Israel,
> Who alone doeth wondrous things,
> And blessed be His glorious Name for ever;
> And let the whole earth be filled with His Glory!
> Amen, and Amen."   (Ps. 72:18–19)

great wondrous things That is, not just wonders but *great* (superlative) wonders, greater than the wonder in the past.

"Blessed be the Lord" *MRS* introduces this quotation with "and it says."

"Who alone doeth wondrous things" Cf. the idiom in the first verse quoted. The verse of course makes a fine doxological conclusion.

The three interpretations of "doing wonders" are manifestly consolation pieces, and one may even detect a kind of crescendo here. First, as again and again in the Mekilta, the clause is made to release a promise for the Future. The second interpretation is an underscoring that not only in the ultimate future is God's mercy extended to Israel, but immediately too, even with us and in every generation. Finally comes the statement which declares that the end deliverance will be not a mere duplication of what took place in the past, but an experience even greater than that. See also the reply of the Sages to Ben Zoma, in T. Berakot 1:12, and cf. *TK*, ad loc., p. 13.

9. Thou Stretchedst out Thy Right Hand

THOU STRETCHEDST OUT THY RIGHT HAND—THE EARTH SWAL-
LOWED THEM: This declares that all souls are in the hand of
Him Who Spake and the World Came to Be, as it is said,
"In whose hand is the soul of every living being" etc.
(Job 12:10), "Into Thy hand I commit my spirit" etc. (Ps.
31:16).

By virtue of what was burial granted to them? By virtue

This declares MRS: "The verse declares."
that all souls . . . "being" The Midrash is commenting on the
non sequitur of the verse if it is taken with absolute literalness:
What connection is there between God's stretching forth His hand
and the earth swallowing the Egyptians? Hence the comment that all
souls are in God's hand, and when He casts them out of His hand,
that is the end of them. If we compare the Mekilta passage with
Sifre Num., 139, p. 185, we can see that the soul entrusted in the
hands of the Creator refers to the human being while *alive*. Note the
imagery in our Mekilta below, and that used by Rashi in his comment on the verse.
"Into Thy hand I commit my spirit" Not quoted by MRS, and the
Job proof-text it quotes without any introductory formula (like "as
it is said").
By virtue of what . . . Cf. AhB, I, 27. Although in the biblical
narrative and in the Shirah too we hear of Pharaoh and his hosts
being drowned in the Sea, here the verse speaks of the *earth* swallowing them; in other words, burial is referred to! (Cf. Cross and Freedman, in *JNES*, xiv, 247, n. 39, and U. Cassuto, *Commentary on Exodus*
[Jerusalem, 1959], p. 122.)
On this and the following interpretation, cf. *Memar Marqah* 2:8
(II, 66) and 2:9 (II, 70): "It was said that when the Egyptians died
the sea cast them onto its bank. Hence He said, '*And Israel saw the
Egyptians dead upon the seashore*' . . . After that the seashore was
split and it swallowed them up." See also Ginzberg, *Legends*, III, 31;

of (Pharaoh's) having said, "The Lord is righteous" etc.
(Exod. 9:27). Said the Holy One, blessed be He, to them:
"You acknowledged the justice of the sentence upon you,
in turn I shall not shortchange you, and I will grant you
burial." As it is said, "Thou stretchedst out Thy right
hand—the earth swallowed them."

Another interpretation of THOU STRETCHEDST OUT THY
RIGHT HAND: This declares that the Sea cast them onto the
dry land and the dry land cast them onto the Sea. The
dry land said: "If when I took in no more than Abel's
blood, and that was an individual, it was said with
reference to me, 'And now cursed art thou (Cain) more
than the earth' etc. (Gen. 4:11): all the more now! How

VI, 11, n. 56. (For still another reason why the Egyptians merited
burial, cf. v, 371, top.) Cf. Be-Shallaḥ, I (I, 169).

burial Lit., "place for burial." *MRS* reads simply "burial."

**By virtue of what (ʾyzh) was burial granted to them? By virtue of
(Pharaoh's) having said** *MRS:* "By virtue of what (*mh*) was burial
granted to them? Because he said . . . ."

On the horror at not being buried, see D. Zlotnick, *The Treatise
"Mourning"* (New Haven, 1966), pp. 104 f., and the references fur-
nished there. See also the quotation from Porphyry in R. M. Grant,
Miracle and Natural Law (Amsterdam, 1952), p. 243. Cf. *MRS*, p. 30.
On the terror at being *drowned*, see Lieberman, "After Life," pp.
527 f.

"in turn I shall not shortchange you" Not in *MRS*.

"burial" Lit., "place for burial, burial ground." *MRS*, again simply
"burial."

Another interpretation In *MRS* what follows is presented as a
simple continuation of the preceding; hence the reading there is,
"For the Sea kept casting them . . ."

cast them Ed. Lauterbach, *zwrqn*, but HR, *zwrqtn*, which is how
MRS reads.

The dry land said . . . Cf. *Memar Marqah* 2:5 (II, 54). *MRS* reads:
"The Sea (kept) saying to the dry land, 'Receive your crowds'; and
the dry land (kept) saying to the Sea, 'Receive your crowds.' Said
the dry land to it (i.e. the Sea), 'If when . . .'" On the dialogue of
earth and sea, cf. V. Aptowitzer, in *HUCA*, III (1926), 151. See also
Ginzberg, *Legends*, v, 140, n. 23.

"it was said with reference to me" *MRS:* "it was said regarding it."

"more than the" So, I believe, *mn hʾdmh* is to be translated. Note
therefore, that as Cain is cursed, the curse of the earth is also spoken
of (quite independently of the curse in Gen. 3:17); and see also Gen.
4:12, cf. Lauterbach's note, ad loc. The reading in HR, p. 145, line
7, is impossible.

can I possibly take in the blood of all these throngs?"
Finally, the Holy One, blessed be He, promised the land
under oath "that I will not bring charges against you," as
it is said, "When Thou didst raise Thy right hand, the
earth swallowed them"—for "right hand" is nothing other
than a reference to an oath, as it is said, "The Lord hath
sworn by His right hand" etc. (Isa. 62:8).

Another interpretation of THOU TURNEST THY RIGHT HAND
ETC.: Scripture declares that when the Holy One, blessed be
He, turns his hand, the wicked are eliminated from the
world, as it is said, "And He will turn His hand on the
north, and destroy Assyria" etc. (Zeph. 2:13), and it says,
"Behold, I will stretch out My hand upon the Philistines,
and I will cut off" etc. (Ezek. 25:16), and it says, "(And) I will
stretch out My hand upon Judah" etc. (Zeph. 1:4), and it
says, "And I will stretch out My hand upon Edom, and I
will cut off" etc. (Ezek. 25:13).

A parable: To what may this be likened? To eggs placed
in a man's hand; if he no more than turns his hand slightly,
they all fall and break—as it is said, "And when the Lord

"the blood of all these throngs" *MRS:* "The blood of all this mob"
(*hmwn hzh*).

"right hand" is nothing other . . . Cf. E. Z. Melamed, in J. Grintz
and J. Liver, eds., *Studies in the Bible* (Jerusalem, 1964), p. 210. See
also Lieberman, in *P'raqim*, I, 99 f.

that when the Holy One, blessed be He *MRS:* "that when the
Holy One."

turns . . . For this translation of *nṭh*, note the parable after the
proof-texts which are now offered.

the wicked are eliminated *MRS:* "the wicked vacate (?)," *pwnyn*.

as it is said, ("And He will turn . . .") *MRS:* "It is written," (And
He will turn . . .).

"Behold, I will stretch out" *MRS:* "And I will stretch out."

"And I will stretch out" So MT. This time *MRS* reads, "Behold, I
will stretch out."

"upon Edom . . ." Not quoted by *MRS.*

if he no more than turns his hand slightly, they all fall *MRS:*
"If he turns his hand from them (? *mhm*), immediately they fall."

as it is said . . . *MRS:* "So it is when God turns His hand, he that
helpeth shall stumble . . ."

The idea expressed by the last interpretation is quite close to that
of the first interpretation; but there is a difference between them. In
the first interpretation the Midrash was primarily emphasizing that

turns His hand, both he that helpeth shall stumble and he that is helped shall fall" etc. (Isa. 31:3).

IN THY LOVE THOU HAST LED: It was an act of love Thou didst perform for us, for we had no works to our credit, as it is said, "The Lord's acts of love I will recall" etc. (Isa. 63:7), "Of the Lord's acts of love I will sing for ever" etc. (Ps. 89:2). And from the very beginning the world was created only with love, as it is said, "For I have said: By love shall the world be built" etc. (Ps. 89:3).

THIS PEOPLE THOU DIDST REDEEM: For although the whole wide world is Thine, there is for Thee no (chosen) people

---

all souls are in God's hands. In the last interpretation the Midrash focuses on the verb *nṭyt*, making vivid what happens when God puts forth or, more exactly, turns His hand on someone or other.

for we had no works to our credit Cf. *AhB*, II, 165, 166. *MRS* reads: *ḥsd šʿśyt ʿmnw, P hyh bydnw mʿśym*. Cf. below, s.v. "were inflicted."

This is the *ḥsd* (*ḥesed*), the love, God acted with, for they had no good works to their credit to merit God's great generosity toward them. On the notion of Israel having no good works to their credit at the time of the exodus, cf. Pisḥa, V (I, 33 f.).

as it is said *MRS*: "even as it is said."

"the Lord's acts of love . . ." See Isaiah 63, through v. 14.

"Of the Lord's acts of love I will sing" Note the form of "I will sing," *ʾšyrh!* *MRS* introduces this proof-text with "and it says," and after this proof-text proceeds to quote also Ps. 119:64 and Ps. 103:17.

And from the very beginning . . . with love Not in *MRS*, though it too quotes Ps. 89:3. Cf. *ARN*, p. 21, and the lovely story, ibid.; *Sifra*, 92d. See also *AhB*, II, 166.

I believe the point of our Mekilta is this: though there was no particular reward Israel was entitled to at the time of their exodus from Egypt, God acted with that very attribute of mercy which from the beginning of Creation He had employed in bringing the universe into existence (on which see also Kaspa, I [III, 151]). For note, Ps. 89:3 follows immediately on the preceding proof-text.

For although *lpy = ʾp ʿl py* (and so indeed *MRS*). The Midrash is commenting on the word *zw* ("this"), which strikes so emphatic a note; cf. also below, p. 228, and see above, 3, p. 108 ff. for a similar idea.

there is for Thee no *wʾyn lk*; *MRS*: *ʾyn lk*.

. . . (chosen) people other than Israel This is clearly the meaning of *ʾyn lk ʿm ʾlʾ yśrʾl*, as the complete Isaiah proof-text bears out; and note by the way the last two words (*ʿmy bḥyry*) in the imme-

other than Israel, as it is said, "This people I formed for Myself" (etc.) (Isa. 43:21).

So too it says, "Threescore are the queens" etc. (Cant. 6:8): "Threescore are the queens" is a reference to the sixty myriads; "And fourscore concubines" is a reference to those of the age of twenty and up; "And maidens without

---

diately preceding verse. Even here, in the first half of the sentence, the Mekilta underscores that "the whole wide world is Thine"; cf. also above, 8, p. 198, "even when all the inhabitants of the world come and cry out before Him, He hears their cries . . ." But only Israel is the Chosen People. See on this subject E. J. Bickerman, "The Historical Foundations of Postbiblical Judaism," in Finkelstein, *The Jews* (3d ed.), pp. 76–77.

Perhaps in this Mekilta statement is also a polemical retort to Christian propaganda that the true Israel is now the Church.

So too it says, "Threescore . . ." Of this passage *MRS* brings only the following (and even that only *after* the section below on Rabbi and his disciple): "And it says, 'Threescore are the queens' etc., and it says, 'My dove, My undefiled, is but one' etc."

"Threescore . . . queens" . . . **the sixty myriads** Who left Egypt; cf. Exod. 12:37, Num. 1:46, 2:32. Cf. also Pisḥa, xiv (I, 108 f.). Josephus, *Antiquities,* II, 15:1: "To estimate the total number of emigrants, including women and children, were no easy task, but those of military age numbered about six hundred thousand" (Loeb, IV, 305).

"And fourscore concubines" . . . **the age of twenty and up** This is exasperatingly difficult, but I do not believe that our text should be "corrected" to coincide with the reading of *Cant. R.* 6:9, 34c, itself in need of clarification! In *PAAJR,* v, 31, L. Finkelstein recommends the correction, suggested by several, of "twenty and up" to "sixty and up." In a private communication (4 April 1968), Professor Finkelstein generously amplifies:

"The problem about the passage in Mekilta seems to be that it is ordinarily assumed that the 600,000 Israelites in the Wilderness were males between the ages of 20 and 60. Actually, the Bible does not say so, so far as I can see. But Lev. 27:3 implies that adult males are within those age limits.

"If therefore the sixty 'queens' of King Solomon were the 600,000 Israelites, the eighty 'concubines' must be someone else. They cannot be those under twenty, for they are alluded to under 'the maidens without number.' Therefore, together with many others, I assumed that the 'concubines' were those above sixty. . . ."

Plausible as this explanation is (but why "concubines"?), I cannot escape the feeling that the Mekilta text as it stands is in some way connected with the statement about the 80,000 young men named Aaron, spoken of in Kallah (ed. Higger [New York, 1936], p. 218); cf.

number" is a reference to the innumerable minors. But for all that, "My dove, My undefiled, is but one" (Cant. 6:9) —that is, Moses, who was the equal of them all.

On one occasion Rabbi sat holding a discourse to the effect that in Egypt one (Hebrew) woman gave birth to sixty myriads. One of the disciples in his company spoke

---

S. Lieberman in his *Supplement to Tosephta*, ed. Zuckermandel (Jerusalem, 1937), p. 52. Note also Aboab, *Menorat ha-Maʾor* (Stetin, 5626), 186d, and the commentary, *Nefesh Yehudah*, ad loc. (I owe this last reference to the commentary on Kallah in the regular Talmud editions.)

Why "concubines" however? "Concubine" is *plgš;* and it seems to me that M. Friedmann (in his Mekilta edition, 42b, note 16) has correctly connected this with *plgs* (*pallags,* vocalized *palges* by Yalon in M. Parah 1:3; Greek, *pállax*), youth (see Aruch Completum, VI, 338b, *plgs*).

(Incidentally, on the number of those named Aaron, contrast the figures in *ARNB,* end of chap. 24, p. 50. As for the stereotype number 80,000, cf. *Lam. R.,* 2, ed. Buber, 54b.)

a reference to the innumerable minors Cf. the final clause in Exodus 12:37. Note also the different interpretations of "maidens without number" in *Cant. R.,* 6:9, 34c. On the number of those leaving Egypt, Philo, *The Special Laws,* II, 146, says, "that great migration from Egypt which was made by more than two millions of men and women" (Loeb, VII, 395; and cf. note, ad loc.). See also *Moses,* I, 147 (Loeb, VI, 353).

But for all that That is, although there are many God loves and cares for (for He certainly was not indifferent to the 600,000 He redeemed from bondage), nevertheless, even among all those He loved, He still has a favorite—to wit, Moses—because Moses devoted himself entirely to Him. Cf. above, s.v. "(chosen) people . . ."

Moses . . . of them all *šqwl kngd hkl;* cf. above, 1, p. 67, s.v. "Moses . . . with Moses" and "Leading all Israel in it."

On one occasion Cf. *Mid. Tan.,* p. 45. From *Cant. R.* 4:1, 23a–b (cf. 1:15, 13a), it would appear that the occasion was one when Rabbi discovered that as he was lecturing the congregation was falling asleep, and he decided to say something startling and extreme in order to wake them up. Cf. *GJP,* p. 161. See also Y. M. Kosovsky, in *Sinai,* XXII (1959), 233 ff., on the terms *drš* and *ʾmr.*

Of course the story and "homily" are introduced here in the Mekilta as an amplification or affirmation of the point just made on Moses being God's favorite among the very people, Israel, whom He loves. On Rabbi's view of Moses, cf. above, 1, p. 66 f.

in Egypt one (Hebrew) woman *MRS:* "one woman of Israel."

sixty myriads *MRS:* "sixty myriads at one birth" (the word "myriads" is added above the line, having been accidentally omitted at first by the copyist; note clearly, ibid., p. 217). See the comments in

up and said to him: "Master, what is of greater import, the
world or a righteous man?"

"The righteous man," Rabbi replied.

"How so?"

Said Rabbi to him: "Take the case of Jochebed, who
gave birth to Moses, (and) he was the equal of them all."

---

the Midrash (e.g. *Exod. R.* 1:8 on Exod. 1:7) on the extraordinary
fertility of the Hebrew women; cf. Pisḥa, XII (I, 95), Be-Shallaḥ, I (I,
175); *Deut. R.*, ed. Lieberman, p. 15; Ginzberg, *Legends*, V, 391, n.
4; Heinemann, p. 24 (and n. 48, ad loc.).

One of the disciples in his company spoke up and said to him
MRS: "And his disciples on that occasion (lit., hour) spoke up and
said," and this plural is continued.

Strictly speaking, there is no direct continuation of Rabbi's remark in the query raised by the student. As the Mekilta reads, we
must assume that the student understood what Rabbi intended by
the "grotesque" statement—namely, that it implied that Moses, one
man, could be regarded as more than the equal of a whole people.
And if so, the student presses on: Is it really so that one *ṣaddiq* can
be held to be of greater weight than a whole people? Yes, answers
Rabbi, and cites the proof-texts to support his view.

While Rabbi's view is not necessarily in conflict with the view
found in Pisḥa, I (I, 13 ff.), certainly the mood of the latter would
hardly encourage the attitude reflected in our present statement by
Rabbi.

Master, what is (*wky my*) **of greater import, the world or a righteous man** (*hṣdyq*) *MRS:* "What is (*my*) of greater import, a righteous man (*ṣdyq*) or all men (*kl ᵓdm*)."

The question raised by Rabbi's student resembles the kind of
question that would arise in schools of rhetoric; for example: "*Theses*
on the other hand are concerned with the comparison of things and
involve questions such as 'Which is preferable, town or country life?'
or 'Which deserves the greatest praise, the lawyer or the soldier?'"
(Quintilian, II, 4:24 [Loeb, I, 237]).

"The righteous man," Rabbi replied On the notion of the dom-
inating role of the righteous in the world, see also *Sifre Deut.*, 47,
p. 106; 306, p. 333. Cf. above, 1, p. 74. Note similarly the statement
by R. Eleazar b. Shammua in B. Ḥagigah 12b, in connection with
which cf. *Legends*, V, 12, n. 28. See too below, X, p. 247. Cf. Bonsirven, II, 307 ff.; Mach, *Der Zaddik*, pp. 110 ff.

"How so (*lmh*)**"** *MRS:* "They said to him: 'In what way' (*bmh*)."

"Take . . . Jochebed, who gave birth to Moses" *MRS:* "We find
that Jochebed, Moses's mother, gave birth to Moses." On Jochebed,
cf. Exod. 6:20, Num. 26:59.

"(and) he was the equal of them all" *MRS:* "who is the equal of
all Israel." Cf. above, 1, s.v. "leading all Israel in it."

And how can we tell that he was the equal of them all?
For it is said, "As the Lord commanded Moses and the
children of Israel" (Num. 26:4), and it says, "Then sang
Moses and the children of Israel" (Exod. 15:1), and it says,
"And there hath not arisen a prophet since in Israel like
unto Moses" (Deut. 34: 10).

BY VIRTUE OF THY STRENGTH THOU HAST GUIDED THEM: By
virtue of the Torah, which they were to receive later. For
"Thy strength" is nothing other than a reference to Torah,
as it is said, "The Lord will give strength unto His people"
(Ps. 29:11), and it says, "The strength also of the King who
loveth justice" (Ps. 99:4).

Another interpretation of BY VIRTUE OF THY STRENGTH
THOU HAST GUIDED THEM: By virtue of the royal house of

And how can we tell Lit., "Now, where do we find." *MRS:* "And so
too we find."

that he was the equal of them all? For it is said . . . *MRS:* "that
Moses was the equal of all Israel, at the time when he recited the
Song, as it is said, 'Then sang Moses and the children of Israel'"
(Exod. 15:1).

Perhaps this is still part of Rabbi's reply, in which case, of course,
the closing quotation marks should not come until the end of the
paragraph. But I believe that from this point on we are listening
to the Midrash homilist and not to Rabbi's own words.

"As the Lord commanded . . . Israel" Not quoted by *MRS;* but
cf. the following note.

The idiom of the proof-text reveals that though all the children
of Israel are referred to, Moses is singled out specifically, and at that,
first; and the same is true of Exod. 15:1. Note also the idiom of
Num. 26:4b.

there hath not arisen a prophet . . . After quoting this verse, *MRS*
proceeds to quote Josh. 11:15 and (as indicated above) Cant. 6:8–9.

By virtue of the Torah Before offering this interpretation, *MRS*
reads: "Thou hast guided us with might, (for) 'my strength' refers
to nothing other than might, as it is said, 'O Lord, my strength, and
my stronghold' etc. (Jer. 16:19), and it says, 'The Lord is my strength
and my shield' etc. (Ps. 28:7)." Cf. above, 3, pp. 107 f.

. . . which they (šhn) were to receive later Cf. above, 3, p. 107,
and note, ad loc., s.v. "As it is said . . . justice" Cf. also below, p.
230, and 10, p. 234.

MRS reads here: "By virtue of Torah which (they) were to receive
later."

For "Thy strength" is . . . to Torah Not in *MRS.*

David, which they were to receive in the future. For "Thy strength" is nothing other than a reference to royalty, as it is said, "O Lord, in Thy strength the king rejoiceth" etc. (Ps. 21:2), and it says, "And He will give strength unto His king" (I Sam. 2:10).

TO THY HOLY HABITATION: By virtue of the Temple which they were to build in the future. For "habitation" is nothing other than a reference to the Temple, as it is said, "And they have laid waste His habitation" (Ps. 79:7), and it says, "Look upon Zion, the city of our solemn gatherings; Thine eyes shall see Jerusalem a peaceful habitation" (Isa. 33:20).

THE PEOPLES HAVE HEARD, THEY TREMBLE: When the Nations of the World heard that Pharaoh and his troops had perished in the Sea, that the empire of Egypt was over and done with, and that disasters were inflicted on their idols, they began to tremble. That is why it is said, "The peoples have heard, they tremble."

By virtue of the royal house of David Cf. above, 3, p. 107 f. *MRS:* "By virtue of the house of David who will receive the royalty in the future."

For "Thy strength" is . . . to royalty Not in *MRS.*

"in Thy strength the king rejoiceth" After this *MRS* quotes Ps. 28:8.

"He will . . . unto His king" *MRS:* "He will give strength unto His people"; but note critical apparatus, ad loc.

which they were to build in the future *MRS:* "which (they) were to build in the future, as it is said, 'To Thy holy habitation'; and it says . . ." See also *Midrash Psalms* 84:2, 185b.

For "habitation" is . . . to the Temple Not in *MRS.*

"a peaceful habitation" Cf. above, 3, p. 115. Although the Mekilta is here presenting commentary on the phrase "to Thy holy habitation," note that the comment is stylistically like the two on the clause "By virtue of Thy strength Thou hast guided them"; in other words, we have again as so often a unit of three statements.

the Nations of the World *MRS:* "(When) they (heard)." Cf. below, s.v. "the Nations of the World."

over and done with (*wbṭlh*) *MRS:* "and perished" (*wᵓbdh*).

were inflicted (*nᶜśw*) *MRS:* "which were inflicted" (*šnᶜśw*). Cf. above, s.v. "for we had no works to our credit."

heard . . . on their idols Cf. above, 8, pp. 190 f.

That is why . . . "they tremble" Not in *MRS.* Cf. *Memar Marqah*, II, 9 (II, 70): "*The people have heard, they tremble,* for the kingdom

Another interpretation of THE PEOPLES HAVE HEARD, THEY RAGE: When the Nations of the World heard that God was crowning Israel with triumph and bringing them into the Land, they fell into a rage. Said the Omnipotent to them: Idiots! How many monarchs of yours occupied the throne, yet Israel never grew angry, as it is said, "And these are the kings that reigned in the land of Edom" (Gen. 36:31)! How many rulers of yours exercised rule, yet Israel never grew angry, as it is said, "The chief of Lotan" etc. (Gen. 36:

---

of the Egyptians has ceased for them, for it was in their estimation a mighty kingdom." Note also how Marqah goes on, through p. 72 (e.g. "They were in terror when they heard that the sea was the executioner of the Egyptians and that Pharaoh's kingdom had been subdued by its fury . . .").

According to this interpretation, then, the Nations were terrified lest what had overtaken so mighty a kingdom as Pharaoh's might now also overtake them. Compare now the next interpretation offered by the Mekilta.

Another interpretation of . . . THEY RAGE *MRS* does not repeat the biblical quotation.

the Nations of the World Not in *MRS;* cf. above, s.v. "the Nations of the World."

that God (*mqwm*) *MRS:* "That the Holy One, blessed be He."

crowning Israel with triumph Lit., "exalting high the horn of Israel." Note how a descriptive term in Dan. 8:3 is made into an expression equivalent to, e.g., Ps. 92:11 or 148:14.

and bringing them into the Land Not in *MRS.* The expression, in effect, explains what the special exaltation consisted of—God's giving Israel possession of the Holy Land.

they fell into a rage Lit., "they began to rage"; *MRS:* "they began to be angry."

According to this interpretation, when the Nations heard what was in store for Israel, they were driven into a rage out of unreasonable envy, for they did not want Israel to have that Land. (Is this Midrash an echo of protest against the fierce suppression of Jewish attempts and revolts to regain independence in Roman times? Note the retort put into God's mouth as the paragraph continues.)

Idiots Not in *MRS.*

of yours occupied the throne *mlkw mkm; MRS:* "of yours arose" (*ᶜmdw mkm*).

yet Israel never grew angry *MRS:* "yet My sons did not rage."

as it is said Not in *MRS.*

"Edom" Referring, almost certainly, to Rome!

of yours exercised rule *MRS:* "of yours arose."

yet Israel never grew angry *MRS:* "yet My sons never grew angry."

as it is said Not in *MRS.*

29)! And do you now grow angry? I will therefore give you cause for an anger in no way to be appeased, as it is said, "The Lord reigneth! Let the peoples rage" (Ps. 99:1)!

PANGS HAVE TAKEN HOLD ON THE INHABITANTS OF PHILISTIA: When the inhabitants of Philistia heard that Israel were entering the Land, they said: Israel are now coming to stir up revenge for what happened to the Ephraimites, as

And do you now grow angry That is, and now when I give Israel a land and kingdom of their own, you are unreasonably enraged? Cf. *Memar Marqah* (II, 70): "This is a true prophecy . . . The kingdom of Israel has now been created!" I will therefore, says God, bring about a state of affairs in the Future which will provoke you to even greater rage.

I will therefore give ʾp ʾny ʾtn; MRS, ʾny nwtn.

you cause for . . . appeased Lauterbach translates, "I too will vent upon you an irreconcilable anger." I believe that what is implied by the expression kᶜs šʾyn bw rṣwn is the following: Out of their rage against Israel's being given the Land, the Nations once upon a time were able to expel Israel from the Land, when the opportunity to expel them presented itself. Hence this former rage served almost as a stimulus for the Nations to get their own satisfaction. But a time will come in the End, says God, when He will finally establish His sovereignty over all the world (cf. Ps. 99:1, which is now cited, and note also 99:2!), and then, rage against this as they might, the Nations will be utterly incapable of doing anything about it.

With the expression kᶜs šʾyn bw rṣwn, cf. PA 4:18, ʾl trṣh . . . bšᶜt kᶜsw.

as it is said Not in MRS.

"The Lord reigneth! . . . rage" That is, in the Future, when God's full triumph will be manifest and Israel's ultimate redemption will have taken place. Cf. *Sifre Deut.*, 333, p. 382, and *Mid. Tan.*, p. 203, on Deut. 32:43a.

PANGS . . . OF PHILISTIA After the general statement in the Shirah, that at Israel's exodus from Egypt the Nations were in a state of turmoil, either out of terror or anger at Israel's good fortune, mention is specifically made of the reactions of Philistines, Edomites, Moabites, and Canaanites. Therefore the Midrash now undertakes to explain what specifically was the cause for the reactions of each of these respective peoples.

When the inhabitants . . . the Land Not in MRS.

to stir up revenge (lᶜwrr ᶜyrwtm) **for what happened to the Ephraimites** MRS: "To take revenge (lgbwt ᶜyyrwtn) for what happened to Ephraim their father." (On the reading ᶜyyrwtn, cf. critical apparatus in MRS, ibid.) The Mekilta is referring to a tradition of the premature exodus of the Ephraimites and their disastrous defeat by

it is said, "And the sons of Ephraim: Shuthelah—and Bered was his son, and his son" etc. (I Chron. 7:20), and it says, "The Ephraimites were as archers handling the bow, and in the day of battle they had to turn back" (Ps. 78:9). —And the reason for that? Because "They kept not the covenant of God, and refused to walk in His Torah" (Ps. 78:10), (that is,) because they trespassed upon the terms for the Appointed Time and because they violated the oath!

Another interpretation: The Philistines said: Israel have no course anywhere save through our country; indeed,

Philistines; cf. Ginzberg, *Legends,* III, 8 f., and notes, ad loc., and Lauterbach's note in Be-Shallaḥ, I (I, 172, n. 6). See also Hengel, p. 129, n. 5.

"Shuthelah . . . and his son . . ." Note how the verse in Chronicles continues. *MRS* does not quote this verse. Cf. Be-Shallaḥ, I (I, 172 f.).

"in the day of battle . . . turn back" In other words, suffered defeat; and note the verses following in Ps. 78, which go on to speak of the ordained exodus, hence, midrashically, as a contrast to what happened to the Ephraimites who undertook an exodus on their own.

and the reason . . . violated the oath None of this in *MRS;* indeed, this comment is irrelevant here, where all that is being discussed is the reason for the fears of the Philistines. On the other hand, see Be-Shallaḥ, I (I, 172 f). In Shirta here, once the verses from Chronicles and Psalms are introduced, the compiler apparently decided to bring the explanation for the defeat of the Ephraimites.

On "because They kept not . . .", note how the midrashic idiom attaches itself to the biblical one.

"Because they trespassed . . . the oath": It is in this regard that they did not keep God's covenant and disobeyed His law. See in this connection *Cant. R.* 2:17, 16c. On the subject of calculating the *qṣ,* see A. H. Silver, *Messianic Speculations in Israel* (New York, 1927), pp. 3-35, 195-206. Cf. also Hengel, 129, and n. 5, ibid.

Regardless of what the political realities may have been to produce an attitude like that reflected by our passage, for the Mekilta on the Shirah it would be a most congenial attitude, since the Mekilta takes every opportunity it can to underscore that the deliverance from Egyptian bondage has all the elements of the supernatural about it. Without God's activity, no deliverance would be possible. See further above, 2, p. 100 f., and the note s.v. "The horse was strapped to his rider."

Another interpretation *MRS:* "Another interpretation of 'Pangs have taken hold on the inhabitants of Philistia.' "

anywhere Not in *MRS.* Since the logical course for the Hebrews would have been by way of the land of the Philistines (Exod. 13:17a), the Philistines naturally assumed that the Hebrews would be coming through their country and plundering it—hence their fears.

they must be coming to plunder us of our possessions and
to ruin our land.

THEN WERE THE CHIEFS OF EDOM AFFRIGHTED: Do you want
to say (it was because the Edomites thought) that "Israel

> **THEN WERE THE CHIEFS OF EDOM AFFRIGHTED** To under-
> stand the Midrash on this and the following biblical clause, several
> points must be noted:
>   (1) Scripture reports that the leaders of Edom (on ᵓ*lwp*, cf. Gen.
> 36:15 ff.) and Moab were in terror. But why, wonders the Midrash—
> what reason could there possibly be for these people to feel threatened?
>   (2) The Midrash constantly proceeds on the assumption that every-
> one was aware of the fact that God redeemed Israel from Egyptian
> bondage to bring them to the Promised Land, the land of Canaan.
> That the Philistines should be disturbed is understandable (see above),
> for it was reasonable to expect Israel's coming through their territory.
> That the Canaanites had good reason to be disturbed (see below) is
> obvious: they were to be dispossessed. But the midrashic *commentator*
> cannot understand why anyone else—specifically Edom and Moab—
> should feel endangered. So *he* says: ᵓ*m t*ᵓ*mr* (note well this expression:
> it is a cliché but must originally have represented either the com-
> mentator thinking out loud or two students in the academy exploring
> a problem), If you might want to say that Edom and Moab were
> in terror because they feared that they too would be dispossessed, that
> is absurd, for *we* know that *at the proper time* specific instructions
> were to be given by God that these countries must not be invaded.
> And—as is often the case with writers and teachers—the midrashic
> commentator simply assumes that what he knows, everyone else knows.
> Since we all know, as it were, that fear of invasion could not have
> been the reason for their reactions, *maybe,* says the commentator, it
> was because Edom and Moab feared they would be compelled (by
> tribute, *annona*) to provide for the needs of Israel, as Israel passed
> through their land; maybe (*dbr* ᵓ*ḥr*) they feared that Israel would
> now recall the ancient quarrel between their ancestor and ours, and
> seek vengeance. Maybe this, maybe that—in other words, the com-
> mentator is himself not sure of what the reason for fear was, and
> admits that he is really baffled: he does not know how adequately
> to explain why, but he must accept the fact that Edom and Moab
> were in fear, for that is what Scripture reports.
>   (3) The word ᵓ*z* ("then") is ambiguous; cf. the very beginning of
> the Mekilta on the Shirah. The word need not necessarily mean
> "then, when the miracle at the Sea occurred," at that moment did
> fear seize the Edomites and Moabites. Whatever the moment when
> fear seized them, why *did* it, the author of the midrashic statement
> wonders.
>   The key to the understanding of the Mekilta on the two clauses,
> "Then were the chiefs of Edom affrighted" and "The mighty men of

are coming to take possession of our land?" But it is plainly stated, "Ye are to pass through the border of your brethren . . . take ye good heed unto yourselves therefore; contend not with them" etc. (Deut. 2:4–5)! Why, then, does Scripture say, "Then were the chiefs of Edom affrighted?" Because (what they feared) was the imposition of annonary imposts.

Another interpretation: The Edomites said: They are now coming to stir up the (old) quarrel between our father and their father, as it is said, "And Esau hated Jacob" (Gen. 27:41).

Moab, trembling taketh hold upon them," is, I believe, in the expression "Do you want to say" (literally, "If you want to say"). Note that on "The peoples have heard, they tremble" the Mekilta reads, "When the Nations . . . heard . . . ," and the identical idiom recurs on "Pangs have taken hold on the inhabitants of Philistia," as well as (below) on "All the inhabitants of Canaan are aghast." But when the Midrash turns to the two clauses, "Then were the chiefs of Edom affrighted" and "The mighty men of Moab, trembling taketh hold upon them," the style changes to "Do you want to say . . . but it is plainly stated . . . Why, then, does Scripture say" (and observe how the one paragraph is simply a repetition of the other). The very change in style discloses that one set of biblical clauses is approached by the Midrash in one way, while the other set of clauses is approached in a different way. (For the expression ʾm tʾmr, cf., for example, Sifre Deut., 311, pp. 351 f., and several times in the Mekilta, e.g. Pisḥa I [I, 5], Be-Shallaḥ II [I, 201], etc.)

"our land" MRS, using indirect discourse: "their land."

but it is plainly stated whlʾ kbr nʾmr; MRS: hry kbr nʾmr. This formula need not necessarily be taken as "it has already been said," but rather as something like, "but is there not in addition a verse to the effect that . . ."

Why, then, does Scripture . . . annonary imposts (ʾnynywt) MRS: "Only because of annonary imposts" (ʾrwnynʾwt). On ʾnynywt, cf. Glossary in MRS, p. 255. See also TK, Long Commentary on T. Ḥallah 1:4, p. 794, and A. Berger, Encyclopedic Dictionary of Roman Law (Philadelphia, 1953), p. 363. On the obsolete English word "annonary," cf. OED, s.v.

For the interpretation offered by Rashi on Exod. 15:15a, see also AhB, I, 32.

Another interpretation Not in MRS, but note critical apparatus, p. 97, esp. l. 21, on interpretation of "The mighty men of Moab."

to stir up . . . quarrel MRS: "to take (vengeance for?) the enmity" (lgbwt śnʾh). Cf. below, s.v. "to stir up . . . quarrel."

As it is said Not in MRS.

"Esau" I.e. Edom; cf. Gen. 36:1. On the notion of the old hatred being recalled, cf. also Memar Marqah, II, 9 (II, 71 ff.).

THE MIGHTY MEN OF MOAB, TREMBLING TAKETH HOLD UPON
THEM: Do you want to say (it was because the Moabites
thought) that "Israel are coming to take possession of our
land?" But it is plainly stated, "Be not at enmity with Moab"
etc. (Deut. 2:9), and also, "And when thou comest nigh
over against Ammonites" etc. (Deut. 2:19)! Why, then, does
Scripture say, "The mighty men of Moab, trembling taketh
hold upon them?" Because it was the imposition of annonary imposts (they feared).

Another interpretation: The Moabites said: They are
coming to stir up the (old) quarrel between our father and
their father, as it is said, "And there was strife between the
herdmen of Abram's cattle" etc. (Gen. 13:7).

ALL THE INHABITANTS OF CANAAN ARE AGHAST: When the
inhabitants of Canaan heard that God had said to Moses,
"Howbeit of the cities of these peoples . . . but thou shalt
utterly destroy" etc. (Deut. 20:16–17), they said: The former

THE MIGHTY MEN OF MOAB, TREMBLING . . . See above,
s.v. "Then were the chiefs of Edom affrighted."

"Our land" *MRS,* again in indirect discourse: "their land."

"And when thou . . . against the Ammonites" *MRS* does not quote
this verse, and of course the Shirah does speak only of Moab.

Why, then, does Scripture . . . Because *MRS,* simply "only because."

to stir up . . . quarrel *MRS:* "to avenge (?) (the) quarrel" (*lgbwt
mrybh*); cf. above, s.v. "to stir up . . . quarrel."

"And there was strife . . ." Lot is the ancestor of Moab and Ammon; cf. Gen. 19:30 ff. *MRS* does not introduce this proof-text with
the formula "as it is said."

**When the inhabitants of Canaan heard that God (*hmqwm*) had
said to Moses** *MRS:* "When they heard that the Holy One, blessed be
He, had said to Moses" (*lw lmšh*).

they said In *MRS,* p. 97, the text for the next several lines is poorly
preserved; literally, after the Deut. 20:16 quotation, it reads: "They
began to melt away (*nmwgym*). The ones said to the others, 'We
are in fear only because of the mob and because of their possessions.'
They began to melt away (*nmwsyn*). 'But they are coming against us
only to wipe us out.' They began to melt away (*nmwgym*)—for *nmygh*
is nothing other than *hmsʾh,* as it is said, 'When the earth and all
the inhabitants thereof are *nmwgym*' etc. (Ps. 75:4), and it says, 'That
their heart be *lmwg,* and their stumblings be multiplied' (Ezek. 21:20).
This is the reason (that) 'All the inhabitants of Canaan are melted
away.'"

and the latter had only to fear for their wealth and for
their possessions; but against us they're coming with no
purpose other than to wipe us out and take possession of
our land! And they began to go to pieces, as it is said, "All
the inhabitants of Canaan are aghast"—for "aghast" is
nothing other than a reference to "going to pieces," as it is
said, "And every heart shall go to pieces" (Ezek. 21:12), and
it says, "When the earth and all the inhabitants thereof
are aghast" (Ps. 75:4), and it says, "That their heart be
aghast" (Ezek. 21:20).

However, cf. ibid., p. 238.

See further, below, s.v. "they began to go to pieces" and "And
every heart shall go to pieces."

The former and the latter Edomites and Moabites.

and take possession of our land Not in *MRS* (cf. above, s.v. "they
said").

They began to go to pieces (*nymsyn*) *MRS:* "They began to
nmwgym."

The midrashic comment seems to grow out of the observation that
in describing the reactions of fear of the different peoples, Scripture
resorts to different terms. For the Philistines it was "pangs take hold,"
for the Edomites "affrighted," for the Moabites "trembling taketh
hold," and now for the Canaanites it is being "aghast." (Moreover, the
Midrash has very likely also observed that in connection with the
Philistines, the verse speaks of "inhabitants"; in connection with the
Edomites, it speaks of "chiefs"; in connection with the Moabites, it
speaks of "mighty men"; but in connection with the Canaanites, the
verse speaks of "*All* the inhabitants" [see also Josh. 2:24]. In other
words, here there is complete panic.) Among the Canaanites, the Midrash tells us, it was a question not only of fear and trembling but of
complete undoing; they literally "melted away," went to pieces, and
lost all capacity to resist. See further below, s.v. "And every heart shall
go to pieces." Cf. Luzzatto, p. 289.

as it is said, "All . . . are aghast" *MRS* quotes this at the conclusion of the comment; cf. above, s.v. "they said."

"going to pieces (*msyyh*)" *MRS, hmsᵓh.*

"And every heart shall go to pieces" *MRS* does not quote this verse.
Cf. *AhB*, I, 32.

What point is there, we may ask, in the Mekilta's explanation that
nmygh (for which we have adopted the translation "aghast") equals
msyyh (literally, "melting away," and we translate "going to pieces")?
It seems to me that while the verb *mwg* occurs quite a number of
times in biblical literature, apparently it was not in much use in tannaite Hebrew (although it continues to appear in Dead Sea literature,
e.g. *Hodayot* 3:34–35; see also *Scroll of the War of Sons of Light* 14:6;

AWE AND TERROR DESCEND UPON THEM: "Awe" on those far
away, and "Terror" on those nearby, even as it is said, "And

---

and note further the Aramaic *mgᵓ*, *mgy* in talmudic lexica), and thus
would be a difficult word. The verb *mss*, on the other hand, does
continue in tannaite Hebrew. Our commentator is therefore explaining that biblical *mwg* means *mss*, and proves it from Scripture itself:
In Ezek. 21:12 we read of the heart *nms*; Ps. 75:4 speaks of a land
and all its inhabitants (cf. our very verse of the Shirah) *nmwgym*; and
Ezek. 21:20 uses this latter verb *mwg* with "heart." *Nmwgw* is thus
the equivalent of *nmsw*, and it applies to the *heart*. "*Nmwgw* all the
inhabitants of Canaan" therefore means, "All the inhabitants of
Canaan lost heart completely."

AWE AND TERROR . . . Resuming also with *MRS*, p. 97.

"Awe" on those far away . . . *MRS:* " 'Awe' on those nearby, and
'terror' on those far away; and so too it says," and now comes quotation of Josh. 5:1, not the verses reporting Rahab's statement. For the
reading of our Mekilta, see also *Sifre Deut.*, 52, p. 118; *Mid. Tan.*,
p. 44; Rashi on Exod. 15:16 and on Deut. 11:25.

The Mekilta is explaining why there are two terms, "awe" and
"terror" (ᵓymth and *phd*), rather than one; is this not an instance of
redundancy? (Note in fact, that though the combination of ᵓymh and
phd occurs in Dead Sea literature—cf. K. G. Kuhn, *Konkordanz zu
den Qumrantexten* [Göttingen, 1960], p. 176; observe also the liturigical
style, "And so, set *phd* of Thee . . . over all Thy works, and ᵓymh
of Thee over all that Thou hast created": Baer, p. 384, and the
reading in *PRE*, chap. 42, f. 100b—in Scripture only here in the
Shirah do ᵓymh and *phd* come together.) Not at all, is the answer;
each term conveys a particular sense.

Perhaps the distinction between ᵓymh and *phd* made by the
Midrash, lies in this: In Josh. 2:9 we read of the ᵓymh of the
inhabitants of Canaan (and note how that verse goes on!) when they
heard (cf. 2:10) of events quite far off from them; and hearing of these
sensational happenings, they not only (v. 11a) lost all courage but
(v. 11b) were led to acknowledge that the Lord alone is God. The
real ᵓymh (awesomeness) would consist of all that Rahab reported. On
the other hand, in 5:1 we hear merely of the "going to pieces" of the
Amorite kings when they hear of what happened at the *crossing of
the Jordan*, something quite close to them: this might then describe
simply the "terror." (But the distinction is not entirely clear to me,
and the interpretation offered remains somewhat labored.)

On the Joshua proof-texts, cf. also above, 3, p. 122 (Simeon ben
Eleazar's statement). Cf. Amalek, III (II, 163). And on the idiom of
the "far away" and the "nearby" see also above, 8, p. 199, and note s.v.
"reverence toward himself . . . nearby."

Finally, note that the Mekilta, in its comment, appropriates the
biblical word ᵓymth (although the word in this form occurs in
Scripture only here).

it came to pass, when all the kings of the Amorites heard"
etc. (Josh. 5:1); but by the same token Rahab said to
Joshua's messengers, "When we heard how the Lord dried
up the water of the Reed Sea" (etc.) (Josh. 2:10), and
continued, "As soon as we had heard it, our hearts went to
pieces" (etc.) (Josh. 2:11).

BY THE GREATNESS OF THINE ARM LET THEM BE REDUCED TO
STONELIKE SILENCE: When Israel came forth from the Sea,
Amalek assembled all the Nations of the World and came
and made battle against Israel. On that occasion Moses
offered up a prayer and all of them were reduced to stone-

Joshua's messengers Cf. above, 3, s.v. "And Rahab . . . Joshua's
messengers."

and continued Lit., "and it says." Note that HR, p. 148, line 3,
does not have this formula.

When Israel came forth from the Sea *MRS:* "When Israel crossed
over the Sea." See Exod. 17:8 ff.

Amalek assembled all the Nations of the World *MRS:* "Amalek
assembled against them all the kings of the Nations of the World."
On Amalek, cf. Be-Shallaḥ, I (I, 172), and Amalek, I (II, 136); see also
Josephus, *Antiquities*, III, 2:1 (Loeb, IV, 339). For still another view
of what Amalek did, cf. Be-Shallaḥ, II (I, 194).

and came and made battle against Israel *MRS:* "to come to make
battle against them." Cf. Exod. 17:8–16.

On that occasion . . . a prayer *(wntpll) MRS* reads, *ntpll.* The
Midrash is obviously interpreting *ydmw* as a jussive; i.e. May they be
reduced to stonelike silence. The thought of Moses praying may be
suggested by his uplifted hands; cf. Exod. 17:11 f. and Palestinian Tg
on 17:12 (and M. Rosh ha-Shanah 3:8). *ZY* suggests: since several of
the verbs in the preceding verses (e.g. "were affrighted") appear in the
perfect tense, the imperfect *ydmw* reflects supplication for something
in the future. See further, next note.

all of them were reduced to stonelike silence It is not clear what
specifically in the verse "By the greatness of Thine arm . . ." suggests
that the reference is to the war with and victory over the Amalekites.
Zayit Raᶜanan, in *Yalkut Shimeoni* (251), on the verse tentatively pro-
poses a connection between God's arm and "the hand upon the
throne of the Lord" of Exod. 17:16. Even more forced is the explanation of *SY:* the stone mentioned in our verse is to be associated with
the stone mentioned in 17:12.

The silencing of Amalek is very likely to be explained in the
light of Yose ben Ḥalafta's statement in Amalek, I (II, 136), that
Amalek undertook to counsel other nations to join in the attack on
Israel.

like silence. That is why it is said, "By the greatness of Thine arm let them be reduced to stonelike silence."

Another interpretation of REDUCED TO STONELIKE SILENCE: When the spies entered the Land, whoever was about to say, "These are Israel's spies," was reduced to stonelike silence.

Another interpretation of BY THE GREATNESS OF THINE ARM . . . : When Israel had crossed the Jordan, all the kings of Canaan gathered together and came and made battle against Israel, as it is said, "And it came to pass, when Jabin king of Hazor heard thereof . . . and to the kings that were on the north" etc. (Josh. 11:1–2), and it also says,

---

On "reduced to . . . silence (*ydmw*)" cf. Y. Kutscher, in *Hadoar,* XLIII (New York, 5 April 1963), p. 378, and Cross and Freedman, in *JNES,* XIV, 249.

That is why it is said *MRS:* "as it is said."

When the spies entered the Land The spies sent by Moses, Num. 13 (*SY* apparently takes this as a reference to the spies sent by Joshua, Josh. 2); cf. above, 3, p. 122, and the note, ad loc., s.v. "And Rahab . . . Joshua's messengers."

MRS reads, "When the spies of Israel entered the Land."

whoever was about to say *MRS:* "whoever wished to say."

was reduced to stonelike silence *MRS:* "were reduced to stonelike silence" (*dwmyn;* cf. critical apparatus, ibid., p. 98, note to line 10, and Melamed's Introduction to *MRS,* p. 41, top); "that is why it is said, 'By the greatness of Thine arm let them be reduced to stonelike silence.' "

(For another explanation of how the spies could spy out the Land and remain undetected, see *Num. R.* 16:13, *Tanḥuma Numbers,* ed. Buber, 34a. On still another miracle in this connection, cf. Ginzberg, *Legends,* VI, 94, n. 515.)

The Mekilta in this comment is led to thoughts of the spies sent by Moses, because it interprets the verse as follows: Let terror overtake all the inhabitants of Canaan, by Thy powerful arm let them be reduced to stonelike silence, until (v. 16b) Thy people, O Lord, have successfully crossed over (into the Promised Land).

When Israel . . . Jordan See Josh. 3, esp. v. 7, 13, 16, and 5:1; cf. *Legends,* IV, 5, and VI, 172, n. 14. See further below, s.v. "On that occasion Joshua offered up a prayer" and " 'pass over' the Jordan."

all the kings of Canaan gathered together and came and made battle against Israel *MRS:* "The kings of Canaan were assembled against them, to come to make battle against them."

"And it came to pass . . . heard" Note that *MRS* quotes Josh. 11 "right up to" verse 5, and does not quote 9:2 as does our Mekilta.

"And they gathered themselves together, to fight with Joshua . . . with one accord" (Josh. 9:2). On that occasion Joshua offered up a prayer and all of them were reduced to stonelike silence. That is why it is said, "By the greatness of Thine arm let them be reduced to stonelike silence."

TILL THY PEOPLE PASS OVER, O LORD, TILL (THESE) PASS OVER: "Till Thy people, O Lord, pass over" the Sea, "Till (these)

"with one accord" Lit. "one mouth"—hence, one speech, one counsel; and of course this leads the Midrash to the thought of *silencing* all these kings.

On that occasion Joshua offered up a prayer (*htpll*) MRS: "Joshua offered up a prayer (*ntpll*) on that occasion."

Once again the Mekilta is obviously drawing attention to the prophetic character of the Shirah (see, by the way, M. Friedmann, in his edition of the Mekilta [Vienna, 1870], p. 43a, n. 42). Is the Mekilta implying that Joshua recited Exod. 15:16 as his prayer? *Sekel Tob, Exod.*, p. 198, seems to be troubled by the same question: "On that occasion Joshua offered up a prayer, and the Holy One, blessed be He, remembered the prayer of Moses and the children of Israel at the Sea, and (the Canaanite kings) were reduced to stonelike silence, and they were unable to counsel one another, and so they fell (in defeat)."

Moreover, when exactly did Joshua offer up his prayer, at the time when the Canaanite kings gathered together to battle against Israel, or at the time of the miraculous crossing of the Jordan? Or is the Mekilta telescoping the two events?

Since the prophetic character of the Shirah will reappear in the Mekilta comment on the last half of Exod. 15:16, an additional observation may be in place. In midrashic compilations, where more than one interpretation of a verse is presented, very often first the interpretations which are not immediately germane are given, and finally the compiler offers that interpretation which *is* immediately relevant or which he is eager to emphasize (cf., e.g., *Lev. R.* 1:1, pp. 1–6). Very likely this is what in the present instance we have in the Mekilta also: it is the third interpretation that the compiler is leading up to all along; hence the commentary on "Till Thy people pass over . . ." continues the mood and point of view of our present passage, and the first two interpretations were essentially introductory to the last one.

TILL THY PEOPLE . . . PASS OVER The Mekilta comment grows out of the repetition of the clause "Till . . . pass over" in the verse. See further below, s.v. "the Arnon streams."

"Till Thy people, O Lord, pass over" the Sea MRS: " 'Till (Thy people) pass over' the Sea."

pass over" the Jordan, "Till (these) pass over" the Arnon streams.

THIS PEOPLE THOU DIDST PRODUCE: For although the whole world is Thine, there is for Thee no (chosen) people other than Israel, as it is said, "This people I formed for Myself" (Isa. 43:21).

> *Four   Were-Designated   Masterpiece*
> Israel   were-designated   Masterpiece
> as it is said, "This people Thou didst produce."

"pass over" the Jordan Cf. Josh. 3:7 ff. Cf. above, s.v. "When Israel . . . Jordan."

the Arnon streams *MRS:* "The (ᵓ*t*) Arnon stream"; but cf. critical apparatus, ad loc.

For the miracle at Arnon, cf. Ginzberg, *Legends,* III, 337 f.

For a similar style, cf. Be-Shallah, I (I, 182), and Amalek, II (II, 151).

However, the reference to the Arnon miracle (Num. 20) *after* those at the Jordan (Josh. 3) is something of a difficulty. For example, note the readings in Tg Onkelos and Palestinian and Jonathan Tg, ad loc. *Lekah Tob* on this verse reads, " 'Till Thy people pass over' the Sea, 'Till this people Thou didst produce pass over' the Jordan." *Sekel Tob, Exod.,* p. 198, has, " 'Till Thy people pass over, O Lord' the streams of Arnon, 'Till this people Thou didst produce pass over' the Jordan." On the other hand, the order in B. Berakot 54a is like the order in the Mekilta.

Perhaps the passage originally read as follows: " 'Till Thy people, O Lord, pass over, till (they) pass over'—'Till Thy people, O Lord, pass over' the Sea, 'till (they) pass over' the Jordan. Another interpretation: 'Till Thy people, O Lord, pass over' the Sea, 'till (they) pass over' the Arnon streams" (cf. the suggestion in HR, p. 148, note to line 13).

But it may be that the Mekilta reads as it does because it wishes first to list the miracles explicitly referred to by Scripture, and only then the miracle reported by "oral tradition."

THIS PEOPLE THOU DIDST PRODUCE *MRS:* " 'This people,' 'this people I formed for Myself.' 'Thou didst produce': the Land of Israel was designated . . ." Note, however, critical apparatus, ad loc.

Cf. above, p. 211 f., and notes, ad loc. On *qnh* as "create," "produce," see also Koehler-Baumgartner, p. 843b, and cf. above, 3, p. 113, and note, ad loc., s.v. "Its Creator." Note also Nahmanides in his comment on Rashi's comment for Gen. 14:19.

Four Were-Designated Masterpiece (*qnyn*) Cf. preceding note and Ps. 104:24.

MRS does not have this opening sentence; it introduces the passage simply by citing the one word *qnyt;* cf. the reading furnished above, s.v. "This people Thou didst produce."

The-Land of-Israel was-designated Masterpiece
as it is said, "Producer of heaven and earth" (Gen. 14:22).

The Temple was-designated Masterpiece
as it is said, "This mountain which His right hand produced" (Ps. 78:54).

The-Torah was-designated Masterpiece
as it is said, "The Lord produced me as the beginning of His way" (Prov. 8:22).

Come O-Israel, who-were-designated Masterpiece

On the style of this poem, cf. above, 6, p. 170 ff.; end of 7, p. 187 f.; and below, 10, p. 233 f. See also Mirsky, pp. 45 ff., 123.

For "parallel" passages, see *Sifre Deut.*, 309, p. 350; PA 6:10; B. Pesaḥim 87b (but cf. R. Ḥananel in *B. Pesaḥim* 87b, and Albeck's note ad PA 6:10 in his edition of the Mishnah, p. 502).

"Masterpiece"—and therefore something which one loves especially.

Israel were-designated . . . The reading in *MRS* is as follows: "The Land of Israel was designated Masterpiece, as it is said, 'Producer of heaven and earth.' Torah was designated Masterpiece, as it is said, 'The Lord produced me as the beginning of His way' etc. Israel were designated Masterpiece, as it is said, 'This people I formed for Myself' etc. The Temple was designated Masterpiece, as it is said, 'And He brought them to His holy border' etc." In what follows, however, the *MRS* reading agrees with that of our Mekilta.

"Producer of heaven and earth" This proof-text certainly creates problems; cf. the critical apparatus in Lauterbach, and note the ed. princeps reading adopted by HR ("The heavens and the earth were designated Masterpiece"), which is of no particular help in the light of the peroration. See the discussion in HR, ad loc., and in Kasher, XIV, 146, no. 192. Lauterbach's note (in his translation, II, 76) is: "According to the Mekilta . . . the phrase qwnh šmym w'rṣ in this verse is to be rendered: The possessors of heaven and the land, i.e., the Land of Israel." (I am not sure if Lauterbach is suggesting that according to our Midrash, in Gen. 14:19, the subject of qwnh is Abraham, as, e.g., in *Gen. R.* 43:7, p. 421.)

"This mountain . . . produced" Note the reading in PA 611; cf. *ARN*, end of chap. 1, p. 8, and *Midrash Psalms* 78:18, 178b.

The-Torah *MRS:* "Torah," without the definite article; and so too below. Cf. below, in 10, s.v. "The Torah."

"The Lord produced . . . of His way" On the equation of Wisdom and Torah, see esp. Ecclus. 24, and cf. H. A. Wolfson, *Philo* (Cambridge, Mass., 1947), I, 20 ff., Heinemann, pp. 115 f.

Come O-Israel While the comment of *SY* on this statement may be homiletical, it is not entirely farfetched: "Perhaps all these statements (of the peroration) are hinted at (by the verses) here: 'This

To-the-Land, which-was-designated Mastedpiece
And-build the Temple, which-was-designated
Masterpiece,
By-virtue-of the-Torah, which-was-designated
Masterpiece!

That is why it is said, "This people Thou didst produce."

---

people Thou didst produce' is a reference to Israel; 'In Thy very own mountain' is a reference to the Land of Israel; 'The exact location . . . Sanctuary' is a reference to the Temple; 'The Lord will be King for ever and ever' is a reference to Torah through which is made known that He is the fashioner of all things and it is His kingship which ruleth over all." For the concluding words, cf. Jer. 10: 16 (also 51:19) and Ps. 103:19.

To-the-Land The editor of *MRS* reads, "to the Land ⟨of Israel⟩."
By-virtue-of the-Torah *MRS:* "by virtue of Torah." Had Israel not previously accepted the Torah, they would not have been worthy of building a house for God—in other words, of having God dwell in their midst. Cf. above, p. 216, and below, 10, p. 234.

10. Thou Wilt Bring Them in and Plant Them

THOU WILT BRING THEM IN AND PLANT THEM: The Fathers uttered a prophecy and did not realize it was prophetic. It is not written here, "Thou wilt bring *us* in and plant *us,*" but "Thou wilt bring *them* in and plant *them,*" which is to say, The children will enter but the fathers will not enter. And so too it says, "If thou know not, O thou fairest among women, go thy way forth by the footsteps of the flock and feed thy kids" etc. (Cant. 1:8), (that is,) the young will enter, but the fully grown will not enter.

Another interpretation of THOU WILT BRING THEM IN AND PLANT THEM: As is done with a vineyard, which is planted in neat rows, as it is said, ". . . From the east side unto the

The Fathers *MRS:* "(the) Fathers," without the definite article, and so too later. The reference is to the older generation of those at the Sea, the ones who were not to enter the Land; cf. Num. 14:22 f., 29 ff.

did not realize it was prophetic On a list of worthies to whom this is applied, see *ARNB*, XLIII, 118, and cf. Ginzberg, *Legends,* V, 250, n. 239.

which is to say Lit., "they said." Not in *MRS.*

"O thou fairest among women" I.e. Moses; cf. *Sifre Num.,* 139, p. 186; *Cant. R.* 1:7, 10a (see also the statement by R. Yose bar Jeremiah, *Cant. R.* 1:7). In answer to the question put to God by Moses (Cant. 1:7), God replies that only the young ones (lit., "kids") will enter the Promised Land, not the fully grown (lit., "goats, bucks"); cf. *Cant. R.* 1:8, 10b–c, and *Exod. R.* 2:4. On the figure of speech of kids and buck for the young and old respectively, see also *ARNA,* XVII, 65.

with a vineyard, which is *kkrm hzh šhwɔ; MRS: bkrm šhwɔ;* but cf. critical apparatus, ad loc.

planted in neat rows Like the properly cultivated vineyard (on Israel as vineyard, cf. Isa. 5:7, and note also the expression at the

west side: Judah, one portion" (Ezek. 48:7), "Dan, one portion" (Ezek. 48:1), "Naphtali, one portion" (Ezek. 48:3), (etc.).

Another interpretation: THOU WILT BRING THEM IN AND PLANT THEM, a planting which will suffer no breakdown, as

---

end of Pisḥa, I [I, 15]), each row clearly laid from one end to the other and not entangled in other rows. (The opposite of such a vineyard is "a vineyard planted pell-mell" [ʿrbwbyꜣ], M. Kilꜣaim 5:1.) On the way Palestinian Jews used to plant their vineyards (as well as orchards), cf. TK, Long Commentary on T. Kilꜣaim 3:5, p. 624.

In the course of discussing style, Quintilian (VIII, 3:9 [Loeb, III, 215]) says: "Is beauty an object of no consideration in the planting of fruit trees? Certainly not! For my trees must be planted in due order and at fixed intervals. What fairer sight is there than rows of trees planted in échelon which present straight lines to the eye from whatever angle they be viewed? But it has an additional advantage, since this form of plantation enables every tree to derive an equal share of moisture from the soil."

The Mekilta is manifestly commenting on the verb tṭʿmw ("Thou wilt plant them"), and the proof-texts from Ezekiel (see below) suggest that it is the ultimate planting which is here being alluded to; in other words, the future tense of the verbs in the verse gives the midrashic commentator still another opportunity to relate the Shirah with the final redemption and permanent establishment of Israel. See also ZY on this passage.

as it is said MRS: "and so too it says."

"From the east side . . ." As the text of our Mekilta now reads, verse 7 is quoted before verses 1 and 3, and one might almost get the impression that other verses in Ezekiel 48 are irrelevant. But that is of course not the case, for the point the Midrash wants to make applies to all the tribes. Note Sifre Deut., 315, p. 357, where the verses are presented in proper order. The way MRS reads ("From the east side, unto the west side [wʿd pꜣt ym]; but cf. MT, ad loc.; Dan, one portion, etc.") also reflects confusion. Note the comment in HR, p. 149, line 8. I believe we have here simply a confusion (due to quoting from memory?) easily created by the repetitions of that Ezekiel chapter. Cf. AhB, I, 34.

Another interpretation: THOU WILT BRING THEM IN AND PLANT THEM MRS begins simply, "And Thou wilt plant them."

which will suffer no breakdown ꜣyn bh ntyšh (cf., however, Lauterbach's critical apparatus, the reading adopted by HR, and AhB, I, 35). MRS: ꜣyn lh ntyšh ("which will suffer no plucking up").

On the significance of the term "planting," see above, Pt. I, pp. 40 ff., and notes, ad loc. Interestingly, although Philo (Preliminary Studies, 56 f. [Loeb, IV, 487]) is talking of something else, he too is struck by the verb "plant": "The mind which truly loves God, that has the vision of Him, He 'plants in,' as a branch of goodly birth,

it is said, "And I will build them, and not pull them down; and I will plant them, and not pluck them up" (Jer. 24:6), and it says, "And I will plant them upon their land, and they shall be no more plucked up" (Amos 9:15).

IN THY VERY OWN MOUNTAIN: In the mountain concerning which Thou hast made us a promise, as it is said, "For in My holy mountain" (etc.) (Ezek. 20:40), and it says, "In the mountain of the Exalted One of Israel will I plant him" (Ezek. 17:23).

THY VERY OWN:

Four	Were-Designated	Very-Own
Israel	were-designated	Very-Own

---

and He deepens its roots to reach to eternity and gives it fruitfulness for the acquisition and enjoyment of virtue. That is why Moses prays in these words, 'Bring them in and plant them in,' that the saplings of God's culture may not be for a day but age-long and immortal." For other reflections by Philo on Exod. 15:17, cf. *Noah's Work as a Planter*, 46 ff. (Loeb, III, 237 ff.).

as it is said *MRS:* "and so too it says."

and it says This formula is omitted by *MRS*, although it also quotes Amos 9:15.

"And I will plant them upon their land . . ." Note that in the preceding verse, Amos speaks of planting vineyards.

In the mountain . . . made us a promise That there Israel would serve God in truth and He would delight in them; see Ezek. 20:40 in full.

as it is said *MRS:* "and so too it says."

and it says, "In the mountain . . ." Not in *MRS*.

Israel is God's *possession* (cf. the following passage). Note also *Memar Marqah*, 2:10 (II, 75): "On Thy own mountain. What is His own? Israel is His own, as He said, His allotted heritage Israel (Deut. 32:9)."

"In the mountain of the Exalted One of Israel" I am virtually certain that so the Midrash takes this expression of the verse, and note too its appearance in 20:40.

THY VERY OWN Lit., "Thine inheritance" (*nḥltk*). *MRS:* "Another interpretation of 'Thy very own mountain.' "

Four Were-Designated Very-Own This sentence is not in *MRS*.

Cf. above, 9, p. 228 ff., and the note, ad loc., s.v. "Four Were Designated Masterpiece." See the nice comment on this passage in *ZY*. On the passage, cf. also Mirsky, p. 45.

Israel were-designated . . ." In *MRS* the reading is as follows: "Torah was designated Very-Own, 'And from the gift God gave me as my Very-Own' etc.; Israel was designated Very-Own, 'Yet they are

as it is said, "Yet they are Thy people, Thy very own" (Deut. 9:29).

The-Land of-Israel was-designated Very-Own as it is said, "In the Land which the Lord thy God is giving thee for thy very own" (Deut. 15:4).

The Temple was-designated Very-Own as it is said, "In Thy very own mountain."

The-Torah was-designated Very-Own as it is said, "And from the gift God gave me as my Very-Own" (Num. 21:19).

> Said the Holy One, blessed be He:
>
> Come, O-Israel, who-were-designated Very-Own,
> To-the-Land of-Israel, which-was-designated Very-Own,
> And-build the Temple, which-was-designated Very-Own,
> By-virtue-of the-Torah, which-was-designated Very-Own!

That is why it is said, "In Thy very own mountain."

THE EXACT LOCATION OF THY ABODE, (that is,) directly facing Thine abode. This is one of the (scriptural) statements to

---

Thy people, Thy Very-Own' etc.; the Land of Israel was designated Very-Own, 'And it shall be when thou art come in unto the Land' etc.; the Temple was designated Very-Own, 'In Thy Very-Own mountain.' " In what follows, the MRS reading agrees with that of our Mekilta.

"In the Land . . . for thy very own" Note that MRS quotes Deut. 26:1, but the idiom and vocabulary are virtually identical.

The-Torah MRS: "Torah," without the definite article, and so too below. Cf. above, 9, s.v. "The Torah."

"And from the gift . . . Very-Own" The midrashic interpretation by means of notarikon of "And from Mattanah" (= "gift") "to Nahaliel" (= El, God, gave me, ly, as a heritage). Cf. HJP, pp. 69 f., 75. See also PA 6:2, and cf. 3:14 (end).

Said the Holy One, blessed be He Not in MRS.

By virtue of the Torah Cf. above, 9, end.

THE EXACT LOCATION OF THINE ABODE MRS quotes the whole clause, "The exact location of Thine abode which Thou hast made, O Lord."

directly facing Thine abode Not in MRS (see also Finkelstein, in PAAJR, v, 11 f.); but cf. Lieberman, in Kirjath Sepher, XII (1935–36), 62, and see also, AhB, I, 35.

As the midrashic comment makes clear, by reading the consonants

the effect that the terrestrial Throne faces over against the celestial Throne. For thus it says: "The Lord is in His holy temple, the Lord, His Throne is in heaven" (Ps. 11:4), and it also says, "I have surely built Thee a house of habitation, directly facing Thine eternal abode" (I Kings 8:13).

WHICH THOU HAST WROUGHT, O LORD: How precious is the Temple in the sight of Him Who Spake and the World

---

mkwn (vocalized *makon*) as *mekuwwan*—a typically midrashic exercise (cf. Heinemann, pp. 128 f.)—the Exodus verse means, Bring them and plant them in the mountain of Thine inheritance which on earth lies over against Thy seat in heaven. On the notion of the heavenly Jerusalem and Temple situated over against the earthly one, see V. Aptowitzer, in *Tarbiz*, II (1930–31), 137–53, 257–87, esp. 145 ff. (note also the quotation, no. 8, p. 258); Bonsirven, II, 112, n. 6. Cf. also Mirsky, pp. 26–28.

. . . statements *MRS:* "places" (and cf. ibid., critical apparatus, as well as the apparatus in Lauterbach).

terrestrial Throne This would seem to be the ark; cf. Aptowitzer, *Tarbiz*, II, 146 f.

For thus it says *MRS:* "as it is said," and proceeds to quote Isa. 66:1 and Ezek. 43:7 before quoting the proof-texts which appear in our Mekilta.

"the Lord . . . in heaven" Thus we see that there is a seating place, a Throne, in the heavens.

"directly facing Thine . . . abode" Once again reading *mkwn* as *mekuwwan* (see above, s.v. "directly facing Thine abode") and as Lauterbach puts it in his footnote (p. 78): "I have built Thee a house of habitation corresponding to . . . Thy eternal throne in heaven."

Cf. *Memar Marqah* 2:10 (II, 75 f.) on this clause.

His Throne being "eternal" reminds us therefore that His sovereignty is too; cf. Ps. 145:13 and Lam. 5:19; note now Exod. 15:19 and cf. below, p. 239.

THOU HAST WROUGHT, O LORD *MRS* having quoted this clause earlier, does not repeat it at this point, but proceeds at once with "How precious is the Temple . . ."

The Mekilta now comments on the verb which speaks of God's *activity* (hence, suggestion of effort and exertion, as it were). Indeed, note the aptness here of the expression "Him Who Spake and the World Came to Be," and then observe that the text continues with "the Holy One, blessed be He" (see however the variants recorded by HR in the critical apparatus); cf. *AhB*, III, 87.

It may well be that the passages which follow, both opening with "How precious is the Temple," are, in part at least, a kind of reply to those who must have said that, since God allowed the Temple to

Came to Be! For when the Holy One, blessed be He, created His world, only by utterance did He create it, as it is said, "By the word of the Lord were the heavens made" (Ps. 33:6). But when He built the Temple, it is as though there were labor on His part, as it is said, "Which Thou hast *wrought*." (And) woe to the Nations of the World at what they hear with their own ears! For lo, the Temple is described as the product of labor on His part, as it is said, "Which Thou has *wrought*, O Lord," yet they rose

---

be destroyed, obviously He no longer cared for it. That even after its destruction, the Temple might be spoken of as though it were still standing, we can see in Josephus, *Against Apion*, II, 193 ff. (and cf. Thackeray's note c in Loeb, I, 371). Cf. also *Sifre Num.*, 92, p. 92.

For when the Holy One, blessed be He, created His world, only by utterance did He create it MRS: "For the whole world, all of it, was created only by the utterance of the Holy One, blessed be He." On God's creation of the world by utterance, see Gen. 1 and Ps. 33:9; PA 5:1.

But (lit., "and") when He built the Temple MRS: "However (ʾbl) when He built the Temple." Note the *editio princeps* reading (kšbʾ, "when He came") adopted by HR (instead of kšbrʾ, "when He built"); cf. below, s.v. "But when He comes to build."

On *waw* as "but," cf. Epstein, *Mabo le-Nusaḥ ha-Mishnah*, pp. 1090 f. The Mekilta is of course aware of the fact that Solomon built the Temple (and see also above, 1, p. 69). But we are dealing here with the tradition that among the seven things created before the Creation of the world, one was the building of the Temple (B. Pesaḥim 54a). As for different views of this very tradition, see Aptowitzer, *Tarbiz*, II, 151 ff. See also Ginzberg, *Legends*, v, 14 ff.

as though there were labor on His part, as it is said kbykwl pʿwlh lpnyw, šnʾmr; MRS: kwykwl pʿwlh hyʾ lpnyw, and it quotes the following verse without any introductory formula. Note how *AhB*, III, 87, cites the proof-text "which Thou hast made, O Lord, the Sanctuary."

(On the spelling kwykwl = kbykwl, cf. Epstein, *Mabo le-Nusaḥ*, pp. 1223 ff.)

woe to the Nations of the World On the tone and nature of this peroration, see above, 4, p. 126. Cf. *AhB*, III, 87.

at what they hear with their own ears mh hn šmʿwt bʾznyhm; MRS: bmh ššwmʿwt ʾznyhm.

For lo, the Temple MRS, "For the Temple."

on His part MRS: "on the part of Him Who Spake and the World Came to Be."

as it is said, "Which Thou hast *wrought*, O Lord" Not in MRS.

and destroyed it. They cried: "Rase it, rase it, even to the foundation thereof" (Ps. 137:7). In regard to this matter, what does it say? "The Lord doth roar from on high, from His holy dwelling He uttereth His voice, He doth mightily roar because of His habitation" (Jer. 25:30).

THE SANCTUARY, O LORD, WHICH THY HANDS ESTABLISH: How precious is the Temple in the sight of Him Who Spake and the World Came to Be! For when the Holy One, blessed be He, created His world, only with one hand did He create it, as it is said, "Yea, My hand hath laid the foundation of the earth" (Isa. 48:13). But when He comes to build the Temple, it will be, as it were, with His two hands, as it is said, "The Sanctuary, O Lord, which Thy *hands* establish, when the Lord will reign." When will *that* be? When Thou

yet they rose and destroyed it (*whḥrybwhw*) *MRS:* "And ('The ones who say, Rase it . . .') destroyed it" (*whḥrybw ʾwtw*).

They cried Lit., "They said." On the *MRS* reading, "The ones who say" (a participle), cf. the Hebrew text of 137:7. Note that the verse speaks of Edom, which for the Midrash equals Rome.

In regard to this matter Not in *MRS.*

what does it say *MRS* quotes after this Jer. 25:30 *and* v. 31. Jer. 25 may indeed be described as referring to the *Nations* (and Edom is referred to, ibid., v. 21), and note too v. 31. See also the note to *MRS,* p. 99, line 24.

SANCTUARY (*mqdš*) And the Temple in Hebrew is *byt hmqdš.*

in the sight of Him . . . Came to Be So too *MRS,* but note the reading ("the Holy One, blessed be He") adopted by HR; cf. above, s.v. "Thou hast wrought, O Lord."

For when the Holy One . . . created His world, only with . . . did He create it *MRS:* For the whole world, all of it, was created only with." Cf. *AhB,* I, 36.

"Yea, My hand" That is, note the singular.

But when He comes to build (*wkšbʾ lbnwt*) *MRS:* "However, when He builds" (*ʾbl kšbnh*); cf. above, s.v. "But when He built the Temple." Here, however, quite vividly, the discussion is of the Temple in the Future. Note further below, s.v., "That is why it is said . . ."

as it were, with His two hands *MRS:* "He will build it (*bnʾw*) only with His two hands." On *bnʾw* in *MRS,* cf. critical apparatus, ad loc.

Thy *hands* establish Note the dual "hands," not "hand."

"when the Lord will reign" Not in *MRS.*

It seems to me that what the Mekilta is doing here is not so much providing what might be called independent commentary on the clause "The Lord will reign," as something else. The words

shalt build it with Thy two hands!—A parable: To what
may this be likened? To brigands who made their way into
the king's palace, plundered his possessions, slew the royal
entourage, and destroyed the royal palace. Some time later
the king brought them to judgment. Some of them he had
imprisoned, some of them he had slain, some of them he

"Thy Sanctuary, O Lord, which Thy hands establish" are in Scripture
followed immediately by "The Lord will reign"; and the Mekilta is
commenting on that very conjunction, thus suggesting that we understand the biblical passage as follows: O Lord, Thy Sanctuary, Thou
establishest it with Thy (two) hands when the Lord reigns—i.e. when
Thy sovereignty will have been universally recognized. Note, for
example, quite clearly *AhB*, I, 36 and 245, and also the conclusion
of the Mekilta passage after the parable; incidentally, compare the
reading at the end of the first chapter of *ARNA*, p. 8. (Hence I
believe that Lauterbach's paragraph arrangement is somewhat mis-
leading.) By omitting the words "The Lord will reign," *MRS* does
read more smoothly (cf. also HR); and stylistically, replying to the
question (literally), "When wilt Thou build it with Thy two hands,"
by "A parable: to what may this be likened," does appear somewhat
awkward. That is why I adopt the translation, "When will *that* be?
When Thou shalt build . . . ," in part taking my cue from the *MRS*
reading. See further, next note.

Incidentally, for "Dead Sea" commentary on this verse, see the
fragment of a Qumran Scroll in *JBL* 77:351 (1958).

When will *that* be? When Thou shalt build it (*tbnyhw*) **with Thy
two hands** *MRS:* "When will *that* be? When Thou shalt build it
(*kštbnnw*) with Thy two hands—'The Lord doth build up Jerusalem,
He gathereth together the dispersed of Israel' (Ps. 147:2)." Then
comes the parable.

A parable *MRS:* "A parable is told." On this parable, cf. Ziegler,
pp. 284 f., and Hengel, p. 41.

who made their way into the king's palace (*lpltyn šl mlk*) *MRS:*
"who made their way into (*ltwk*) the king's palace."

plundered his possessions . . . the royal palace (*pltryn*) *MRS:*
"(and) of his servants whom they seized, some of them they slew,
some of them they crucified, and some of them they burned (to
death), and they destroyed his palace" (*pltyn*). Note the reading in
AhB, I, 37.

"Entourage", *pmly*ᵓ, is an excellent word in this context. On the
MRS reading, cf. preceding note.

Some time later the king brought them to judgment *MRS:* "Some
time later the king came and brought them to judgment." "Brought
to judgment" is to be understood as imposed their penalties upon
them.

had crucified: once again he took up residence in His palace, and thereafter His sovereignty was recognized in the world. That is why it is said, "The sanctuary, O Lord, which Thy hands establish, when the Lord will reign for ever and ever."

THE LORD WILL BE KING FOR EVER AND EVER: Rabbi Yose the Galilean says: If only at the Sea Israel had proclaimed, "The Lord *is* King for ever and ever!" Not a nationality or empire would ever after have ruled over them! Alas, they

some of them he had crucified After this MRS adds, "and some of them he burned" to death.

once again he took up residence in his palace MRS: "once again he took up residence [in] his palace"; but cf. critical apparatus to line 7, ibid.

and thereafter . . . was recognized (ntwdᶜh) MRS: "and (thereafter) . . . was recognized" (wnwdᶜh).

That is why it is said . . . Not in MRS.

This conjunction of "The sanctuary, O Lord, which Thy hands establish" and "The Lord will be King for ever and ever," is worth looking at in Memar Marqah 2:10 (II, 75 ff., esp. pp. 76 f.) also, where a kind of ecstatic note is struck. (Marqah's comment, p. 76, on "O Lord, which Thy hands have established": "a great prophecy since He did not establish it until after the destruction," I am not sure I understand. Does he mean, After destruction of the Egyptians because they were disobedient?)

A review of the comments on the verses "Directly facing . . ." will reveal that the Mekilta is reflecting on a threefold theme. (1) In connection with "directly facing Thine abode," we learn of the Temple on high; (2) in connection with "Thou hast wrought, O Lord," we learn of the terrestrial Temple; (3) in connection with "The sanctuary, O Lord . . . ," we learn of the Temple to be built in the Future.

The Lord will be King for ever and ever MRS does not quote the verse at this point. In any event, the Mekilta is now proceeding to offer commentary on Exod. 15:18; cf. above, s.v. "when the Lord will reign."

Yose the Galilean MRS, simply "Yose"; and note the comment in the critical apparatus, ibid. On the other hand, cf. AhB, I, 40.

If only . . . had proclaimed Note, however, the view expressed in Be-Shallaḥ, VI (I, 235).

The phrase "at the Sea" is not in MRS.

"The Lord *is* King for ever and ever" Cf. Ps. 10:16a.

Not a nationality or empire would ever after have ruled (hyth . . . šwlṭt . . . lᶜwlm) over them MRS: "Not a nationality or empire would have ruled (šlṭh) over them."

said, "The Lord *will* be King for ever and ever," in the
Age to Come.—

> But verily over Thy people,
> Thy flock, Thy sheep,
> The sheep of Thy pasture,

See on this passage Hengel, pp. 113 f. According to R. Yose, had
Israel spoken of God as Sovereign in the present tense (as *mlk, melek,*
rather than *ymlk,* the verb in the imperfect, future, tense), redemption from Egyptian bondage would never have been succeeded by
subjugation or defeat; note indeed the idiom of Ps. 10:16b.

Alas, they said Lit., "But they said"; *MRS:* "But," without "they
said."

in the Age to Come By proclaiming *ymlwk,* He *will* reign, Israel as
it were caused the postponement of the universal recognition of
God's sovereignty. Note however the Targumim on the verse (and in
connection with 2 Tg Yerushalmi, cf. Ginzberg, *Legends,* v, 437, n.
235), and observe also how this Shirah verse is amplified in the
liturgy (Baer, p. 74), as well as the reading in the prayer *wbꜣ lṣywn*
(Baer, p. 128). See Schechter, *Aspects,* pp. 86 ff.
Immediately after this, *MRS* continues: "And the grounds for that
(lit., why so)? 'For the horses of Pharaoh' (Exod. 15:19) etc., up to
'the waters of the sea' (ibid.)" (note our Mekilta, below). The text,
ibid., also seems to be defective; cf. critical apparatus, p. 100, note
to line 10.

But verily over Thy people . . . The reading in *MRS* is: "But we
are Thy people and Thy heritage, the sheep of Thy pasture, the
children of Abraham who loved Thee, the seed of Isaac Thy favorite,
the family of Jacob Thy first-born, the vine whom Thou didst pluck
out of Egypt, the stock that Thy right hand hath planted, 'and the
children of Israel walked on dry land in the midst of the Sea' (Exod.
15:19)."

On the "flavor" of this passage, see also above, 5, p. 145 and note,
s.v. "But as for Thee, Thy goodness, Thy manifold mercies etc."; cf.
also Melamed, in *Tarbiz,* vi, 119; and significantly, this exclamation
comes at the end of comment on the Shirah. See further, below.

On "But verily," see the note in Baer, p. 45, and *TK* ad T. ꜥErubin
4:1, Long Commentary, p. 363. In the Mekilta, however, it might well
be intended as an emphatic contrast between recognitions of God's
sovereignty in the Future by all, and that recognition even now, by
Israel. See further, below.

On "Thy people," e.g. Exod. 15:16 (for the reading of *MRS,* see
the idiom, e.g., in Deut. 9:29).

Thy flock E.g. Jer. 13:17 or Zech. 10:3.

Thy sheep E.g. Ezek. 34:31 or Micah 7:14 (cf. also Pisḥa, I, end [1,
15]).

sheep of Thy pasture E.g. Ps. 79:13 or 100:3; Ezek. 34:31.

The seed of Abraham who loved Thee,
The children of Isaac Thy favorite,
The community of Jacob Thy first-born son,
The vine Thou didst pluck out of Egypt
And the stock which Thy right hand hath planted,

seed of Abraham who loved Thee II Chron. 20:7; cf. Isa. 41:8. See also Ginzberg, *Legends*, v, 207, n. 4.

children of Isaac Thy favorite Cf. Gen. 22:2, 12, 16 (on the *MRS* reading, cf. Baer, p. 45; and see also, Gen. 21:12). Our Mekilta expression may even include a kind of word play on Gen. 21:10, end, as well as Gen. 22:2.

The community of Jacob Thy first-born son On Israel being referred to as *ᶜdh*, see, e.g., Lev. 8:4, 5; Num. 27:15 f.; and frequently. On Jacob as first-born, cf. Exod. 4:22 (and Israel = Jacob, Gen. 32:29). In the expression there may be a deliberate innuendo: Jacob, not Esau (= Rome?) is the legitimate first-born (Gen. 25:31–34, and note esp. 34b). On *ᶜdh*, see also the "concluding" poem in the *Passover Haggadah* (*Haggadah Shelemah*, ed. M. Kasher [Jerusalem, 1960], p. 83 of the text), "The Passover Seder Is Ended," where we read, "Raise up the assembly of the *ᶜdh* whom none can number" (cf. Num. 23:10); but that reading is not in the *Haggadah*, ed. Goldschmidt (p. 136; cf. p. 97), and even Kasher apparently has some doubts about it, as is evident from the smaller type adopted for that word.

(The reading of *MRS*, "the *family* of Jacob Thy first-born," seems to me to be an adaptation: note the biblical concordance, s.v. *mšpḥh*, for the term in connection with the tribes, the sons of Jacob.)

On the three epithets descriptive of the descent of Israel ("seed," "children," "community"—representing a kind of crescendo, from seed to sons, to the community: which bears witness?) from the three patriarchs, see also the prayer in Baer, p. 45.

The vine . . . out of Egypt Cf. Ps. 80:9.

The stock . . . planted Ps. 80:16.

These last two characterizations are particularly apt in the present context, which celebrates the exodus from Egypt, and where the vocabulary of the Shirah includes "Thy right hand" (three times!), as well as the references to planting, to *mkwn*, and to *kwnnw*.

As already suggested (cf. above, s.v. "But verily over Thy people"), having arrived at the end of the Shirah, strictly speaking, and at its concluding *acclamatio*, a kind of prayer bursts forth, even somewhat melancholy in undertone, at the realization of the great contrast between the triumphant time when Israel was redeemed from bondage, and the present which is not yet the point of the ultimate triumph, when God's sovereignty will be acknowledged on all the earth. The prayer is an obvious product of the brilliant combination of biblical phrases (as is so much of the classical Jewish liturgy); and if the

"May the Lord reign for ever and ever!"

And the grounds for that? "For the horses of Pharaoh went"
etc. (Exod. 15:19).

---

reading in the Lauterbach edition (cf. variants in HR, p. 150) is correct (as I think it is; cf. the *MRS* reading above, s.v. "But verily over
Thy people," despite minor variants in *its* version), then what we
have is nine (in other words, three times three) epithets for Israel,
thus: (1) Thy people, (2) Thy flock, (3) Thy sheep, (4) The sheep
of Thy pasture, (5) seed of Abraham, (6) children of Isaac, (7) community of Jacob, (8) vine plucked out of Egypt, (9) stock Thy right
hand planted. This is not accidental and must be deliberate. *MRS*
has eight terms, but note "Thy heritage" (ibid.), which does not appear in our text; the reading adopted by HR furnishes seven (!)
terms. (Perhaps the pleonasm of "Thy flock, Thy sheep, The sheep
of Thy pasture" has bothered the copyists, though as poetic diction
goes, this is not disturbing.)

Now, this liturgical passage (beginning with *ᵓbl*, "But verily") is
not, in my opinion, part of R. Yose the Galilean's statement. It seems
to me that the very note struck by R. Yose was so sad and depressing
that the homilist or compiler felt virtually compelled to add a statement which would emphasize Israel's enduring loyalty to God, even
before the arrival of the Age to Come. Furthermore, this liturgical
piece is most likely to be taken with what follows, still another
comment on the verse, "The Lord *ymlwk*"—this time, however,
understood not as verb in the future tense but as a jussive, with a
present tense application—i.e. Oh, may the Lord reign (from this
moment) for ever and ever. See further, below.

"May the Lord reign for ever and ever" Instead of this verse, *MRS*,
after "and the stock which Thy right hand hath planted," reads:
"But (and) the children of Israel walked on dry land in the midst of
the Sea" (Exod. 15:19b).

In our Mekilta, the words *ᵓdny ymlwk* are best taken with what
preceded (representing at the same time "another interpretation" of
the verse), thus: But over Thy people, Thy flock, and so on, do Thou
Lord reign from this moment on. To some extent this interpretation is borne out, I believe, by the *MRS* reading, despite its deviation
from our Mekilta reading. The idea suggested by *MRS* is something
like the following: (Lord, reign over us now!—God's sovereignty being
recognized in what happened to Pharaoh and his hosts at the Sea,
Exod. 15:19a;) but us, Thy people, Thy heritage, and so on, Exod.
15:19b declares what happened to us.

And the grounds for that That is, in what specifically was God's
sovereignty recognized when Israel made that proclamation? Verse 19:
in His punishment of Pharaoh and His deliverance of Israel. Thus

AND MIRIAM THE PROPHETESS TOOK: But where do we find of Miriam that she uttered prophecies? Here: She had said to her father, "You will yet beget a son who will arise and save Israel from the power of Egypt." Forthwith, "And there went a man of the house of Levi, and took . . . And the woman conceived and bore a son . . . And when she could not longer hide him" (etc.) (Exod. 2:1–3). (At which point) her father rebuked her, saying: "Miriam, what about your prophecies!" But she held fast to her prophetic statement, as it is said, "And his sister stationed herself at a

---

the Mekilta has even supplied an explanation for the connection between Exod. 15:18 and 19.

AND MIRIAM THE PROPHETESS *MRS* continues quoting, "Aaron's sister."

But where do we find of Miriam that she uttered prophecies *MRS:* "Where did Miriam utter prophecies?" Immediately after the question, *MRS* quotes Exod. 2:1. Note the order in our Mekilta.

The Midrash is asking, Why should Miriam be called a prophet? Is there anywhere in Scripture an event revealing her in the act of prophesying?

Here: She had said to her father Lit., "However, she had said . . ." (ʾlʾ ʾmrh lʾbyh). *MRS:* "She said to her father" (ʾmrh lw lʾbyh).

On Miriam as prophet, see Ginzberg, *Legends*, II, 264 f., and notes, ad loc.

"You will yet beget a son" *swpk ʾt mwlyd bn;* MRS: *swpk lhwlyd bn.*

"who will arise and save Israel from the power of Egypt" *MRS:* "who in the future will redeem Israel from Egypt."

Forthwith Not in *MRS.*

On the significance of the term *myd* ("forthwith") here, see the story in *Legends*, II, 258–63. Anecdotes in Midrash and Talmud often like to highlight dramatic effect by using this term *myd.*

"And there went a man . . . In *MRS*, after Miriam's prediction to her father of the son who will redeem Israel (cf. above, s.v. "Who will arise . . ."), the text continues: "Her father answered her and said to her, 'What about your prophecy?' But still (wʿdyyn) she insisted on her prophecy (hyʾ bnbwʾth ʿwmdt), as it is said . . ." (quoting Exod. 2:4).

"your prophecies" *nbwʾtyk;* but it may well be that the *yod* (*y*) in the word is intended as a vowel sign, in which event the word would be in the singular ("your prophecy"), second person, feminine.

But she held fast to her prophetic statement For the idiom, cf. Job 2:9. *MRS:* "But still she insisted on her prophecy"; cf. above, s.v. "And there went a man . . ."

distance, to learn what would befall him" (Exod. 2:4):

Now, "taking up a station" is nothing other than a reference to the Holy Spirit, as it is said, "I saw the Lord station Himself beside the altar" (Amos 9:1), and it says, "And the Lord came and stationed Himself" (I Sam 3:10), and it says, "Call Joshua, and station yourselves" etc. (Deut. 31:14).

"At a distance"—Everywhere "at a distance" is nothing other than a reference to the Holy Spirit, as it is said, "At a distance the Lord appeared unto me" (Jer. 31:2).

"To learn"—"Learning to know" is nothing other than

"to learn" Ed. Lauterbach, *ld⁄t,* but this may be a misprint. MT, *ld⁄h,* and so too our Mekilta a few lines further on; cf. below, s.v. "To learn."

Now, "taking up a station" is nothing other than . . . the Holy Spirit *MRS:* "Everywhere 'taking up a station' is nothing other than . . ."

On "the Holy Spirit"—i.e. Prophecy, see also *ARN,* p. 102. Cf. Be-Shallaḥ, III (I, 210). As the proof-texts which follow indicate, the homilist says that where the verb *yṣb* (*nṣb*) occurs, there we encounter a communication from the deity to the person standing by; and that communication is here called prophecy. (For Exod. 2:4 being quoted in the Mekilta and not being connected with prophecy, cf. Be-Shallaḥ, I [I, 177].)

"I saw the Lord station Himself" *MRS* quotes this after quoting Gen. 28:13; see further, next note.

"And the Lord . . . stationed Himself" *MRS* first quotes Deut. 31: 14, then this verse from I Samuel, and then Gen. 28:13.

"Call Joshua . . ." I do not understand why the Mekilta cites the biblical verses in this order—Amos, Samuel, and Deuteronomy. Perhaps, to put it tentatively, first the Midrash wishes to show the verb in connection with God, then it furnishes a verse where the verb in connection with God appears in *hitpa⁄el* form (cf. the form in Exod. 2:4), and finally, it uses the same form of the verb in connection with human beings other than Miriam.

"at a distance" Once the Mekilta has quoted Exod. 2:4 to justify calling Miriam a prophet, it proceeds to interpret the other terms of the verse in a way which would confirm her prophetic status. (Cf. also Philo, *On Dreams,* II, 142 [Loeb, V, 507].) In a sense, therefore, this is a brief digression.

Everywhere This time *MRS* omits the expression.

"At a distance the Lord . . ." Note God's promise in the succeeding verses.

"To learn" The next expression in Exod. 2:4. (This time ed. Lauterbach also reads *ld⁄h;* cf. above, s.v. "To learn.")

"Learning to know" is nothing . . . *⁾yn d⁄h; MRS: ⁾yn ld⁄h.*

a reference to the Holy Spirit, as it is said, "For the earth shall be full of learning to know the Lord" etc. (Isa. 11:9), and it says, "For the earth shall be filled with learning to know the Glory of the Lord, as the waters cover the sea" (Hab. 2:14).

"What would befall him"—"Befalling" is nothing other than a reference to the Holy Spirit, as it is said, "For the Lord God will let nothing befall" etc. (Amos 3:7).

AARON'S SISTER: But was she not, in fact, the sister of both of them? Why, then, does Scripture say, "Aaron's sister?" However, since he was ready to give his life for his sister's sake, she goes by his name.

The same you have to say of "Simeon and Levi, Dinah's brothers" (Gen. 34:25). But was she not, in fact, the sister of all the tribes? Why, then, does Scripture say, " (Simeon

"For the earth shall be full . . ." Note the context in Isaiah; and such "knowledge" is prophecy. See also Joel 3:1–2 for the end of days.

"For the earth shall be filled with . . ." *MRS* neither quotes this verse nor proceeds to interpret the clause, "What would befall him." In Habakkuk the word is *ld‘t,* and this verse is probably quoted because of its similarity to the Isaiah idiom. Note also the expression "the Glory of the Lord"; it may well be that this verse is quoted because of the reference to God's Glory and the Sea (otherwise, the verse would seem to add nothing to what the Isaiah verse had already established).

"the Lord God will let nothing befall" That is to say, before God acts, He first communicates with the prophets. Cf. above, s.v. "the Holy Spirit."

But was (*hyth***) she not . . . of both of them** Of Moses and Aaron. (Cf. also *Barhebraeus,* pp. 121, 123.) Before this question, *MRS* reads: "Now, was she (only) Aaron's sister?" The word *hyth* in "was she not . . ." is not in *MRS*; but cf. ibid., critical apparatus. Observe how Noth, 97, explains the mention of Aaron and not Moses; on the other hand, observe the "gallantry" in Abarbanel's explanation!

for his sister's sake *MRS:* "for her sake." On Aaron giving his life for his sister, see Ginzberg, *Legends,* III, 259 f., and notes, ad loc. Note particularly the idiom at the beginning of Num. 12:11 and 12. On the idea of giving one's life for someone (and some things), cf. above, 1, p. 69 ff.

Observe that now two more examples follow, thus making a total of three.

But was she not . . . of all the tribes Before this question, *MRS* reads: "Now was she (only) the sister of these two?" The sister of the

and Levi,) Dinah's brothers?" However, since they were ready to give their lives for their sister's sake, their sister goes by their name.

The same you have to say of "In the matter of Cozbi, the daughter of the prince of Midian, their sister" (Num. 25:18). But was she their sister? In fact, was she not a chief of her people, as it is said, "He was the tribal head of an ancestral house in Midian" (Num. 25:15)? Why, then, does Scripture say, "their sister?" However, since she gave her life for her people's sake, her people go by her name.

---

tribes is of course the sister of the twelve sons of Jacob, who are the heads of tribes.

they were ready . . . See the whole story in Gen. 34, and in the last verse Simeon and Levi's retort to Jacob.

for their sister's sake MRS: "for her sake."

their sister goes by MRS: "she goes by."

But was she their sister? . . . MRS, lit.: "But was she their sister? The daughter of her people was she. However, because her people gave (their?) life for her . . ." But see the critical apparatus, ibid.

The question, "But was she their sister," seems to be, How could she possibly be the sister of all the Midianites (cf. also SY and Landau); in MhG, Num., ed. Fisch, II, 217, the reading is: " 'In the matter of Cozbi, the daughter of the prince of Midian, their sister': But was she the sister of her whole people? However, since she gave her life for her people's sake, she is recalled by their name."

In fact . . . a chief of her people If this reading is correct (cf. the critical apparatus in Lauterbach, II, 82, to line 81, and see also L. Finkelstein, in Proceedings, AAJR, v, 12), the meaning must be, But was she not a member of a principal family of her people.

"was the tribal head of an ancestral house" That is, her father was. Perhaps, however (to put it very hesitantly), the Midrash reads the last word of Num. 25:15 as hiɔ (she) rather than huɔ (he), making the reference to Cozbi directly (?). That hwɔ can be read as hiɔ is perfectly obvious in many places of MT; and cf. ARN, pp. 101 f.

since . . . for her people's sake In connection with the story in Num. 25, see the narrative in Ginzberg, Legends, III, 380 et seq. (and the notes, ad loc.); and note especially the way Balaam's counsel is formulated in ARN, p. 3 ("Go, therefore, fix booths for them . . . have the booths occupied by beautiful women, royal women . . ."); and for the benefit of her people, says the Mekilta, Cozbi was ready to play this degrading role.

her people go by her name MRS: "It (her people?) went by her name." See also the variant reading in ed. Lauterbach, II, 82, to line 83. The text of our Mekilta here will have to mean something like,

A TIMBREL IN HER HAND: Now, where in the wilderness could
Israel get timbrels for choral dances? However, the righteous were confident, and they knew that God would be
performing miracles and mighty deeds for them at their
exodus from Egypt. So in advance they prepared timbrels
for choral dances.

AND MIRIAM STRUCK UP THE SONG FOR THEM: The verse declares that even as it was Moses who led in recitation of the

---

Her whole people came to be identified as her relations; hence she
may be referred to as their sister. Note the reading recommended by
L. Finkelstein, in *Proceedings, AAJR*, V, 12.

Note, incidentally, that in discussing the notion of one's being
named by what he gives his life to, the Midrash here adopts what
might be called a thoroughly neutral position: it simply reports what
happens—and therefore does not hesitate to bring examples of situations it hardly admires.

**Now, where (mnyn) in the wilderness . . . timbrels for choral
dances** MRS: "Now, where (m'yn) did Israel get timbrels at the Sea."
On the expression "timbrels for choral dances," cf. Exod. 15:20, end.

On "choral dances," cf. Tg Onkelos and Jonathan, and also
LXX on Exod. 15:20, end. For the interpretation adopted by Lauterbach (II, 83, n. 3); see also Cassuto in his *Commentary on Exodus*, p.
126 (and p. 343); *Barhebraeus*, p. 123.

the righteous (ṣdyqym) Rashi on this verse deliberately speaks
not of ṣdyqym (masculine plural) but of ṣdqnywt (feminine plural),
the righteous women!

However, the righteous were confident . . . MRS: "However, because at their exodus from Egypt the righteous were confident that
God would be performing for them miracles and mighty deeds; therefore they took along in their hands timbrels (ṭwpyn! but cf. critical
apparatus, ibid.) for choral dances."

On the confidence (and faith), even before the exodus, that deliverance was at hand, cf. Be-Shallaḥ, VII, end (I, 252 ff.).

miracles and mighty deeds Cf. above, 8, pp. 191 and 206, and p. 191 f.,
s.v. "The likes of Thee . . . deeds."

they prepared timbrels for choral dances On praising God in this
fashion, cf. Ps. 150:4. On tqn ("prepare"), cf. also *TK* on T. Shabbat
1:12, Long Commentary, p. 11, n. 38 (cf. p. 129, n. 1).

The verse declares It seems that the homilist is led to make his
comment because, in addition to what verse 20 reports of Miriam's
going out with the women, he notices in verse 21a that the reading
is *lhm* ("for them," in the masculine) rather than *lhn* (in the feminine); see too the Midrash quoted by Kasher, XIV, 159, no. 240—
therefore the emphasis: no celebrations in mixed company took place
at the Sea; rather the men were by themselves, the women likewise

Song among the men, so it was Miriam who led in recitation of the Song among the women,
    "Sing to the Lord for He is highly exalted" etc.

---

were by themselves. And as verse 21b reveals, the Song Miriam invited the women to join her in is the same as the Shirah of the men, Scripture simply furnishing this time only the opening line, for it has already quoted the Song in full (cf. also ZY in 1, s.v. whP *ʿšr šyrwt hn*).

that even as it was Moses . . . of the Song *kšm ʾmr mšh šyrh*. It seems to me that this statement of the Mekilta need not at all be taken as rejection of the view that when they recited the Song, Israel was on a par with Moses; cf. above, 1, p. 67, for the two views, with either of which our statement can agree.

among the I so translate the prefix *lamed* (*l*). I am indebted to Professor E. Y. Kutscher for the following observation: "As to šyrh Pnšym, šyrh lnšym, note the reading of the verse, wtʿn lhm mrym."

. . . men As Exod. 15:1 states plainly, Then sang Moses and *bny*—literally, the *sons* of, Israel.

it was Miriam MRS: "It was his sister" (but cf. also critical apparatus, ibid.). On keeping the sexes apart even when one and the same activity is involved, see, e.g., *Gen. R.* 39:14, p. 379. On Miriam teaching women as Moses (and Aaron) taught men, cf. *Sifre Z.*, p. 277.

. . . among the women For Philo's view, see *Moses*, I, 180; II, 256 (Loeb, VI, 369, 577 f.); and also *On Husbandry*, Secs. 79–83 (Loeb, III, 149 f.), and *Contemplative Life*, Secs. 85 ff. (Loeb, IX, 165 f.); cf. Ginzberg, *Legends*, VI, 13, n. 70. Note too *Memar Marqah* 2:7 (II, 58): "[The Israelites] would then fall silent and the prophet Moses would begin to sing. In the same way Miriam would sing and say *Sing to the Lord*, along with the Elders, and the women would say with the Israelites, *My strength and my song* (v. 2) to the end of it. (She) *For He has triumphed gloriously* (v. 1, 2nd part), they *Pharaoh and his chariots* whose power was great against the Israelites, *The horse and his rider He has thrown into the sea* (v. 1, 3rd part)." Cf. ibid. 2:11 (II, 80). See also *Barhebraeus*, p. 121 (on Exod. 15:1).

And so, commentary on the Shirah closes as it began, with the exaltation of God and His triumph over His enemies (cf. on v. 1b, end; 21b, end; Ps. 20:8), with the women's choir led (cf. esp. *Lekah Tob*, 50b, on "And all the women went out after her" [Exod. 15: 20]—Miriam *kngd kwlm*) by a prophet, even as was the men's choir, one leader the sister of Aaron and the other his brother, with the same words and in the same style—and the same mood no less: "Who is like unto Thee, O Lord!"

Such was the Song at the Sea, with this additional observation perhaps: unlike the celebrations at other triumphs, here was festivity that did not degenerate into an orgy; rather, the men were on one side and the women on the other—their own—side, with only God's praises on their mind, unlike even the Israelite women of a later day who made Saul and David the theme of their song (see above, 1, p. 76).

INDEX OF PRIMARY SOURCES

Entries for this index are arranged in roughly chronological order, except under the last two headings, Post-Talmudic Sources and Non-Jewish Sources, where they are alphabetized.

Hebrew Bible

GENESIS

1; 236	18:20 f.; 148
1:1; 202	19:24; 148
1:2; 139	19:24 f.; 91
1:20; 203	19:25; 93
2:6; 90, 91	19:30; 93
3:17; 209	19:30 ff.; 222
4:11; 209	19:32 ff.; 93
4:12; 209	19:33; 93
4:26; 65, 66	21:10; 241
6:2; 90	21:12; 241
6:3; 147	22:2; 241
7:11; 91	22:12; 241
7:12; 90	22:16; 241
8:21; 196	25:31–34; 241
11:4; 91	25:34b; 241
11:6; 147	27:41; 221
11:8; 91	28:13; 244
13:7; 222	32:29; 241
13:10; 93	34; 246
14:1; 156	34:25; 245
14:9; 156	35:22; 49
14:9 ff.; 156	36:1; 221
14:15; 156	36:15 ff.; 220
14:15 f.; 156	36:29; 217 f.
14:18; 157	36:31; 217
14:19; 228, 229	37; 49
14:22; 229	37:3; 49
15:1; 157	37:30; 49
15:13 f.; 7	46:4; 118

EXODUS

1:7; 214	1:13; 137, 171
1:10; 165 f.	1:13 f.; 170

LEVITICUS

NUMBERS

DEUTERONOMY

JOSHUA

JUDGES

I SAMUEL

II KINGS

ISAIAH

JEREMIAH

EZEKIEL

HOSEA

JOEL

AMOS

OBADIAH

PROVERBS

JOB

CANTICLES

Ancient Versions

SEPTUAGINT

VERSIO ANTIQUA

VULGATE

SAMARITAN VERSION

PESHITTA

AQUILA

THEODOTION

Targum

ONKELOS

Apocrypha and Pseudepigrapha

WISDOM OF SOLOMON

"Dead Sea Scrolls"

HODAYOT

SCROLL OF THE WAR

GENESIS APOCRYPHON (ED. FITZMYER)

QUMRAN SCROLL (4Q FLORILEGIUM)

FRAGMENT, DISCOVERIES

New Testament

MATTHEW

MARK

LUKE

JOHN

MEKILTA DE-RABBI SIMEON

(by page number)

SIFRA (ED. WEISS)

(by page and column)

SIFRE NUMBERS (ED. HOROVITZ)

(by section and page)

SIFRE ZUTA

(by page)

SIFRE DEUTERONOMY (ED. FINKELSTEIN)

(by section and page)

MIDRASH TANNAIM

(by page)

Mishnah

BERAKOT

KIL'AIM

SHABBAT

PESAḤIM

YOMA

SUKKAH

ROSH HA-SHANAH (ED. LOWE)

MEGILLAH

KETUBOT

NEDARIM

NAZIR

SOTAH

BABA MEṢIAᶜ

Tosefta

BERAKOT

KIL°AIM

HALLAH

SHABBAT

°ERUBIN

PESAḤIM

MEGILLAH

SOṬAH

Palestinian Talmud

BERAKOT

Minor Tractates

ARNA (ED. SCHECHTER)

ARNB

FATHERS ACCORDING TO RABBI NATHAN

SOFERIM (ED. HIGGER)

SEMAḤOT (ED. ZLOTNICK)

KALLAH (ED. HIGGER)

Midrash Rabba

GENESIS RABBA

Tanḥuma

WA-ʾERA

5, end; 136

BE-SHALLAḤ

10; 65, 68	14; 139
11; 76, 80	16; 153, 156, 157
12; 97	

NAŚO

25; 84

EXODUS (ED. BUBER)

30b; 66, 76   31b; 7

NUMBERS (ED. BUBER)

19b; 84   34a; 226

DEUTERONOMY (ED. BUBER)

16b; 189

Bible as Read (= Midrash Ḥadash ʿal ha-Torah)

I, 227–30; 102	I, 230; 106
I, 229; 75	

Pesikta de-R. Kahana (ed. Mandelbaum)

P. 220; 84   P. 223; 128

Pesikta Rabbati (ed. Friedmann)

8a; 41	100b; 128
14b; 71	196b; 156
22a; 120	

Midrash Psalms (ed. Buber)

Midrash Mishle (ed. Buber)

Pirke de-R. Eliezer

Seder Eliyahu R. (ed. Friedmann)

Seder Eliyahu Z.

Midrash Shir ha-Shirim (ed. Grünhut)

Agadat Shir ha-Shirim (ed. Schechter)

Midrash Wa-Yoshaʿ (= Jellinek, Bet ha-Midrasch)

Lekaḥ Tob (Exod.)

Sekel Tob

Yalkut Shimeoni

ʿArugat ha-Bośem

(by volume and page)

Midrash ha-Gadol, Exodus (ed. Margulies)

Numbers (ed. Fisch)

Post-Talmudic Sources

Non-Jewish Sources

INDEX OF MIDRASHIC-
TALMUDIC AUTHORITIES

INDEX OF SUBJECTS